OUTWA...

RETURN JOURNEY

GERMANY

POLAND

BOHEMIA

FRANKFURT

PRAGUE

HEIDELBERG

HEILBRONN

LUDWIGSBURG

...RT

AUGSBURG

MELK

ULM

MUNICH

LINZ

ST. PÖLTEN

VIENNA

SALZBURG

...ZERLAND

AUSTRIA

VV 9MS, 94 8D
Nov

A MOZART PILGRIMAGE

Being the Travel Diaries of
Vincent & Mary Novello
in the year 1829

TRANSCRIBED AND COMPILED BY
NERINA MEDICI DI MARIGNANO

EDITED BY
ROSEMARY HUGHES

LONDON
NOVELLO AND COMPANY LTD
160 WARDOUR STREET W.1

First printed in 1955

Copyright 1955 *by Novello & Company Ltd*

SET IN MONOTYPE BASKERVILLE AND
PRINTED AND BOUND IN GREAT BRITAIN
BY NOVELLO AND COMPANY LIMITED
LONDON W.I

To the dear memory of
the great-aunts and
great-uncles of Genoa
and of the long-since
vanished Villa Novello.

Vernon Medici Gigliucci

CONTENTS

ACKNOWLEDGMENTS

The grateful thanks of the Compiler and Editor are due to the following : MR A. HYATT KING, MR EDWARD CROFT MURRAY, and MR C. B. OLDMAN, *of the British Museum, for their kind and constant help and guidance ;* DONNA CATULLA *and* DON IGNAZIO VIGONI, SIR GEORGE DYSON, *the* REV. DON GUALBERTO VIGOTTI, MRS HANNAH ATKINSON, MR ERIC BLOM, *the late* PROFESSOR ARNALDO BONAVENTURA, DR WALTER BREITENFELD, PROFESSOR PIERO REBORA, MR RODERICK ENTHOVEN, MRS RICHARD HARVEY, MR ARTHUR LANE, *of the Victoria and Albert Museum,* MR NEIL MCLAREN, *of the National Gallery, and* MR GEORGE HAILEY WILLIAMS, *for their help over points of detail and in lending books ; the* REV. SEBASTIAN BULLOUGH, O.P., MR CECIL CLUTTON, *and* MR RALPH DOWNES, *for advice and detailed information regarding the history and literature of Gregorian chant and of the organ, and* MISS VIRGINIA WIMPERIS *and the late* MR GRAHAM RAWSON *for their skilful help with numerous details of research ;* MRS PETER BEVAN, MISS HELENA LIFSZYC, MRS GRAHAM RAWSON, MISS NESTA DE ROBECK, *and* MISS LUCY WARE, *who at various times have read the entire book in typescript and offered invaluable advice ;* MISS JEAN CUNNINGHAM *for her help and advice over the correcting of the proofs ; and* MRS NORMAN YATES-FISH, *in whose car and in whose company the Editor followed the Novellos' route from Boulogne to Salzburg in August* 1952.

In addition, the Compiler wishes to express her gratitude to her husband, GENERAL GIAN ANGELO MEDICI DI MARIGNANO, *her cousin* DONNA BEATRICE NOTABARTOLO *and her friend* SIGNORINA LINA ANAU, *for their help in copying, typing, and arranging the original transcripts.*

NERINA MEDICI DI MARIGNANO
ROSEMARY HUGHES

June 1954

LIST OF ILLUSTRATIONS

ix

FOREWORD

BEFORE I introduce Vincent and Mary Novello, the authors of these diaries, the reader may be interested to know how it was that the journals of an English couple travelling in Germany early in the nineteenth century came to be found, half way through the twentieth, in a little hill-town on the Adriatic, in the southern part of that region of Central Italy known as *Le Marche*.

Why fate had carried them so far will be related in the Afterword, since, oddly enough, the events of the last few days of the diarists' journey have something to do with it. We are here concerned with the manner of their discovery, which is, just as oddly, connected with the second World War—that ruthless destroyer of so many things of far greater value. But for it they might easily have gone on sleeping forgotten in the archives of an old Italian house, probably to be destroyed after the passing away of the present and last generation of the family.

This house is the home of the Gigliucci family in Fermo. To it the celebrated singer Clara Novello (daughter of the diarists, and my grandmother) was brought as a bride by her Italian husband Count Giovanni Battista Gigliucci, and it was her home until her death in 1908. But the first step towards the discovery of her parents' diaries was taken not there, but in Florence, in the house (15 Piazza Savonarola) designed and built for himself and his family by Clara's son, my dear father Mario Gigliucci ; he, with his elder brother Giovanni, had been living in Florence since 1879.

At that time the family chain stretched across Italy to the Riviera. In 1849 Vincent and Mary Novello them-

selves, for reasons of health, had come to Nice, which was
then still part of the Kingdom of Sardinia. They brought
with them Sabilla, their youngest surviving child, and
were later joined by the eldest, Mary, with her husband
Charles Cowden Clarke ; also by Alfred Novello, co-
founder, with his father Vincent, of the firm of Novello
and Company. Mary Novello died in 1854, Vincent in
1861 ; and in the latter year Nice was ceded to France by
the new Kingdom of Italy. Alfred Novello accordingly
decided to leave Nice, and bought a villa in Genoa ; and
here he, with the Cowden Clarkes and my delightful, witty
great-aunt Sabilla Novello, settled for the rest of their
long lives.

I myself fondly remember these 'Genoa Novellos',
though Florence was my home until I married, late in life.
My grandmother Clara's children—my father, his only
brother Giovanni, and their two sisters Porzia and
Valeria—were devoted to and dearly beloved by them all,
including ' dear Uncle Charlie ' or ' Uncle Clarky ', Keats'
friend and early teacher ; he died, alas, in 1877, a year
before I was born. Clara's children had lived in Nice—
not actually with the Novellos, but as it were ' under
their wing '—during my grandfather Gigliucci's self-
imposed exile from the Pontifical States for the cause of
Italian independence and unity, when Clara resumed her
musical career to support the family. Later on, it was
in the lovely eighteenth-century music room of the
Villa Novello in Genoa that these four young Italians
met and made friends with a bevy of charming, music-
loving English sisters, the Mozleys ; they were wintering
on the Riviera, and had become great favourites at the
Villa long before two of them, my aunt Charlotte and
Edith, my dear mother, became the Novellos' nieces-in-
law. And thus it was that we, the third generation (to

whom the elderly people in Genoa, who then seemed to us very old indeed, generously extended much affection and interest) grew up in the tradition of their peculiar charm and that of the beautiful Villa Novello, until we were old enough to appreciate it fully ourselves.

Meanwhile my great-grandparents' diaries must have been lying, unknown to all of us, among the papers and books and pictures and music, and living memories of bygone days, which helped to form that delightful atmosphere. But when my story opens in the latter part of 1944 —after that incredible and saddest of sad episodes, the Battle of Florence—all the Novellos had long since passed away ; and of the Gigliuccis, the sole members of the family in the old home on the Piazza Savonarola were my only brother Donatello and his English wife Dorothea. It was they from whom Mr (then Major) Edward Croft Murray, who was one of several British officers quartered in the house, borrowed a small English volume, bound in its original green and gold : *The Life and Labours of Vincent Novello, by his daughter Mary Cowden Clarke*. The Major seemed very much struck by it, and particularly by the quotations from Vincent and Mary Novello's accounts of their journey to Salzburg in 1829. He had already been much interested in the Novello family portraits in the house, as also to learn that we—myself and my brother and sister, and our cousin Beatrice Notabartolo—were the last living descendants of Vincent and Mary Novello ; eleven children were born to them, but none of the sons had married, and only three of the daughters, and of these two alone ' had issue ', as the official phrase runs—Clara and Cecilia. Clara Gigliucci's two daughters and Cecilia Serle's children, all girls, died unmarried.

Mr Croft Murray inquired eagerly after Vincent Novello's diary, since it was likely to contain many points

of interest to scholars like himself. But my brother knew
nothing about it ; and indeed, it seemed to all of us highly
improbable that it still existed. Apart from Vincent and
Mary's several changes of abode in London after 1829,
there had been their final migration to Nice, and the
subsequent move to Genoa by Alfred, Sabilla, and the
Cowden Clarkes. After the death of Sabilla in 1904, the
Villa Novello, with all its contents, passed to the Gigliucci
nieces, our maiden aunts Porzia and Valeria ; they never
went to live there, and sold it in 1913. (It has since been
destroyed, owing to the growth of the city.) To our knowledge much had been given away or otherwise discarded
at that time, and even long before. All these dear ladies,
our aunts and great-aunts, were as lavish in bestowing
things right and left, where they saw or thought they
might please, as apt, sometimes, to destroy things that they
considered of no particular interest to anyone, or to be
no one else's business. It was indeed unlikely that great-
grandfather Vincent's diary should have survived so many
uprootings and vicissitudes.

Yet survived it had ; and it came to light, without any
special search for it, in Fermo—'the miracled city', as
the devout Poles called it when they entered it unscathed
in the summer of 1944 along the line of the advancing
Allied forces on and above the east coast of Italy. My
unmarried sister, Bona, had been in Fermo since 1943,
taking care of our aunt Valeria, last of her generation, to
whom the old family home then belonged. Valeria
Gigliucci died, at ninety-six, on 10 March 1945 ; but
during the previous winter Bona had been able to visit
her home in Florence for a very short spell, had met Mr
Croft Murray, and had heard about the diary. After our
aunt's death she was held up in the *Marche* for some time
by war and post-war conditions, and began to look through

the family papers, which were left jointly to herself and to me. Her attention was at once arrested by a packet which, but for her visit to Florence, might have escaped particular notice. It was tied with a faded blue ribbon and marked ' Vincent Novello's MS. relative to his tour in Germany in 1829 '. She brought it home with her to Florence at the end of May, but though the English troops remained for many months longer, Mr Croft Murray had been moved on.

That very summer I came to Florence with my husband from our Lombard home after the terrible separation, by the curtain of fire of the Gothic Line, from all news from beyond the Appennines. My sister and I wrote to Mr Croft Murray, but he was unable to come and see the manuscript before being recalled to England. I then thought I should like to read it myself. It seemed so restful, after the long pain and anxiety, and in the still dark uncertainty for the immediate future of our beloved country, to plunge and forget oneself in the account of this peaceful, far-away journey.

But I found at once that it would be impossible for me to master the contents of Vincent Novello's diary except by copying it out slowly and carefully with the aid of a magnifying glass. The handwriting, mostly in pencil, is very minute, often faded or shaky from having evidently been scribbled in a jolting vehicle, or on the writer's knees, or perhaps against the seat or pew when taking notes in church or at the theatre. It is full of abbreviations, corrections, and cross-references. More than half of it is written on unnumbered, unbound sheets of letter paper, and on leaves torn out of notebooks. In some cases he has written on the last sheet first and continued further back. In the end I copied everything as it stood, and proceeded to put it into chronological order afterwards. Luckily for me, Mary Novello's notebook had also been preserved, and I soon discovered that her account, in a small but much more legible handwriting, and written mostly in ink, acted as a counter-check to her husband's. It tallies with his diary, but contains some details, and records some incidents and anecdotes, which he either omitted or merely jotted down in an almost unintelligible manner. It thus makes the story of the journey much clearer and more complete.

Of course it was obvious to us at once that the manuscripts, and the other papers found with them—letters, memoranda, playbills—must eventually be handed over to some collection or library in England and thus made available to scholars and students. But as the story of this summer trip pieced itself together under my delighted eyes, it struck me that the two diaries, welded together, might afford a pleasure almost equal to our own to a wider circle outside the world of specialists : to people who, though neither members of the family nor scholars, might yet be interested in the period at which the diaries were written, in anecdotal history generally speaking, and in music in particular.

I had, I must confess, some hesitation and qualms of conscience about what my great-grandparents would have thought of the idea of publishing what they had written down hastily, and for themselves alone. We shall find the mild Vincent Novello vigorously proclaiming his dislike of anything savouring of ' impertinent curiosity, prying and indiscretion ' ; and I had come upon some words of Heine's, in the dedication to his own Memoirs, which had almost seemed to warn me off: ' It is not permissible to publish even a single line of any writer if he has not himself destined it for the larger public '. It was a great relief to my scruples to learn that parts of Mary

Novello's diary had already appeared in print during her own lifetime. But ultimately, it was in loving remembrance of the ' dear children ' for whom she originally wrote, who had treasured the diaries to the end of their own long lives and beyond, that I decided to carry on.

In the end, after many months of single-handed work, I went to England at the close of 1951, to be most kindly received by the directors of Novello and Company in the person of Mr Harold Brooke—a grandson, on his mother's side, of Henry Littleton, who was at first our great-uncle Alfred's assistant, then his partner, and finally his successor in the business—and by Mr Hyatt King and Mr Croft Murray at the British Museum. At their suggestion, Miss Rosemary Hughes undertook to edit and revise the book from the musical angle, and in the summer of 1952 she came out to me in Italy, having, on her outward journey, joined forces with a motorist friend and followed the Novellos' route from Boulogne to Salzburg, as closely as the changes wrought by the passage of nearly a century and a quarter, and by two world wars, would permit. Our work together, side by side, has been carried on at long range during the ensuing months, and thus, in collaboration, the task has been completed. Whatever the reader may think of its result, this collaboration has proved, to myself, a most happy, interesting, and fruitful experience, turning the somewhat formidable figure of ' my Editor ' into that of a valued and invaluable, albeit so very much younger, ' guide, philosopher and friend '.

The long and detailed work which the task has entailed has been amply compensated by discovering (alas, too late in life) the fascination of such laborious transcriptions and researches ; still more, by the thought that there are indeed, in the Diaries, some little sidelights whose significance, I verily believe, could only have been apparent

xvii

to that family tradition which we are the last to possess ; but, more than anything, in the remembrance of some all too kind words written to me by Edmund Blunden, whom I had been fortunate enough to meet during my brief stay in London :

'Allow me to say that the Novellos must be feeling happy somewhere in your great devotion to them.'

But then Mr Blunden is not only a scholar : he is a poet.

NERINA MEDICI DI MARIGNANO
(*Née* Gigliucci)

Briosco, 1953

EDITOR'S NOTE

THE problem of editing the diaries of Vincent and Mary Novello was twofold : that of presenting a pair of diaries in double harness, and that of allowing their story to unfold at a normal speed while at the same time taking account of Vincent Novello's long and detailed musical criticisms, which, while they throw much light on the state of music at the time, hold up the movement of the narrative.

The method of presentation finally adopted by compiler and editor was to allow the two diarists to tell the story of their journey, and of their personal encounters, in extracts linked by a running commentary which, besides giving any necessary explanations, indicates which diarist is speaking. In certain passages the initials V.N. and M.N. are used to identify them. From this story, Novello's longer and more specialized comments on the music he heard in church and theatre have for the most part been omitted, or represented by brief extracts only, in order to present them in a separate section, entitled *The Musical Scene in Europe in 1829.* Here, grouped together instead of being scattered throughout the book, they throw more light on each other and on the general musical picture. In the same way, the copious notes made by both Vincent and Mary Novello about the circumstances under which Mozart's Requiem was composed, and the dispute then current concerning its authenticity, have been gathered into a section of their own. The diaries have thus been reproduced practically uncut, save in a few places where illegible words, or the disconnected character of the notes, have made the sense unintelligible.

Such minor changes have been made as the diarists themselves would have made in presenting their material for publication (and such as Mary Novello actually did make in the extracts from her diaries published in the *Musical World* in 1837): abbreviations have been expanded, punctuation inserted where lacking, words obviously omitted by inadvertence have been inserted in square brackets, and the spelling of foreign names has been corrected. Otherwise, spelling which the writers themselves would have regarded as correct has been left intact. The many musical quotations which Novello noted down by ear in church, opera-house or village inn have also been reproduced without correction.

R. H.

June 1954

PUBLISHER'S NOTE

EXTRACTS from the diaries of Vincent and Mary Novello have been set to the full width of the page. The editorial commentary is indented on *both* sides. This distinction has not been applied to pp. 119-125 and the Appendices.

INTRODUCTION

THE story that emerges from the diaries of Vincent and Mary Sabilla Novello is that of a journey across Europe —to Salzburg, Vienna, Paris, and back—made in the year 1829. Their journey had a threefold purpose : to present to Mozart's aged and invalid sister a modest sum of money subscribed by Novello and his brother musicians in London : to collect materials for a projected Life of the composer himself : and to make arrangements, in Paris, for the musical education of their little daughter Clara, soon to become one of the most famous singers of her time.

Vincent Novello himself, at forty-eight, was something of a celebrity. As organist and choirmaster to the Portuguese Embassy, he had made South Street a magnet to music-loving Londoners, whose carriages, Sunday by Sunday, blocked the approaches to the little chapel where the masses of Haydn and Mozart were sung to admiration, and the organ voluntaries, instead of playing the congregation out, held them in their seats until the very last note. He was a prolific composer, a pianist and viola-player, and a well-known teacher ; as one of the founders of the Philharmonic Society, he frequently ' presided at the Piano Forte ' at the Society's orchestral concerts. But it was as a scholar, editor, and publisher that he served posterity as well as his own generation. His published selections from the manuscript music at the Fitzwilliam Museum at Cambridge—which he had been called in by the Museum authorities to examine—and his great edition of *Purcell's Sacred Works*, were pioneer enterprises ; still more, his editions of Haydn's and Mozart's Masses in vocal score, with separately printed orchestral parts. Choral works, normally published only in full score, were costly and difficult of access, and this venture on Novello's part, undertaken at his own risk and expense and followed up by other similar publications, was destined to contribute more than any other single factor to the diffusion of great music in cheap and accessible form during the next hundred years.

His wife, whom he had married in 1808, was what the French would call the *maîtresse-femme* of his household, a notable housewife as well as an authoress in her own right. In their twenty-one years of married life she had given him eleven children, of whom eight were still living.[1]

The Novellos had a genius for friendship. The choicest spirits of the age met under their roof: Mendelssohn, Paganini (who called Vincent *il divino maestro Novello*), Liszt, Dragonetti, Malibran and de Bériot, Douglas Jerrold, Shelley, and later, his widow, Mary Wollstonecraft Shelley. With Leigh Hunt their intimacy was of long standing, and Hunt's friend Charles Cowden Clarke revered Novello not only as the ' golden-hearted musician ' of his *Recollections of Writers*, but, after his marriage to the Novellos' eldest daughter Mary in 1828, as a beloved father-in-law. True, the young Keats (whom Cowden Clarke had introduced not only to the Novellos and Leigh Hunt but—as his schoolmaster—to poetry itself) went away after an evening in their company exhausted by ' a complete set of Mozart and punning.' But it was just such an evening that drew from Charles Lamb that picture of Vincent and Mary Novello (in *A Chapter on Ears*), which brings them most vividly before us:

. . . Something like this *scene-turning* I have experienced at the evening parties at the house of my good Catholic friend Nov-, who, by the aid of a capital organ, himself the most finished of players, converts his drawing-room into a chapel, his weekdays into Sundays, and these latter into minor heavens. When my friend commences upon one of those solemn anthems, which peradventure struck upon my heedless ear, rambling in the side aisles of the dim abbey some five-and-thirty years since . . . a holy calm pervadeth me. I am for the time

—rapt above earth
And possess joys not promised at my birth.

But when this master of the spell, not content to have laid a soul prostrate, goes on, in his power, to inflict more bliss than lies in her capacity to receive . . . still pouring in, for protracted hours, fresh waves and fresh from the sea of sound, or from that inexhausted *German* ocean above which, in triumphant progress, dolphin-seated, ride those Arions *Haydn* and *Mozart*, with their attendant tritons *Bach, Beethoven* and a countless tribe, whom to attempt to reckon up would but plunge me again in the deeps—I stagger under the weight of harmony . . . clouds, as of frankincense, oppress me . . . the genius of *his* religion hath me in her toils—a shadowy triple tiara invests the brow of my friend, late so naked, so ingenuous—he is Pope—and by him sits, like as in the anomaly of dreams, a she-Pope too, tri-coroneted like himself! I am converted, and yet a Protestant— at once *malleus hereticorum* and myself grand heresiarch . . . till the coming in of the friendly supper tray dissipates the figment, and a draught of true Lutheran beer (in which chiefly my friend shows himself no bigot) at once reconciles me to the rationalities of a purer faith ; and restores to me the genuine unterrifying aspects of my pleasant-countenanced host and hostess.

Vincent Novello was, indeed, the mildest of men: modest, hard-working, a devoted husband and father—as he had been, to the end, an excellent son to his own widowed father, Giuseppe Novello, a Piedmontese of humble origin who had come to London in 1771 and eventually set up as a pastry-cook in what was then the Oxford Road[2]. From early youth Vincent had been an artist to his finger-tips; yet he found time, while giving lessons, copying, editing, and composing, besides attending to his professional duties as organist, to write ' little dance tunes for his little chicks ', for whose establishment in life

he cared and worked so hard. Unlike most fathers of his
generation, he treated his children as friends and companions, admitted them to the company of his brilliant
friends, and shared with them his own love of books and
the theatre. Mary Cowden Clarke, in her *Life and Labours
of Vincent Novello*, recalls ' once, riding home on his shoulder,
tired and sleepy, after the glory of going " to see the play " ;
so young was then the rememberer, so kind the good
father.' Thus he had enkindled in the future compiler of
the famous Shakespeare Concordance his own loving
familiarity with Shakespeare, apparent in the quotations
and allusions scattered throughout his diary, which indeed
constantly reveals a width of reading and general knowledge little short of miraculous in a man of his unremitting
professional activity. As his daughter describes him, ' in
looks and stature he was of middle height, in person somewhat stout, his carriage and walk wonderfully energetic
and purposeful, his hands and feet remarkably small and
white . . .' His portrait by his son Edward, which she
describes as ' the youth's first attempt in oil painting ', is
a fine one, and known to be very like him.

Mary Novello had made herself in every respect ' his
beloved helpmate and comfort ', and was adored both by
him and by her children ; though we know, from the
Reminiscences of her daughter Clara, that she was a strict
disciplinarian. Mary Cowden Clarke depicts her as taking
part in all Vincent's interests and friendships : ' She read
to him when he could listen ; talked with him when he
had time for conversation ; walked with him when he
took air, exercise or recreation '. Moreover, ' that he might
have none of the petty details of income, outlay, or domestic
affairs, she made them all her province '. Her vigorous
personality, indeed, earned for her the nickname of
' Wilful Woman ' from Leigh Hunt, with whom she was

a great favourite. Though not as lovely as her sister Catherine—later Mrs Collins—she was, says her eldest daughter, ' tall, finely proportioned . . . graceful in movement ; dignified, yet of extreme suavity in demeanour.' That she looked young for her age we shall repeatedly hear during the journey. Her descendants possess many portraits of her as she must have appeared about that time, painted or drawn mostly by her son Edward, who evidently had a predilection for taking his mother as a subject ; but the little portrait in oils, here reproduced for the first time, is unsigned. It depicts her very much as she must have appeared when dressed for theatre or opera or the hospitable dining-rooms of their Viennese hosts, with an almost Elizabethan lace collar and a scarf thrown over her arm, and wearing the large white cap, ornamented with gaily-coloured ribbons, in which she is always portrayed. This was the sign of matronhood, donned immediately after marriage, just as the toga was the sign of manhood to the boy of ancient Rome.

Their children, as Mary Cowden Clarke makes clear, had inherited a full share of their parents' gifts. She herself, at twenty, had been for a year ' the happy wife of a man of letters . . . confirming her early ambition to make literature her profession ', and had already begun work on the *Complete Concordance to Shakespeare*, which was to take her another sixteen years to complete. The eldest son, Joseph Alfred, had been set ' to the cultivation and acquirement of such knowledge as should best fit him for becoming a music publisher '. He was indeed destined to carry on his father's work : that same year (1829) saw the modest opening of ' Alfred's shop ', in Frith Street, Soho, soon to develop into the firm still known throughout the musical world as Novello and Company—though, as already related, the family died out in the male line at the end of the last century. Cecilia (Celia), later Mrs Serle, was meanwhile ' having her sweet voice and predilection for the stage trained by Mrs Blane Hunt, a former pupil of Thomas Welsh '. Edward, aged sixteen—who, had he outlived his twenty-fourth year, would certainly have become one of the great English painters of his time, to judge by the family portraits he left—was already (says his sister) ' a student of drawing at Mr Sass', the first master for young artists before they became colorists ', where he was later followed by his younger sister Emma Aloysia, who also drew and painted with a certain ability.

And now, after twenty-one years of marriage, and after having, according to Mary Cowden Clarke,

. . . promoted their elder children's establishment in suitable channels for happily, honorably, and independently earning future livelihood [sic], Mr and Mrs Novello, in the year 1829, took a pleasant journey together to Germany, for the fulfilment of a no less pleasant purpose. This was the presentation of a sum of money to Mozart's sister, Madame Sonnenburg, which sum had been subscribed by some musical admirers of the great composer, who had heard with deep sympathy and concern that she was then in poor health and poorer means. These gentlemen entrusted their friend and brother-sub-scriber (indeed he was the original proposer of the subscription and undertook all its contingent expenses himself) Vincent Novello, with the execution of what they knew would be a most welcome commission to him—the conveyance of this contribution to Mozart's sister.

The sum entrusted to Novello for the widowed Frau Hofrath Maria Anna von Berchtold zu Sonnenburg (once the gifted little ' Nannerl ' who, with her miraculous younger brother Wolfgang, had dazzled the courts of Vienna, Paris, and London in the 1760's) appears to us no very large one. Even in that day it amounted only to a little present—' un petit cadeau ', as Novello himself calls it in his letter to her : sixty guineas all told. It was, in fact, raised by the private generosity of a small circle of seventeen subscribers. The list of their names was carefully written out by Novello to serve as a receipt, and was duly signed on behalf of Madame Sonnenburg (now blind) by her sister-in-law, Mozart's widow. It presents a cross-section of the London musical world;[3] among the names are those of Thomas Attwood (organist of St Paul's Cathedral and formerly Mozart's pupil), J. B. Cramer, Ignaz Moscheles, Richard Stevens (organist at the Temple Church), the singer Braham, Cipriani Potter (pianoforte professor at the Royal Academy of Music), and J. A. Stumpff (harp-maker, collector of Mozart autographs, and Beethoven's faithful friend). According to Mary Novello's subsequent account it was Stumpff (who corresponded intermittently with Mozart's widow) who had found out that Mozart's sister was ' blind, bedridden and out of sorts with fortune ',[4] and it was he who, with Novello himself, contributed the highest sum—£10 each.

Novello, indeed, idolized Mozart—to him ' the Shakespeare of music '—and his journey had another object beyond its immediate aim. In the postscript of his draft letter to Madame Sonnenburg—written in French, with many corrections, and carried in the pocket of the ' little green leather book with clasp ', as he calls it, in which he begins his diary—he mentions this further purpose, which for some reason was never fulfilled : ' Je me propose de faire une esquisse biographique de Mozart, fondée sur les memoires qui ont été dernièrement publiées par Madame sa veuve '. The *Biographie W. A. Mozart's* written by Georg Nikolaus von Nissen, the Danish diplomat who was Constanze Mozart's second husband, had in fact been brought out by her in the previous year (1828) ; she was then a widow for the second time. This was the only large-scale life of Mozart to appear in the thirty-eight years since his death, though a notice had appeared in Schlichtegroll's *Nekrolog* in 1793, and shorter memoirs had been produced by Niemetschek (1798), Arnold (1803) and Beyle (1814, stolen from Schlichtegroll). Novello had eagerly acquired it when the first copies reached London ; at one time he even planned to bring out a translation.[5] But that project, too, was abandoned, and ultimately it was his pupil Edward Holmes—Keats' schoolfellow at the Cowden Clarke school at Enfield—whose *Life of Mozart*, published in 1845, became what Ernest Newman calls ' the first complete and adequate account of the composer to appear in English.' Holmes' work is based mainly on Nissen and his own researches ; but Novello's attitude and influence shine through his approach. Moreover, some of the actual memories of the Novellos' visit to Salzburg had been placed on record in 1837, when Mary Novello rewrote extracts from her diary and published them in Alfred Novello's little weekly journal, the *Musical World*, and Holmes expressly acknowledges his debt to these extracts ' for some original sayings of Mozart and traits of his character '.

Our travellers had a third and, to them, no less important task to be carried out before their return to England : one which in the end was to affect the fate of their diaries. The precocious abilities of the eleven-year-old Clara, fourth daughter and seventh child of their gifted brood, were crying out for development. Since earliest childhood, as her sister relates, she had given tokens of possessing ' a voice and musical ability very rare in their order ', even in that family of delightful singing voices and well-trained artistic capacities, where music—and especially part-singing round the father's instrument and at their picnics with the Leigh Hunts on Hampstead Heath—was a regular recreation. Edward Holmes had taught her to sing ' as a baby ' (so she herself has noted under a letter of his received in Rome in 1857), probably in consequence of her having, at three years old, startled her family by singing the famous air *Di tanti palpiti* from Rossini's *Tancredi* after having heard it ground out on a barrel-organ. At seven, she had been sent to York and entrusted to the care of Miss Betsy Hill, the singer, to be taught by her and by the pianist John Robinson, organist of the little Catholic chapel in the city. In the early months of 1829 Fétis, of the Paris Conservatoire (whose *Biographie Universelle des Musiciens* is still a classic work of reference) had visited her father and had heard her sing ; she herself has related in her *Reminiscences* how, ' sitting on my usual square footstool, a doll in my arms, I had been suddenly told to sing Dr Arne's *The Soldier Tired*, which goes up to D, also Mozart's *Agnus Dei.*' Fétis had promptly recommended her parents to allow her, although only eleven, to compete for a vacancy at the Institution Royale de Musique Religieuse, founded in 1817 by Alexandre Choron for the training of church choristers and choirmasters, and since 1825 sub-sidized by King Charles X. The voice trials were to be held in mid-August, and Vincent and Mary Novello, returning from their travels by way of Paris, counted on making all the necessary arrangements then. Meanwhile Clara was sent to improve her French at Boulogne : doubtless with the Bonnefoys, who kept a sort of private school much frequented by English pupils.

Going to Boulogne-sur-Mer was an institution with the Novellos. So were the Bonnefoys. Vincent himself, and his elder brother Francis, had been sent to that neighbour-hood as boys ; his eldest son Alfred, in his turn, had been left for a twelvemonth at the Bonnefoys. Mary Cowden Clarke, in her own autobiography, speaks of ' dear old Monsieur Bonnefoy ', when she too, at sixteen, had been ' confided to the care of that estimable family ' before starting on her brief career as a governess—of all delightful coincidences, at Cranford. Emma Novello has left some sketches of Boulogne and the Bonnefoys (probably made at a later period) ; and twenty years after the Novellos' Salzburg journey, Clara's children in their turn were left with the Bonnefoy family, while their parents crossed to England—Clara having just resumed her musical career during her husband's political exile.

★   ★   ★

To Vincent and Mary Novello, standing on the threshold of the Continent in 1829, Europe presented a very different aspect even from that which their children and grand-children knew, and worlds apart, geographically and politically as well as morally, from the Europe which over a hundred years of upheavals and wars have left us today.

In 1829 Napoleon had been lying buried, these eight years past, under a weeping willow in far-off St. Helena, and the surface appearance of Europe was of a continent restored to its former self, by England and the Holy Alliance, almost as if the French Revolution and the Napoleonic era had never been. But beneath that surface a new Europe was seething.

The England the Novellos had left behind them—not yet an Empire, far less a Commonwealth of Nations—was, in all men's eyes, the victorious, all-powerful Kingdom of Great Britain, ' Britannia ruling the waves '. At home, the Georgian era was nearing its close, and little Princess Victoria of Kent growing up, quietly enough, in Kensington Palace, under the shadow of her Mamma and Baroness Lehzen. Like most of their circle the Novellos were, to say the least of it, no great admirers of the House of Hanover under George IV.

xxx

In France, the Bourbon restoration was fifteen years old and the reactionary ' Ultras ' were in full bloom under the reigning monarch Charles X, brother to the hapless Louis XVI and to Louis XVIII, the Restoration's first king. Charles X and the party he affected were going their way, heedless of the new revolution which was to burst in the month of July of the very next year, and to drive the elder branch of the Bourbon line off the throne. The First Lady of the land (Charles X's wife having died in exile in 1805) was Madame la Dauphine, his niece and daughter-in-law : that Duchesse d'Angoulême who visited Choron's establishment a few months later and kissed the reluctant Clara, who always regretted not having been told that the ' very ugly Princess ' from whom she recoiled was so interesting a person as Marie Antoinette's daughter, ' l'orpheline du Temple '. To us also it may be difficult to recognize, in the somewhat severe-looking elderly lady, that poor young fainting curly-headed maiden in muslin and ribbons with whom we are familiar in the pathetic prints of Louis XVI's farewell to his family.

Belgium, as a separate state, did not exist in 1829. After the Treaty of Vienna in 1815 it became one with Luxemburg and Holland (more than a century before Benelux) under the name of Kingdom of the Netherlands ; the King, whom we shall all but meet in Louvain, was William I of Orange. He, like Charles X of France, lost his throne in 1830. Italy, which the two diaries mention but casually, had been divided by the Treaty of Vienna into seven states, nearly all, either directly or indirectly, under Austrian domination. Indeed, according to Prince Metternich, the word Italy was ' nothing more than a geographical expression '.[6] The other Mediterranean countries do not come into the picture at all ; but it is worth recording that the Balkans (except Greece, newly freed from Turkish domination) were still divided between the Sultan of Turkey and the Emperor of Austria, who was also King of Hungary and Bohemia.

As for Germany and Austria, of which we shall hear most, the Novellos make no clear distinction between them, but write of Austria and her people invariably as ' Germany ' and ' Germans '. So did everyone in those days : Chateaubriand, when arriving at Salzburg in 1833 after travelling through Carinthia on his way to Linz, writes (in his *Mémoires d'outre-tombe*) : ' L'Allemagne s'est voulue venger de ma mauvaise humeur. Dans la plaine de Salzbourg, le soleil parut '. So too did the oppressed Italians, and to this day the Austrian oppressors of the time of the Risorgimento are spoken of as ' the Germans ' —*i Tedeschi*—a term comprising even those soldiers and officials who, as natives of Bohemia or Croatia, were of Slavonic race.

The term ' Germany ' did not, and would not for many decades, denote a political unit—though to some extent already an economic one since the creation of the *Zollverein* (Customs Union) in 1819 between the greater number of its various kingdoms, grand-duchies, duchies and Hanseatic towns. And the Germany of our modern experience and consciousness seems worlds apart from the Germany of the early nineteenth century, which we see through the eyes of Thackeray's Becky Sharp, Pendennis and Clive Newcome, and of the Novellos' real-life British tourists— with one solitary young American—as they journey along the Rhine. To them, it was simply a land of mediaeval castles and picturesque towns and romantic legends and quaint principalities, larger or smaller : of artistically- minded princes and of great poets, philosophers and musicians : of beautiful woods and pleasantly shady, gay international watering-places : the home of Rhine wine and beer, wandering, light-hearted students, and much *Gemütlichkeit*. Even Queen Victoria, years later, narrowing it down to her knowledge of the courts of her beloved husband and mother, cousins and uncles, could still speak of it, with naive enthusiasm, as ' dear little Germany '.

There was but one Empire in Europe and one Kaiser in his *Kaiserstadt* of Vienna (not counting that other Caesar, the Czar of All the Russias, who, after all, resembled the Grand Turk in being but half a European potentate). The ' Roman Emperors of German race ' as the Italians had called them for centuries, hereditary since the sixteenth century in the Hapsburg line, held sway, of course, over many non-German lands ; we shall find Mozart's widow and her elder and younger son living respectively in Salzburg, Milan, and Poland under the same ruler. In 1829 this was the Emperor Francis I, Napoleon's father-in-law and grandfather of Francis, Duke of Reichstadt (' l'Aiglon '), already well on his way to his early death in that golden captivity. The ' power behind the throne ' was Prince Metternich. Nine years later, when Clara Novello was a much-feted young soprano, she and her mother were to be entertained by Metternich and his third wife, Princess Melanie, at a private dinner-party in their palace. But for the moment, in Vienna, we shall find the Novellos mingling only with the bourgeois society of bankers and musicians, music publishers, and pianoforte makers, most of whom were hardly *hoffähig* (eligible for presentation at Court) as the phrase ran all over German lands, even as late as my own young days.

The Novellos themselves, though anything but bourgeois in outlook as the word is often understood, belonged to the bourgeoisie. Vincent Novello's father, indeed, as we have seen, was a man of the people. And whoever Mrs Novello's German grandfather may have been—a matter of mystery

xxxiii

and surmise—her father, Simon Hehl, was a self-made intellectual of the middle class ; he, like Giuseppe Novello, had settled in London in the second half of the eighteenth century.[7] Although Mary Novello's brother became a captain in the Guards (through whose influence we know not) she and her sister Catherine had been brought up as governesses, ' the only profession then open to a girl of good family ', as Professor Altick says in his account of her daughter Mary.[8] In fact, the Novellos would be best described as belonging to the world of intellectuals and artists. There was, however, nothing about them of the Bohemian attitude, and their moral standard was a very strict one. It had been no obstacle to their deep friendship for the Shelleys (they never knew Byron, who was anathema to them in any case), but Shelley's self-proclaimed ' atheism ' had not so much as touched them. Vincent Novello's canon, *Give thanks to God and praise His name for ever*, was to become part of the daily family repertory, and his wife's favourite motto, ' Trust in God ', was written in the hearts of all her children, as appears in many letters of theirs long after her death ; her son Alfred even had it worked into the marble floor of the gallery of the lovely Villa Novello in Genoa.

Their religious outlook, in its simple, undogmatic idealism, was in fact very much that of Leigh Hunt. But by allegiance, as we learn from Lamb, both were Catholics : members of a small, heavily circumscribed religious minority of which the Embassy Chapels had long been the main strongholds in London, and whose members did not receive full civil rights until the Catholic Emancipation Act of that very year, 1829. Deprived of educational facilities and political and professional opportunity, English Catholics had, in the course of years, learned the art of retaining their private faith and practice in a watertight compartment while otherwise absorbing the ideas and taking on the colour of their surroundings. The Novellos' friendship with Leigh Hunt and Shelley brought them into sympathy with the liberal movements of the time all over Europe, towards which the Church was politically antagonistic. Mary Novello's sentiments constantly reflect the humanitarianism of her adored Leigh Hunt, as her husband's echo his political radicalism ; indeed, Vincent Novello's fellow-organist and lifelong friend Samuel Wesley (himself, for a while, a convert to Catholicism) wrote of him that he ' as much merits the title of one of the faithful (in the Roman Catholic sense, which always signifies a bigoted Papist) as you or I, for he believes not a word of Purgatory, Priestly Absolution, Transubstantiation, Extreme Unction nor any other extreme of such extreme absurdities '. Yet neither they, nor any of their children, ever changed their religion. Their daughter Mary, though married to the son of a one-time Baptist preacher, John Cowden Clarke, remained the affectionate godchild of her father's very good friend Monsignor Victor Fryer, first chaplain of the Portuguese Embassy, who had married Vincent and Mary Novello in 1808, baptized nearly all the little Novellos, and stood sponsor to several of them. At least two of the girls, Emma and Sabilla, were sent to school at the Augustinian convent at Bruges, where one of their Hehl cousins, Agnes—a sister of Mrs Stirling the actress—was at one time Mother Superior.

Yet, members though they were of a Church regarded by many Englishmen, then and now, as somehow foreign, un-English and subversive, the Novellos were both English to the core. Their grandson Mario Gigliucci used to say of all the Novellos, whom he loved dearly, that never had he known people more English than these, who yet had so little English blood in their veins : just that fourth part which came to them through Vincent's mother (for Mary Hehl's mother was Irish). This seems to lend weight to the observation made by Violet Paget (Vernon Lee) in her charming essay *Bayeux and the Tapestry* in *Genius Loci*: that 'race is nothing and language all ; for the blood carries only physical resemblance,which is simple and very individual, while the word carries thought, custom, law and prejudice, which are complex and universal '. Indeed, the intense Englishness of the Novellos' prejudices appears nowhere more strongly than in their remarks on the Catholic life of Europe, as if they considered the Church on the Continent to be somehow different from the same Church in England. The superficial differences must in fact have been considerable, and compared with the small, unadorned Catholic chapels of pre-Emancipation England, the richly-decorated churches of Europe must have seemed to abound in ' tawdriness, golden ornaments and finery '— the Novellos' recurring complaint, and that of travelling Britons from that day to this.

★   ★   ★

Both diaries seem pervaded by something of that pleasant feeling of momentary freedom from home worries which a well-assorted middle-aged couple experiences on achieving what one may term a second and, if less exciting, more serene and secure honeymoon after years of married life, with its joys and sorrows (they had already lost three beloved little ones). Nevertheless, Mrs Novello's journal begins ' My dear children ', and never does either of them look out upon some beautiful prospect from the many seats ' judiciously placed ' on hills or in gardens, never do they return from enjoying wonderful sights and sounds, never does an apt quotation, amusing or poetical, occur to them, but their thoughts fly at once to the dear ' young folks at home '. More often than not it is of the valued friend and dear son-in-law ' Charlie ' that they seem to be thinking ; to his tender care, and that of his young wife, those of their children still in London must have been left, for at that time the Cowden Clarkes lived in the Novello household.

A comparison between the two diaries is illuminating. Mary Novello's record, as the opening indicates, was kept in the first place for her family. But she was enough of a professional authoress to have an eye to the possibility of publishing it, whole or in part—a possibility eventually realized in the extracts she prepared for the *Musical World* in 1837. Her husband, on the other hand, with his projected biography of Mozart in mind, set out equipped for systematic note-taking ; but his entries, whether in his notebook or on the loose sheets into which his ' diary ' degenerated, vary enormously. Sometimes they are ample, and corrected and polished with an eye to their ultimate literary form ; at other times they are mere jottings made to refresh his memory. His ' Memoranda ' and ' Heads of Conversations ', indeed, are often scribbled down at random among his daily entries as they recurred to him, perhaps days after the conversation had taken place. Mary Novello, by contrast, usually writes up her diary immediately after the events she records ; it is therefore invaluable in ordering and dating her husband's more disconnected notes. The similarities between their two accounts, and the conscientiousness with which they relate what was told them, are all the more remarkable, and certainly vouch for the authenticity of their record-keeping.

The two diaries show their tastes and interests to have been very much the same, or at any rate (as is usual with well-assorted couples) to have become so. But the personal character of each soon becomes apparent. It is entertaining, from a human rather than a musical standpoint, to notice, among other things, the different tones in which husband and wife speak of Rossini and Beethoven when quoting practically the same remarks made by Mozart's widow and son, and by the Abbé Stadler and the Streichers in Vienna ; as the French say, ' c'est le ton qui fait la chanson '.

Neither of them cares for Rossini : it is a family tradition that Vincent Novello described part of his masterpiece *The Barber of Seville* as ' ridiculous '. But even when criticizing his music in the diary, Novello always analyses it most carefully and objectively, while his wife dismisses it almost with a shrug, and is ready to believe the worst of Rossini's marriage, a private matter that her husband does not even stop to consider. As for Beethoven, Mary Novello evidently does not realize his full stature—no more, apparently, did Prince Metternich—therefore she does not stop to make allowance for his character and his physical misfortune. On the other hand, as she does not like what is told them of the man, she makes little effort to appreciate the artist ; a somewhat feminine trait, I fear, and one which her daughter Clara, whom Rossini was to call his ' adorable interprête ', applied in exactly the same manner to Wagner—a curious instance of the strength of heredity, and an object-lesson in the evolution of artistic taste and understanding down the generations.

Mary Novello is certainly only repeating what she had heard when she writes, in Vienna, that ' Streicher considers Beethoven ungrateful . . .' ; but she is less than just when she implies that her husband joined her in feeling that ' What we hear of Beethoven does not increase our love for him '. For a note of pity for the physical misfortune and unhappiness which explain so many of the asperities and vagaries of Beethoven's character, and one of great admiration for his art, pierces through all that Novello repeats of what was told them by the composer's friends. Although to him, as well as to the Abbé Stadler, Beethoven's greatness may not seem to loom as gigantic as it has done to the generations that have followed (*nemo propheta in patria* can be no less true in relation to time than to place), yet both musicians are fully aware that it is a wonderful genius of whom they are speaking.

It is a characteristic of Novello's—a very pleasant and perhaps a rather unusual one—that this ' golden-hearted musician ' is so often disappointed to *be* disappointed in people or things, especially where music or brother musicians are concerned. ' Habitually,' says Maeterlinck in *La Sagesse et la Destinée*, ' man will issue from his home in search of joy, beauty, truth, love, and not re-enter thoroughly satisfied unless he can tell his children that he has met with nothing at all.' With Vincent Novello it is just the reverse : he is always thoroughly dissatisfied when unable to tell his children—and himself to start with— that he has met with something, be it great or small, to admire or to learn from.

★   ★   ★

As we shall see, the Novellos' diaries describe neither the beginning of their journey nor its end.

The tale of their stay in Paris from the 10th to the 17th of August is told in a somewhat summary and erratic manner. Mary, indeed, breaks off what appears to be merely a *resumé* of the first two days, written late on the afternoon of Tuesday the 11th, and does not continue it either before her departure for Boulogne on the 15th or on her return to Paris with little Clara. As for Vincent, his daily entries—more precise, though often laconic and desultory—tail off and cease abruptly on the 17th, leaving three pages blank which he never took up his pen or pencil to fill in. Paris was no novelty to them—nor, it is clear, to Charles Cowden Clarke and others, perhaps, of the home circle for whom (apart from their subsequent usefulness for reference purposes) the Novellos' records were intended. There was therefore no need to take note of the many particulars that were unchanged : only of the changes and innovations they noticed, the people of interest they met, and the stray thoughts that occurred to them during the period of interviews and waiting before Clara's arrival. Once Clara had arrived, their time must have been fully taken up by the last interviews before her final acceptance at Choron's institution, the business of settling her at Madame Tardieu's boarding establishment, and the arrangements for their own return to London, and they probably thought that their recollections would last long enough to enable them to recount all this on their return. The breaking-off of the diaries, and Clara's account in her *Reminiscences*, give an impression of haste, as if their last days had been very few. Their treasured autograph album, however, of which we shall hear so much, contains an *Ave Regina caelorum* signed by Sir Henry Bishop and dated ' Paris, August 26th 1829 ' : nine whole days after Vincent's diary comes to its abrupt end. Did they really stay so long? Or did they leave their album behind for Sir Henry to write in?

The vague, unfinished ending to Vincent Novello's notes, as he wanders among the tombstones of Père Lachaise, leaves us with a very pleasing picture of the writer ; like some water-colour sketch—slightly faded, as are his pencilled lines—which one might come upon in an old scrapbook. A man's figure against the background of a cemetery —a picture characteristic at once of the man and of his period : a period lasting one and almost two generations after his own, which tended to revel in graveyards and weeping willows and relics of the beloved ; a man of sentiment and sensibility, as sensitive and over-sensitive to kindness as to rough behaviour, to himself or others ; who cherished memories and mementoes, but delighted in things pleasant and gay and gracious, provided they were also noble and benevolent ; who worshipped God thankfully and believed (God bless his memory) in the ultimate progress of mankind.

PART I

THE JOURNEY TO SALZBURG

London—Boulogne—Antwerp, June 24-28

Neither Vincent nor Mary Novello mention their departure from London. But the list of subscribers to the 'petit cadeau' for Mozart's sister is dated 'London, Wed. June 24, 1829', and the probability that they left London on that day is strengthened by the opening of Mary Novello's first paragraph, written at Cologne on July 1st:

My dear children,

I have now been out a week and with the exception of last night have known no alloy to the pleasure of this journey. We were a little weary with 2 nights travelling and shall endeavour to avoid it for the future. The children at Boulogne appear well and happy.

From this it is also apparent that not only little Clara but a contingent of the Novello family was at the Bonnefoys' establishment that summer ;[9] probably the others were Cecilia, then seventeen, and Clara's devoted big brother Edward, for among the memoranda scribbled by Mrs Novello inside the cover of her notebook as she hurried to Boulogne at the end of their trip, to fetch Clara to Paris for her voice trials, we find ' Cecy to speak to Miss Shelby about Miss Mapleson' and 'Edward to know what Michelangiolo he wants'. The little notebook itself looks as if ' the children at Boulogne' had presented it to their mother, for the first page bears a sort of dedication in French verse:

I

Cette Femme charmante,
Aussi bonne épouse que tendre mère,
Par des actions bienfaisantes
Marque sa vie entière :
Les rejetons d'une âme si belle
Doivent a l'envie l'imiter. . . .

Bravo, M. Bonnefoy! One somehow suspects his authorship. But the careful round copybook handwriting is that of a young person. It looks as if the father, too, had been furnished by his offspring with food for his pen and pencil ; the little paper exercise-book in which his diary is carried forward from the green leather notebook bears, in red ink on the outside cover, the words ' E. P. Novello, 1827 ', while inside Edward has written ' Dramatis Personae—Don Ambrogio, an old Miser, Donna Eugenia, a Widdow . . .' No doubt Papa Vincent had begged, borrowed or stolen it, for his convenience, from the youthful dramatist.

Meanwhile, his first, undated entry in the little green book is clearly made on the seashore at Boulogne. Characteristically, though neither about the journey, nor about music, properly speaking, it is a meditation on sounds, to which, of whatever kind or quality, we shall find his ear and mind constantly and most sensitively attentive :

In Cowper some lines I remember comparing the wind among the trees of a wood to the rush of the sea on the beach

> Mighty winds
> That sweep the skirt of some far spreading wood
> Of ancient growth, make music not unlike
> The dash of ocean on his windy shore.

Not only the rush of the water when, heavily and with pauses, it breaks on the shore, is solemnly pleasing ; but the low half-heard murmur of the small waves, that just rock the sea weed as it floats upon them, before it.is

2

deposited on the shingles, is a sound almost as soothing as that we listen to, when the low summer wind sighs among woods and copses—a sound, for which I think the English language wants an expressive word—we say indeed the sighing or the murmuring of the trees, but the wind among the Trees seems better and much more elegantly expressed by the Italian *sussurrare* :

Frangersi l'acqua, e sussurrar le foglie[10]

After thus revealing his sensibility to the sounds of Nature, as well as to the niceties not only of his own language and literature but of Italian—his father's native tongue and, by consent and use, the international language of music—Novello continues briskly :

June 26th. Left Boulogne 6 in the evening, arrived Calais 10, 5 fr. each, 1 fr. to guide. *Dunkerque* arrived 3 in the morning, Saturday, June 27th, from Calais 10 Leagues, left Dunkerque 4 in the Morning.

From Dunkirk his brief remarks plot their route as, turning inland, they pass through Bergues, Warmouth, Cassel, Castor and Bailleul, arriving at Lille at 1.30 in the afternoon. As the diligence trots past in the early morning light, he covers page after page of his note-book with observations, laconically jotted down and, with the movement of the carriage, very hard to decipher. But nothing escapes him :

Carriages pass on the *left* of each other not *right*—puzzling to an English driver.

Carts of very novel form and picturesque figures—good combinations of colour, blue smock frocks . . . short fat sleek Horses partaking of the *Mule* shape.

Cuckoo.

Girl drawing the Boat on Canal near Dunkerque—very

flat tedious landscape—Picturesque old Fort on the banks of the Canal . . .

Beyond Berze (or Bergues) Road very pleasant, with large fir trees on each side—well cultivated . . .

Bergues is a well-built place, several fine Houses. Well fortified but however in a state of decay.

At Cassel, which stands on a solitary ridge falling away to the level country on either side, Novello's comments reveal the inveterately pictorial eye inherited by his son Edward, and his keen appreciation of contemporary art as well as of the great artists of the past. The church, on which he comments so disparagingly, is a solid, undistinguished early Gothic structure, and as such falls outside the scope of his appreciation, which is focused on the later and more florid Gothic.

Cassel—highest ground we passed. General Vandamme has a Château here and lives quite retired.[11] Beautifully situated and the winding road full of the most changing, varied and extensive views, especially one looking towards another eminence which rises abruptly on the left side near the extreme height of the Hill. This is by far the finest Prospect I have yet met with. The point of view looking *through the Gate* on reaching the top of the Hill and turning round, is quite a picture and would have formed an admirable subject for Claude or our own excellent artist Turner.

The Church is an antique looking affair and disfigured by one of those melancholy representations of the Crucifixion which are so prevalent in this quarter and which invariably produce a feeling of sadness whenever I meet with one of these proofs of the continuance of ignorance and bigotry.

The Chimes which happened to strike while I was

looking at the Church are detestable. They have not the least reference to any regular scale, either diatonic, chromatic or enharmonic, but are a mere discordant jingle.

Left Lille at 2—cold Fowl, Wine . . . entered Belgium at Menin. Pleasant *Conducteur* who had been in Italy, Germany, etc. Intelligent fellow.

Left Menin at 5. Blackguard Custom House—toss the Property about without your leave and then demand payment for the impertinent interference—stupid and useless system.

Sudden and violent hailstorm.

Courtrai—pretty and large place. Left after taking coffee at 6.

At length, after two consecutive nights on the road, they reached the Scheldt:

Arrived at Antwerp at ½ past 6. Crossed in Steam Boat.

Mary Novello, summing up their thirty-six hours of travel, has been delighted to meet, in the ' pleasant conducteur ' of their diligence, the embodiment of one of her own literary creations—Narcisse, the all-knowing postilion who figures in her book of stories, *A Day in Stowe Gardens* (dedicated to Leigh Hunt and published anonymously by the Hunt brothers in 1825).

Our route through Dunkirk, Cassel, etc., had many delightful views. At Lille a pleasant *conducteur*, who reminded me of my own Narcisse, had he sat for the portrait he could not have yielded a truer, or more agreeable likeness. At Antwerp, through his recommendation we were well lodged at the Ville d'Ostende—the woman of the house amused me by saying she took Vincenzo and myself for a newly married couple, come out on a visit of amusement during the *printemps* of marriage, so much for the complaisance of dear Papa.

Of their hotel her husband merely notes that it was in the ' Rue des Israélites, près de la Bourse ' and had ' iron gratings to the Parlour windows, like Prison '.

Antwerp, Sunday, June 28—Monday, June 29

The Novellos allowed themselves little respite after their early-morning arrival; but the chance of seeing Rubens' *Elevation of the Cross* and *Descent from the Cross* in the Cathedral uncovered on the eve of his name-day —the feast of SS. Peter and Paul on June 29th—was one not to be missed, especially as their tastes in painting obviously incline towards the great masters of colour—Rubens, Titian, and Guido Reni among the old masters, Turner among their own contemporaries. In the afternoon, too, Sunday vespers are combined with a visit to the Rubens chapel in St. Jacques. In its famous altar-piece, a Madonna with saints, St. George bears the painter's own features and—according to a tradition now discredited but evidently one of long standing—two of the female saints represent his two wives, Isabella Brant and Hélène Fourment. Mary Novello describes their strenuous day.

At Antwerp we lost no time, but it being fortunately the festival of St. Peter and St. Paul we not only saw those divine paintings of Rubens but heard an instrumental Mass and Vespers, and a military Mass. Vespers also at St. Jacques where dwells the family picture of Rubens, an everlasting monument of his superior genius, conferring a halo on the church itself where it is kept, which is however otherwise rich in marble and sculpture, and some heads of Vandyk and a St. Roch.[12] But the organ is

I. VINCENT NOVELLO

2. MARY SABILLA NOVELLO

worse than bad, its detestable growling almost forced me to abandon the place from whence issued such sounds, resembling the discordant tones of a spirit in agony.

At Mass in Antwerp Cathedral Vincent Novello found a vantage point near the front of the nave from which he could feast his eyes on the two great Rubens canvases in the north and south transepts, while making notes on the music as it proceeded (see below, p. 287). His comparison of the stained glass in the Cathedral with that of King's College Chapel and York Minster springs from personal observation while at work in Cambridge on the Fitzwilliam music and in York on the materials for his great Purcell edition. Where he is at fault on points of fact—as in attributing the windows in Antwerp Cathedral to Roger van der Weyden and Dürer—he has probably been misled by his reference books ('see Burney, p. 28, and Guide for Cathedral'): Burney's *The Present State of Music in Germany, the Netherlands and the United Provinces* (1773) was the obvious travel book for a musician to take with him, but it has given him the erroneous dating of Roger van der Weyden as contemporary with Holbein. The 'curious carving' on the pulpit—a mass of naturalistic birds and foliage—is by Michael van der Voort (1667-1737).

Placed so as to command view of *both* paintings.
Pulpit curious carving.
Painted glass more like King's than York—probably done by Roger contemporary with Holbein (see Dr. Burney, p. 51)—only North transept—and two out of six in the nave Albert Dürer.

A most beautiful girl passed us just before the conclusion of the service. Her hood was very artfully disposed, and the head altogether reminded me of one of Guido's exquisite Madonnas. She was a most charming creature, more like an Italian than a Flemish woman.

7

At St Jacques' the ' Rubens family picture ' suggests, to his associative mind, comparisons with other paintings—the self-portrait in the Royal Collection, now at Windsor Castle, the famous *Chapeau de Paille* portrait of Susanna Fourment, his second wife's sister, in the National Gallery, and *The Shepherd and Shepherdess* (also known as *Le croc en jambe*) at the Alte Pinakothek in Munich. It was the engraver's art which, until the coming of the colour print, brought the masterpieces of painting to the cultured middle classes ; of this we are reminded by the mention of Titian's *Venus blinding Cupid* in the Borghese Palace in Rome, which Novello might never have known but for Sir Robert Strange (1721-92), acknowledged as the greatest English classical engraver, who, driven abroad for a period by his Jacobite sympathies, engraved this work in 1769.

St. Jacques—Rubens interesting monument ; buried in a place worthy of him. Family picture. Portrait in armour like him, but I prefer the one in His Majesty's Collection, formerly at Carlton House, and the one representing him [*illegible*] with one of his wives looking round over his shoulder at the spectator. The latter is perhaps more generally known under the title of the ' Shepherd and Shepherdess '. I don't much admire the *Chapeau de Paille*, but the second wife is a very pretty creature, and the little angel with his wings leaning against the lower limbs of the old man is so exquisitely tastely as to be worthy of Titian himself. It is only exceeded by the incomparable Cupid by the latter fine artist in his admirable painting of ' Venus blinding Cupid ', which has been engraved in so masterly a manner by Strange.

I regret not to be able to speak favourably of the musical performance at this fine church. I heard the whole of the Vespers which was accompanied by a small orchestra; but throughout the entire collection of pieces there was not a single one worthy of a musician's attention. The Choir Organ is poor and meagre in its tone and the Full Organ is without exception the very worst I ever heard. The Reed Stops were buzz combs,[13] harsh and detestably out of tune. A pretty voice among the trebles—pity not to employ *women* as in England.

The Music was by some obscure composer whose name I was unwilling to ascertain exactly for his sake [*deleted but legible* : and the careless inefficient hand and common manner with which it was accompanied did not at all compensate for the poverty of the composition].

Civil Swiss seemed anxious for the honour of his church. Told him of the removal of Rubens' ceiling from Whitehall to National Gallery at which he seemed delighted.[14]

Two portraits by Vandyk—pity there are not more pictures by him—likeness to *Milton*.

On the conclusion of the Vespers at St. Jacques, which began at 4 and terminated about 20 minutes before 5, I hurried to the Cathedral once more in order to be present at the afternoon [service] there also which began at 5.

★   ★   ★

The Procession was altogether a most pompous and imposing ceremony. There was first the Swiss to clear the way—then embroidered flags surrounded by large lamps of gold and silver—then upwards of 40 or 50 large wax tapers carried by Priests and the respectable class of Citizens of the place ; the acolytes alternately swinging the incense and kneeling down after every three steps, walking backwards all the way.

Rubens glorious paintings especially the Descent.

An isolated, undated and somewhat cryptic entry on the first page of Novello's second notebook (the little

9

exercise book which had belonged to Edward) proves, by its musical allusions, to refer to this day (cf. pp. 289-90). The reference to ' children singing *Youth's the season made for joy* ' is explained by the fact that this tune, familiar to Novello as the cotillon sung and danced by the Ladies of the Town, in *The Beggar's Opera*, is described by Macheath as ' the French tune Mrs. Slammekin was so fond of ', and is actually the song *Ma commère quand je danse*, well-known all over Europe in the seventeenth century[15]. Antwerp was probably *en fête* for the feast of SS. Peter and Paul, which would also account for the odd scrap of French conversation recorded by Novello, for ' ducasse ' (or ' ducaze ') is the term for *Kermesse* on the Franco-Flemish border.

Vespers at Cathedral, Cimarosa—best movement the one in E flat for tenor voice solo with choral accompaniment : the best voice heard. Children are now singing ' Youth's the season made for joy '. Organ all outside show, large case to which additions seem making, tone poor in quality and totally deficient in power, especially bass.

' Comment vous quittez votre ducaze ' was the natural expression of one lady to another (for every woman by courtesy is a lady).

Mary Novello's account of their next day's round of sightseeing and services takes in two more churches— St Charles and the late Gothic church of St Paul, formerly that of the Dominicans. Her ' fifteen paintings representing the life of Christ ' are in fact a series by various artists depicting the fifteen Mysteries of the Rosary. The original of the Flagellation by Rubens, of which a copy is in this series, is in the North transept. In the courtyard outside is the artificial mound representing Calvary and the Holy Sepulchre, referred to with not unjustified disparagement by Vincent Novello.

The Church of St Charles was built in the seven-

teenth century, in the Baroque style, from the designs
of the Jesuit Pierre Huyssens. Rubens painted the
ceiling panels and altar-pieces, but nearly all his work
(save for two altar-pieces now in Vienna) was destroyed in the fire of 1718. The Assumption and
Presentation to which Mary Novello refers are, respectively, by Cornelis Schut and Jean Joseph Delin.

At the Dominicans on the Monday we heard a good
service, it is really a magnificent church. The choir being
separated from the aisles, and the altar much raised, has a
very imposing effect more especially with the appendage
of acolytes in cortège. The sculpture here is also good, and
the fifteen paintings representing the life of Christ, more
especially the Salutation, the Christ being mocked by the
soldiers and the copy from Rubens of the Flagellation—but
the original is here and I defy anyone to look unmoved
upon this heartrending painting, this Man of sorrows and
of deep intents so maltreated by bigotry and intolerance,
behold and blush, persecutors of any age and faith.

The Church of St Charles, late the Jesuits, is a noble
building and resplendent with marble, sculpture and
paintings. The best are an Assumption of the Virgin, and
a Presentation ; the St Simeon and the Virgin delightful.

Vincent Novello, besides commenting on the mass
they heard at St Paul's (below, pp. 290-91), continues
to keep his eyes open. His remarks on the type of
churchgoer here, as earlier at the Cathedral, provide
an interesting comparison with what he will find in
Catholic Germany and Austria. And at the end of the
service he voices what is to become a recurring
complaint.

Good effect of the steps going up to the Grand Altar.
Flagellation most exquisite Painting. Good copy—and
other Pictures—Presentation. Calvary—childish trumpery.
Fine statues, particularly St. Paul. Original Guido [?][16]

Beggars—Mary to notice . . .

Polite *procession* of Town people to see who are the friends of the Priests, etc. . . . (Collected money *twice*).

I have heard nothing yet by Haydn, Mozart, Beethoven, Cherubini, Hummel or other of the most elevated class of composers.

For the charming gallery at the Museum (Convent of Recollet) see my remarks in the Guide Book.

From St Paul's it is only a short way, down the Canal des Recollets, to the Museum, part of which incorporates the church of the former Franciscan (Recollet) monastery. Novello's note suggests that they went there straight from St Paul's that morning, especially as they were due to leave Antwerp in the afternoon:

Quitted Antwerp at 5 evening by the diligence from the Hotel d'Angleterre. 64 fr. 35 cents to Cologne.

Antwerp to Cologne, June 29-July 1

Another thirty-six hours of non-stop travel lay before them, again with two nights running in the stage-coach. But Mrs Novello's capacity for enjoyment remained undimmed:

We have been very fortunate with the exception of a little cold rain and that I left my much-wished-for cloak behind, but luckily the King of the Netherlands chose to pass through Louvain the same night as we did and the place was gaily illuminated in consequence. The *coup-d'oeuil* was exceedingly picturesque, as though we had waked upon England in the days of Queen Bess. The Town Hall which is beautiful gothic, lit up in every window with a crown and so presenting an entire front of light, which reflecting upon the opposite houses showed their scalloped gable points filled with females at every window in the showy colours peculiar to the continent. Beneath were ranged the military like a gay but uniform parterre and crowds of gaping peasants filled the surrounding area. Our *conducteur* would fain have regaled them with a triumphant strain, but his cracked tones savoured more of our old friend Punchinello.

There must be something very rejuvenilating [*sic*] in the continental air, for I have twice been addressed by the title of Mademoiselle, I can hardly believe I am turned of forty and the mother of a married daughter.

Liège is a pretty town, the whole populace speak French, the market is very large and well supplied, bought a basket of strawberries and cherries at double its value, because the girl looked so pretty, and coaxed so well with her ' Chère Madame '.

As on the first lap of their journey, Vincent Novello's notes trace this second phase, point by point—first from Antwerp to Malines, then along the straight Roman road to Louvain. The ' beautiful Gothic tower ' to St Rombaut's Cathedral at Malines is, as his fellow-passenger told him, incomplete. An engraving by Wenzel Hollar shows the original design, which, if carried out, would certainly have made it a rival to Antwerp Cathedral.

Monday, June 29th. . . . Arrived Malines 7 o'clock. Beautiful Gothic tower to the church, a little like the one at Antwerp Cathedral. Shawls principal manufacture.

A Passenger told me that it was originally intended to have been much higher, and if the design had been completed it would have been nearly if not quite as fine as Antwerp. The *lower* part is, I think, more beautiful than the Antwerp tower. The tracery of the windows, especially the one at the South transept, is far more elegant and graceful than those at the Cathedral at Antwerp.

13

Road from Malines to Louvain straight as an arrow without once turning the whole distance, which is no less than 12 miles.

At 10 o'clock arrived at Louvain—entrance to the town very picturesque down the rapid descent of a hill, on the summit of which to the left as you enter are the remains of a castle said to have been built by Julius Caesar. The Hotel de Ville is a remarkably fine specimen of ancient architecture which we were particularly fortunate in seeing under very peculiar and favourable circumstances —for in consequence of the King passing through Louvain this evening, the Hotel and the surrounding neighbourhood were brilliantly illuminated, and the upper part covered with Flags which, waving high up in the air above the weird light produced by the Lamps, had a very striking effect. Before the gates of the Hotel were the six Horses [which] belonged to the King waiting ready for his arrival. The Square was surrounded by Military, and although the rain was pouring down, the whole Town seemed gathered together to gaze at the illuminations and enjoy the show.

Tirlemont 12 o'clock at night, Saintrond $\frac{1}{2}$ past 12 o'clock at night. Changed to the cabriolet.

Driving all night through the rain, they reached Tongres early next morning, and their halt for breakfast gave them an opportunity to glance at the outside of the Basilica of Notre Dame. Its Gothic tower, as Novello surmised, had originally been crowned by a steeple; but two successive steeples had been destroyed by fire, in 1598 and 1677. The little belvedere turret that the Novellos saw—and which is shown in prints of the eighteenth and early nineteenth century—was erected in 1703 and again destroyed in 1877. At the final restoration in 1877 the tower was completed by a stone balustrade, as seen today. The brickwork in the bell-loft window, to which Novello took exception, has been removed.

Streaming rain all the way to Tongres. *Tuesday morning* at ½ past 5—to breakfast. Handsome Tower to the Church, as far as the clock. The remainder to the top is evidently a mere temporary addition put up after the original height had been diminished by some accident. The beauty of the Tower is much deteriorated by the destruction of the *tracery* of the large opening to the Bell loft, etc., the deficiency being supplied by the aperture being merely bricked up, gives a look of great poverty and meanness.

Only 1 franc and ½ for *both* to Breakfast—excellent Coffee and plenty of good Bread, Milk, etc.

Left Tongres after changing diligence at ¼ before 6. Continued rain. Road uninteresting till we arrived at Liège ½ past 7, but the view on descending the steep Hill overhanging the Town amply repaid the previous insipidity of the Landscape, for it forms one of the most extensive, varied and beautiful Prospects which we have met with since Cassel. In the abruptness and magnificence of its principal features, it reminded me of the charming Scenery of Fairlight Glen near Hastings.

During their two hours and a half at Liège, besides touring the streets and parks, and the market that had so beguiled Mary, the Novellos found time for an architectural pilgrimage also. Novello's objection to the Cathedral is doubtless due to its squat, ill-proportioned tower. St Martin's church, a very old foundation, was rebuilt in 1542 ; the ' gorgeously attired ' Madonna to which Novello refers is probably the mediaeval statue of Notre Dame Mère de Tous, then but newly brought back from St. Séverin to this church, its original home. The central rood screen with its sculptures has now been removed, and the present organ, of nineteenth-century construction, is in the

15

south transept. Though he had no time to hear any music, Novello at least had the satisfaction of recalling that he was in the native city of André Ernest Modeste Grétry (1742-1813), one of the leading eighteenth-century composers of *opéra comique*.

More proofs of the universal passion for Flowers which is so creditable to the People's taste. Shops decorated with large Bouquets which seemed just gathered. Fine Market. Beautiful clean Brass cans for milk . . . Brass vessels like the ancient Etruscan Vases. *Grétry born here*. Extraordinary number of Billiard Tables. The Banks of the River very tastefully laid out in Gardens.

Cathedral in the low town is hideously ugly, but church of St Martin situated in the highest part of the Town good specimen of old Gothic style and is in the form of a Cathedral with transepts, etc. The high altar is rich, and at the East end are some good windows in stained Glass. A Madonna and Child most gorgeously attired are situated under the centre, and on the place where the Organ screen is generally placed in our English Cathedrals are the admirable pieces of Sculpture representing Popes in their Pontifical Robes and other figures of Saints, etc. At the West end is situated the Choir with a rather large organ in a handsome Case.

This is altogether [a] very fine old Church though it appears to have suffered much during the revolution and is now in a decaying state.

If I could have spared the time, I would have touched the Organ Keys to ascertain what kind of instrument it was, but I was obliged to hurry back to the diligence which was to leave at 10 o'clock.

Another proof of the Liègeois' love of plants was afforded by the great nave of this church being surrounded with Orange Trees and other Shrubs in large Boxes.

Left Liège at 10. The environs are very picturesque and the numerous hills with which the town is surrounded form . . . [*sentence unfinished*].

Novello's pictorial eye, his quick associative faculty and his wide knowledge of painting, past and present, are constantly in evidence, together with that ready response to the picturesque elements in late Gothic architecture which the Romantic movement had engendered; hence his appreciation of Samuel Prout (1783-1852), whose water-colour studies had familiarized cultured Englishmen with the mediaeval churches and houses of the Continent.

Arrived at Anze [?] 1 o'clock. Curious old place with an ancient but not handsome church. Some of the houses would have afforded good subjects for Prout's pencil. Number of Birds in Cages especially *Larks*. Fine Brass work—singular shape of wooden Shoes, or sabots. *Fat* Beggars very troublesome.

Four very handsome white and iron grey Horses just like what Wouwermans was so fond of painting. At the foot of a Hill further on a fifth Horse was added which was a facsimile of the fine animal in Cuyp['s picture] of a Cavalier mounting.[17]

I have not yet heard any striking instance of that tendency to sing in parts, which is said to be so peculiarly characteristic of the common People on the Continent.

Very pleasant road abounding with beautiful and extensive views, some of which strongly reminded us of English scenery.

Douane de Belge (Custom House) 3 o'clock. The officer merely enquired whether we had anything to declare, and on our stating that we had nothing, he did not even look at our Luggage. Mary purchased a couple of Bottles of Eau de Cologne of him (at his request) for his civility.

At Aix, Novello's comments reveal the limitations of his romantic appreciation of Gothic architecture. In the Cathedral he has eyes only for the late Gothic choir, which, for him, completely obliterates the venerable Octagon, built in the Byzantine style at the close of the eighth century, and containing the tomb of the Emperor Charlemagne himself. In his reactions, moreover, he shows himself a scholar and purist as well as a romantic. The romantic as such delighted in the picturesque clutter of old houses and booths built up against cathedral walls, as shown in so many of Prout's water-colours. Novello wishes them removed— a measure since largely carried out, partly in the interests of hygiene and town-planning, partly in those of tidy scholarly restoration. He also objects continually to the admixture of architectural styles. He does not dislike the classical revival as such : he praises the Madeleine in Paris and Barth's public buildings at Stuttgart, and if, in Cologne, he refers to Buckingham Palace as ' the Pimlico deformity ', it is probably a mixture of distaste for its occupant and for Nash's designs for its reconstruction. But here, at Aix, and throughout the journey, his severest criticisms are invariably levelled against ' Grecian ' additions to Gothic churches.

St Paul's, the other church the Novellos visited in Aix, was severely damaged in the second World War.

Arrived at Aix-la-Chapelle 5 [in the] afternoon. St Paul's (opposite the Poste Royale) handsome interior— good sculpture in wood painted in imitation of stone. Good Copy of Rubens' ' Descent ', and a remarkably fine Painting of the Flagellation, different from Rubens and apparently an original by one of the great Italian masters.

Cathedral very fine at the *east* end and resembles the Cathedral at Cologne. *West* end very bad—evidently modern addition and in the very worst *Grecian* taste. The upper part of the East End has a most strikingly novel and

18

light effect, the whole of the sides consisting of *Glass windows* and the *Buttresses* to support them, so that there are no side *walls* whatever.

Quite disfigured like the Tower at Antwerp by the mean houses built up against it.

Hotel de Ville at Aix good old style, but much decayed.

Handsome fountain, with a Statue of Charlemagne at the centre and two other fountains on each side with the Prussian Eagle surmounting them. Took coffee at the Hotel de Tourelle near the Post Office where we took a cold Fowl and a good Vin de Bordeaux (charges high, 1 Thaler and 30 Groschen).

The fountain was erected in 1620. The statue is still standing, but the side fountains surmounted by the Prussian eagles are no longer there. The Town Hall, to which both Novello and his wife refer, was begun in the fourteenth century, and was built on the site, and partly with the fragments, of Charlemagne's palace.

Mary Novello sums up the city and the second weary night of travel.

At Aix la Chapelle, in the church of St Paul there are some good carved figures and a copy of Rubens descent from the cross, very good. The exterior of the cathedral is much disfigured by the repairs of brick and mortar, what is untouched of the old Tower is good. The Platz has a fine fountain, or rather three—the principal one surmounted by a figure of Charlemagne, which the French carried off, but this must have been more in spite than for its beauty which is only mediocre. The town house good, probably the remains of Charlemagne's palace.

Left at eight in the evening in a miserable chaise called extra-post, but a relief one way as there were some horrid persons in the diligence with dogs and birds. Recognized by a fellow traveller who had seen me two years ago at supper at Heidelberg[18] (what a thing it is for a middle-aged gentlewoman to cause such a sensation).

Her husband also records the incidents of the night, and their arrival at Cologne.

Left Aix at 8 o'clock evening. Very brutal manner of the official people at the Post Coach Bureau.

A very disagreeable road between Aix and Cologne, rendered still more so by the incommodious and worn-out Chaise into which they placed us under the name of the extra Post—the Diligence being quite full.

A gentleman (by a curious coincidence) rode with us who remembered travelling with Mary from Heidelberg when she was in Germany before.

Wednesday, July 1st. Arrived at Cologne 5 o'clock morning, went to Bed at our Hotel (de Vienne) at $\frac{1}{2}$ past 5 and slept till $\frac{1}{2}$ past 8.

Cologne, July 1-2

After their two nights on the road—for the second time within the week—the travellers might well have allowed themselves more than three hours' sleep. But there was too much to be seen, besides business calls to be made. Mary Novello continues:

Cologne, at the Hotel de Vienne were comfortably lodged and attended by a good-natured waiter, excellent wine, particularly the Hochheimer. Went to the Cathedral, the beauty of the choir struck me as much as ever, but the remainder seems hastening to decay. They are busy working on the exterior but will never restore its intended splendour which would render it the first gothic Cathedral in the world. No organ or bell heard.

20

Rubens divine painting of the crucifixion of St Peter in the church of that name, what a superior artist is Rubens, more especially in his groupings and colouring, but to see him to perfection it is certainly necessary to visit the continent, for I greatly suspect many of those in England are either copies or his earliest performances.

Found our way wonderfully through the intricacies of Cologne and went to our banker's which was in a narrow lane resembling our Thames Street filled with warehouses, and indeed many of these foreign bankers are merchants— this one a wine merchant, at Munich a tobacconist.

In Cologne Vincent Novello, disappointed of music, consoled himself with the visual arts. Rubens, and the unfinished Cathedral, dominate his imagination. It is curious, however, that he assumes that the Cathedral has once been complete and is now a ruin, whereas it was, in fact, in an unfinished state, although the nave was temporarily fitted up for service in 1388 and a temporary roof provided about 1508. But the work was suspended, and engravings by Wenzel Hollar, and a painting by Jan van der Heyden dated 1694, show one unfinished West tower with a crane still in position—as still depicted in a vignette by Clarkson Stanfield in Heath's Picturesque Annual for 1832. In 1824, however, King Frederick William III of Prussia had begun the work of restoration on which the Novellos cast so pessimistic an eye. The project of completing it was then put forward, the foundation stone of the new part of the building being laid in 1842 and its completion celebrated in 1880.

St. Peter's Church, which they also visited, was reduced to a shell during the second World War.

St Peter's Church, St Cecilia Street, charming quiet Cloister, and beautiful garden. The Painting of the Crucifixion of St Peter with his head downwards is one of the finest productions of Rubens, the head of St Peter is full of expression, which is best perceived by looking from beneath a desk which the sacristan brings to you—a most quaint [?] looking squalid little fellow—he ought to have a Description book printed for visitors. All the five Executioners are fine especially the one lifting the left arm of St Peter—and the one *hammering* the nails into the feet of the Martyr—the head and face of the latter Executioner appear to have been studied from the same individual as that of the old man in the ' Descent ' who is looking over the top of the Cross, and supporting the sheet with his mouth and teeth.

The composition, grouping, energy, colouring, expression are all of the very highest order—and if Cologne contained nothing but this exquisite and masterly production, it would be well worth the trouble of visiting.

The more I see of Rubens the more highly I think of the extraordinary energy and universality of his genius— no one can have a just idea of his great superiority, who judges only from the Paintings which are to be met with from his hand in England.

The Cathedral when in its complete state must have been one of the most magnificent specimens of gothic architecture in the world. The Choir or East End, both exteriorly and interiorly, is one of the most beautiful specimens of the florid Gothic that I ever saw ; the tracery is of the most exquisite and tasteful description, the forms and proportions of the windows and the flying Buttresses are of the most graceful kind—the stained Glass windows are of the most brilliant, deep and rich Colours especially those which are at the extremity of the small Chapel in which (it is said) are contained the remains of the Magi—or three Kings who after paying their adoration at the Manger in Bethlehem, wandered together as far as Cologne, where they all died and were buried in this very building.

3. MARY NOVELLO AND HER DAUGHTER CLARA

Of the west end there now remain only the ruins of *one* Tower—but those ruins are of so grand and beautiful a description that one hardly knows which feeling is the predominant one, whether admiration at what is still remaining or regret for what has been destroyed.

The masterly view of Cologne taken from the [*illegible*] by Stanfield (which is worthy of Turner himself) will give you a very accurate idea of the general appearance of this fine old Town[19]—but you ought to see the Cathedral on the spot to appreciate the peculiar charm conveyed by its mixture of perfect beauty and sad mutilation.

I should much like to see an accurate painting or engraving of this superb Building in its *complete* state, in the meantime I should be well satisfied to see a series of Drawings [*several words illegible*] drawn by Prout and engraved by Le Keux.[20]

Horridly disfigured by the houses built up against it especially on the south side—how beautiful it would be if it were completely restored (instead of patching it up in the interior with a *low* ceiling of wood) and then laid open entirely by a grand square to the River Rhine.

It would certainly require a long while and cost perhaps as much money as the Pimlico deformity called the new Palace,[21] but the Cologne affair would be well worth the time, trouble and money bestowed upon it.

Several of the windows reminded me of the fine ones in the nave of York Minster and others were very like those delicately tinted and pale coloured slim slips of [*blank*] known by the name of the Five Sisters in the north transept of the same ' glorious Minster of old Ebor '.

I am sorry to add that Music seems to be completely ' at a stand ' here or rather in a state of retrogradation. I could not find out there was anything of any kind in

23

5

the musical way that was in the least degree prominent or worthy of notice.

The celebrated Bell or what has been very well called [*blank*] kept its beauty to itself. I suppose it was under repair or that the clock machinery connected with it was out of order as it never once struck during the whole time I remained here. I regret this as I should have liked to have heard this Rival of our Bow Bell.[22]

So the only music Novello was able to record in Cologne, on the pages he had prepared with blank staves in his notebook, was the following :

Melody played on the Trumpet by the Postilion at Cologne.

His tone was very like that of Mr. *Punch*.

The pleasant weather on which he comments added to the enjoyment of their sight-seeing. Of the inn where they spent so short a time he makes a single characteristic observation.

Very fine weather at Cologne ; the day was what Rousseau calls ' un jour des Dames ' or neither sultry, windy nor wet, so that a Lady can walk about without being annoyed in any of those three ways.

Staircase at our Inn was a very curious one of the Corkscrew kind, and reminded me of the circular one in Rembrandt's painting of the old Philosopher, and another by Ostade representing an old Lady coming down the stairs with a strong light in her hand.[23]

Journey up the Rhine, Cologne to Mannheim, July 2-4

The following day, after only one night's rest, they continued their journey up the Rhine. Between Cologne and Mainz they travelled by steamboat—a service that had only been in existence since 1827. The voyage is recorded in a very different manner by husband and wife. For Novello, there is no music to take note of or dissect, no architecture save that of the distant castles, no painting ; so he remains quietly and happily on deck, watching one lovely landscape melt into the next, through rain and sunshine, as the boat glides past, and somewhat detached from his travelling companions. Indeed, when he mentions his fellow-travellers at all, it is usually when they are ' amiable ' or ' well-informed ', so that he has been able to learn from them something of interest.

Thursday, July 2nd. Left Cologne at 6 o'clock in the morning by the Dampfschiff or Steam Boat—up the Rhine.

Arrived at Bonn at 11 o'clock after a quiet voyage of 5 hours during which we had several showers of rain. Although the weather was not very favourable yet the journey was a very placid and agreeable one. The Banks of the fine River have been hitherto much flatter than what I expected to find them, but the Seven Hills [Siebengebirge] are now at a very little distance and the views promise to become much more picturesque and interesting.

We remained but such a short time (only 10 minutes just to take in passengers) that I had no opportunity of going on shore, otherwise I should have liked to have paid a visit to the Establishment of Mr. Simrock who is (I understand) so great and enthusiastic an admirer of Mozart that he always moves his hat whenever Mozart's name is mentioned. It would have also afforded me much pleasure to have called upon my friend and Brother

25

Professor Mr Ries, but that I understood from his Brother before I left England that Mr Ries had left Bonn for the present on a little professional excursion to Aix-la-Chapelle, etc. This very ingenious Professor and estimable private individual has retired to live here after having acquired a handsome and well-deserved competency by his meritorious Professional exertions in England.

Nicholas Simrock (1752-1834), a native of Bonn, had founded his well-known publishing house in 1790, and published some of the earliest piano arrangements of Mozart's operas. *Die Entführung, Figaro, Così fan tutte* and *Die Zauberflöte* all appeared in this form under his imprint before 1800.

Ferdinand Ries (1784-1838) had studied the piano with Beethoven in Vienna. Like him a native of Bonn, he came to London, and in 1813 was introduced by Salomon to the newly-formed Philharmonic Society, of which he, like Novello, became one of the most active members. He retired to Bad Godesberg in 1824, but remained active and for several years was in charge of the Lower Rhine Festival. His younger brother Peter, a friend of Lamb's, remained in London with Broadwoods, the firm of piano manufacturers.

The term ' Professor ' was used in the musical world at this period to denote a professional musician.

Just after quitting Bonn and on approaching the celebrated ' Drachenfels ' (see Campbell's Lines)[24] we were overtaken by one of the most sudden and violent showers of Rain that I ever was in. Several of the Passengers were wet before they could get below—and I was the only Passenger at last who remained on Deck, but I did not by any means regret this, as it afforded me an opportunity of enjoying some of the grandest sights during the voyage ; the effect of a Storm on this River and amongst these singular and abrupt elevations was quite sublime. In the course of the day we had every variety of weather from a

Storm to a beautiful and brilliant Sunshine. The two finest points of this day's voyage were the ' Drachenfels ' and the Fortress of Ehrenbreitstein, of which Turner made so admirable a Drawing and an engraving of which appeared last year in one [of] the Annuals.[25]

> Mary Novello, on the contrary, is always vastly interested in the men and women she meets, whether or not she likes them, as befits an authoress. Her account starts with one of those bad Novello puns with which Keats was ' devastated and excruciated ' when taken to visit the family.[26]

The Dampschiffe [sic] verified its name, for we were overtaken by the most furious rain storm, which wet everyone through who had not sheltered themselves in time in the cabin. We were passing the Drachenfels so that it was very tantalising to peep at these beauties through round holes like the Panorama and a veil of mist.[27] Dear Papa kept the deck stoutly, fortunately there was an awning and he had his umbrella, besides it was his whim, from which no element (particularly a violent one) could move him. The cabin was full—one party of six, an Irish family in search of the picturesque, were very polite considering they had two carriages on board. They were very modest, but it must be owned, nature had been very niggardly to them, they seemed to have but little brains in the party and their carriage and air might have indicated them for assistants at Flint's. They seemed goodnatured but their whole discourse, whether upon the places they had visited, or their intended route, was concerning Inns— the sole purport of their tour seemed to discover where they could best be lodged, and their albums were produced for no other purpose than to take note of the ' Lion D'or ', the ' Cerf Blanc ', the ' Coq rouge ' etc., etc., etc. An Amsterdam Jewess, who spoke Whitechapel English, was in their eyes an admirable cicerone, she had visited Switzerland, whither they were hastening, and furnished them with a long list of guides, Inns, prices, etc. Not one of the party spoke any other than their mother tongue, except the elder son, and his French was very English and his German almost as *schlecht* as mine.

The only foreign language Mrs. Novello seems to have been proficient in was French, although her father was German-born and a teacher of languages. In Italian she writes Vicenzia for Vicenza and Vincenzio for Vincenzo ; but usually she calls her husband Vin.

An English general of simple appearance, and very well informed, had the discernment to fasten himself upon Vincenzio, they were deep in discourse, most of the day, upon Italy, where this gentleman had resided for some years.

After all my preconceived notions of Americans being great bores, conceive my astonishment to meet with one on board, in person resembling young Pinto's portrait,[28] his voice sweet and low like a woman's, and his manner and conversation well informed, easy and gentlemanly.

An old, military *roué* of the sister kingdom, with a red face, an invincible brogue, and a measureless impudence, several Germans and their wives and children, one nice young man, but very plain, kept eyeing us English—he had just returned from a visit to England : this was our party until we arrived at Coblenz where we were to sleep, and then such a confusion to get suited at the different hotels. Not liking our room at the ' Trois Suisses ', we were for going to the ' Post ', but it was full, and the porter took us to the ' Cour du Rhin '. Here we found our Hibernian *roué* in a great fume, he entreated us to come and sleep in the adjoining room to him, for he did not like the people of the house, they were extortionate, vulgar, etc., etc. ;

had we been in the heart of the Schwarzwald, or the wilds of Calabria, he could not have worn a more agitated aspect, I verily believe had any one in sport stalked him with a sausage he would have dropped down dead in real earnest. In pure compassion I followed him to the chamber he wished us to have, but as it looked only over a garden, my complaisance could not extend so far as to exchange it for the previous one showed by the waiter, exactly facing the Thal Ehrenbreitstein, and I very naively told him, I thought there was nothing to fear. ' Not exactly to fear, but I do not like the appearance of the house, and wish you could be near me '. Now this man had very much the appearance of a bully, a sharper, and a fortune hunter, only that his ugly and battered appearance was something against this latter pursuit, except like Sir Ulic Macshane [*sic*], he made his court to old spinsters with lap dogs;[29] he was going to Ems, doubtless with a view in that resort of the idle and the thoughtless to resuscitate his funds and his health.

Vincent Novello's brief note on their arrival elliptic-ally bears out the story :

We arrived at Coblenz at 8 in the evening. Hotel ' Cour du Rhin ' exactly opposite the grand fortress of Ehrenbreitstein. Irishman very nervous about sleeping in the next room to where we were.

Mary Novello continues :

When we got rid of him, for he paid us a second visit, we enjoyed the fine view our room afforded us over the Rhine, the sunset was fine and the twilight lasted until nearly 10—the grand fortress seen by its light became doubly aweful, and one by one the twinkling lights from the bridge and the opposite houses announced the increas-

ing gloom of night, sounds on the river and the banks
became fainter, and left the sublime scenery of nature in
solitude and delicious repose. Had we not been forced to
rise at 4 next morning we should not have quitted it for
hours, but we left our window open, so that whenever we
wakened our eyes might light upon the delicious scene.
Germany is the only place to see the sunrise, for you cannot
sleep much after 3, there is such a stirring among all the
people, both in the Inn, and the Town.

Vincent Novello therefore records:

Friday, July [3]:
Rose at $\frac{1}{2}$ past 4, took a look round the Town. Curious
fountain with inscription erected in 1814 in commemoration of the Campaign against the Russians. Beautiful
morning. Left by steam Boat at 6. Stolzenfels particularly
fine Ruin, large fort blown up by the French . . . restored
by Prince Friedrich.[30] Echo. Fine altogether though
restored—as fine as B[*illegible*] where the Bank similar.

Mary Novello continues her account:

The views today on the river surpassed even those of
yesterday. The Stolzenfels is one of the most beautiful,
and here a young Englishman came on board, who had
been a companion of the young American's, and whom he
was to accompany in a walking tour through Switzerland.
He had remained in this little village strolling amongst the
heights, and amused us much by his stories and the cool
manner of narrating his hair breadth escapes from various
perils by mountain and river. I have not had a heartier
laugh since the stories of Leigh Hunt, though he did not
otherwise resemble him. One was of an upset he had in the
Thames, his young companion and himself soon swam to
shore, but an old gentleman and his baggage who were in

the boat with them sank. ' I began to be alarmed,' he said,
' when I saw the old man going down with the stream, so
we fished him up and *hung him on a rail to dry*, for we thought
it was all up with him, and it was a long while before he
came to '. The oddity of hanging the old gentleman on a
rail to dry, like so much wet linen, tickled my fancy
amazingly, and I laughed outright. ' It was an awkward
job,' he added, ' for I should not have liked it to appear
in the newspaper, it would have looked so odd '. This
seemed his only apprehension or reflection after such a
narrow escape.

Vincent Novello sums up the American, his English
friend and his story in an even more elliptical note
than that about the Irishman, which would not even
make sense without his wife's account, but does give
the American's name :

Pleasant American Mr. Potter (very like Pinto) and his
friend—(hung up to dry).

New and less congenial travelling companions joined
them, and are described by Mrs. Novello :

A little further on our company was reinforced by two
English families—one the most disgusting set, with ' foreheads villainously low ',[31] and the lower part quite
brutal, voices, men's sullen and the girls snappish. Thank
God they sat in their carriage all the time on deck and even
wanted dinner brought to them. I wish they could have
obtained their piggish desire, for unfortunately they sat
opposite us, and spoiled Vincent's dinner completely, with
their brutal looks and manners. What could these people
be originally, Vin thinks they had come into a fortune
suddenly and had gone a-voyaging to acquire polish—but
this was an odd way truly, to remain shut up in the fore
part of the Vessel, where they could only watch the cooks,

scullions and sailors with other singular proceedings too numerous to mention.

In contrast to these the other English party were working for taste and *les belles lettres* and *les arts*, with a 40-horsepower of exertion. The Papa seemed a reasonable sleepy old gentleman enough, but the Mama was most amusing, a little woman eternally besetting someone for information. They came on board loaded with cloaks, eye glasses, telescopes, albums, Walter Scott's works, Byron and T. Moore (Galignani's edition) to show that they had been in Paris,[32] and that not a moment must be lost by the hopefuls to catch a smattering of these authors between each view, and then Miss must sketch in her album each passing view. The first thing I heard the good bustling little dame say, a few minutes after her arrival, was ' Come directly, Caroline, here is a Swiss lady who speaks French very well, and she will tell you all about it.' By her manner you might have imagined the life of someone in a convulsion fit was at stake for this intelligence ; and yet, poor woman, her four children were the weakest-looking mortals, body and mind, imaginable.

At dinner time, in contrast to these fantastical English, were a party of Germans who, though they had never met before, grew merry over their wine, clicked their glasses, drank bottle after bottle of Rhenish, told odd stories, and set their end of the table in a roar, they would have sung some Rhine wine songs, but I verily believe the staid faces of the English damped the fumes of their wine, and after an attempt or two they desisted from further melody, but their harmony was complete until they divided and then as the boat carried off a part they cheered and waved caps bravely.

Another elliptical note in her husband's notebook sums up the German party :

32

Divine and disciples sat opposite to us (merry set of Germans) who tried to sing afterwards.

Mayence at $\frac{1}{2}$ past 8 at night.

The following day they completed their journey by coach to Mannheim, their next stopping place, travelling in company with the German (' nice young man, very plain ') whom Mary Novello had already noticed on the steamboat :

From Mayence to Mannheim we travelled in company with the young German who proved a pleasant companion, he was from Weimar where Goethe and Hummel live.

Johann Nepomuk Hummel (1778-1837), whom, as Mozart's pupil, Novello was to hear discussed in Salzburg and Vienna, had a great contemporary reputation as pianist and composer. He was musical director to the Court of Weimar in 1820-2 and again in 1833-7, undertaking extensive concert tours in between, during which he had visited London. Edward Holmes met him on his travels and gives an enthusiastic account of his improvisation[33] ; but it was rather as a composer of ' sterling ' church music that Novello (whose account amplifies his wife's) held him in such high esteem.

Saturday, July [4th]. Left Mayence at $\frac{1}{2}$ past 7—by a kind of hired carriage something like a Cabriolet but larger and more commodious. A very well-behaved German Gentleman was our companion, who had been with us on board the Steam Boat from Cologne to Mayence. He spoke French very fluently, had been in England, and was altogether a well-informed and tasteful person. In the course of our conversation he told me that he was personally acquainted with Goethe and Hummel and (what was very pleasant for me to hear) he also said that I was very like Hummel in personal appearance. There was also

33

a German returning to see his birth place after having been
absent from it for 36 years, during which he had lived in
England.

> At Worms, Novello appears to have been as much
> struck with the Salvator Rosa engraving at the inn
> where they dined as with the noble Romanesque
> Cathedral, which dates from the twelfth century ; the
> Gothic south portal, to which he takes exception for
> its inconsistency of style, was rebuilt in the fourteenth
> century.

Salvator Rosa, Jason, engraved in 1765 by Boydell—
from the original formerly in the Collection of the Earl of
Bessborough,[34] in the Inn *Der Roemer* (the Roman) at
Worms where we arrived at $\frac{1}{2}$ past 12, after a very pleasant
journey in a kind of Glass Coach.[35] Saw the Cathedral—
in the Saxon style, handsome circular Tower[s]—the additions to the Building are inconsistently made in the
Gothic style.

Frauen Milk [*sic*] Wine from the name of a Convent
dedicated to the Virgin in the neighbourhood formerly.

Arrived at Mannheim $\frac{1}{2}$ past 5. Inn of the Paladin.[36]
Birthplace of John Cramer.

Mannheim, July 4-6

After settling at their inn there was still time for the
Novellos to see something of Mannheim—not yet the
manufacturing centre which was to form a target for
Allied bombs in the second World War, but a quiet
little town, laid out (on the rectangular plan to
which Novello calls attention) and built in the seventeenth century by the Electors Palatine. As their
residence, in the eighteenth century, it reached its
heyday as a cultural and musical centre. Mozart was
vastly impressed with its famous orchestra, which he

34

heard on his way to Paris in 1778, and its musicians—such as Wilhelm Cramer, father of Novello's friend the pianist, composer and publisher J. B. Cramer (1771-1858)—brought a high reputation with them when they settled in England. But in 1778 the Elector Carl Theodor also became Elector of Bavaria and transferred his Court to Munich : hence Novello's observation on the ' neglected appearance ' of the Palace, (further damaged by French gunfire in 1792), and the fact that Mozart's *Idomeneo* was first produced at Munich, and not in the squat, horse-shoe-shaped Mannheim Theatre, with its tiers of boxes, where the Novellos were to hear Auber's *La Muette de Portici*. The Jesuit Church, which they attended on the Sunday, was built in 1733-36.

Vincent Novello describes the town as they saw it during their evening stroll.

Very pleasant place, agreeable airy walk lined on each side with Trees. Very large Palace of which the part formerly occupied by the Theatre was unfortunately burnt down at the time that this place was bombarded by Custine—it has never been restored and is now a complete ruin.

The Palace itself has a neglected appearance but the Gardens behind it are both extensive and well laid out. We took a stroll in them for about an hour in the evening and proceeded along a large mound which has been erected to check the incursions of the Rhine which occasionally overflows its banks so as to cause considerable injury. The view from the Banks of the River just in this spot is particularly fine especially towards that point looking towards Heidelberg—on the height of one of the mountains are seen at the distance of twelve miles the remains of a Roman watch tower[37]—and on the other side of the valley can be clearly distinguished the Castle of Heidelberg itself. On our return from a most delightful little walk we saw the observatory attached to the Palace, the arsenal and the Hotel de Ville—both very handsome specimens of architecture. Indeed the whole Town appears to be particularly well built. The whole is built at right angles and divided into small portions, which are all *lettered* and *numbered* so that the Police can refer to any particular quarter with the greatest facility.

It was while exploring Mannheim that Novello first observed symptoms of the all-prevalent 'Rossini fever' that swept the musical world from Vienna to London in the 1820's:

Heard Rossini's Overture to 'Barbiere di Siviglia' on the Piano Forte concerted [?] with Violoncello—and the Introduction to the same Opera. Violoncello poor player —but Piano Forte good—brilliant fingers and accurate timist. I should have preferred hearing something by their celebrated townsman John Cramer, but *sterling* music appears to be at a very low ebb here, as well as everywhere else on the Continent as far as I can hitherto judge. The tone of the Piano was thin and wiry and very inferior to those I have been accustomed to hear by Broadwood and other excellent *London* makers.

But the associations linked with the all-pervasive Italian are not so easily to be shaken off; a tiny sketch of a hat in Novello's notebook is preceded by the words

In walking through *Mannheim*—*Hats* worn like those by Pippo in the ' Gazza Ladra '.

The next day, Sunday, July 5th, was given up to the strenuous pursuit of music, sacred and profane. (Novello's detailed comments are to be found on pp. 292-95.)

Sunday, July 5th. Went to the principal Church (formerly that of the Jesuits whose order is now suppressed) [38] to High Mass which began at 9 o'clock. There was no Orchestra—and the Music merely consisted of a kind of Chant, but not Gregorian . . . The musical part of the service was remarkably short as it was all over in little more than half an hour.

The Church is splendidly decorated with marble in the interior and (making allowance for the usual tendency to gaudiness and finery so general in the Catholic Churches all over the Continent) the effect is altogether handsome and striking. The Paintings were not remarkable but the sculpture over the high altar was in good taste and well executed.

As I wished to hear some of the fine old German Chorales I endeavoured to procure admission to the Lutheran Church—but the service had taken place at the same time as at the Cathedral and was concluded before I had arrived.

Charles Lamb would have crowed over this admission on the part of his ' good Catholic friend Nov— ', of whom he had written teasingly to Leigh Hunt in 1825 : ' Something has touched the right organ in Vincentio at last. He attends a Wesleyan chapel on Kingsland Green. He at first tried to laugh it off—he only went for the singing . . .'[39]

Between 11 and 12 I went to hear the Military Band which played for about half an hour in the public square before the Palace. The Instruments were well in tune (a rare thing in a collection of wind Instruments) and the band consists of expert performers—but they wasted their talents upon trumpery waltzes, commonplace trifles, country Dances—and paltry jigs in $\frac{6}{8}$ time. There was not a single movement played that at all approached the elevated style of composition or that was worth a moment's attention from a musician.

On his way back to the hotel he evidently passed ' the club called " Harmony ",' whose reading room is mentioned in Murray's Guide to North Germany of 1877 as still being ' thrown open to strangers, properly introduced ' :

' Harmonie ' written over a House I found meant a ' Club ' where people met not for *musical* purposes but to eat, drink and play cards.

Over the ' Table D'Hôte at our Inn, Niederstein wine, 3 Thalers each ', they fell into conversation with a fellow-countryman :

Pleasant fellow who talked French like a native and who told us that he had a good deal of fun in passing himself off occasionally among the surly [?] English as of a different nation.

Lutheran Church—afternoon service began at 2. Having been detained talking with the agreeable person at the table d'Hôte, I was rather later than I wished to be—but still I was in time to hear a very charming old chorale steadily sung and judiciously accompanied. . . .

I had the curiosity to stop and hear the sermon ; the Preacher seemed to be in earnest and more intent upon instructing his congregation than in exhibiting his own eloquence (rather a rare occurrence amongst the Parsons). His face and person reminded me of the eminent unitarian Preacher and liberal Patriot [?] Mr Fox.

It was probably the influence of Leigh Hunt's radical-ism that had brought the Novellos within the orbit of William Johnson Fox, first minister of South Place Unitarian Chapel (built in 1824) and as much of a liberal in theology as in politics. In the 1830's, when the Novellos and Cowden Clarkes had settled in Craven Hill, they became next-door neighbours to the

38

high-minded but irregular *ménage* shared by Fox with the gifted Eliza and Sarah Flower, and abandoned by the jealous and hostile Mrs Fox in 1834.

Afternoon service at the Jesuits began at 3. It is quite a different service from our Vespers. The commencement was a Hymn in the same style as the morning service—after which came a long sermon of which the congregation seemed as weary as I was, who had the advantage of not understanding it. The Preacher was a most unconscionable fellow and went on in the most persevering droning manner for near an hour. To my great relief, however, he left off at last—when the Litany of Loretto began; it was recited by one of the Priests, and answered by the Congregation not by the Choir—and without any accompaniment whatever. After some dreary prayers, during which most of the People round me seemed inclined to indulge in a Nap, came the Benediction.

That evening we enter a theatre with them for the first time during their journey as they arrive to hear *La Muette de Portici*, Auber's latest opera, which had had its first performance in Paris only the previous year and was now sweeping Europe. From Novello's account they had evidently taken seats in the parterre :

The present Opera House is an extensive building occupying the entire side of the Square opposite the Church of the Jesuits. The Portico is rather heavy—but the building altogether has an air of magnificence arising principally from the Statues and other Sculpture with which it is ornamented. Amongst the Figures which appeared to me best executed were four sphinxes.

In the evening we went to the Opera which began at 6. The performance was the ' Muette de Portici ' (or ' Masaniello ' at Drury Lane) . . .

Price of entrance : Boxes, 1st circle, 1 fl. 20 k., 2nd circle,

6

1 fl., Parterre 48 k., Loge du 4th [*sic*] Rang 24, Gallerie 18, Seitenbänke daselbst [i.e., slips] 12.

The Pit was well filled with respectable Company, but there is not the same advantage here as at Munich, Vienna and other places, where the place may be previously taken and booked up till the persons arrive. The audience part is remarkably heavy and very ill-lighted. The Boxes appear crushed down by the tiers immediately above them, and I should think that the sound must be much deteriorated and nearly smothered before it reaches the Persons seated in them.

The custom of placing a candle *inside* of each box gives a very singular and not agreeable effect.

At the commencement of the Opera the chandelier in the Pit was drawn up entirely out of sight, leaving the audience almost in darkness, in order, I suppose, to give more effect to the light thrown on the stage.

> This was clearly as new to them as it seems old-fashioned to those of the older generation of opera-goers who still remember it. And even today the boxes at La Scala and at other Italian opera houses remain dimly lit as the strong lights in the house subside until the curtain rises, giving an aquarium-like aspect of which it is by no means certain the Novellos would have approved.
>
> Mary Novello's summing-up of the performance is confirmed and amplified by her husband's running comments (below, pp. 264-67).

The present opera house is an ugly heavy interior and so dark on entering that you are literally obliged to feel your way. The centre chandelier is so badly lit that once it went entirely out, to the great amusement of the audience, who applauded as loudly as if some great feat had been achieved, yet this is the only light in the house except the

footlights which seldom appear but during the performance, there are indeed a few rush-lights placed at the back
of the boxes but these were only partially lighted. The
performance was a mediocre representation of the ' Muette
de Portici '. The Princess was rather elderly for a bride,
but she had small regular features and was very thin, her
voice had once been good and with the exception of a little
tremor in the upper part was still flexible and pleasant.
The Prince had a fine nasal tone and the Masaniello was
but indifferently good. The Muette was below mediocrity
infinitely, and was fit only for Sanders' troop.[40] The most
pleasing voice was a baritone who played one of the
fishermen. The house was very crowded and the applause
vociferous especially when any of the commonplace arias
were sung, yet whenever their singers failed in a passage
they laughed outright without any ceremony.

Mannheim—Heidelberg—Heilbronn. July 6

Early next morning they were once again on their way.
Novello describes the day's travel :

Monday, July 6, left Mannheim at 7 in the morning
and arrived at Heidelberg about 9 after a most delightful
ride. The road runs through cultivated fields on either side
[and] is lined all the way with a mixture of Linden and
Fruit trees and occasionally the River on one side, the views
on approaching Heidelberg are particularly beautiful.
Hotel de Portugal to wait for the Diligence to Munich.

As the diligence was not due to leave till 2 that
afternoon, they passed their waiting time in characteristic fashion. ' The principal church ' was probably
the Heilig-Geist-Kirche, of which the nave was
separated from the choir by a wall in 1705, the
Catholics using the choir and the Lutherans the nave.

At the principal Church heard a Requiem Mass. It was the fine Gregorian Mass for the Dead. . . .

The building in which the Requiem was performed was only a portion of the former church, the West end and tower being now shut up and fast falling into decay. Nearly the whole congregation consisted of Females—there being not above four or five men present out of 60 or 70 Persons.

Near the Church is a fountain with a statue of Hercules taken from the Hercules Farnese.

We took a stroll through the town and by the side of the River, the banks and scenery on each side of which are particularly beautiful—and the view is finely terminated by the remains of the Castle, which is one of the most extensive, interesting and picturesque Ruins I ever saw. Heidelberg is altogether a very curious old Town and most charmingly situated. Unfortunately a Shower came on as [we] were enjoying the beauty of the Landscape but our walk was notwithstanding a very delightful one.

(Little Bird in the Road, and refuge in House near the Gateway).

They were probably on the *Philosophenweg*, the road leading up the right bank of the Neckar opposite the town and castle. Unfortunately Mrs Novello's account throws no light on the incident of the little bird in the road. Vincent Novello continues:

Fine as was the walk which I took this morning, the one round and *above* the Palace is still more beautiful. The view from one particular spot where a seat is very judiciously placed was one of the very finest Landscapes I ever beheld. In front are the ruins of the Palace forming a most noble foreground—below is situated the ancient Town with the *Stadtring* and the River 'wandering at its own sweet will' (Wordsworth)[41]. On each side the hills rise with the utmost grandeur and magnificence and are clothed to their very summit by trees and foliage [of] the most beautiful forms and every possible variety of tints of green and other colours. On the eminence to the right was an old Tower built by the Romans. Beyond the Ruins of the Palace is a Claude-like distance with the River glancing on the eye at different points as it winds away in the most graceful curves, and the remote horizon is terminated with the view of Mannheim and other Towns with mountains of the most elegant shape rising beyond them as far as the eye can reach.

I wish, dear Charles,* that you had been with me to have enjoyed this exquisite scene, or that I possessed the power of Turner to have made you a worthy sketch of it to bring home with me in order to present to you.

Left Heidelberg about 2 o'clock in a hired coach—the Postilion of which offered to take us to Stuttgart for the same price as the Diligence (only 17 Thalers).

The Road by the side of the River Neckar (which runs through the valley of that name) is a very charming one forming a complete succession of beautiful views on both sides of the River. We travelled on the right side, which is perhaps the finer of the two, and is formed of immense blocks of granite interspersed with beautiful foliage which has found a nestling place in the crannys and interstices of the Rocks.

About two miles from the Town we passed a particularly beautiful Garden in which was a fountain which perfectly corresponded with the one described in ' Rimini ' as ' shaking its loosening silver in the Sun ' (see the rest of the passage in the poem).[42] There were also several statues visible in different parts of these grounds, which evidently belonged to some Person of cultivated and refined taste.

* Charles Cowden Clarke.

The Scenery continued to be of the most romantic and picturesque description for several miles, each opening occasioned by the winding of the River presenting some new object of admiration.

A carriage appears to me much too quick a mode of conveyance in scenes like these. I quite longed to be on foot, that I might linger on the most interesting spots, instead of being whisked off and hurried out of sight almost immediately they become visible. Few things would afford me higher gratification than to *walk* at my leisure with some tasteful and cordial friend through the whole of this beautiful valley.

In the evening we stopped to take a bottle of ' Landwein ' at a very common little Inn, where no one could speak a word of any other language than German. The wine which seemed to have been just drawn from the large cask, was brought in a singular Decanter something like a Water Bottle, but it was delicious. The Bread also was excellent, which with a slice of Cheese (they had not any meat or Butter) afforded us a very primitive but refreshing Meal. The whole was charged only 36 kreutzers and the maidservant appeared quite surprised when Mary offered her 6 kreutzers and at first actually refused to accept it.

We arrived about 11 o'clock at Heilbronn and after taking a little Cold Bouillon and an excellent Bottle of Rhein Wein we went to Bed.

Mary Novello sums up their day :

On Monday at Heidelberg we had a most delightful walk by the Neckar and after dinner went to Heilbronn in a hired carriage, the road all the way was delightful through the most exquisite scenery of river, woods, and mountains—did not arrive until 12 at night and got a most funny three-cornered room to sleep in.

44

Heilbronn—Ludwigsburg—Stuttgart.   July 7

Their next day's journey was slightly shorter and allowed plenty of time for strolling and sightseeing through Ludwigsburg and Stuttgart. The former, laid out in squares and built to an uniform Italian design in the eighteenth century as the residence of the Dukes of Württemberg, is still very much as they saw it, quiet and untouched. Duke Frederick II, who, as Novello recalls, had married Princess Charlotte Augusta, eldest daughter of King George II, had been made Prince Elector and then King by Napoleon, and the Stuttgart they entered was thus the capital of a kingdom ; but Novello's comments reveal the liberal-humanitarian and critical attitude towards royalty characteristic of the Leigh Hunt circle.

Tuesday, July 7th. Left Heilbronn at $\frac{1}{2}$ past 7. In the morning we heard a very simple and melodious Chorale played by the small Band of wind Instruments which, as our Host afterwards informed us, belonged to a Monastery adjoining our Inn. It was tastefully played and well in tune—I have preserved it (see Music).[43]

There is a very handsome and large Church here, the tracery of the windows very graceful and remarkably elegant in design.

12 o'clock arrived at Ludwigsburg, walked over the

45

Palace and Garden (formerly the residence I believe of our Princess Royal), which are very pleasantly laid out, and the Public have free access and there are seats and tables provided for their accommodation and refreshment and in various parts of the garden are swings, rocking horses and other little objects of amusement.

In the court is a fountain with four lions cast in bronze and the Palace itself is rather a handsome structure, ornamented with Statuary and other pieces of Sculpture. Jommelli was *Maestro di Capella* here for 7 years, but [I] could find none who knew anything about him or his music.[44]

The place is altogether a very pretty one with plenty of foliage and agreeable walks under the Linden Trees and it has a remarkably clean and genteel look about it.

The only thing I disliked was the quantity of Soldiers, who seemed to be more numerous than the inhabitants. I have an invincible repugnance to these outward signs of the power of the ' privileged few ', which power is so likely to be abused and to be turned against the liberty, happiness and best interests of the people at large.

There is a very fine Road amongst the hills covered with vineyards and abundant cultivation on all sides to Stuttgart where we arrived at 3 o'clock (Hotel of the ' Moon '). It is a large and well-built Town, the residence of the Court.

Of the buildings Novello describes, the eighteenth-century New Palace, the sturdily walled Old Castle built in 1553-78 and the Stiftskirche were all severely damaged in the second World War. The seventeenth-century Prinzenbau (the Crown Prince's Palace) is still intact, as also Barth's chastely classic State Archives and Natural History Museum, which had only been completed in 1821.

The Palace of the King, at the left hand just as you enter the Town is not deficient in grandeur and would be better still if the golden (or rather gingerbread, tawdry looking) Crown were removed from the central entrance.

The residence of the Crown Prince, further on, to the right, is a handsome edifice in the modern style, but without pretensions, or exhibiting any signs of its belonging to any of the Royal Family.

The old Palace, which is close to the principal Church, is a good specimen of the ancient style of architecture in this part of the world and is nearly surrounded with Trees, which in my opinion always add to the beauty and interest of a building. The Theatre is of a rather large size and I would have visited it but that, unfortunately, it was closed and the Opera Company were absent on a strolling tour, which it seems is not unusual here.

There is a respectable-looking Concert Room near the entrance of the town, but as there was no performance, I was prevented from forming any opinion of the state of musical taste or of the general feeling on the subject amongst the people of this place.

The principal church is not prepossessing in its appearance, but the windows have some good tracery and over the south west door are some fair specimens of Gothic sculpture. On the West Tower under the clock are several dates painted in large figures from 1530 to 1804 which I presume are intended to recall the various periods at which alterations or additions were made to the building. On the Northern side is a covered Staircase on the outside, very like the one leading to the Jerusalem Chamber at Westminster Abbey and that forming the entrance to Crosby House, mentioned by Shakespeare in Richard III and still extant in a court near Bishopsgate Church— although it is now converted into a mere warehouse belonging to some city merchant.[45]

What appeared to me most singular at Stuttgart was

47

the South Eastern Tower of the Church, the top of which is fitted up like a parlour with window shutters—above, the roof has an opening like an attic and the very summit of all is formed into a kind of summer house. Along the gable end runs a cord and the same rope is continued and stretched at an immense height from tower to tower, that the Gentleman who resides in the East Cupola may occasionally swing himself along over the roof to the other Tower. It is one of the most curious residences I ever saw and I should think it rather inconvenient for anyone but a Rope Dancer.

The King's Library is very liberally open to the Public as is also the collection of subjects of Natural History and they are both contained in adjacent buildings of modern structure, tasteful design and symmetrical form.

Mary Novello appears to have exhausted her capacity for comment by the time they reached Stuttgart.

At Ludwigsburg the next day we had a delightful stroll through the public gardens which like the Champs Elysées at Paris are full of swings and roundabouts to amuse children and common people of a Sunday. At Stuttgart there is nothing remarkable except that the charges are rather high.

Her shrewd eye for character comes into its own once more, however, on the long drive from Stuttgart to Munich, which began at 6 the next morning, July 8th, and continued without a break until 1.30 p.m. on July 9th:

Travelled till we reached Ulm through most delightful scenery—the Cathedral here is certainly fine but much out of repair. The company from hence by the *Eilwagen* [Post Coach] was much improved although we were 5— a good-natured bigoted *royaliste* of the old school and his

German wife, a lively countryman of his, who had served under Prince Eugene [Beauharnais],[46] had been at Moscow, and was evidently still a Napoleonist, but since the death of his beloved master Prince Eugene had married and was settled at Munich. He was very gay and told us many droll naive stories, in good contrast with the other who however told his stories well, which were mostly in honour of the reigning family and were full of love and romantic adventures and always about a *belle fille*, the other seemed delighted when he could throw in a little contrast and give his romance (which was somewhat tedious) a rather burlesque turn. The old gentleman very gravely assured me that the English were obliged to go to France to *buy our cottons and prints* both for cheapness and superior make—they all seem to think we have no vegetables or common fruits. Another merchant laughed at my ignorance because I thought cotton goods were cheaper in England than on the continent, and told me the reason was evident, that ours were charged with a heavy duty which was taken off upon exports. It is in vain to urge your experience to the contrary, they believe you not, England they are determined in all things is the dearest place in the world and their envy makes them deny the superiority she has acquired in all manufactories—but this feeling is most predominant among travelling dealers and tradespeople. Bankers and the better informed, though unwilling, are forced to confess the fact.

Vincent Novello, as usual, sketches in the descriptive and architectural details of their ride through the Swabian Jura:

Wednesday, July 8. Left Stuttgart by the Diligence at 6 in the morning. The weather was remarkably fine and we enjoyed our Ride, which was through orchards, cornfields and high Hills, covered to the very summits with innumerable quantities of Vineyards.

Geislingen in the mountains seems a most romantic place.

Ulm Cathedral, fine old Tower which forms the central entrance at the west end. The Architect has avoided the mistake of placing the circular Staircase so as to block up a part of the windows (which oversight forms such a draw-back to the beauty of the Tower at Antwerp). The *projecting* tracery all over the Tower produces a remarkably light and elegant effect.

The other entrances are disfigured by very coarse carvings in wood painted white—of subjects from the Crucifixion, etc. They are so badly executed and mix so ill with the Stone sculpture that they are quite a deformity.

The Choir at the East end, as well as the greater portion of the rest of the building, has an appearance of poverty from the exterior being of *brick* instead of Stone—and the whole is now evidently going fast to decay.

Thursday, July 9th, arrived at Augsburg 4 in the morning—Church well decorated with Painting, marble Columns—Houses painted al fresco—Bronze fountains, Mercury, Hercules, nymphs—tasteful place altogether. High houses, five storys—capital subjects for Prout.

The Road from Augsburg to Munich is rather flat and uninteresting and for the last 20 miles there was a very violent storm of Rain with Thunder and Lightning.

Munich, July 9-13

Once at Munich they were already, in Vincent Novello's eyes, ' in the country of Mozart ' ; for not only were political boundaries fluid and national differences slight between Bavaria and the Austrian regions to the south, but Mozart himself had seen his first mature opera, *Idomeneo*, produced there, and had angled vainly for an appointment under the cultured Elector Carl Theodor, whom he had already encountered at Mannheim as Elector Palatine. Hence Novello's musical expectations quicken—only to be disappointed.

We arrived at Munich about ½ past 1 o'clock and selected the 'Golden Cock' as our Hotel. The table d'Hôte was over so that we were obliged to take our Dinner in our own Room.

On the Gallery were stationed three itinerant Musicians —a woman who played the Harp, a man who played the Violin and another the Clarionet.* The latter produced a very fair quality of tone and was not deficient in taste, but the Pieces they played were of the most commonplace kind—Waltzes, Quadrilles from Rossini, Pacini and other poor stuff fit only for the amusement of little school girls. The effect was rendered still more monotonous by their being all played in the same key, viz., C, with the exception of one movement which was performed in G.

At 5 o'clock went to the Cathedral but the service was only the Litany followed by Benediction without any Singing or Music whatsoever.

The exterior of the building is of brick, and the forms are not at all distinguished by their beauty or symmetry, neither is the interior remarkable for its grandeur or magnificence. The Paintings seemed to me of a mediocre class with the exception of a Madonna and Child, which group forms the altar piece of the first chapel on the left going in at the great West Door.

The construction is favourable to sound, as far as I can judge from the resonance produced by [the] Voices of the

*This form of the word, though now obsolete, was in normal use at the period, and has therefore been retained.

Congregation when they were united in answering the Priest in the Versicles and Responsories.

In passing through the Town I heard a young Lady practising her songs with a Piano Forte accompaniment—but the Pieces she was singing were from the compositions of Mercadante or other 'illustrious obscures' of the Modern school.

Not a single chord have I heard to remind me that I am now in the Country of Mozart. Not once has his name ever been mentioned except by myself, nor have I heard even one note performed of his inimitable compositions.

From Mary Novello's brief record it seems that their hotel was near the Cathedral, whither they had ventured forth in the rain on that first afternoon :

At Munich the rain kept us close to the house. . . . The people of the house (Coq D'or) are very obliging, particularly the waiter.

The next day was spent surprisingly quietly for such insatiable sightseers—perhaps because of the persistent rain, to which Novello again refers. The Königliche Hof- und Nationaltheater, whither they went that evening to see one of the prolific Kotzebue's forgotten plays, was built in 1818, burned down only five years later, but rebuilt and reopened in January 1825, so was relatively new when they saw it. Novello's enthusiastic comparison of its architectural features with those of St. Martin-in-the-Fields shows once more that he can enjoy contemporary classicism provided it does not encroach on Gothic antiquity. The famous drop-scene with its copy of Guido Reni's 'Phoebus and Aurora' was one of its most distinctive features until its destruction in the air raids of the second World War.

Friday, July 10. Went to the great square to hear the military Band but as it had been a rainy morning the musicians as well as the troops were covered up in their great Coats and they seemed in a hurry to get through their performance—if such it can be called—for they only played about five minutes and then dispersed. Here as elsewhere the Performers were good, but they played bad compositions.

In the evening went to the Theatre . . . a very large one *showy* in its style of ornament. There are five tiers of Boxes, beside the lower tier which is like our Cellarets at Covent Garden. The general form is that of a Lyre, and is somewhat like the interior of Drury Lane. The Stage Boxes and the Royal Box in the Centre of the House are peculiarly elegant in shape and magnificent in effect, but the projecting range of Boxes under the Royal Box is apparently an intrusion put for those who wish to be conspicuous and stand out, and quite spoils the symmetry of the general form of the house. The Drop Scene with a very tasteful and well-executed Copy of Guido's Aurora (a piece of refinement which might afford a very useful hint to Stanfield and other of our English Scene Painters.)[47]

The extension of the Theatre is in a good style of modern architecture, and is adorned with an elegant Portico, supported by eight columns of noble dimensions; the effect they produce is somewhat like the fine Portico to St. Martin's Church, which is in my opinion one of the best proportioned and [most] symmetrical in London.

The only part that I felt to be deficient in the Portico at Munich was the Pediment, which had a naked effect, being left without any Statues or Sculpture whatever.

There were but 4 Acts to the piece which was the 'Casket of Jewels' [*Das Schmuckkästchen*] by Kotzebue. The Lady (Mad. [Fries])[48] who played the old Mother was a good Actress and both in voice and manner reminded me strongly of our clever Actress Mrs. Sparkes who used to play the same sort of parts at Drury, some years since. Mamselle [Hagn] also was a handsome woman and of a very pleasing figure, but her dramatic talents did not appear to be of a very high order. The remainder of the performers did not exceed that negative kind of merit which is generally termed 'respectable'. . . .

The whole performance was over by a little after nine o'clock, and after a short stroll by moonlight we returned to our Inn and went to bed.

Mary Novello succinctly sums up :

. . . next day we saw The Casket and not understanding German it seemed a dull affair.

The next morning they intended to begin their sight-seeing in real earnest; but Novello has another disappointment to record :

Saturday, July 11. Rose at $\frac{1}{2}$ past 6 and after Breakfast we went to the Gallery of Paintings, as we had been informed by the Sentry on the preceding evening that it would be open from 8 till 2, but on our arrival we were much disappointed on being told that Saturday was the day appointed for cleaning, sweeping, etc., and that we could not be admitted till to-morrow morning.

We took a walk instead in the English Gardens as they are called. They are very pleasantly laid out, and are considerately furnished with seats which are placed in very judicious situations for the accommodation of the Public. Several of the Students were resting on the Benches reading quietly in the Shade, and I was quite surprised at the numbers of People lounging about in the most indolent manner who really seemed to have nothing whatever to do.

A branch of the River Isar runs through these agreeable Gardens—its course is remarkably rapid, and in one particular spot where two streams unite there is a very picturesque cascade—a bridge situated near it affords a good view of it, and the Landscape altogether would form a very pretty little Landscape.* On the other side of the Bridge the scenery is of the most simple and rural character forming a complete contrast to the refined and Park-like style of the Gardens. Over the course of the River there were several water Birds of the Gull species flying about and fishing. Their mode of waving about and wheeling round in the most graceful curves formed a most elegant and complete climax to the peculiar beauty of the Scene.

These Gardens are very creditable to the taste of Count Rumford (one of the most sensible and tasteful originators of the ' utilitarian school ') who constructed them on what was formerly a mere dreary and unwholesome marsh. There is an obelisk erected to his memory with an inscription recording the gratitude of the people for this successful and beneficent improvement.[49]

For such enthusiastic lovers of Gothic architecture the Novellos are remarkably open-minded towards later styles. They are repelled by the over-ornate, as in the exuberant rococo remodelling by the Asam brothers of the fifteenth-century Heilig-Geist-Kirche, but they invariably respond to that nobility of proportion which is the glory of the best Baroque, and which characterized the Italianate Theatiner-Kirche and Michaels-Kirche, both severely damaged in the air-raids of the second World War.

On strolling through the Town we found a church of the Holy Ghost open, and we accordingly walked in. There was only low Mass going on at one of the side Chapels. The Paintings are not remarkable for beauty or talent, and the Church altogether seems to have [been]

*Sic: he is clearly thinking in terms of painting.

55

fitted up principally for the gratification of the poorer Class, who are more especially fond of tawdriness, golden ornaments and finery.

The Church of the ' Theatines ' nearly opposite the Royal Palace is in my opinion by far the handsomest in Munich. The exterior is, both in its form and style, like the Jesuits' Church at Mannheim, and the interior, though rather overloaded with ornament, is symmetrical, of noble proportions, and has a striking air of grandeur and magnificence, especially the upper part containing the High Altar and the two adjoining Chapels. The paintings too are of a superior school, and are far from deficient in beauty of colouring and appropriate expression—one especially of St Roch and the Angel (although not equal to the charming painting on that subject by Lodovico Caracci in the Fitzwilliam Museum at Cambridge) is remarkably well painted, especially the figure and coun- tenance of St Roch. There are also near the Altar some colossal figures of Popes and Saints which are good speci- mens of that style of sculpture, and add much to [the] general look of vastness and elevation produced by the large scale upon which the proportions of the Edifice is [sic] constructed.

At 12 o'clock I went to the Grand Place, in hopes not only that I should hear the Military Band again, but that I should be able (without sacrificing what is due to impar- tiality and truth) to give a more favourable account of their performance, but to my great disappointment there were only the common Drums and fifes, and the Band itself did not play at all.

The costume of the Bavarian Peasants is very peculiar and picturesque—it seemed not to have been changed for the last 500 years. They wear a kind of plush or velvet breeches of a dark green, waistcoats of a bright colour, single-breasted jackets with rows of bright Buttons, short thick curly hair, and steeple crowned Hats like the Cavaliers of England in the time of Charles the 1st.

St Michael's Church, formerly that of the Jesuits—there is nothing remarkable or striking about the exterior of this Edifice, but the interior is distinguished by a very singular peculiarity, viz., there being no side aisles and not a single Column to be seen. The result of this unusual construction is to produce an uncommon effect of *spaciousness* and unencumbered *openness*. If you can fancy walking up the nave of St. Paul's Cathedral with the aisles on each side filled with Chapels, you may form some idea of the curious effect consequent upon the whimsical design of the Architect of this building. There are three Chapels in the kind of niches with a very elevated Gallery over them, two transepts and the High Altar. The Paintings were of the inferior class and the ornaments of the most gaudy kind.

I attended the Vespers which began at 3 o'clock but the Service was not interesting.

★   ★   ★

In the evening at 6 o'clock we went to the Gardens belonging to the King's Palace (the Hof Garten) to hear the Military Band.

Novello's detailed musical criticisms of the music in church and public gardens are given below (pp. 274-5, 296-9). His wife echoes and sums up his views :

On Saturday strolled for some hours in the gardens, at 3 attended Vespers at St. Michael's, a very hurried affair. The church is magnificent though rather gaudy in its ornaments. The military music in the gardens, very poor pieces but well performed, especially the clarionet ; overture to *Preciosa* well performed.

Her husband continues his account of their Saturday evening :

We intended to have visited the Gymnasium where there were some curious feats of Horsemanship to be seen but by the time the Military music was terminated it was too late to go to the *Theatre Equestrien* which was situated near the Botanical Garden at the other end of the Town. We therefore again strolled on to the English Garden, at the entrance of which I forgot before to notice that there is a very graceful little marble statue, in an attitude like that of the Antinous. It stands most placidly with its hand inclined towards the tranquil and retired Garden as if it were inviting the Passenger to enter and enjoy its quiet beauty.

I was sorry to observe one piece of bad taste amongst the people of Munich, viz., that out of the hundreds of Persons we met there was scarcely an instance of a Lady and Gentleman walking together arm in arm. We saw crowds of men altogether and women in numbers but solitary and apparently neglected. One Group of no less than *seven* young ladies passed me, who had not even *one* young man with them.

It seems so natural that persons who like and admire each other should wish to be together, that I own this circumstance (of the Gentlemen and Ladies keeping separate from one another) considerably shakes my belief in the truth of what has been said of the gallantry and good breeding of the Germans in their behaviour towards the Ladies, or of that partiality and devotedness to the fair sex to which the Germans lay claim.

During Dinner, some itinerant Musicians played at the Door of the antechamber. There were two Clarionets and two Horns. The performers were much better than what we had heard on the preceding day or two. The piece which pleased me best was the charming Air in Der Freischütz ' Through the Forest ',[50] which was played with feeling and appropriate expression especially by the 1st Clarionet ; on this occasion it was transposed to F, but I prefer it in its original key of E flat.

Their Sunday, as usual, combined churchgoing with aesthetic pleasures, of which the first was the mass they heard at the Cathedral in the morning. This, as Novello found out on making inquiries after Vespers, was by Benedict Schack (1758-1826), the tenor who had sung Tamino in the first production of *The Magic Flute* in 1791. Schack was a good musician and something of a composer ; Mozart wrote variations on his song *Ein Weib ist das herrlichste Ding* and—so Nissen relates—would sometimes add a phrase here and there to his manuscripts. Novello fastened on this hint, corroborated by his informant at the Cathedral, to confirm his determination to discover Mozart's part-authorship behind the Mozartian influence he had sensed in the work, and in his preface to the edition of the mass which he brought out in 1831, he attributes to Mozart not only, as at first, the *Kyrie* and part of the *Agnus Dei*, but also the *Crucifixus* and *Sanctus*.[51] As, however, Schack was not appointed to the Cathedral Choir at Munich, for which his six masses were written, until 1796, five years after Mozart's death, and previously had written mainly *Singspiele*, it is most unlikely that the mass contains any of Mozart's work.

Novello's record of the Mass itself consists entirely of musical extracts and disjointed comments, but he pursued his inquiries that afternoon when Vespers were over.

After the Service I endeavoured to meet with the Organist of the Cathedral, who, I was told, was Mr Stadler, but he had escaped before I could get to the foot of the staircase leading to the Organ loft. I however was

59

so fortunate as to accost a young man of very prepossessing appearance, whose good-natured face encouraged me to ask him who was the Composer of the Musical part of the vespers, and he informed me that it was L'Abbé Stadler of Vienna. This led to a conversation, in the course of which he invited [me] to walk with him to his apartments near the Cathedral, when I found that he was the son of the Gentleman who had directed the Mass in the morning, and who had *himself* directed the music of the afternoon Service. His name was Schreifel (or something that sounded like it) and he turned out to be a most unceremonious pleasant fellow. He took great pains to show me his Collection of Music, which was a very valuable and select one, amongst which was the score of the Mass which Righini wrote for the Coronation of the Emperor, and that which Méhul wrote for the coronation of Napoleon, and which Mr Schreifel told me he had himself got up at Munich with a very large Orchestra. No. 3 of Haydn (in D minor) he told me was known in Germany under the name of Nelson's Mass, but the reason why it had acquired this particular title he could not explain to me.[52]

He showed me also the scores of two Masses which he seemed to prize very highly and which he said were composed by a young man of much promise of the name of Dobschreiter (or something like that sound) and which he said were about to be published by Falter and Son of Munich. I intend to order them as soon as they are brought out. He showed me also a Mass by Michael Haydn (brother to the great Joseph Haydn) called the ' Hieronymus ' Mass, and said that he had 7 or 8 masses by Michael [Haydn] which were in good estimation.[53]

On my expressing a wish to purchase a copy of the Mass which was performed in the morning, he informed me that he thought it would be difficult to obtain, as in the first place it had been written expressly for the Cathedral at Munich, and even if I could obtain permission to have a copy transcribed it would take some time to make a score of it, as the only copy they had was in *parts* only, from which it would be necessary for the Copyist to condense the score.

The Composer of it was (with the exception of the Graduale and offertory which were by an inferior writer) Mr Schack, who was not a professor, but only a Cantor belonging to the Church and who had written it for his amusement. He added that Mr Schack had been an intimate friend of Mozart, from whom he seems to have caught some of his enchanting melody and exquisite beauty of style, and it is not improbable that Mozart had added a few touches to the composition of his friend ; indeed, the Kyrie, and the first part of the Agnus Dei, are not unworthy of Mozart himself.

It is quite a pity that such a charming composition should remain unpublished while the Public are deluged with a daily inundation of Quadrilles and other contemptible trash without a single musical idea in a wagon load of the spoiled waste paper. However, as I was obliged to depart for Salzburg the next morning and there was not sufficient time either to obtain permission for the copy to be made, or to make a copy if permission could be procured, I was obliged to give up the hope of taking home with me a copy of Mr Schack's clever composition.

Young Mr Schreifel, however, was better than his word. A triumphant entry, ' Got Schack's Mass ' in Novello's diary after his visit to the music publisher Haslinger in Vienna a fortnight later, coupled with his record of 'leaving a note of thanks to Mr. Schreifel' on his return journey through Munich, indicates that

Schreifel had had a copy made and sent it after him to Vienna. Novello also gratefully acknowledges his help in the preface to his edition of the work.

Mary Novello, who outlines their day, echoes her husband's suppositions regarding Mozart's share in Schack's Mass. From the reason she gives for not accompanying him to Rossini's *Ricciardo e Zoraide* at the Opera that night, evening dress was obviously *de rigueur*; Novello himself made extensive notes on the opera (below, pp. 258, 267-9) and if he summed up his impressions even more unfavourably to her than at the time, it was probably from a kindly wish to assure her that she had not missed much.

On Sunday at the Cathedral by 9, a beautiful Mass of Schack's well performed, in Mozart's style, especially the Kyrie and Agnus. He was an intimate friend of Mozart's and probably some touches were added by him as Schack was but a singer.

The Military Mass at St. Michael's was next, the drums made me start at first and there was a grand roulade at the Elevation, but this is nothing considering that the pieces played during the service were, first, ballet music, and secondly a bravura, the solo parts so sweetly played by the clarionet, with so much delicacy and expression that I question if any prima donna could have given it equal effect.

The picture gallery was our next visit—oh how I wished for Charles, I really believe it would have been too much for him, such an assemblage of divine paintings. Rubens is here great, Monk, Snyders and Titian, P. Aretino and Van Dyck, and Murillo and Velasquez, Eeckhout and many others.

The opera I missed being obliged to send our clothes forward by the *Eilwagen*, but Vin went and it was but a poor affair.

Munich to Salzburg.   July 13

The following morning, July 13th, they left Munich for an eighteen-hour drive through the Bavarian highlands to Salzburg.

As those will remember who have had occasion to motor through them, the heights and valleys of Upper Bavaria merge into the Salzkammergut near Salzburg itself without any perceptible natural barrier, and if the Novellos—to whom Munich was already ' the country of Mozart '—seem to confuse Bavaria, the Tyrol and the Salzkammergut, they had every reason to do so, for both the Salzkammergut and the Tyrol had been given to Bavaria by Napoleon, returning to Austria in 1814 and 1816 respectively.

Vincent Novello's impressions, scribbled in the carriage, once more reveal his observant and pictorial eye:

Monday, July 13. Left Munich for Salzburg at 6 in the morning. The country in the immediate vicinity of Munich is flat, but at the distance of eight or ten miles the road becomes pleasant, and further on there [are] some very agreeable rides through Forests of Fir, with openings occasionally affording picturesque Landscapes with the Tyrolese mountains on our right hand, forming a most noble background, on the distant horizon. The Houses gradually change their form and approach more to the Swiss Character, such as those which are represented in the view of the village of Sarnen at the Diorama.[54]

We passed an old man who had a fine head for a Painter, it was somewhat similar, but of a more elevated character, to the old man's head for which Sir Joshua made a study for his ' Count Ugolino.'[55]

The Dress of the Peasants is very grotesque and wild— the *shape* of the Hats was like those worn by the Tyrolese

63

Minstrels who exhibited in London, but instead of being made of green velvet they were only common chip or straw or felt. Neither did I perceive any of the gaudy embroidered waistbands which the Rainer family wore at their performance. Some of the females had much the appearance of Welsh girls.[56]

Mary Novello's account of the day's journey shows, in its opening sentence, that the travelling Briton's character has not changed with the means of transport:

Fortunately the next day we had the Cabriolet to ourselves all the way to Salzburg, the day was fine, and after a time the scenery improved to great beauty. The peasantry wear the costume of the Tyrol and are hearty and good-natured, but the women not handsome, indeed I am not an admirer of the German style of beauty. The peasantry in some parts are really shocking looking, so coarse and sunburnt, and in the towns though their features are delicate and regular, and their complexions fair, they want expression terribly. Mademoiselle Sontag and Mrs Hutchison are facsimiles of the general character,[57] there is no such thing apparent, as fine figures, or a graceful air. The better class walk in the fidgeting French manner which arises probably from the dreadful pavement.

Vincent Novello's notes, which bring them to their journey's goal, show that they followed the route by way of Wasserburg, as described in the 1840 edition of Murray's *Handbook for Travellers in Southern Germany*. The 'large Place' where they arrived at half-past six in the evening cannot be identified with certainty, since no such place as Oelburg appears in modern maps or in Murray's Handbook. Traunstein corresponds most nearly to his description, the route as given by Murray, and the distance covered in the time.

12 o'clock, arrived at Wasserburg, a remarkably pretty place situated in a most agreeable and picturesque manner in the midst of an amphitheatre of Hills and Rocks with the River ' Inn ' flowing entirely round it.

Arrived at Oelburg [?] at ½ past 6, a large Place, beautifully situated just at the foot of the Tyrol mountains. The approach to it is through a fine Forest of Fir Trees full of charming views of which the adjacent mountains form the most prominent feature.

After one of the most delightful rides I ever enjoyed through one of the finest days I ever saw, concluding with a bright Moonlight Night, we arrived at the object of our Pilgrimage—Salzburg the Birthplace of Mozart.

PART II

THE FIRST VISIT TO SALZBURG

Ah, did you once see Shelley plain?
And did he stop and speak to you?

For the Novellos, whose friendship with Leigh Hunt
had brought Shelley as a visitor to their hospitable
drawing-room and who had sheltered and cheered his
widow on her return from Italy, time had not yet
thrown that aura of breathless wonder round the poet
whose short life—shorter even than Mozart's—had
ended but seven years before. But it was in just such a
spirit of veneration that they walked the streets of
Salzburg, and made their pilgrimage to Mozart's
untenanted birthplace, and to those living ' relics of
the divine man ' (to borrow Mary Novello's phrase),
his widow and his sister.

Mozart's Constanze, at this time, was 66 and again
a widow, her second husband, the Danish State
Councillor Georg Nikolaus von Nissen, having died in
1826. For some years after her marriage to her former
lodger in Vienna they had lived in Copenhagen; but
in 1820 they came to Salzburg, where Nissen took the
baths at Gastein and worked at his sprawling biography of Mozart, aided by Constanze, whose
genuine if limited affection for Mozart had, with the
passing of the years, merged with a keen awareness of
her own interesting position as the widow of an acknowledged genius. After Nissen's death her widowed
younger sister, Sophie Haibl, who as a girl had
helped her nurse Mozart in his last illness, came to
share her home.

Mozart's sister Marianne, who during her marriage

66

to Baron Johann Baptist von Berchtold zu Sonnenburg had lived at St. Gilgen, her mother's birthplace, had returned to Salzburg with her two children on her husband's death in 1801. She took an apartment in the Kirchgasse (now Sigmund-Haffnergasse), almost opposite the house where she and Wolfgang were born, and added to her income by giving piano lessons. She had never liked Mozart's wife, and had only heard of her remarriage through strangers.

When Constanze and her second husband came to live in Salzburg their relationship remained one of mere civility. It was further strained when, on Nissen's death, Constanze claimed the family grave (the resting-place of her aunt Genoveva Weber, Carl Maria's mother, of Leopold Mozart, and of Nannerl's daughter) for her husband, and erected over it an elaborate monument—to which she piously conducted the Novellos—on which no mention was made of the grave's earlier occupants. But by this time Mozart's sister was already blind, and was soon to become partly paralysed. It speaks well for the essential decency and dutifulness of Mozart's plodding second son, who had hurried to Salzburg from his teaching at Lemberg to conduct his father's Requiem in Nissen's memory, that under such circumstances he retained his aunt's affection and showed her the tender solicitude which so impressed the Novellos when he again came to visit his family in 1829.

None of these cross-currents seem to have impinged on the Novellos ; even Mary's shrewdness almost succumbs under the impact of meeting Mozart's widow in the flesh. Both of them spent their three days in Salzburg in a state of bemused beatitude, and the incidents of their not uneventful first night gained an added zest from ' happening at the birth place of Mozart '. Mary Novello tells the story:

We did not reach Salzburg until 12 at night—only one Inn open, the Golden Ox. At first I believe there was a proposition of sleeping all the passengers in one room, but as *der Herr* and *die Frau* objected, we were shown into a prodigious room with six windows and hung round with portraits of knights and dames in armour and silks, with plated sconces between and a chandelier suspended from the centre, containing three beds. We had scarcely surveyed this enormous apartment and were waiting our supper, when the landlady entered and very unceremoniously introduced two women to sleep in the same room, it was no use remonstrating, the *Herr* could sleep she said in one corner, myself in another, and the two women in a third. The other hotels were closed and she fairly told us we had no choice. Here was a dilemma for how did we know but that they might rise in the night and strangle us—for I must tell you, that in this part of the country, the coach always travels well armed with pistols, and certainly some of the woods through which we passed must be rather aweful for a single passenger, as for many miles not a house is to be seen. The poor women were however very harmless. They rose next morning by 4, and one of them, seeing me awake, spoke something very energetically to me, but I was sorry to answer ' nichts verstehn '. She clasped her hands in great sorrow at this intelligence and departed, but afterwards when I was dressed and Vin had gone out rambling, she returned and by her manner I perceived she was much agitated. I therefore exerted all my wits to understand and relieve her distress which I soon found was occasioned by her ignorance of the way to her uncle's, who was a priest in the Tyrol and had written to her saying he was ill and requesting her to come to him. There was no coach to this place, she must walk on foot and it was 33 *stunde** off— and she knew only it lay among the mountains. I could

*Hours, i.e., hours' journey.

not assist the poor girl for I was myself ignorant of the place she named but I soon guessed that poverty was added to her other evils, I asked her if she had breakfasted. *Nein* she added shaking her head, and it struck me perhaps that she had scarcely eaten yesterday as she never appeared where we stopped to dine and sup. Fortunately there was a large slice of batter pudding with cherries untouched from our last night's supper on the table, this I offered her and she ate it with avidity, convincing me she had not breakfasted. All the provisions I had in the basket I pressed upon her for her journey. Money she at first refused, saying she could not return it, but I assured her that was unnecessary and I hope it rendered her journey less painful, as among the mountains hospitality prevails and coarse provisions are cheap. Her tone when she said ' es ist sehr traueriche ' [traurig]—it is very melancholy— was very touching. Before we parted I gave her a print out of my pocket book, as a souvenir, she kissed it, and said she would show it to her Uncle the priest, it was ' schoen ', he would pray for me—doubtless poor girl it will be placed with the ' lieb frau ' in her prayer book and as it represents fashionable ladies, may stand a chance hereafter of being considered the veritable portraits of three saints.

It was a pleasant event for me to help the poor girl, and happening at the birth place of Mozart seemed even more delightful, and soon after came in dear Vin looking all eager pleasure because he had explored the town of his favourite Mozart, seen the house where he was born, and found out the directions of his widow and sister. He was unwashed and unshaved, unbreakfasted, our luggage to be got from the custom house officers, our passport to be fetched (for we had entered Austria) but nothing of these sublunary affairs could touch Vin, and I would not awaken him from this reverie. I paid our bill at the *Ox* and we departed for the *Ship*, as I did not wish to be intruded upon a second night.

Contrary to expectation, the officers were not troublesome and no impertinent questions were asked at the Police, perhaps as we were well dressed when we fetched our passport it might have some effect, for the Germans are much taken by outside show. We left our letters at Madame Sonnenburg, who we were told was very ill, and soon after received a very friendly note from the widow saying that as her sister-in-law was so unwell she requested to see us at her house and her servant would attend at 9 to conduct us to her house.

Of his early, unkempt rambling, Novello merely writes:

Salzburg, Tuesday, July 14. This day has been one of the most delightful and interesting that I ever passed. I rose early and found my way into a Bookseller's Shop where I procured a description and Plan of the town. I also ascertained that the house in which Mozart was born was situated in the Getreidegasse no 225, that Madame Sonnenburg (his sister) resided at no. 214 Kirchgasse and that Madame von Nissen (Mozart's widow) lived at no. 23 Nonnberg.[58]

I first left the following letter to the Sister, saying that we would return again for an answer at 3, if she was well enough to receive us, and soon after came the following note from Madame Nissen the widow.

Constanze von Nissen's note, inviting Novello to call upon her 'cet après dinné' is now in the Mozart Museum (no. 832). Novello's copy of his letter to Mozart's sister, in which the warmth of his feelings struggles through the refractory medium of the French language, is reproduced as it stands.

70

5. EHRENBREITSTEIN

6. SALZBURG

7. AIGEN

A Mad. Sonnenburg.

Madame,

J'ai le plaisir de vous remettre une Lettre de Mr Stumpff, et la liste de quelques-un de mes Amis a Londres, qui sont (comme moi-meme) admirateurs enthousiastiques des compositions incomparables de Mozart, et qui m'ont confié un petit cadeau pour mettre entre vos propre mains, Madame, si vous voulez avoir la bonté de me permettre l'honneur de vous faire une petite visite, quand il vous conviendra le mieux, pour me reçevoir sans façon—et dans la maniere qui vous genera le moins possible.

Je serai charmé Madame si vous voulez me traiter comme un ancien et cordial Ami de votre illustre frere, pour qui c'est impossible que personne au monde peut sentir un plus profond respect ou un admiration plus vif que celui que je me loue d'entretenir pour sa memoire.

En attendant la faveur d'une ligne en reponse,

J'ai l'honneur d'etre

Madame votre tres obligé

V. NOVELLO.

P.S.—Je me propose l'honneur de faire un ' esquisse Biographique ' de Mozart, fondé sur les Memoires qui ont eté dernierement publié par Madame sa Veuve.

Je suis venu faire un petit tour en Allemagne avec ma femme expres pour avoir le plaisir de vous faire une visite et d'enjouir la gratification d'avoir un peu de conversation avec vous, Madame, et avec Made. von Nissen, sur le sujet du plus grand Genie Musical qui ait jamais existé ; et de qui [sentence unfinished]

Comme je n'ai pas l'habitude d'ecrire en Français— j'espere Madame que vous aurez la bonté d'excuser les fautes que, sans doute, vous trouverez dans la communication presente. Je ne m'exprime pas comme je veut, mais comme je peut.

71

8

In the event, the first meeting with Constanze von Nissen did not take place until the afternoon, and Novello therefore, with the morning free, spent the time in drafting two sets of ' Questions relative to the Biography of Mozart ' (amplifying the notes he had scribbled at the end of his green notebook), one for Constanze and one for Mozart's sister, in the hope that their replies would enable him ' to render his intended " Sketch of the Life of Mozart " as complete as possible for the gratification of the Musical World.' Madame von Sonnenburg, as he soon found, was in no state to reply, so he retrieved his letter. His questions to Constanze, of which he kept a copy, were— apart from those relating to Mozart's childhood and youth—on parallel lines ; to these also he appears to have received no written reply.

Novello, however, clearly seized the opportunity of asking some of his questions verbally, for many apparently unrelated pieces of information embedded in the copious notes made by both Vincent and Mary Novello after their meetings with Mozart's widow and son reveal themselves, on examination, as being answers to questions contained in the two questionnaires. Those questions which were thus asked and answered have been used, in the following pages, as ' conversational openings ' within the relevant interview, in order to provide a framework and context for the replies they elicited. Where an answer is recorded by both diarists, the initials V.N. and M.N. are used to distinguish the two records.

Unfortunately, while many of Novello's questions were pertinent and sensible, his reverence for his subject, his native delicacy and his lack of the born biographer's flair for the essential issue, kept his inquiries from penetrating much farther below the surface than those of a respectful radio interviewer. In any case, he could have found the answers to most of them in Nissen's biography, which he had so eagerly acquired on its publication in 1828. Perhaps his admittedly scanty German had prevented him from ploughing through the fat and ill-arranged volume from cover to cover. That he had dipped extensively into it, however, appears from his repeated requests for the confirmation of anecdotes related in it.

At last the long-awaited moment arrived and the pilgrims climbed the narrow lane running along the side of the Mönchsberg, immediately beneath the towering walls of the Hohensalzburg fortress, towards the lower spur of the Nonnberg and Madame von Nissen's house.

V.N. She [Madame von Nissen] very politely sent her servant to conduct us to her house, a little after 2 o'clock. She was a very cheerful pleasant-looking Girl but could only speak German. The road leading to the House is of the most uncommon and picturesque description, and the House itself is placed in one of the most exquisite spots I ever saw (describe it).

Madame Nissen who was waiting for us in the Room on the first floor received us in the most cordial and unceremonious manner. She had with her, her own Sister [Sophie Haibl] and Mozart's youngest Son (Wolfgang Amadeus—who was about 5 months old when his father died) who by a fortunate coincidence happened to be on a visit to his Mother just at this time.

An animated and (to me) most interesting conversation immediately began.

M.N. We have just seen Mozart's widow—oh what a world of sensations has this interview excited—the woman that was so dear to him, whom he has so often fondly caressed, for whom his anxiety and tender solicitude urged on [*sic*] to such great and glorious efforts of his genius, next to seeing himself it was the nearest approach to his earthly remains, and I felt during the whole interview as if his spirit were with us ; how could it be otherwise as I held his portrait in my hand which breathes of life and of him. When I first entered I was so overcome with various emotions that I could do nothing but weep and embrace her. She seemed also affected and said repeatedly in French ' oh quelle bonheur pour moi, de voir les enthousiastes pour mon Mozart '. She speaks French fluently though with a German accent, in Italian she thinks better but as I do not converse in that language she politely continued in French. She is indeed completely a well bred Lady, and though no remains of beauty appear except in her eyes such as the engraving prefixed to her biography of Mozart would indicate, yet she keeps her figure and a certain air, well, for a woman of her age, which I suppose must be 65. She is charmingly lodged in the Nuns' street, half way up a cliff from which a most extensive and charming view is gained scarcely to be equalled in the world. The apartments, like most foreign ones, are not encumbered with furniture and the room she received us in opened to a cabinet which contained her bed, but it was tastefully covered with a bright green silk counterpane forming a nice unison with some flowers round the room. She lamented that her ' belle-soeur ' could not enjoy the pleasure of seeing and thanking us for the handsome *cadeau* which Vin brought with him from her friends in England, ' ma pauvre soeur quelle malheur pour elle '. She however promised her son should introduce us to Madame Sonnenburg on the morrow, as it would be doubtless interesting to us.

At this point Vincent Novello, who had made a note among his memoranda to inquire about the possibility of giving a concert for Madame von Sonnenburg's benefit, probably raised the question, for he records the following :

Sister of Mozart (Sonnenburg) has been ill for the last

three years, and has for the last six months [been] confined to her bed quite blind, and infirm. André offered to make a subscription, but Sonnenburg refused, saying she had enough to live upon and would not be made the subject of public observation. Madame Nissen thinks she would *not* like a concert to be given for her.

Johann Anton André, of Offenbach, was the music publisher who in 1799, on Haydn's calling his attention to the poverty of Mozart's widow, bought her entire collection of Mozart MSS., including his thematic catalogue, for 3,150 gulden (about £320). (His offer to organize a benefit concert for Mozart's sister had been made through Nissen, through whom she had returned a grateful refusal). The curious story of how the collector and scholar in him triumphed over the music publisher is told by C. B. Oldman in introducing his selection of Constanze's letters to André published in the *Letters of Mozart and his Family* edited by Emily Anderson (Vol. III, pp. 1453ff). André kept the precious MSS. locked in a special cabinet, carefully catalogued them, and persistently importuned Constanze with letters in his quest for missing items. Köchel was to acknowledge his debt to him in the preface to his Thematic Catalogue of Mozart's works ; but André actually published so few of his treasures that the musical public at large—like the Mozart family—criticized him for keeping the collection ' hermetically sealed '. The autograph score of *Don Giovanni*, which was the subject of Novello's first inquiry, was one of those in André's possession— though Constanze appears to have forgotten that she had sold it to him.

QUESTION. *Whether the original scores of ' Il Don Giovanni ' or any of his other operas have been preserved, and, if so, whether any of them can now be purchased?*

V.N. Score of ' Don Giovanni ' probably at Prague. André who has a large pile half a yard high of Mozart's

MSS., amongst which his son told me was the sketch of an Opera with several of the Movements quite completed ; that he supposed André had disposed of several of the MSS. in England, and both he and his Mother seemed to unite with me in regretting that André had kept all these MSS. in obscurity instead of publishing [them] for the gratification of the musical world.

QUESTION. *The same question as to his Masses, sinfonias and other works.*

V.N. Showed me original MSS. of two Kyries in Score, one in E flat, and the other in C (different from any that I have published). He was about 22 when he wrote them.[59]

> André had acquired not one but three unfinished operas—*Zaide, L'Oca del Cairo* and *Lo Sposo Deluso.* The MSS. disposed of in England were those of the string quartets sold to J. A. Stumpff (the ' Haydn ' set, the three dedicated to the King of Prussia, and K499); but this can have been no news to Novello.

QUESTION. *What is become of his own Piano Forte?*

V.N. The other son at Milan has the Piano Forte—not a Professor but employee.[60]

Madame Nissen expected to receive the Harpsichord on which he composed his ' Clemenza, Zauberflöte ', etc.

QUESTION. *Which were the greatest favourites with him of his own compositions?*

> The previous question, ' Which were his favourite pieces by *other* composers? ' was apparently not asked.

V.N. She said he was fond of ' Don Giovanni,' ' Figaro ' and perhaps most of all ' Idomeneo,' as he had some delightful associations with the time and circumstances under which it was composed.

There were three of his Sinfonias which he liked nearly

equally and preferred to all the others. She could not tell me in what keys, but as well as I could make out they were the ones in G minor, that in E flat, and the ' Jupiter ' in C.[61]

M.N. ' Il Don Giovanni ' she thinks altogether he preferred of his compositions, but she is not certain, ' Figaro ' was also his principal favourite, and ' Idomeneo ' sometimes he preferred, this latter was written for Munich and when he was most happy.

> The commission to compose *Idomeneo* for the Bavarian Court, and its production in Munich in 1781, had brought Mozart, at twenty-five, a taste of liberty from his uncongenial Salzburg employment and the first unalloyed success he had known since his child-prodigy days.

QUESTION. *Whether he was in the habit of playing and singing much, and what particular pieces he most frequently performed, or whether he generally played* extempore *when alone—any particularities in his mode of performance?*

V.N. He did not play much in private, but would occasionally extemporise when he was sitting alone with her, and would often play over the songs which he wished her to learn ; nor did he like playing to strangers, except he knew them to be *good judges*, when he would exert himself to the utmost for their gratification.

M.N. He seldom played on the Pianoforte, scarcely in company unless he found someone who could appreciate him, but he would sometimes extemporise when alone with her.

QUESTION. *In composing, whether he sat at the instrument and tried over different passages as they occurred to him, or whether he deferred writing down any piece until he had completely constructed and finished it in his own mind, and then* scored *it at once?*

   . . . *Whether it was necessary for him to be alone when he wrote, or if he could abstract himself so as to compose with many persons present?*

V.N. He seldom went to the Instrument when he composed . . . In composing, he would get up and walk about the Room quite abstracted from everything that was going on about him. He would then come and sit down by her, tell her to give him his inkstand and paper and say ' Ma chère femme, ayez la bonté de me dire de quoi on a parlé ' ; then went on writing by her side while she talked to him, without the conversation at all impeding his occupation.

M.N. When some grand conception was working in his brain he was purely abstracted, walked about the apartment and knew not what was passing around, but when once arranged in his mind, he needed no Piano Forte but would take music paper and whilst he wrote would say to her, ' Now, my dear wife, have the goodness to repeat what has been talked of ', and her conversation never interrupted him, he wrote on, ' which is more ', she added, ' than I can do with the commonest letter '.

V.N. Description of the Room—hung round with the Portraits.[62] Over the sofa, the one containing Mozart and his sister playing a Duett with the father sitting down and the Mother's portrait in a picture frame, over that the Portrait of her second Husband Mr von Nissen. In the other Room, the portrait of Mozart as a Boy with an embroidered waist and sword, and the picture of his two Sons in a very affectionate and graceful attitude as if they were fondly attached to each other.

The Youngest who stood by me just as I was looking at it, told me that he was about five years old when it was done.

QUESTION. *How many portraits, busts, engravings, etc., have been made of him and which does Mme. von Nissen consider the best likeness of him?*

78

V.N. By far the best likeness of him in [Madame] Nissen's opinion the painting in oils done by the Husband of Madame Lange (the eldest sister of Mrs. Nissen) from which the portrait of Mozart contained in her Biography [*sic*]—is *unfinished* but admirably done . . . in a wooden case as if it had been travelling.

Some good Likenesses done in Wax, by an Artist at Berlin.

M.N. The originals of all the engravings she has given to his life are hung round the rooms, Mr. Nissen's portrait, her two sons, Mozart when a boy of seven, the family playing and singing, but the divine portrait of Mozart she has kept in a case and very wisely has refused to have it finished for fear the divine expression should be lost by some unlucky touch ; it was done by Monsieur Lange her sister's husband. Madame Lange was Mozart's first choice. She assured us that it exactly resembled him, and it is much more beautiful than the engraving, the forehead is high and ample in the extreme, full of genius, the mouth of sweetness and beauty, both this latter feature and the nose are exaggerated in the engraving, they are much more delicate in the painting . . . Mozart had very delicate hands.

Mary Novello's reference to Mozart's hands was almost certainly an outcome of their discussion of the unfinished portrait of Mozart by Josef Lange, whom Aloysia Weber, Constanze's sister and Mozart's first love, had married ; for when, on their return journey through Salzburg, the Novellos again called on Madame von Nissen, Novello records that ' on my expressing my regret that the painter had not preserved the form of his hands, which I understood were particularly delicate and beautifully shaped, she corroborated the truth of this report . . .' Novello had also included in his questionnaire an inquiry regarding the possibility of purchasing this picture, but finding the portrait in Constanze's possession, and obviously valued, he doubtless refrained from pressing the inquiry.

The ' good Likenesses done in Wax, by an Artist at Berlin ' were probably the medallions made by Leonhard Posch. The wax medallion now in the Mozart Museum was presented by him to Mozart's younger son, and his bronze medallion of the same date (1788) was the prototype for the print in Madame von Sonnenburg's possession, which she eventually presented to Vincent Novello, and which is repeatedly mentioned as being the best likeness of the composer.

QUESTION. *Whether his general disposition was lively and playful—or melancholy—whether he could draw, or paint well —or possessed any particular talent for any other art or pursuit than his own science.*

V.N. She said ' Il etoit toujours si gai '.

Was fond of Painting—Sculpture—and could draw himself. ' Indeed ' she added—' he had superior talents for all the Arts.'

M.N. She told us that he drew a little and was very fond of the arts, that he had indeed a talent for all the arts—that he was always in good humour, rarely melancholy but of a very gay humour, indeed he was an angel she exclaimed, and is one now—there was no affectation about this, but said quite simply.

She showed us Mozart's album,[63] but as most of the lines were written in German they were sealed to us, but some lines of his own were delicious to look at. His signature and indeed the whole of his writing was like Vin's, or rather more like my own when I imitate his and have a wretched pen and no kind Vin to mend it—*Mozart* like this.

V.N. Showed me a Book which belonged to him, it

was a kind of album containing some short Pieces of a Literary nature and various Drawings, Paintings, etc., that had been inserted in it at different times by his friends. In one part were some remarks in Mozart's own handwriting—but unfortunately the whole was in German.

It is not clear what train of thought led the conversation from the Mozart relics which Constanze was showing the Novellos, to Thomas Attwood ; but evidently Novello mentioned that Attwood (who between 1785 and 1787, as a young man in his early twenties, had been Mozart's pupil in Vienna) had given him an introduction to Aloysia Lange. Attwood had also subscribed to the sum presented to Madame von Sonnenburg, so perhaps Constanze was feeling a little out of it.

V.N. [She] showed me the words (in his own writing) of a Trio in Il Seraglio the first few notes of which she hummed very naturally. She [was] surprised at Attwood not having written to her—read over his Letter to Madame Lange, and then said it was probable that he did not think she was at Salzburg.

Seemed pleased when I told her that there were copies already of her Biography of Mozart in England and that the very first Copy which arrived in England was in my possession.

The King of Prussia (Frederick II) offered Mozart 16 hundred zechins a year to come [and] live at his Court, but Mozart was so much attached to the Emperor (Joseph II) that he preferred remaining with the latter from whom, however, Mozart received no salary whatever.

M.N. He was very fond of Joseph II and though that emperor allowed him no salary, he refused an offer of the King of Prussia to reside at his court with a salary of 1,600 sequins because he would not leave Joseph—it is to be hoped this generous sacrifice will not go unrewarded to his family by the Austrian court.

Constanze probably told the Novellos this story, as she had told it to Nissen, in all good faith, since, according to Rochlitz, she had had it from the King of Prussia himself when, in 1796, he placed the Royal Opera House and orchestra at her disposal for a benefit concert. But as no mention of the episode is made in any of Mozart's letters to her in 1789, the year of his visit to Berlin, it is now generally regarded as legendary, though some casual proposition thrown out by the King of Prussia may be at the root of it.

Mozart's post as Chamber Musician and Court Composer to the Imperial Court of Vienna, which chiefly involved the writing of dances for court balls, carried a small salary of 800 florins a year ; on one of the receipts he noted ' Too much for what I do, too little for what I could do.'

V.N. Description of Madame Nissen. In youth her Eyes must have been very brilliant and are still fine. Her face does not resemble the portrait given of her in the Biography.[64] It is thin and has the traces of great care and anxiety in it, but when her features relax into a smile, the expression is a remarkably pleasant one. She is of a rather small stature, slim figure, and looks much younger than what I expected to find her. Her voice is low and gentle, her manners well-bred and prepossessing, unconstrained like a person who has lived much in society and seen a good deal of the world, and the way in which she spoke of her illustrious Husband (though not quite so enthusiastic as I should have expected in one ' so near and dear ' to him) was tender and affectionate, and I could perceive a little tremor in her voice whilst she was looking with me at his portrait and on two or three occasions when she was alluding to some of the last years of his Life, which was not the less affecting or pathetic, from its being involuntary, unobtrusive and partly repressed. Nothing could be more kind, friendly and even cordial than her behaviour to me during the whole visit. Altogether this Lady is, to me, one of the most interesting Persons now in existence.

She said she had given away nearly everything to the numerous persons who had applied to her at different times for a Memorial of him. Relics she gave me—a small portion of the little Hairbrush with which he arranged his Hair every Morning, a part of a Letter addressed by him to his Father[65] I wished to have had a lock of his Hair but she said it had all crumbled away.

Novello, a great lover of relics and mementoes (like Leigh Hunt with his famous collection of locks of hair) had noted at the end of his questions addressed to Constanze that he was ' very anxious to procure some little relic of Mozart, to preserve for his sake, such as a lock of his hair, a letter or piece of music in his own handwriting, a pen or pencil case, his inkstand . . . or any other little ornament which once belonged to him '. In the end Constanze's evident liking for the Novellos made her think better of her white lie about Mozart's hair. Meanwhile Novello had to be content with the tuft from his hairbrush, which cost him some gentle teasing from Lamb when the latter was returning to him, the following June, the precious album of which we shall hear so much in Salzburg and Vienna, after himself writing in it his poem *Free Thoughts on some Eminent Composers* :

Pray write immediately to say ' the book has come safe '. I am anxious, not so much for the autographs, as for that bit of the hair brush. I inclose a cinder which belonged to *Shield*, when he was poor, and lit his own fires. Any memorial of a great Musical Genius, I know, is acceptable. . . .

Novello, who obviously took such teasing in good part, endorsed the letter ' A very characteristic note from Dear Charles Lamb, who always pretended to Rate all kinds of memorials and Relics, and assumed a look of fright and horror whenever he reproached me with being a *Papist* instead of a Quaker, which sect he pretended to dote upon '.[66]

The son told me he would give me a Letter to Haslinger, who could give me a great deal of information relative to his father, and another Letter to L'Abbé Stadler.

These introductions provided the Novellos with two of their most valuable contacts in Vienna. Tobias Haslinger was one of the city's leading music publishers, and the Abbé Maximilian Stadler (1748-1833), an active and devoted Benedictine and priest and an excellent musician, had been a friend of the Mozart family and, after the composer's death, his widow's chief adviser in musical matters. By completing and arranging a number of Mozart's unfinished works he made these incomplete MSS. into a saleable commodity for her.

. . . told me [he] resided at some distance but that he came regularly to pay his Mother a visit, and that this just happened to be the time. He showed me that Cantata (at his Mother's request) which he had dedicated to [*blank*].[67] It is in D and published by Haslinger, Op. 28. Score still in his own possession. Breitkopf has published most of his work.

Best Biographies of Mozart (after Nissen) which the son wrote down for me.

The slip of paper on which Mozart's son noted down for Novello ' Niemtschek—Biographie de Mozart, Schlichtegroll's Nekrolog (Gotha 1791) ' is still extant and in the possession of Messrs Novello & Company. On it Novello has written :
' The above is the handwriting of the youngest son

of Mozart . . . he gave it me himself in the course of a most interesting and delightful interview which I had with him and his Mother . . . at Salzburg on Tuesday the 14th of July, 1829.

' I was enquiring which works relative to the Biography of Mozart were the best written and most authentic (after those published by his own widow) when both he and his Mother mentioned the above, which he wrote down for me ; they also spoke highly of another work which I mentioned to them, " Mozart's Geist ".[68] '

' Young Mozart is a melancholy thoughtful-looking Person—he is short and rather stout, with very frank, and unaffected, quiet manners, his face somewhat resembling his Father's, especially the forehead. He is (*unfortunately*, I think) a Professor of Music, and seems to be impressed with the idea, that everything he can possibly do, will be so greatly inferior to what was accomplished by the wonderful genius of his illustrious father, that he feels disinclined to write much, or to publish what he produces.'

Mary Novello confirms her husband's impression of Mozart's overshadowed son :

In the room was also another sister of Madame's, and her youngest son, who though somewhat resembling his father seems to have no genius, and this feeling perhaps may cast a shade over his countenance rendering it rather heavy, and damps the ardour of his musical works reducing them to mediocrity; something of this despair of effecting anything worthy his father's name seemed to hang over him, otherwise he appears goodnatured, modest, easy of access and frank.

The Novellos' day was fittingly rounded off by a visit to Mozart's birthplace.

V.N. After having visited Madame Nissen (on Tuesday, July 14) we went in the Evening to the house in which

Mozart was born, and of which an engraving is given in the Biography.* It is situated in the Getreidegasse No. 225 [present numbering, 9], the lower part is now occupied by Joseph Lorenz [Hagenauer][69] . . . On the 3rd floor are four Rooms, one large and one small in the front of the house—one at the back which commands a fine View of the handsome Church belonging to the University, and one chamber in the middle between the front and back Rooms ; it was in this central apartment that Mozart was born. On entering the House we saw only a Maid servant belonging to the Person who occupied some other floor— but she very civilly went to call the woman who lives in the second floor and who also owns that above it. She was a most polite and chatty person (but unfortunately could only speak German) and in the kindest manner got up from her supper on purpose to show us the Apartments we so much wished to see.

These Rooms are now entirely unoccupied—there was not a single piece of furniture in any of them—but they had just been fresh cleaned and painted, and as well as I could make out, were intended to be let as Lodgings. There are few things that I should like better if I were independent (and could bring my friends with me) than to come and occupy these very apartments, and pass the remainder of my life amongst this exquisitely beautiful scenery, filled with so many interesting and delightful associations.

M.N. Vin and I made a pilgrimage to the house where Mozart was born, it is well-given in the print.* I ventured to accost a *mädchen* who observed us staring, with my broken German, and she soon understood my drift, indeed we have hardly ever been at a loss, so expressive I must believe are my looks and nods and ' wreathed smiles '

*The reference is to the engraving of the house in Nissen's *Biographie W. A. Mozarts*.

CONSTANZE WEBER IN 1782

8.   *from the portrait by Josef Lange*

9.   *from the Nissen engraving*

10. *from the Nissen engraving* MOZART AT THE KEYBOARD 11. *from the portrait by Josef Lange*

for my German is detestable. A goodnatured little fat woman, in dress and manner resembling an English-woman, left her supper to accompany us up the stairs. There are four rooms, two in front, the middle one is that where the divine Mozart first drew breath. I cannot describe my feelings, indeed we are both in a complete trance since our arrival in Salzburg. I wish much we could live for 12 months here, but that fate denies.

On the following day Novello was able to carry out his mission to Mozart's sister.[70]

V.N. Wednesday, July 15. A still more delightful day if possible than yesterday. Mozart's son came to us about 11 to conduct us to his Aunt Sonnenburg. After a little chat we accompanied him to her house which was within a few Yards of where we resided. It seemed that she had passed a very restless and sleepless night for fear we should not come to see her, and had repeatedly expressed her regret that we had not been admitted when we first called. On entering the Room, the Sister of Mozart was reclining placidly in Bed—but blind, languid, exhausted, feeble and nearly speechless. Her nephew kindly explained to her who we were and she seemed to derive much gratification from the intelligence he conveyed to her. During the whole time, I held her poor thin hand in mine and pressed it with the sincere cordiality of an old friend of her Brother. She appeared particularly pleased that the little present we had brought her should have arrived just before her own Saint's Day (St Anne the 26th of the month). Her own birthday is on the 30th on which day she will have completed her 78th year. Her voice is nearly extinct, and she appears to be fast approaching ' that bourne whence no traveller returns '.

Her face, though much changed by illness and drawn

9

by age, still bears a strong resemblance to the portraits that have been engraved of her, but it was difficult to believe that the helpless and languid figure which was extended before us was formerly the little girl represented as standing by the side of her Brother, and singing to his boyish accompaniment.

Vincent Novello is here referring to Carmontelle's water-colour, painted while the Mozart children were in Paris in 1764 ; it was engraved by Delafosse.

Novello's diagnosis was more accurate than his quotation. Mozart's sister died three months later, on October 29th, 1829, and Novello directed a performance of Mozart's Requiem in her memory at the Portuguese Embassy Chapel.

M.N. Another most delightful day has been spent in company with the Mozarts.

The son came to introduce us to his aunt, she had been very uneasy all night and could not sleep because she feared we would not call upon her. She is quite blind but suffers no pain, hers is entirely a decay of nature. She remains in bed like a person ready for the death stroke and will probably expire in her sleep. Her countenance, though much changed, even rather ugly, has something resembling her portrait. She is very fair and has most delicate hands. Like most blind people she is always alive to touch and kept our hands locked in hers, asking which was *der Herr* and which Madame, grieved very much that we could not speak German, ' kann nichts Deutsch '. Her voice is scarcely intelligible it is so low. She seemed like a child delighted with the *cadeau* from England, conceiving it was sent for her approaching name's day the 26th—the feast of St Anne, repeatedly called her nephew and begged he would thank us. Begged them to show her portrait, and the one of the family.

' Begged *them* '—because, though the Novellos do not mention him, there was yet another person present at the interview : doubtless that ' Joseph Metzger, Privatier ', who on July 16th wrote, in courteous but execrable French, to convey Madame von Sonnenburg's renewed thanks to Novello and his fellow-subscribers ; for, when Novello called again, on the return journey, to inquire after her, he ' met with the Gentleman, who spoke French, and who had before behaved with so much politeness '. Mary Novello, re-writing parts of her diary for publication in the *Musical World* in 1837, also adds to her account of this visit :

> I should mention, that the poverty and loneliness of Madame Sonnenburg are pitied and alleviated by the kindness of a fellow-lodger, who, himself in humble circumstances, ministers to her greater needs, by the occasional present of some little dainty, and the more frequent meed of sympathy and cheerful conversation. I could not catch his exact name and did not like to appear too curious, more especially that he shrunk, with genuine delicacy, from making his little services apparent.'

V.N. Near the Bed was the original Painting of which Madame Nissen has a small copy and which has been engraved in the Biography, represents Mozart and his sister playing a Duet on the Piano the likeness of Mozart's Mother in a frame and the Father leaning on the Piano Forte with a Violin in his hand.

In the adjoining apartment over the sofa was the Print . . . which his son told me was generally considered the best likeness[71] after that in Madame Nissen['s possession] (in which opinion he himself coincided). Around the room hung a very numerous Collection of Portraits of the greatest painters—amongst whom I particularly noticed those of Vandyk and Rembrandt. In another part of the Room was a Miniature of herself—another of her

Son (who had some resemblance to Leigh Hunt) and another likeness in Miniature of Mozart).

In the middle of the Room stood the Instrument on which she had often played Duetts with her Brother. It was a kind of Clavichord, with black keys for the naturals and white ones for the sharps like on old English cathedral organs. The compass was from ♮ to ♮ and had evidently been constructed before the additional keys were invented.[72] The tone was soft and some of the Bass notes, especially those of the lowest Octave C's ♮ were of a good quality ; at the time it was made it was no doubt considered an excellent Instrument. You may be sure that I touched the keys (which had been pressed by Mozart's fingers) with great interest. Mozart's son also played a few Chords upon it with evident pleasure. The key he chose was that of C minor, and what he did, though short, was quite sufficient to show the accomplished Musician. On the desk were two pieces of music the last which Mozart's sister had ever played before she took to her bed six months ago. They were the O Cara Armonia [i.e. *Das klinget so herrlich*] from her brother's opera of the ' Zauberflöte ' and the Minuet in his ' Don Giovanni '. This to me was a most touching proof of her continued sisterly attachment to him to the last, and of her tasteful partiality for his inimitable productions.

About two days before we arrived she had desired to be carried from her Bed and placed at the Instrument. On trying to play she found that although she could still execute a few passages with her *right* hand, yet with her *left* hand she could no longer press down the keys, and it was but too evident that her powers on that side were entirely gone.

90

On leaving this estimable and interesting Lady both Mary and myself could not refrain from kissing her weak and emaciated hand with tender respect, convinced as we were that we should never again behold her.

I fear that she cannot continue much longer in her present exhausted state—but whenever the hour arrives which no one living can ultimately avoid, I can only hope that it will not be attended with the least suffering, and that she will calmly cease to breathe as if she were merely sinking into a tranquil sleep.

I was particularly charmed by the respectful and kind cordiality with [which] Mozart's son behaved to her, calling her repeatedly ' meine liebe Tante ' and exerting himself to the utmost to ascertain and fulfil all her wishes.

> With Mozart's son as their guest at the mid-day meal, and afterwards at coffee with Constanze, the Novellos resumed their role of eager questioners.

M.N.   After our visit the son dined with us, he improves much on acquaintance—is a quiet but amiable character. He lives in Poland and comes to see his Mother but once in three or four years so that we may consider ourselves fortunate to meet him. He resembles Henry Nyren a little only that his skull is wider and his nose is more like his father's . . . he told us that Gall on seeing him had been astonished at his skull, which is certainly remarkable[73] . . . He speaks with enthusiasm of his father although he was but five months old when he died, but says that so much is expected of him from the circumstance of his name that it has become a burthen to him. . . . He complains of giving lessons and says it destroys all ideas worth committing to paper.

V.N.   . . . very temperate liver, seldom takes wine,

prefers the plainest food, and ordered the common household bread in preference to the whiter and more delicate
kind at table . . . at his Mother's took no coffee but a
kind of thick milk like curds. After Dinner I had the
pleasure of drinking the three following toasts with Mozart's
own son—the immortal memory of Mozart, Mozart's
widow, Joseph Haydn and Mozart's other favourite
friends.

QUESTION. *Who were his most intimate and cordial friends
amongst his brother professors, etc., and which seemed most
completely to appreciate his incomparable genius?*

M.N. Haydn he thinks his father's greatest admirer,
and said he never saw him as a child but he wept.

V.N. Spoke highly of Haydn—never saw him but he
wept. Seven Last Words and the Vocal Quartets and
Trios.[74] Haydn told him that if he (Mozart) went to
England first (as Salomon at one time wished) it would be
of no use for him (Haydn) to go there as ' nothing would
do after Mozart's compositions '. Haydn often visited them
and repeatedly declared that Mozart was the greatest
musical genius that ever existed.

Haydn's devotion to Mozart, and to the interests of his
orphaned family, lasted until increasing age and weakness—which prevented him from appearing at the
younger Mozart's benefit concert in 1805—checked its
active expression. It is not clear, from its context
among Novello's random notes, whether the story of
Haydn's anxiety to make his London visit before
Mozart was told now or later ; it was repeated to the
Novellos in Vienna by the Abbé Stadler.

M.N. In the afternoon we went to take coffee with
Madame. On our first arrival she was in her garden,
which is beautifully situated half way up the mountain
and full of flowers, with Vines trellised up the sides and

several seats which command the most delightful view perhaps in the world—the fine Town, Palace and church to the left, the mountains covered with snows before and the Salzach river flowing beneath in a beautiful Valley. She received me very affectionately and answered my innumerable questions with the greatest readiness, pressed us to stay a few days longer at Salzburg and as an inducement promised to accompany us on a little excursion in the neighbourhood. She had written in our Album some lines in French and moreover gave us some of Mozart's hair. She had very little she said, but she would divide with Vincent.

This is the first allusion in either diary to the Novellos' treasured Album, now in the possession of Messrs Novello & Company,[75] in which Novello collected the autographs of nearly all the leading figures of his day. It was clearly bought for this trip, for it is Mozart's widow who leads off, on the first page, with a typical autograph-album commonplace:

La Misère des pauvres, le bonheur des riches,
La gloire des Héros, la Majesté des Rois,
    Tout finit par : Ci-gît.

Saltzbourg ce 15 juillet Souvenez vous Monsieur et
        1829 Madame de votre tres humble
Servante Constance de Nissen
Veuve Mozart.

V.N. The widow who had but a very small quantity left of Mozart's own hair was so kind as to share it with me (which I esteem as a very high and flattering compliment). She consented to accept in return a little gold Brooch, which I had now in my bosom for many years past, and which I had the gratification of seeing transferred to a much more honourable post, that of forming an ornament for her own neck.

The conversation inevitably turned once more to Mozart; apparently Novello pursued his previous question whether Mozart played or sang much when at home, and this in turn led on to the subject of his operas.

M.N. She told us that Mozart when he finished an opera brought it to her and begged she would study it, after which he would play it over and sing with her, so that not only the songs but the words she knew by heart, but one air in the ' Idomeneo ' he preferred to hear her sing and on that account she prefers it also, ' se il Padre perdei '[76] . . . The most happy time of his life was whilst at Munich during which he wrote Idomeneo which may account for the affection he entertained towards the work.

V.N. The widow seemed pleased when I mentioned so many pieces out of his operas—' Oh, I see you know them all by heart as I do '—she knows all the words by memory as well as the music . . . told me that ' Non so più ' in ' Figaro ' was a great favourite with Mozart also ' Riconosci a questo amplesso '.

In ' Così fan tutte ' she remarked that in ' Di scrivermi '[77] (which I guessed was one of his great favourites) you could actually fancy the sobs and tears of the performers—also noticed the extraordinary *difference* of the melodies he has assigned to the various characters and the wonderful appropriateness of them—that passages of the Ghost part of Don Giovanni made one's hair stand on end. . . . She does not admire the plot of ' Così fan ', but agreed with me that such music would carry any piece through. . . .

QUESTION. *Whether he was fond of reading, and what kind of literature he preferred—Poetry, prose, fiction or history?*

M.N. Mozart was fond of reading and well acquainted with Shakespeare in the translation. One of his favourite

94

authors is at present in her possession, and which she most frequently peruses, it is in 9 volumes but being a forbidden fruit in the Austrian states she did not name it—I suspect some of the French revolutionary works.

QUESTION. *Was he a great performer on any other Instrument than the Piano Forte?*

Whether he occasionally attended to play the organ, or accompany any of his own Masses, and if so, at what churches?

V.N. Widow told me that Mozart's favourite Instrument was the Organ—upon which she said he played with the most incomparable skill.

M.N. He played upon several of the organs both at Salzburg and Vienna, the Cathedrals of both—the organ was his favourite instrument.

This was corroborated by the Abbé Stadler, whom Mary Novello records as saying that Haydn ' played but little on the Piano Forte. Mozart preferred the Organ and played divinely on that instrument '.

QUESTION. *Which were his favourite amusements, when he wished to relax from his severe studies, and intense application to composition and his other professional avocations?*

Whether he was an early riser, and if he generally composed late at night or early in the morning?

M.N. It is quite evident that Mozart killed himself with over-exertion. He could never entirely abstract himself from his musical thoughts. Billiards he was very fond of, but he composed whilst he played, if he conversed with his friends, he always was at work in his mind. Necessity and the duties of his situation induced this habit, which evidently wore out the system and would have produced death had he not been attacked with the fever which killed him suddenly. . . .

Madame confirmed the truth of her sitting up all night

95

with him whilst he wrote the overture to ' Don Giovanni.' He frequently sat up composing until 2 and rose at 4, an exertion which assisted to destroy him. At present she rises at the same hour, but goes to bed, her son says, with the chickens.

QUESTION. *On what occasion was the ' Davidde Penitente ' written, and which of the movements were originally composed as a Mass?*

V.N. The ' Davidde Penitente ' originally a grand Mass which he wrote in consequence of a vow that he had made to do so, on her safe recovery after the birth of their first child—relative to whom he had been particularly anxious. This Mass was performed in the Cathedral at Salzburg and Madame Mozart herself sang all the principal solos. Mozart thought so highly of this production that he afterwards made several additions and adapted new words to make it a complete Cantata, or rather Oratorio, for the former is too modest a title for so elevated, elaborate and masterly a work.

Constanze's account is not entirely correct. The Mass was indeed composed in fulfilment of a vow, but the occasion was an illness of hers during her engagement to Mozart, and the condition was that she should recover and become his wife. When, in 1783, the young couple visited his still disapproving family in Salzburg the work was unfinished, and had to be completed by the inclusion of numbers from earlier works for its performance in St. Peter's Church on August 25th, when Constanze sang the soprano solos.

It was the *Kyrie* and *Gloria* which were subsequently converted into the oratorio *Davidde Penitente* ; the words, according to the account given in Vienna by the Abbé Stadler, were by da Ponte (see below, p. 158).

Mary Novello's version of the story is identical but much condensed. But among her miscellaneous notes

she has written : ' How touching is the anecdote of
Mozart's writing a Mass in thanksgiving for the
recovery of his wife from the perils of child birth—how
delicious are these offerings of genius to conjugal love ;
riches may purchase many pleasures, and many
casual gratifications, but only talent combined with
exquisite tenderness can elicit emotions which while
they last are little short of divine anticipations—love
and its pleasures are God's best gift to human nature,
but failing of tenderness, which outlives possession and
decay, it knows but half the sublime emotions of
which it is capable '. The alterations and corrections
suggest the authoress at work, but the passage is none
the less Mary Novello's profession of faith.

After some time the little group apparently split
up ; the two gentlemen, with Sophie Haibl in attendance, went over to the pianoforte while Constanze
and Mary Novello remained in conversation.

M.N. The son spoke with great enthusiasm of his
father's music, and played several things for Vincent, he
said there had been many fine musicians in the world, but
he might be allowed to say but one Mozart, that he was
the Shakespeare of music—(this is often an expression of
Vin's) . . . Madame Mozart regretted that her son is so
lazy a character—his father she says was of the sweetest
disposition, but he was full of energy and vivacity . . .
I asked her if she did not mean to give a biographical
sketch of her own life. No, she said, it was too fatiguing to
write about herself—if she had any one to write she would
dictate, for there were many interesting particulars.

She said his death was at last sudden, but a few moments
before he had spoken so gaily, and in a few moments after
he was dead—she could not believe it, but threw herself
on the bed and sought to catch the fever of which he died,
but it was not to be. There were moments, she declared,
when she not only prayed sincerely to die but that she did

97

not love her children, every thing was hateful to her in the world, yet here I am still, and have gone through all this suffering . . . Mozart not only died poor, but left some debts, when the youngest son was 13 he took a benefit concert and the receipts went among the creditors—how few but the widow and child of a professional man would have after such a lapse of time dedicated the money to such a purpose, for it must be recollected they had nothing, except a trifling pension allowed by the Emperor of Austria—all Mozart's operas were either given, or stolen, the remainder of his music was sold for a mere trifle.

She said Mr. Nissen was as amiable in his character as Mozart, that she could not say which had been most kind to her, she could have wished to live for both. . . . The biography was undertaken with a view to make a small sum for the two sons, but unfortunately it has not yet paid its expenses. . . . . There is no monument erected to him at Vienna ; although the Emperor gave 1,000 florins in part, not a sufficient sum has yet been raised, and this is their enthusiasm for the cause of good music.

The Emperor asked him why he did not marry a rich wife—he said he hoped he should be able always to gain sufficient by his genius to maintain the woman he loved. He repeatedly told her he should not have known what to do with a rich wife—she would have expected his undivided attention and he must have neglected his compositions. He frequently compared his married fate with that of others, particularly the two Haydns, Joseph and Michael ' But no one is so happy as I am in a wife ' he would exclaim.

Joseph Haydn's uncongenial and shrewish wife was a legend even in her husband's lifetime. That similar tales were current of Michael Haydn's wife—perhaps

98

through mere association of ideas—we shall shortly learn from Mary Novello.

Meanwhile, at the piano, Mozart's son played and Novello listened and questioned. Unfortunately the recorded answers are in many places illegible.

V.N. The sister of Mozart's widow sat by our side . . . his own portrait quite close to us over Piano Forte.

Opinions of Mozart's Son—Liked that best (of his father's compositions) which he had last played to me, Fantasia in C minor and Rondo in A minor . . . Fantasia in C minor written for Madame (see memo in son's handwriting), Rondo in A minor not written for any particular person, but a great favourite of his own.[78]

Jupiter sinfonia the triumph of Art especially the finale (the subject one for Bach) [?] . . . although he thought he preferred G minor sinfonia.

Novello shared this opinion of Mozart's last symphony for he recalls it on the return journey, on a page of isolated memoranda dated August 7th (and incidentally tells us that it owes its nickname to Haydn's friend Salomon) :

Mozart's son said he considered the Finale to his father's sinfonia in C—which Salomon christened the Jupiter—to be the highest triumph of Instrumental Composition, and I agree with him.

I mentioned [*illegible*][79] which he said that if his Father had written nothing more he would have deserved immortality.

Although some of the airs in Idomeneo are rather old-fashioned yet he esteemed some of the Pieces as much as any that his father has written.

Mozart's son is in possession of 8 or 9 of his father's Masses of which he promised to send me a catalogue *thématique,* and I am not without hope of finding some of them to be different from those already in my possession. He has also several sketches of Masses, etc., in Mozart's own handwriting, of which he likewise promised to send me a List. He played me (and sang in a pleasing soft tenor voice) the subject of a Motett for four voices in F the words beginning [*blank*] and which he said was 'a delicious composition'. He afterwards at my request wrote down the *motivo* [?] and said I could probably get a copy at Breitkopf.[80]

I endeavoured to persuade him to undertake a *complete* Collection of all his father's works, which after his death might be deposited in the national Library of Germany or in the British Museum as the best monument to the memory of his father's genius, and where it might be safely preserved [as] a genuine collection of authentic documents for public reference, and the eternal admiration of the whole Musical world.[81]

I flatter myself that my persuasions had some weight with him—and should he ever undertake the glorious Collection I have suggested I sincerely wish him success in the fulfilment of his enviable task, which will be equally honourable to himself, to his immortal father, and to his native country, of which that father is the most brilliant ornament.

Novello's disjointed notes suggest that the conversation continued on more personal lines. Mozart's son told Novello about the choral society which he conducted in Lemberg, 'nearly 50 voices to perform Classical Music, especially his father's Davidde Penitente— difficult double chorus in G minor'. He then appears to have spoken of his former teacher of counterpoint, Gallus[82] and to have mentioned the famous pianist Moscheles (who had studied with Albrechtsberger) as 'an excellent contrapuntist'. Moscheles had by this time settled permanently in England (and had subscribed to the present for Mozart's sister), and this perhaps led on to young Mozart's struggles with the English language.

Learnt a little English of Dignam [?] but when he came to the pronunciation of the *th* he gave it up.

Liked the old German text or characters for printing, and thought it was best that every language should preserve its peculiarities, otherwise there would ultimately be no distinction or originality of character.

Thought he could have done something if he had met with encouragement—but now *too late*. Widow told me he wanted courage. His elder brother at Milan who has Mozart's Piano Forte is a fine performer and has great natural [?] talent for whatever he undertakes.

Walked arm in arm with him in the afternoon and afterward had the same pleasure of having Mozart's widow as a companion in a stroll. She walked between Mary and myself having hold of an arm of each. He spoke very affectionately of his Mother (his father unfortunately he never knew) and of Mr Nissen who brought him up like his own son and to whom he said he owed everything.

The stroll through Salzburg by which the party was prolonged—and which, according to Mary Novello's published account, ended with them all supping together at their inn—was the occasion for further questions and anecdotes.

M.N. The son said, when I was remarking how much younger his Mother looked than she really was, she is my Mother but it must be allowed that she has great qualities to secure the esteem of two such husbands as she has had . . . she is really a delightful woman. When we left she would accompany us for a little walk—and behold Vin and I supporting the wife of Mozart. It was a delicious recompense for my dear Vin after all his exertions in behalf of Mozart's music to render this token of respect to this relic of the divine man. Our walk was most delightful. Great respect is shown to her by the inhabitants of Salzburg although she seldom quits home, having such a delicious house and garden, where she can quietly enjoy the air without fatigue. She showed us the ancient *manège* which is curiously cut out of the solid rock, and further on a gate of the city called Maximilian's Gate. [It] is cut through the solid rocks, forming a grotto like the Pausilippo at Naples, for a considerable distance, it is lit up at night, and is wide enough to admit two carriages abreast.

> Conversation seems to have turned on the iniquitous ' Behaviour of Rolla and the Female Singers ', and his ' treatment of young Mozart about a benefit together with the prima donna ' in Milan, as a result of which young Mozart told Novello that he ' was too disgusted to to go on in Italy '. The trouble seems to have been the lack of rehearsal (' no rehearsal required ') and this may have led on to other questions of performance.

M.N. Mozart particularly disliked the hurried manner in which some orchestras accompanied his operas, and Madame thinks they are now generally spoiled by their being played too fast and each sound cut too short, many of the wind instruments she declared were mere *puffs*, no effect whatever produced.

Madame declares she could not bear to hear either the Requiem or ' Idomeneo ' performed, the last time she heard ' Il Don Giovanni ', she was not calm for a fortnight afterwards. At Prague she thinks the operas have been best performed, and very well sometimes at Vienna, but at present whilst the Italian singers are there, there is no chance of hearing Mozart's operas, when they leave, they are performed. If we do not visit Prague our regret will be lessened because the son thinks they are few who recollect his father and these we might not discover. The band are the most probable to have been acquainted with him.

Prague had been on the Novello's original itinerary, scribbled in pencil on the end-paper of Mary Novello's notebook somewhere before they reached Coblenz:

> At Coblenz, Thursday, July 2nd.
> Mayence, Friday, 3rd.
> Mannheim, Saturday, 4th.
> Stuttgart, Monday, 6th.
> Ulm, Tuesday evening, 7th.
> Munich, Wednesday, 8th.
> Leave Munich for Salzburg so as to arrive in the afternoon of Saturday, 11th.
> Get to Linz on Wednesday morning, 15th.
> On to Vienna, on Thursday, 16th.
> Leave on Monday night, 20th.
> Reach Prague, Wednesday, 22nd.
> Leave on Thursday morning, 23rd.
> Get to Dresden, Friday, 24th—Crown Inn.
> Leave on Sunday evening, 26th.

But since they had stayed an extra night at Mannheim—probably for the sake of the opera on Sunday, July 5th—they had been running steadily behind their time-table, and were clearly debating whether to give up the idea of returning by way of Prague and Dresden. Madame von Nissen's promise over the coffee-cups to accompany them to Aigen probably persuaded them, nothing loth, to take an extra day in Salzburg, and eventually the Prague plan was abandoned.

The Aigen excursion was fixed for the following afternoon, and the Novellos thus had the morning free. As the day, Thursday, July 16th, was the Feast of Our Lady of Mount Carmel, the Novellos were able to satisfy their appetite for music with two High Masses, as well as seeing some of the sights of the town.

103

10

V.N. Thursday, July 16th, at 7 in the morning. Went to hear the high Mass at the Church belonging to a Convent of Nuns close to the present residence of Mozart's widow, which derives its name of the ' Nonnberg ' from its vicinity to this Nunnery. . . . It is here that Mozart's widow frequently comes to hear Mass at 7 in the morning. She is a very early riser I understand, indeed she herself told me that she generally gets up every morning at 4 o'clock to enjoy the fine effects of the Morning sun upon the exquisite scenery in front of her house and garden.

On the preceding Morning she told me that the Choir had performed one of Mozart's Masses in B flat (probably No. 7 or No. 10 of my edition)[83] but I did not regret not having been present as she added that the performance was so very unsatisfactory she could scarcely recognize it as the composition of Mozart.

Cathedral, Salzburg. Mass. July 16, 9 o'clock.

The service began with the Procession round the Church carrying the Sacrament under a Canopy, surrounded with Priests chanting a Gregorian Hymn. A fine effect was produced by the Choristers stopping at intervals, and then breaking out again with their solemn strain, which was sung by men's voices only, and entirely unaccompanied.

The Orchestra was placed in the right-hand Gallery near the Altar. . . . The best Performers were the three Trombone players, who produced a fine tone and added much grandeur to the general effect. The next best Player was on the Double Bass. He was a Priest and it appeared to me quite a novel and singular thing to see this Instrument played by a Person in a Cassock and other sacerdotal habiliments which however did not seem in the least to impede the freedom of his bowing.

The Mass was in C but contained nothing very striking

. . . I own I was disappointed at not having heard a single Piece of Mozart's composition at any of the Churches in his own native town.

M.N. The town is really magnificent and was in the time of that cursed vulgar-minded Archbishop who ill-treated Mozart so, kept in a style of more than princely splendour—but now the houses are many of them uninhabited, and many hastening to ruin. The situation is most delicious, far exceeding the finest scenery on the Rhine, as many of the mountains are covered with perpetual snows, and the fortress overlooking the town is in better preservation than either the Rheinfels or the Ehrenbreitstein. The church of St Peter where Michael Haydn is buried, has some good paintings, and his monument is worth seeing. The burial ground is very picturesque, as it is a succession of small chapels, containing monuments, built against the side of the mountain, which overhangs it fearfully, threatening one day to overwhelm it.

In the famous cemetery of St Peter's, with its arcaded niches built against the rocky face of the Mönchsberg, Mozart's sister was soon to be laid to rest, as Michael Haydn had been 23 years before ; the monument in the church itself, described by Vincent Novello, contains his skull. He was born, not at Salzburg as the Novellos thought, but, like his brother Joseph, at Rohrau. He lived and worked in Salzburg, however, for 44 years, having been appointed to the Archbishop's musical establishment in 1762. A memorial tablet marks his house at the foot of the Mönchsberg, adjoining the cable railway to the Fortress. His wife, against whom Mary Novello launches so fierce a diatribe, was the Court singer Maria Magdalena Lipp, who, so far from being a drunkard, was—according to Mozart—a *dévote* well on the way to ruining her voice with her excessive penances. Mary Novello probably had confused her with Joseph Haydn's notoriously unsympathetic wife, who however, shrewish and spendthrift as she appears to have been, was never accused of spending her money on drink. It was in fact poor Michael Haydn himself who in middle life, if Leopold Mozart can be trusted, drifted into mildly drunken habits. But of such confusions are legends born.

V.N. Inscription on the Monument of Michael Haydn in the church of St Peter at Salzburg:

Michaeli
Haydn
Nato Die 14 Sept.
1737
Vita functo
die 10 Augt
1806

The Names of 20 Pieces of his Sacred Music which he had written expressly for this Church, were inscribed on scrolls which were distributed over the lower part of the Monument.

He was born and died in a small white House which was beautifully situated quite close to the Church (of which he was Organist for a great number of years) with a most magnificent background formed by a perpendicular Rock of granite and foliage intermixed—and the ancient fortress of Salzburg towering over the very highest summit.

M.N. From the churchyard is seen the house where Michael Haydn was born and died. Poor man, he was plagued with a wretch of a wife, who made away with everything he earned, sold his work and his furniture to procure a glass of beer, miserable creature—it is not fair to be hard upon any vice, since we may all have some hidden cherished one, which we think not so heinous ; but certain it is, that some are more disgusting than others, and cause greater misery and disgrace to those with whom they are connected. What a companion must this swinish creature have been for a musician's leisure moments, when he would fain have been met with tenderness and his great genius appreciated—now her disgrace lives with his fame.

I wish I could describe Salzburg so as to give you some idea of it but I fear that is impossible for it resembles no other place. The river Salzach, from which the town takes its name, runs with great rapidity between immense cliffs but the town lies only partly on the river side, it extends inward on the right and leads to the most romantic Valley surrounded by rocks rising one over another, some nearly bald of vegetation, others covered with dark vegetation, and the higher and more distant ones covered with snow, which at sunrise and sunset, reflect the light in beautiful colours, and at other times the clouds hang round them, literally like a wreath. The principal ones are named Untersberg, Watzmann, the Devil's Horn, the Capuziner-berg and the Nonnberg, this latter is crowned with a most noble fortress[84] and half way down is situated Madame Nissen's house. The whole resembles an immense Pano-rama, so that from her window you look at these covered with snow, etc., and may imagine the prospect she enjoys. In the winter she has a lodging in the town on the Platz.

In the afternoon, before their excursion to Aigen, the insatiable Vincent Novello went once again to the Cathedral.

Salzburg Cathedral—2 o'clock afternoon.

I expected the vespers to have begun at the above hour and accordingly attended punctually, but I found the Person at the Cathedral tuning the reed stops of the large Organ at the west end of the Church. . . .

The Priest who had played the Double Bass in the morning came out of the Sacristy to tune his Instrument beforehand. He seemed to be a genuine lover of the grand notes that are to be pulled out by a skilful hand from this noble Instrument. He brought out some very fine soft, subdued and rich notes before he had tuned it to his mind, and as he leaned over it he appeared to doat upon its full round and deep tones nor did he leave it till he had put it into most admirable order.

The Choir Boys of which there were about a dozen, had cocked hats like the Choir Boys belonging to the King's Chapel Royal in England.

At ½ past 3 the Service began. There was a Catafalque under the Dome with a Mitre, Cardinal's Cap, etc., and the Service seemed to be in commemoration of some elevated Ecclesiastic. The painting at the high Altar was covered with black cloth and the Priests wore dresses similar to those I have seen in England when there has been a Requiem or Service for the dead celebrated.

Amid the wild beauties of the natural park surrounding Schloss Aigen, their conversation with Constanze von Nissen posthumously invested Mozart with a romantic love of nature of which no trace appears in his own letters. Mozart was, in fact, essentially a townsman and one to whom ' the proper study of mankind is man '. But to the Novellos, not to have been attuned to natural beauty would have been a deficiency, unthinkable in Mozart, and in their eyes his exquisite sensibilities only cast a harsher light on the coarseness of Rossini, about whom Mozart's son complacently retailed the current gossip.

As usual, there was a grain of truth in it ; Mozart's son stressed the difference in age between Rossini and his wife, and it is true that in 1822, when Rossini married the singer Isabella Colbran, he was thirty and she thirty-seven. But their marriage was simply the legalization of a relationship which had begun in Naples some seven years earlier, when Colbran, at the height of her vocal powers and her dark Spanish beauty, had dazzled the Court and the San Carlo Opera House in the rôle of *Elisabetta Regina d'Inghilterra* created for her by the handsome and successful young *maestro* from Pesaro. Later her voice degenerated, and Stendhal was excruciated by her habit of singing out of tune ; she retired from the stage in 1824, immediately after she and Rossini had visited England.

M.N. Thursday. At 4 o'clock Madame Nissen came to accompany us to Aigen, a charming Park situated on the opposite side of the town. We went by the Capuzinerberg and all along our prospect was most delicious, yet excelled I think at the different points of the garden where seats are placed commanding the most picturesque point of view ; a mountain stream falls between rocks from a prodigious height and forms several cascades [which] are crossed by rustic bridges.

V.N. [Mozart and his wife] lived a twelvemonth together at Salzburg,[85] he was very fond of its picturesque scenery—especially of the romantic grounds at Aigen now belonging to Prince Schwarzenberg and which we had afterwards the pleasure of visiting together and strolling arm in arm with her in the identical places she had visited with Mozart. If he had not been an enthusiastic admirer of nature he could not have written what he has done. Especially fond of flowers, as is also his widow—she gathered a beautiful bouquet out of her own garden on purpose to bring to Mary. There is a little summer house in it where she often passes many hours with a book . . .

. . . [Mozart was] extremely fond of the country and a passionate admirer of everything that was beautiful in nature—liked little excursions and passed much of their time out of town.

M.N. She does not like Italy, it is certain, the modern

109

Italians bear a bad name from all travellers. She says they have spoiled Rossini and that nothing was to be heard but his operas ; the son I think spoke of him truly, he said he could not be a man of any sentiment or he would not have married when quite young, an old woman merely for gain, who had no charms of any kind—yet such was the nationality of the Italians[86] that although she never by any chance sang in tune, nay once continued throughout $\frac{1}{2}$ a note too flat, yet they applauded with the utmost vehemence.

On their way homeward they stopped at the church of St Sebastian, the burial-place not only of Paracelsus but also of Mozart's father. The family grave, as already related, also housed Constanze's second husband, and she herself was eventually buried there.

Madame took us to the grave of Mr Nissen—it is a simple pyramid, with four inscriptions, and as usual surrounded by flowers. In this church is also the monument of Paracelsus. By a singular coincidence the husband of the sister who lives with her at present, and who appears very amiable, died the same day as Mr Nissen, a circumstance which must unite them closer from sympathy.

Madame speaks with great pleasure of the society of Copenhagen, and of the time she spent there, although she was there twice while the English attacked that city. She appears to have been terribly ill used by the booksellers respecting this biography, so that the tribe of Barabbas does not seem to be confined to England, on the contrary there was a pettiness in some of the dealings she mentioned that any respectable house in London would have been ashamed to practise.

Friday, July 17th, was the day of the Novellos' departure for Vienna. They were not due to leave until the afternoon, so the morning was devoted to a final visit to Mozart's widow. Before this, Vincent Novello had been to Mass once more at the convent church on the Nonnberg and (if an undated entry among his loose papers belongs, as seems probable, to this morning) at the Cathedral also.

Responsive, as ever, to the beauties of Gothic architecture, he makes a few notes on the charming fifteenth-century convent church. His eye is caught by the grille separating the nuns' chapel from the main church, and by the steps descending beneath the slightly raised choir to the crypt below. Nor does he fail to spot the twelfth-century murals. But his silences are revealing too : the only thing he mentions about the Cathedral is the music, and, save for a casual reference to Fischer von Erlach's Kollegienkirche (' the handsome church belonging to the University '), Baroque Salzburg passes him by.

Mass in Nonnberg, Morning, Thursday*, 7 o'clock. Mass De Angelis, Gregorian—too short. No orchestra.

Church very antique—Gothic style. Good effect of Painted Glass window behind the figure of the Virgin placed at the altar. Crypt under the choir seen through the steps. Confined cages for the nuns. Floor covered with curious stones. Side Chapels—opposite to Confessionals. Eight Portraits of Female Saints at the top of the columns in Choir—old paintings.

Salzburg Cathedral. Went at 9 expecting to hear High Mass—but there was no Choir or Orchestra—merely a few Priests singing in the Plain Chant without even the Organ to accompany them.

Music indeed is in a very sad state of decay in this, the very birthplace of the most enchanting composer that ever existed.

*A slip of the pen ; Thursday's Mass at the Nonnberg is dated and fully described.

At Madame von Nissen's, they made the most of their last opportunity to ask questions and secure her confirmation of the more dramatic episodes related in Nissen's biography, such as the writing of the D minor string quartet during the birth of her first child. (In this connection it has been pointed out that, with Mozart, the act of writing was the purely mechanical recording of a work already composed mentally; Constanze herself described this process to the Novellos at their first interview, but it doubtless pleased her to think that her labour-pangs had been immortalized in music.) The most dramatic story of all, Mozart's death, the mysterious commissioning of the Requiem and its completion by Süssmayr, was prominent in all their minds, both for its human interest and on account of the controversy that had just been raging around the authenticity of the work, and the very next week the Novellos' encounter with Mozart's old friend the Abbé Stadler was to bring them a mass of additional information. For the sake of coherence, the entire story has been gathered together in a separate section.

M.N. Friday, 17th. We have bade farewell to Mozart's widow and his son, but not I trust a last farewell. We went to her Town lodging to see the inkstand of Mozart—it is in the condition he left it, with the same ink spots which his Requiem caused. She confirmed the truth of his writing the *quatuor* whilst she was in child birth of her first son, and declares that the agitation he suffered and her cries are to be traced in several passages.

V.N. She confirmed the truth . . . of his writing the Quartet in D minor while she was in labour with their first child; several passages indicative of her sufferings especially the Minuet (a part of which she sang to us).

QUESTION. *Whether he was well acquainted with the works of the English composer Purcell, and the oratorios of Handel? . . .*

*Whether he ever began or finished any oratorios like Handel's,
and if so, what is become of them?*

V.N. Mozart [was a] great admirer of Handel, well
acquainted with his works especially his oratorios. . . .

Son thought higher of Handel's oratorios than of any
other Compositions after his father's, and said that he
should have purchased the whole of his works in score but
that [they] were difficult to procure and at too high a
price for a Professor who like himself was not rich.

M.N. He contemplated writing oratorios in the style
of Handel and it seems as if fate had determined the latter
should remain single in that department by removing the
one who could best have outshone him.

QUESTION. *What kind of speaking voice, whether high or low,
loud or soft, and his singing voice, whether contralto, tenor or
bass—powerful or delicate?*

M.N. His singing voice was a tenor, his speaking voice
gentle, unless he was directing, then he was energetic and
would occasionally stamp with his feet, and once he was
so loud in the Cathedral that Madame heard him at an
immense distance.

V.N. His voice was a Tenor, rather soft in speaking
and delicate in singing, but when anything excited him,
or it became necessary to exert it, it was both powerful
and energetic. His usual exclamation was ' Saperlotte ',
and occasionally [he] would stamp with his foot when
impatient, or things did not go correctly in the orchestra.
With him at the opera ' Il Seraglio ' when they took the
time of one of the Movements too fast—he became quite
impatient and called out to the Orchestra without seeming
to fear or to be aware of the presence of the audience.

Two anecdotes (both related by Nissen) are telescoped,
somewhat confusedly, into this account. At Berlin, in

1789, during a performance of *Die Entführung aus dem Serail* (*Il Seraglio*), in Pedrillo's aria *Frisch zum Kampfe, frisch zum Streit*, the second violins, by playing D sharp instead of D natural at the words *Nur ein feiger Tropf versagt*, were turning a fresh and piquant progression into a mere cliché ; Mozart astonished the house, and revealed his identity, by crying out ' Damn it, play D natural ! ' At Leipzig, on his way thither, in order to spur on an elderly and sluggish orchestra, he drove the tempo of one of his symphonies excessively fast, stamping so violently that he lost a shoe-buckle (normally, as Constanze had already told the Novellos, he was averse to over-rapid tempi in the performance of his works). Constanze did not accompany him on this journey, so she cannot have been present on either occasion ; it is, however, just possible that a similar incident may have occurred in her presence.

The conversation seems to have developed naturally into a discussion of Mozart's personality and temperament, in which, through the inevitable idealization of the dead, we suddenly hear his living voice, as marriage breaks the mysterious equilibrium of joy and sorrow within him : that equilibrium which he himself recognized when, at twenty-one, he wrote to his father that he had so far been ' neither happy nor unhappy—and I thank God for it '. And the waters are troubled once more as Constanze relates how, during their uneasy visit to Salzburg in 1783, their singing of the great quartet in Act III of *Idomeneo*, in which the young Idamante faces exile and disaster, had brought upon him a wave of overwhelming and unaccountable emotion, like a presage of woe.

V.N. [He was] not difficult to please or at all particular respecting ' les plaisirs de la table ' . . . never had the least dispute of any consequence with him—he was of so sweet a disposition altogether that it was impossible to quarrel with him. . . . At one time of his Life he said [he] was too happy for it to last.

M.N. She told us that after their marriage they paid a visit to Salzburg and were singing the Quartet of 'Andrò ramingo' when he was so overcome that he burst into tears and quitted the chamber and it was some time before she could console him.

All his operas he liked the best when they were finished ; he would say, 'I shall not gain much by this but I am pleased and that is my recompense '—he was frequently requested to write more for the common lot, but he would never comply—' I shall always try to do what pleases myself.'

V.N. . . . Not devoid of 'amour propre '—propre amour [*sic*]

With characteristic warm-heartedness Novello seems to have told Constanze and her son all he thought it would please them to hear of what his brother musicians in England were doing for Mozart's music—J. B. Cramer as pianist and conductor of the Philharmonic Orchestra, and his old friend the Rev. C. J. Latrobe as fellow editor, and ardent (if somewhat uncritical) collector of Haydn's and Mozart's church music. His library was, indeed, the source of some of the MSS. of Haydn's and Mozart's Masses, both genuine and spurious, which Novello, as his daughter writes, ' with the zeal of a true musical enthusiast . . . edited and published, at his own cost of time and money, in order to introduce them, in accessible form, among his countrymen in England.'

The singer Ernst August Kellner, though of German extraction, was also a native of London. Mozart's son must have heard him on one of his European tours.

V.N. Kellner's singing of ' Madamina ' in ' Don Giovanni ' [and] another [aria] from ' Il Sacrificio d'Abramo '[87] so pathetically as to excite tears in several of the Company—Mozart's son included.

Both he and his Mother seemed pleased when I informed them of John Cramer so frequently selecting Mozart's Concertos, etc., to perform in public (Sinfonia in E flat at his last concert). They had heard of his admirable style of playing which I had the pleasure of confirming in the most unqualified manner.

Latrobe and what he had done towards turning the attention of the English public to the sacred music of Mozart, Haydn and other German [?] composers.

[Mozart's widow] wishes much for an English Piano Forte, in Mozart's time the Instruments not very good.

[She] shewed me the first watch which had been made a present to him at Paris, and which he had given to her as a bridal present—it is a small gold one, going remarkably well, and though she had several presented to her since has never worn any but that one (she had it at that very time in her bosom). She playfully asked me ' voulez-vous l'avoir? ' . .

She also shewed me the Inkstand out of which he had written most of his works amongst others the ' Figaro ', ' Don Giovanni ', the ' Tito ', ' Zauberflöte '—and the Requiem—she has had the good taste to preserve it just in the same state as he left it, with all the blots running from the time he wrote the last page just before he died.

This interesting relic consists of a little dark marble slab of an oblong shape, upon which is placed the silver metal vessel for the ink—it contains about the same quantity as a wine glass and is of the shape of a small tumbler. On the opposite side is a vessel of the same shape, containing sand, and between the two is a little silver Bell forming a cover for the wafers. At each end is a raised branch, something like a small Lyre, for the pens to be placed lengthways when he [had] done with them. As I evidently admired this relic (which is like the fountain whence had issued such exquisitely beautiful creations) Madame was so kind as to ask me whether she should give it me. The offer was so tempting a one that I rather hesitated in saying that I should be sorry to deprive her of what she valued so much, and had she repeated the offer I own I would not then have been able to resist accepting what would have been such an invaluable treasure to me —but as nothing further was said I was fearful of being thought encroaching or indelicate if I had ventured to renew any petition for it.

I shall certainly envy whoever ultimately becomes possessed of this curious inkstand, as well as the person who may be the inheritor of the Portrait of Mozart by M. Lange.

M.N. The inkstand she offered to Vin but it seemed more an offer of complaisance and Vin very wisely did not avail himself of it. The ' Davidde Penitente ' she kindly procured for Vin which has much delighted him—she wrote her name in it, as did also her son and sister. Her son has written in the album a trio,[88] and Vin gave him a seal at parting.

V.N. Mutilated copies published [of *Davidde Penitente*] but the widow was so kind as to procure me a very fine MS. Copy of the *complete* work in score, which was formerly in the possession of Mozart's own son—the latter was so good as to write his name in the title page, as did also Mozart's widow and her sister, and with these three rare Autographs of the Mozart family I now prize this volume as one of the most valuable MSS. in my possession.

. . . He [Mozart's son] wrote a most charming [?] little Trio of his own composition . . . in my album and I had the pleasure of [*illegible*] his acceptance of my watch seals to wear for my sake as a little reminder [?] of the very high gratification I had derived from having so fortunately formed his acquaintance.

M.N. Madame said that Mozart had he been alive would have been much gratified by our visit and have much liked Vin. This, though a compliment perhaps, was very gratifying to hear and more true as regards Vincent's merit, which Mozart could not fail to have discovered, than she was aware of. We planned together a pleasant society, if we could have settled at Salzburg, to have met each evening, and played over an opera of Mozart. The idea seemed much to please her.

V.N. Made her promise to make my house her home in case she should visit London, which she has some idea of doing for the sake of her son to whom she seems very affectionately attached. . . . Mentioned Victoria and [the] other children—offered to take Edward if he came to Salzburg and treat him as her own son. . . . Indeed if I had been her own Brother, she could not have behaved towards me with more familiar friendship and kind cordiality.

We at last parted with mutual anticipation of meeting again soon, whether at Salzburg or in London and with mutual promises of becoming in the meantime frequent correspondents. Altogether the three days I have passed at Salzburg with the widow and son of Mozart have [been] some of the most interesting, satisfying and gratifying that I ever enjoyed.

An echo of this leavetaking is heard in Constanze's diary: July 17, 1829. Sent reply to Stumpff by Novello, very attractive man and altogether charming wife . . . these good people left today, July 17[89].

PART III

THE AUTHENTICITY OF THE REQUIEM

The tragedy of Mozart's unfinished Requiem, which fascinated and perplexed the Novellos as it has fascinated and perplexed succeeding generations of scholars and music-lovers, might itself be described as an unfinished drama, in which the Novellos cross the stage towards the end of the third act.

The first act was played out during the last six months of Mozart's life. The *dramatis personae*, besides the composer himself, were his wife, the anonymous patron who commissioned the work, the messenger who brought the commission, and a little group of pupils and friends, chief among them Joseph Eybler and Franz Xaver Süssmayr. As we now know, the mysterious grey-liveried messenger— to Mozart's overwrought imagination an emissary of death —was merely the steward of a certain Count von Walsegg zu Stuppach, who was in the habit of commissioning works by professional composers and having them performed as his own, and intended the composition he was now ordering to figure as his own Requiem Mass for his wife, who had recently died. The work was commissioned in July 1791 and duly begun, but Mozart laid it aside in order to compose *La Clemenza di Tito* for the coronation of Leopold II as King of Bohemia. He returned to it, however, in October, and worked at it feverishly during the last two months of his life, discussing its details with his pupil Süssmayr and getting his family and friends—including Benedict Schack, his first Tamino—to rehearse sections of it at his bedside.

At his death, however, the Requiem lay unfinished, and the second act of the drama opens on the widowed Constanze, beside herself with grief and the menace of unpaid debts, and desperately anxious lest the unknown patron should demand the repayment of the sum he had paid out in advance if she could not deliver the completed work. She conceived the expedient of asking one of her husband's pupils to finish the work, and turned first to Joseph Eybler. He began work on the uncompleted scoring of the sections already complete in outline, and added a few bars to the unfinished *Lacrymosa*. But eventually he gave it up, and she then turned to Süssmayr, who undertook and carried out the job.

The position at this point was as follows : the Introit (*Requiem Aeternam*) and *Kyrie* were complete and fully scored ; the *Dies Irae* (save for the final, unfinished section *Lacrymosa*) was also complete as far as the vocal parts and figured bass were concerned, but only partly scored, and the Offertory and its versicle (*Domine Jesu Christe* and *Hostias et preces*) were in the same state. No score existed at all of the *Sanctus*, *Benedictus* and *Agnus Dei*. Süssmayr, so Constanze asserted later, had already received Mozart's instructions regarding the completion of the work in the event of his death (including the advice to repeat the *Kyrie* fugue, as was often done, for the final section, *Lux aeternam*) ; though why, if that were so, she had turned first to Eybler, is unexplained. Süssmayr began by recopying, from Mozart's draft MS. with Eybler's additions,[90] all the incomplete sections—i.e., all those of the *Dies Irae*, with the *Domine Jesu Christe* and *Hostias*—and completing the scoring. He then also finished the *Lacrymosa*, wrote the *Sanctus*, *Benedictus* and *Agnus Dei*—what help he had received in this from Mozart's instructions or sketches, if any, is still disputed[91]—and duly repeated the Kyrie fugue in the *Lux aeternam* at the words *cum sanctis tuis*. His hand-writing was so like Mozart's that his score and Mozart's own autograph score of the first two movements appeared to be by the same hand, and the composite MS. was duly handed over and accepted without question by the anonymous patron.

The work was, however, performed as Mozart's in Vienna in 1792, and it was even then an open secret that Süssmayr had had a hand in it. When, in 1800, the firm of Breitkopf and Härtel came to publish it, they asked Constanze for information and she referred them to Süss-mayr. His reply, published by the firm in their organ, the *Allgemeine musikalische Zeitung*, in October 1801, protests his reluctance ' to allow a composition, the greater part of which is my work, to appear as his, for I am convinced that my work is unworthy of this great man '. He continues :

> In the *Requiem* and *Kyrie*, *Dies Irae* and *Domine Jesu Christe*, Mozart had completed the four vocal parts and the figured bass, but in the scoring had only indicated a point here and there. In the *Dies Irae* the last line set by him was ' Qua resurget ex favilla ' . . . from the line ' judicandus homo reus ' onwards I completed the *Dies Irae*. The *Sanctus*, *Benedictus* and *Agnus Dei* were all newly composed by me. . . .

This statement was, as we now know, in the main correct, though in stating that the *Requiem aeternam* and *Kyrie* were also, like the *Dies Irae*, incomplete as to instru-mentation, Süssmayr (perhaps inadvertently) overstepped the bounds of truth, and if he had received any help from Mozart's instructions or actual drafts in the composing of the *Sanctus*, *Benedictus* and *Agnus Dei* he says nothing about it.[92] Count Walsegg demanded an explanation. Von Nissen, who had by this time appeared upon the scene and assumed the role of Constanze's man of affairs, went with the Abbé Stadler (who, as an old friend of the Mozart family and a good musician acted throughout as Constanze's musical adviser) to interview the Count's attorney, and told the whole story, freely admitting Süssmayr's share. The Count handsomely declared that he would regard the episode as closed, Süssmayr's letter aroused little attention otherwise, and the Requiem was generally accepted for close on a quarter of a century as *opus summum viri summi*.

Then, in 1825, the third act opens with the appearance of a new character—Gottfried Weber, a namesake and friend, but no relation of Carl Maria von Weber, to whose family he had given refuge when they had fled to Mannheim on their banishment from Stuttgart. A lawyer and civil servant by profession, he was in his presumably abundant spare time a musical theorist and composer and the editor of a musical periodical, *Cäcilia*, which was a useful vehicle for his own opinions. In 1825 he published, in no. 11 of *Cäcilia*, an article querying the authenticity of the Requiem.

Weber's theory was that Mozart had in fact completed the work, but that the ' priceless jewel ' had disappeared and that the current published version was in fact, to a large extent, Süssmayr's work. In his attempt to allocate their respective shares, it is interesting that, on aesthetic grounds, he attributed to Süssmayr precisely those portions which the autograph has since revealed to be entirely Mozart's, critizing the ' tortuousness ' and ' pedantry ' of the *Kyrie* fugue and pointing to it, and to the opening of the *Requiem aeternam*, as being in any case borrowed from Handel. Clearly he had no idea of the character and extent of Bach's influence on Mozart in his last years, nor did he understand the nature and use of such contrapuntal formulae as this fugue theme, which in Bach's and Handel's time were common property. Moreover he held strong and unorthodox views on church music, and had himself composed a Requiem which in one respect oddly presages Brahms, for he sets only a selection from the liturgical text, attempting to give it a unity of thought, which he feels to be lacking, by linking the various sections with appropriate German chorales. Unorthodox also in religious matters, he conceived the *Dies Irae* as a superb vision of elemental terror marred by monkish servility ; he himself only set the first six strophes, and Mozart's tender and poignant *Recordare* was repugnant both to his religious and his aesthetic outlook.

Weber was, however, a conscientious man honestly desirous of getting to the bottom of the question, and published a request for further information. This not only brought him a flood of misleading reminiscences, but provoked a reply from the Abbé Stadler, in the form of a pamphlet, *Eine Vertheidigung der Echtheit des Mozartschen Requiem* (In Defence of the Authenticity of Mozart's Requiem). From personal knowledge Stadler expressly confirms Süssmayr's account in the main, describing in detail his method of proceeding, though he states that the *Requiem aeternam, Kyrie* and *Dies Irae* were ' largely scored by Mozart himself' (true as regards the first two but not as regards the *Dies Irae*), and suggests that the various scraps of manuscript given by Constanze to Süssmayr may have contained drafts or sketches of the missing movements. He also gives an account of his and Nissen's interview with Count Walsegg's attorney, in which, as already mentioned, he had admitted Süssmayr's share and actually pointed out which sections were by Mozart and which by Süssmayr. In the pamphlet, however, his attitude was that of a champion of his hero's wounded honour, and he broadly hinted that Weber's attack was caused by jealousy.

Weber chose to regard Stadler's pamphlet as a confirmation, rather than a refutation, of his thesis, and seized on
Stadler's reference to Mozart's early study of Handel to
reinforce his contention either that Süssmayr had put the
work together from youthful fragments and Handelian
transcriptions made by Mozart for purposes of study, or
that Mozart himself had drawn on earlier material,
knowing the use to which the work would be put. Stadler,
furious, returned to the charge, and the controversy—into
which Beethoven was eventually to be drawn in support
of Stadler—raged acrimoniously for almost three years ;
Süssmayr, who alone could have settled the question, had
died long since, in 1803.

It was not until 1838 that the existence of the original
MS. delivered to Count Walsegg, with the first two movements in Mozart's own hand, came to the knowledge of
the Curator of the Imperial Library in Vienna—the same
Count Dietrichstein who was to receive the Novellos with
such courtesy—and his acquisition of it settled at least a
part of the problem. But by that time Stadler was dead,
and Weber, who had jubilantly announced the finding of
the ' lost ' Mozart original, died in 1839, probably before
its actual contents, so disastrous to his theory, had come to
his knowledge. Meanwhile, in 1829, the only autograph
portions of the work known to be in existence were the
drafts of the *Dies Irae* and Offertory, and it was these that
Novello was to feast his eyes on in Vienna : the Offertory,
with the close of the *Dies Irae* (the incomplete *Lacrymosa*)
in the possession of Eybler, who later gave it to the
Imperial Library,[93] and the rest of the *Dies Irae* in the
Imperial Library, to which it had been presented by
Stadler, together with the copy he had made of the
definitely Mozartian sections of the work before it had been
sent to Count Walsegg. Stadler had acquired his treasure

as a gift from an unnamed friend in 1827 ; previously it had been in Süssmayr's possession, and then returned by him to Constanze. What had happened to it in the interval is uncertain. Eybler had, of course, received his portion from her with the other when he undertook work on it. It is puzzling that he did not hand it back with the remaining drafts to Constanze—though Süssmayr obviously had access to it—and that Constanze, in her subsequent correspondence with André on the subject, appears to have forgotten not only Eybler's attempts but the very fact that her husband had drafted the *Domine* and *Hostias* at all.

It is in the light of these facts that Constanze's story of Mozart's last days, and the Novellos' animadversions on it, must be understood.

★   ★   ★

M.N. (July 17th). Some six months before his death he was possessed with the idea of his being poisoned—' I know I must die ', he exclaimed, ' someone has given me acqua toffana[94] and has calculated the precise time of my death—for which they have ordered a Requiem, it is for myself I am writing this '. His wife entreated him to let her put it aside, saying that he was ill, otherwise he would not have such an absurd idea. He agreed she should and wrote a masonic ode* which so delighted the company for whom it was written that he returned quite elate ; ' Did I not know that I have written better I should think this the best of my work, but I will put it in score. Yes I see I was ill to have had such an absurd idea of having taken poison, give me back the Requiem and I will go on with it.' But in a few days he was as ill as ever and possessed with the same idea. . . .

But three days before his death he received the order

*The ' Little Masonic Cantata ', K 623.

of his appointment from the emperor of being music director at St Stephen[95] which at once relieved him from the cabal and intrigue of Salieri and the singers. He wept bitterly : ' Now that I am appointed to a situation where I could please myself in my writings, and feel I could do something worthy, I must die ' . . .

A short time before his death he sang with Madame and Süssmayr the Requiem, several of the movements oppressed him to tears, he wrote the *Recordare* and principal parts first, saying, ' If I do not live these are of most consequence '. When they had finished he called Süssmayr to him and desired that if he died before he had completed the work, that the fugue he had written at the commencement might be repeated and pointed out where and how other parts should be filled up that were already sketched. It was in consequence of this, that Süssmayr afterwards wrote to Breitkopf of Leipzig that he had written the principal part of this Requiem, but as Madame justly observed, any one could have written what he had done, after the sketching and precise directions of Mozart, and nothing Süssmayr ever did, before or after, proved him to have any talent of a similar kind.

The abuse that has by some persons been heaped upon this last work of Mozart's, originated in Weber, the director of the *Cäcilia* (no relation of C. M. Weber), who has written also a Requiem but not being of the same *genre* as Mozart's was not liked. Envy made him wish to decry this standard of perfection which he could not reach, but this was a difficult affair, as people would but laugh at him for his pains ; his object therefore was to deny that Mozart ever wrote it and this he asserted in one of the numbers of the periodical which he edits. There are always plenty of envious poor souls ready to join in the hue and cry raised against a great genius, whom they can never imitate or appreciate, and on this occasion there were some who lent an ear to this scribbler's assertion. This point gained, he ventured to attack its merits and in short proved his ignorance by denying it to possess any as the work of Süssmayr—yet not perceiving that if it had originated with this latter, how came it, that he never before or after wrote anything else like it.

July 15*th*. Salieri's enmity arose from Mozart's setting the *Così fan tutte* which he had originally commenced and given up as unworthy [of] musical invention. The son denies he poisoned him although his father thought so and Salieri himself confessed the fact in his last moments, but as he was embittered all his life by cabals and intrigues, he may truly be said to have poisoned his life and this thought, the son thinks, pressed upon the wretched man when dying.

Antonio Salieri (1750-1825) was undoubtedly Mozart's rival, and had been so for some years before the composition of *Così fan tutte* in 1790 ; but there is no foundation for the widespread rumour that he poisoned him, or any evidence, other than this statement by Mozart's son (who was five months old at his father's death) that Mozart, though he thought he had been poisoned, actually suspected Salieri. The statement that Salieri ' confessed the fact in his last moments ', though also widely rumoured—it was related to Beethoven by Schindler—was denied by Carpani on the evidence of the two men who had attended him in his last illness. Süssmayr was at one time Salieri's pupil.

V.N. July 15*th*. Salieri first tried to set this opera but failed, and the great success of Mozart in accomplishing what he could make nothing of is supposed to have excited his envy and hatred, and have been the first origin of his enmity and malice towards Mozart (Süssmayr a friend of

Salieri). It was about six months before he died that he was impressed with the horrid idea that someone had poisoned him with acqua toffana—he came to her one day and complained that he felt great pain in his loins and a general languor spreading over him by degrees—that some one of his enemies had succeeded in administering the deleterious mixture which would cause his death and that they could already calculate at what precise time it would infallibly take place. The engagement for the Requiem hurt him much as it fed these sad thoughts that naturally resulted from his weak state of health.

The great success of a little Masonic ode which he wrote at this instant cheered his spirits for a time, but his melancholy forebodings again returned in a few days, when he again set to work on the Requiem. On one occasion he himself with Süssmayr and Madame Mozart tried over part of the Requiem together, but some of the passages so excited him that he could not refrain from tears, and was unable to proceed.

I was pleased to find that I had guessed right in supposing that the ' Recordare ' (one of the most divine and enchanting movements ever written) was one of his own greatest favourites.

She also confirmed the truth of his having said only three days before he died, ' I am appointed to a situation which will afford me leisure to write in future *just what I like myself*, and I feel I am capable of doing something worthy of the fame I have acquired, but instead of that I find that I must die.'[96]

What glorious productions have been lost to the world by his unfortunate early death—for incomparable as his works are I have not the least doubt but that he would [have] written still finer things such as Oratorios and other extensive works (of the Epic class) had he lived.

Among the first people the Novellos called on in Vienna was Joseph Eybler, the first to try his hand at the completion of the Requiem. The old Abbé Stadler they met at dinner at the house of their banker Henickstein, and soon became their firm friend ; from him, the Requiem story can have lost nothing in the telling.

V.N. *July 23rd.* Eybler has the original MS. of Mozart's Requiem beginning at the Lacrymosa and ending [with] the *fac eas* modulation into A dominant to D,[97] part of the offertorium, vocal parts complete with a few of the leading features of the accompaniment sketched in. I tried all I could to persuade Eybler to have a facsimile engraved of the last Page which Mozart wrote before the pen dropped from his weak hand—this would be [a] most interesting engraving to all lovers of Mozart.

July 24th. He [the Abbé Stadler] at one time was in possession of the first part of the Requiem, beginning at the ' Requiem aeternam ', the ' Kyrie ', and the ' Dies Irae ' as far as the ' Lacrymosa '[98] (the latter movement and the Offertorium, ' Domine Jesu Christe ', the versicle ' Hostias et preces tibi Domine ' terminating with ' fac eas in aeternum ' with the direction to repeat the fugue ' Quam olim Abrahae ' which were the last words Mozart wrote just before he died, are in the possession of Mr Eybler, the Capellmeister to the Chapel Royal, as I have already mentioned).

But L'Abbé Stadler has in the very highest taste (preferring the fame and reputation of Mozart to his own private gratification) sent Mozart's original score to be preserved in the Imperial Library for public reference, as the most satisfactory and incontrovertible answer to those who insinuate that Mozart did not write his own Requiem.

The ' Sanctus ', ' Benedictus ', ' Agnus Dei ' and ' Dona

eis requiem ' bear such internal proofs of their having been written by Mozart that I never for a moment believed they could have been produced by another composer, especially such an obscure writer as Süssmayr of whom nothing whatever can be shewn as having the least resemblance to the style of Mozart's Requiem. My own opinion is that Mozart wrote the ' Sanctus ', ' Agnus Dei ', etc., *before* he had done the ' Offertorium ' and, finding his death approaching, gave directions (as his widow distinctly and decidedly asserted to me that he did) to Süssmayr to fill up the mere *remplissage* of the leading features which Mozart himself had indicated : that he also told Süssmayr to repeat the Fugue at the end, as such a mode of terminating a Mass was by no means unusual and would save time in composing another adaptation of the words, and that Mozart then went on writing the ' Offertorium ' till he arrived at the words ' fac eas in aeternum ', when the Pen dropped from his hand and he expired.

The circumstance of Süssmayr's coming forward *after* Mozart was dead and claiming the merit of having written the last part of this justly celebrated composition appeared to me so suspicious that I could not refrain from asking the widow of Mozart whether he was not possibly some envious and concealed enemy [rather] than a sincere friend and grateful pupil, and when the widow owned that although Süssmayr had a few Lessons from Mozart yet that he was also a pupil and friend of Salieri's (Mozart's bitterest foe), my suspicions were at once confirmed of his treachery, easily traced and naturally accounted for.

I hope that Mr Eybler will follow the generous and noble example of L'Abbé Stadler and that he also will send the part which he possesses of the Requiem in Mozart's own handwriting to the same Institution, in order not only that these precious MSS. may be safely and carefully preserved, but [that] they may also be at all times accessible as documents of public reference and thus put a stop to all further dispute and cavil on the part of Mozart's jealous and mean-spirited calumniators.

I trust also that at some future day the *remainder* of this exquisite Mass will be found in Mozart's own handwriting, unless (as is but too probable) the original Copy of the 'Sanctus', etc. was destroyed by Süssmayr to give some air of plausibility to the improbable falsehood he has endeavoured to propagate against the memory of his too kind and indulgent Master.

Novello's last mention of the Requiem is dated July 28th, after he and his wife had visited the Imperial Library with the Abbé Stadler.

The first part of the Requiem in Mozart's handwriting is not now to be found, but fortunately before it was sent off to the Baron who ordered it, L'Abbé Stadler made a Copy of the MS., which copy he has now presented to the Imperial Library. The sketch of the 'Dies Irae' *in Mozart's handwriting* is preserved. It contains the whole *vocal score* complete of the 'Dies Irae', the 'Tuba Mirum', 'Recordare', 'Rex Tremendae', 'Confutatis' (Query, their proper order of succession?) and the first 8 bars of the 'Lacrymosa', with the principal features of the Accompaniment marked out. Here and there where there was a symphony* or particular effect required, there are also figures added to the Bass, to indicate the proper chords he wanted, so that it was easy for Süssmayr or any other person who had been taught scoring by Mozart to fill in the mere *remplissage*.

The 'Offertorium', beginning 'Domine Jesu Christe',

*An orchestral passage or interlude.

the Fugue 'Quam olim Abrahae', the verse 'Hostias' and the direction for the repetition of the Fugue 'Quam olim' (which were the last words that Mozart ever wrote) were also copied by the Abbé Stadler, who has likewise presented his copy to the Imperial Library.

The original Copy is in the possession of Eybler the Capellmeister of the Imperial Chapel, who I earnestly hope will follow the noble example of L'Abbé Stadler and present this interesting MS. to the Imperial Library for preservation with the rest of this inestimable work.

That the 'Sanctus', 'Benedictus' and 'Agnus Dei' were also written by Mozart I feel not the least doubt, and I can account for the disappearance of the original score in the same manner as the commencement of the Requiem, with this unfortunate difference, however, that the Score was sent off to the Baron who ordered it *before* L'Abbé Stadler saw it or had any opportunity of preserving a Copy as he had done of the Kyrie, etc.

I can only add my earnest hope that the Baron Walsegg, or whoever else is in possession of this invaluable MS., will have the good feeling and honourable liberality to leave it at his death (for it is perhaps too much to expect any person to part with such a precious treasure while living) to the Imperial Library also, to do justice to Mozart's Memory and to put a stop at once to all further cavil and dispute upon the subject.

PART IV

THROUGH AUSTRIA TO VIENNA

Salzburg to Vienna.   July 17th-21st

V.N.   Friday, July 17th.   ½ past 1 left Salzburg after a most delightful morning with the Mozarts . . . and arrived at a pleasant village called [*illegible*]* at 5 o'clock. The scenery for upwards of two or three miles around Salzburg is of the same romantic and charming description as that surrounding the town. The weather was agreeably serene and cool from the rain which had fallen in the night and we travelled on calmly and quietly after our three days' enjoyment and high excitement in a kind of tranquil dream.

At 8 arrived at Frankenmarkt (pretty village) supped (on a roast fowl and salad which was our most usual food) and went to bed. In the room pictures: Adam and Eve, Angels and Madonna and child, Titian's Adonis.

Mary Novello says little about this part of the journey and seems to have remained in a retrospective reverie, half Mozartian and half housewifely.

Our journey from Salzburg was very pleasant in a return coach. Living at Salzburg is cheap in the extreme and by a singular coincidence we were lodged in the same room that Madame and M. Nissen were in when they first came to Salzburg.

Lodged the first night at Frankenmarkt, where the girl

*The name is completely indistinct. Neumarkt or Steindorf are geographically possible.

133

amused me by saying I spoke better German than Vin ;
it would be difficult to say which was the worst.

The rest of the tale as far as Linz is told by her
husband. The 'remarkably handsome' church at
Lambach is that of the Benedictine Abbey, built in
1652-56. The altar-pieces on which Novello comments
are by Joachim von Sandrart (1606-88).

Saturday, July 18th. Rose at 4 (beautiful sunrise) ;
breakfasted and were off by a quarter before 5. Very
picturesque straggling houses with projecting eaves over
the wood piled up to the roof and so contrived as to leave
the windows clear like the Organ at the west window of
the Salzburg cathedral. Charming landscape from the old
Rustic bridge looking down the stream. Remarkably fine
large Dogs around here of the Staghound kind. Walter
Scott would have been delighted with these noble specimens of his favourite animals.

Curious turnpike gates made with a huge single Beam
of wood placed across the road with a weight at one end to
assist in raising the opposite lever. The tolls throughout
Germany appeared to be a mere trifle and even thus
occurred but very sparely. I should guess that our coachman did not pay for our progress all over Germany more
than what would have been demanded for a single toll at
the bridge over the Ouse at York (now very properly done
away with), or at Kingsland toll where they charge nearly
2 shillings if you happen to be later than 6 in the evening.

Numerous pretty villages between Salzburg and Lambach, where we arrived and *dined* at ½ past 10 in the morning, rather an earlier hour than what is fashionable in
Grosvenor, but a much more rational one. Whilst our
roast fowl was getting ready I strolled into the church
where service was going on. It is a remarkably handsome
one in the interior and is decorated with some very good

134

paintings especially the large ones on the left side as you go up the nave.

By the side of the church towards the south is a most picturesque walk, commanding a charming view of a winding stream about the same size as the Wye near Chepstow, the banks of which it much resembles.

The country after passing Lambach is rather flat and uninteresting till it approaches Linz, where we arrived between 6 and 7 in the evening.

But here, on arrival, their tone abruptly changes ; unusually, for them, they are both disgusted with the place, and their one idea is to get out of it as soon as possible—and for the most unexpected of reasons, for according to Novello :

Linz itself is a pretty place, situated in a picturesque manner on both sides of the Danube. The best views I obtained of it were from the bridge (which took me upwards of 400 paces to cross) and from the highest points of a steep little path leading up towards an old building in ruins.

It is not the town, but the townspeople, who are detestable, and both husband and wife are vehement in their denunciation :

V.N. I have met with idle loungers and rude starers in various parts of the continent but never did I see such a quantity of lazy and indolent people lounging about or such illbred rude and impudent starers as at Linz.

The inn where we supped was the most ill-conducted one we had yet met with, although reckoned one of the best in the place, and the intrusive prying and peeping about and impertinent curiosity was almost beyond endurance : we could not open a door without a head being thrust forth from the neighbouring room to watch what was going forward and once when the servant brought some message I perceived on her leaving the room that a woman had the effrontery to have stationed herself at the door and had been listening to the orders I gave the servant. There are few things so irritating and disgusting to me as this mean and contemptible prying spirit.

In my opinion a person who would steal a secret from another against his will, would pick his pocket if he thought he could do it without detection.

In order to vary the scene and become acquainted with the manners of as many classes of the Germans as possible we resolved on proceeding hence to Vienna by water on one of the passenger boats which ply regularly on the Danube between Ratisbon and Vienna.

Everything had been arranged for our journey, which was to begin as early as 3 in the morning, but during the night a most furious storm of rain came on, which of course altered our plans as the bad weather would have rendered our otherwise pleasant journey a most disagreeable one.[99]

About 4 o'clock the ' Hausknecht ' (an attendant similar to our ' Boots ' at an inn) knocked at our door and then actually fell on his *knees* to ask our pardon for not having called us at 2 o'clock as he ought to have done.

M.N. Arrived at Linz and lodged at the ' Canon ', where the master is a fool and a coxcomb. We were so disgusted that we resolved to go by the Danube at 3 on Sunday morning but it rained so hard that we gave up our purpose. The *hausknecht*, who is a sort of boots in a German inn, and who we had desired to wake us at 2 in the morning never knocked at the door till 4. I repeatedly called to him that we did not go but he still remained and I was forced to open to him although in my nightgown ; no sooner was the door opened than he popped upon his knees put up his folded hands and implored my pardon by all manner of gesticulations for not calling us sooner. Vin did not recognise him, but thought he was some importunate beggar and kept calling from his bed ' allez, allez ', which the man understood about as much as Chaldeac. At length I quietened him by saying that we did not journey on account of the rain ; he really looked like one possessed, yet I could hardly forbear laughing between him and Vin who afterwards said that P[*illegible*] would have been much amused at the scene.

Never was there such a disagreeable inn as this ' Canon ' so we have agreed to quit it with our *cocher* from Salzburg though we shall be 3 days on the road.

They try to make a joke of their broken night as Vincent leans forward to write in her notebook :

We were as much tormented at this Inn as Don Quixote and Sancho were at that where the ' enchanted Moor ' travelled over them all night at a brisk trot.

His wife retorts :

Not so bad, dear Vin, for no one came near us even when we rang.

As a result of their decision to continue by road they were detained at Linz for part of Sunday, July 19th ; and Novello fills in the time in characteristic fashion :

On taking my usual walk round the town the next morning (Sunday, 19th July) I found the same extraordinary number of indolent people lounging and staring about and in one of the public places near the bridge the rooms were full of persons who were smoking and drinking beer although it was only 6 o'clock. Before 7 the people were pouring out from their houses [and] the churches in all directions and the streets were as crowded as if there

137

had been a fair. It is by far the most populous place I have yet seen in Germany. Plenty of churches and priests.

He went to Mass at the Cathedral, where, besides making his usual notes on the music, he observes:

Cathedral at Linz . . . not very large size; no transepts, only six side chapels, three on each side. High altar and side altars of dark coloured marble with sculptured figures of angels in white. . . . Paintings mediocre. Rich pulpit, dark wood. Fine print [?] with Raphael's portrait of Julius II . . . [The rest is illegible].

A few dressed-up people; the greater part poor.

As we had been detained here against our wishes I should have attempted to have made the best of our delay by availing myself of the opportunity of hearing vespers at another church near the Cathedral and intended also to have visited the theatre in the evening.

A pleasant walk under the trees of the town to the theatre which is a prepossessing building on the outside. I therefore obtained a bill of the performance[100] which I hoped would have afforded me some compensation for my disappointment hitherto in this place, but as we afterwards found an opportunity of going on to Vienna by a more private and pleasant carriage than the diligence (which did not leave till Monday), we therefore quitted Linz at about [2] o'clock and were glad to get rid of the impolite rude illbred people we had encountered and rid of the disagreeable associations we had with the place altogether.

What was there about this quiet unobtrusive couple to awaken so much 'prying and peeping' and 'rude staring', let alone the servile terror of the *Hausknecht?* Nowhere else on the whole journey do either of them notice anything of the kind; and as Linz lay on one of the main roads to Vienna, the inhabitants must have been used to the sight of travellers and tourists.

138

A possible, albeit somewhat fantastic, explanation suggests itself. Mary Novello's father, Simon Hehl (whose name, there is reason to suppose, was not Hehl[101]), belonged to a high-born German family. As far as is known, he did not come from that region ; but the fact remains that high-born families frequently intermarry. Cases of one person being taken for another by general consent do sometimes occur even outside fiction and the stage, and there may have been an extraordinary likeness between Mary Novello and some distinguished personage whose features were well known in Linz, strong enough to create a suspicion that she was such a personage travelling incognito.

Once away from Linz, their journey, and Vincent Novello's account of it, continue placidly enough :

Left Linz at 2 by the same private coach and civil driver as those by which we arrived from Salzburg. The country immediately round Linz is not remarkably attractive but improves as you proceed towards Vienna. We passed [Ebelsberg] where a very severe battle took place with the French.[102] At Enns there is a curious old tower in the centre of the Grande Platz with a very good-toned bell in it. Beyond the town is a bridge over the river Enns which latter had overflowed its banks not long since and had buried the whole of the country and neighbourhood under water for 6 weeks. Nothing could pass that way for 15 days which must have occasioned great incovenience as Enns is on the high road between Vienna and Paris.

At the time we passed the bridge had just been completed and from the rapid rate at which the river was running under it at this comparatively temperate season of the year I can easily imagine that after a sudden thaw in winter time the violence and velocity of the stream must be almost irresistible.

Met a very singular figure which seemed to me to be a

139

most extraordinary figure of incongruity : he was without *shoes* or *stockings* and yet was carrying an umbrella in a slight shower.

We had much rain during the last part of our journey today, but it finally cleared up and a most beautiful rainbow appeared over the Danube on our left before we got to Strengberg a most quiet little village where we arrived about 8 o'clock, supped and went to bed.

A drummer round the town for the Players like the old English comedians.

M.N.   I was but poorly so kind Vin rejoiced that I did not go by the *Eilpost* which is always fatiguing. Nothing particular occurred on the journey ; we slept on Sunday night at a small country inn but got a capital duck and salad for supper.

The next day brought them a fleeting glimpse of the great Benedictine Abbey of Melk, superbly set on a cliff overlooking the Danube, and one of Austria's noblest specimens of Baroque architecture (which Novello, here and elsewhere, terms ' the Roman style ').

V.N.   Monday, July 20. We were travelling the whole of this day from a little after 4 in the morning till 8 in the evening. We had the Danube on our left the greater part of the way and some of the scenery was very beautiful. We should have enjoyed it more but for a very heavy rain which lasted the whole day ; it however cleared up as we approached Melk, which is most charmingly situated on the banks of the River (Danube). At this place is the most magnificent convent I ever saw; it belongs to the order of the Benedictines, and you may get some idea of its extent, though not of its beautiful architecture and position, when I tell you that in one façade alone there are about 60 windows in a row and there are 3 rows making altogether nearly 200 windows.

The church attached to it is a fine one in the Roman style of architecture and I should have been much pleased to have had an opportunity of hearing the service performed there ; but my time would not admit of it as our carriage merely passed through the town. This Establishment which is more like a palace than a convent appears to have swallowed all the riches of the place as the rest of the buildings are only poor miserable looking houses.

Banks of the Danube though like in some features to those of the Rhine yet are different in their general appearance especially in the circumstance of there being but few vineyards which latter form the most striking and peculiar feature of the Rhine.

Novello did after all, as we shall see, have an opportunity of seeing more of Melk on their homeward journey, and was to return there nine years later. He, his wife, and their daughters Clara and Emma, were then received as honoured guests by the Abbot and the community after Clara's triumphal appearance in Vienna, where she had sung in aid of the victims of the recent floods at Pesth.[103] On this occasion she was invited to sing for the Abbot in his private apartments, and Emma made a little pen and ink sketch of the monastery, with its three times sixty windows, apparently from the very angle from which her father had seen it for the first time.

Arrived at St Pölten at 8. Black tin steeple. I am still surprised at finding no music nor any single person ever attempting to sing or even humming a tune.

Our postillion was a remarkably merry fellow but he never even tried to get up a song or tune of any kind whatever.

At this point after sharply criticising the local military band (see p. 275) Novello plunges again into pages of random recollections of Salzburg and what had been told him there ; so wrapped up in these is he that he entirely omits the date of Tuesday 21st, from his diary and says nothing about this last stage of their journey, or of their arrival at Vienna. So it is left to Mary to sum up the last lap.

The 'gold helmet' worn by the woman who served them at St. Pölten was simply the local head-dress, made of golden material, and shaped rather like a Phrygian cap.

On Monday at St Pölten where we were waited upon by a woman in a gold helmet ; yet notwithstanding she was very gentle and civil. Tuesday we arrived at Vienna which appears very gay and bustling, delivered our letters and settled with the police, which is always a bore ; but fortunately we have escaped very well at the customs house, etc. Have an invitation to dine tomorrow at our banker's who knew Mozart and will invite Abbé Stadler to meet us. No letters and much depends upon the one from Paris.

Vienna. July 21-30

The tiresome formalities on arrival, it must be owned, loom larger in retrospect. In her published version of her diary in the *Musical World* of 1837 Mary Novello writes :

' Of all the troublesome cities to travellers this is surely the worst : pestered at the gates with searching the luggage ; fretted with impertinent questions by the police respecting your age, station and fortune ; and, to crown all, insulted by a *permit* to remain a stated time in their trumpery city, which if you exceed, you are likely to visit the interior of their well-contrived prisons . . . but to make up for the little provocations upon entering this capital, it must be confessed that the inhabitants are very friendly and hospitable.'

The last sentence explains everything: a week crowded with social contacts and musical experiences lay before them—so crowded as to drive all else from their minds. Indeed, although they remark on nearly every other inn they stopped at, even for a meal, they never think to mention their hotel in Vienna, save for a casual remark of Novello's that it was near the Dominican Church. But a note of his to the Abbé Stadler (which he evidently decided not to send) asking him to reply to the questionnaire originally prepared for Madame von Sonnenburg, gives us the missing information, for it is dated, 'Hotel Stadt London, No. 23, July 24/29.'

Although they were disappointed of the 'letter from Paris' (presumably from Fétis, about Clara's prospects of admission to Choron's institution), the letters of introduction which they themselves delivered proved most fruitful. Their banker, Joseph Henickstein, was an amateur musician of some standing in that city of gifted amateurs, and one of the original members of the *Gesellschaft der Musikfreunde*; he had been personally acquainted with Mozart and Beethoven, and, as Mary Novello relates, promptly invited the Novellos to dinner to meet the Abbé Stadler, to whom Mozart's son had, in any case, given them an introduction. Attwood's letter to Aloysia Lange brought about a meeting between Mary Novello and Mozart's first love, and Mozart's son, besides his introduction to the publisher Haslinger, had probably given them messages for his former piano teacher, the pianoforte maker Andreas Streicher, and his wife Nanette, though the Novellos' official introduction to these old friends of Beethoven's was undoubtedly from J. A. Stumpff.[104]

Even in the course of the Novellos' first business call on Henickstein the conversation inevitably turned on Mozart.

V.N. Mr Henickstein our Banker invited us to Dinner to meet L'Abbé Stadler. Knew Mozart who gave his

sister lessons. Mozart would not take pains in giving
Lessons to any Ladies but those he was in love with. Did
not show the great genius in his conversation—was of the
most gay and lively character. Had moderately good Tenor
voice.

Madame Mozart was *not* an Actress and had not great
powers as a singer—Mr Henickstein used often to call
upon Mozart when he was composing ' Don Giovanni ',
he used to try over the different pieces as they were written,
Mozart accompanying from the MS. score.

Henickstein sang the part of Leporello having a Bass
Voice ; mentioned ' Madamina il catalogo è questo '.

Mozart played the Violin very well and the viola still
better, he often heard him play that part in pieces of his
own writing.

But if Vienna, like Salzburg, was rich in memories of
Mozart, it had other and more recent associations as
well. Only two years before, in March, 1827, the
Philharmonic Society, of which Vincent Novello was
a founder member, had sent £100 to Beethoven as he
lay dying in the rooms he had rented on the north-
western outskirts of the city. Novello had noted
among his memoranda the address of these, the last of
Beethoven's innumerable lodgings in Vienna : ' Beethoven House No. 200 on Glacis (Schwarzspanierhaus)
before the Schotten Thor ' ; and on his first morning
in Vienna, with characteristic piety towards a departed
greatness which he recognised and revered (albeit
with less of love and insight than he had for Mozart)
he was up early to find the place.

Wednesday, July 22. At 7 o'clock Walk along the Bastion.
Woman at the Schottenstrasse within a few yards of
Beethoven's house had never heard of him ; called another
person, who was equally ignorant.

Later that day the quest for music, sacred and secular, is already in full swing—and the usual frustrations are encountered.

Benediction at Augustinians Wednesday, July 22 . . . no last Voluntary. Poor organ.

Visited the principal Garden (Volksgarten) as we were told that there was to be an Orchestra of wind. To our great disappointment there were only 2 Clarionets, 2 Horns, 2 Bassoons with a Double Fagotto. As we entered they were playing a poor commonplace Waltz. On requesting they would be so good as to play something of Mozart or Haydn the man said, ' O yes, Mozart or Rossini '—but I said, ' No Rossini—some air of Mozart '. He accordingly went away for the purpose of telling his companions our wishes—but instead of what we had requested they played the Cavatina in A flat (transposed and thereby spoiled to the key of C) and I really believe that they had not a single piece by Mozart in all their book and probably thought we should not detect the difference. They next played two pieces from Auber's ' Muette de Portici ' which seems to be all the rage here as well as in every other place I have yet been at in Germany—the performance was in every respect totally unworthy of a musician's notice.

Novello had been prompt in presenting his letter of introduction to Tobias Haslinger, who in 1826 had succeeded to the proprietorship of the music publishing firm of S. A. Steiner & Co. During his long period of partnership the firm had published many of the major works of Beethoven's second period, and he himself had been the composer's friend and the butt of his extravagant humour. His establishment was the rendezvous of the leading musicians of Vienna, whom Novello was to meet there, under the eye of that imposing array of busts of the great dead which so impressed him that he reverted to it on the return journey: 'Haslinger's shop, four busts, Handel, Gluck, Haydn, Mozart—not like. Try to get them for Alfred's shop.'

Haslinger at once arranged to take the Novellos to visit Joseph Eybler, whom, as Mozart's pupil and as Court Capellmeister, Novello was doubly anxious to meet.

V.N. Thursday, July 23. Introduced by Haslinger to Eybler, Capellmeister to the Royal Chapel. He did not speak French but as he could converse very fluently in Italian we managed to chat very pleasantly and freely together. He is now upwards of 75, but has not the appearance of being so old [105]; remarkably agreeable manner without the least ceremony or formality. He was an intimate friend of Mozart's and spoke of him with enthusiasm and admiration. He also was formerly acquainted with Haydn (Don't forget that Haslinger showed me a bust of Haydn in wax, strikingly like, clothed in a part of the clothes which he himself wore, and the imitation of his wig is made of his own hair.[106] Also busts of Mozart, Haydn, Gluck and Handel).

Haydn advised Eybler to go to England and he seemed to wish to be able to follow the advice, but he added ' I am now too old '. Showed me his Requiem in C minor, which he wrote about 25 years since, and it is now published by Haslinger (seemed to be a fine composition). He also showed me the score of a new Mass in F upon which he was at work when we called upon him (it was not much after 8 and he was writing quietly in his room in his *Robe de Chambre*). He had proceeded to the end of the first Movement of the *Agnus Dei*, so that he had only one more movement (the *Dona Nobis*) to finish.

He told me that Haydn died and was buried at Gumpendorf, but that on opening his grave some time since his head was found to have been removed from the coffin. He seemed to think the general opinion was that it had been taken to Paris for phrenological studies.[107]

In another Room he had the portraits of Sebastian Bach, Handel, Gluck, Michael Haydn, Joseph Haydn, Graun (of whose *Tod Jesu* he spoke with great admiration), Cherubini, Albrechtsberger, Stadler. On my enquiring whether he had the Mass in F by the latter, he said he had, but that as it was only three vocal parts the effect was unsatisfactory to him—without the fourth voice there always seemed to be something wanting.

The laws of survival in music operate unaccountably. Karl Heinrich Graun's Passion oratorio *Der Tod Jesu*, now but rarely revived, was admired and repeatedly performed by a generation which remembered J. S. Bach simply as a great theorist and virtuoso, and to which the *St Matthew Passion*, lying hidden in manuscript, was not even a name. Another great theorist and virtuoso, Johann Georg Albrechtsberger, is now chiefly remembered because he gave the young Beethoven lessons in counterpoint, while church composers famous in their day—the Abbé Stadler, Ignaz Seyfried, Johann Gänsbacher, and Eybler himself— are now barely remembered save by historians. Eybler, to judge by the composers whose names arose in conversation, seems to have shared Novello's scholarly interest in the Italian masters of the seventeenth and early eighteenth centuries.

Eybler studied with Albrechtsberger, who, he said, was by far the greatest Organist he had ever heard. Spoke of Durante, Carissimi, Leo, Caldara (he seemed pleased when I mentioned the duet of 'Placidissime Catene'), Jommelli, Steffani. Promised to write something in Album.[108]

He knew of about seven or eight masses of Mozart—he had adapted the one in D for a full orchestra for his own

Chapel. He will have it performed at Mass next Sunday with the graduale and offertorium of Michael Haydn.[109]

Eybler has the original MS. of Mozart's Requiem, beginning at the *Lacrymosa* and ending with *fac eas*[110] . . . I tried all I could to persuade Eybler to have a facsimile engraved of the last page which Mozart wrote before the pen dropped from his weak hand—this would be a most interesting engraving to all the admirers of Mozart.

' Where is Mozart's monument? ' ' Where *indeed?* ' said he and Haslinger.

Mozart's portrait (published by Artaria, with set of keys under) the best likeness.[111] Mozart's favourite opera ' Don Giovanni '.

Eybler was so polite as to express his regret at my short stay and invited me very cordially to call upon him again in case I should remain longer. He has composed 24 Masses (that he was at work upon was the 25th) but only five have yet been published.[112] Haslinger told me that Seyfried and Eybler were the two best composers for the church now. Gänsbacher also in high esteem.

M.N. Thursday, July 23rd. Went this morning to Capellmeister Eybler who has the latter part of Mozart's Requiem and the last note he ever wrote—what a treasure— I was quite sorry for dear Vin's envious feeling, he so much coveted this possession. Eybler is a very agreeable gay old man and as he speaks Italian fluently, Vin and he got on very well. He is a pupil of Albrechtsberger and a great lover of fugue. He gives the preference to Mozart's ' Don Giovanni ' of all his works.

It was apparently while writing up her journal at the hotel between their morning expedition and their dinner party that Mary Novello received a visit which her husband does not even mention, and from her account it is evident that he was not present. Probably he had gone out again exploring on his own while his wife rested ; but had he guessed that Attwood's letter was to bring to their door, that very day, the woman who won Mozart's youthful devotion as a lover and mature admiration as a musician, nothing would have induced him to leave the spot.

In Aloysia Lange's memories of her relationship with Mozart, even more than in Constanze's case, distance had lent enchantment to the view. There had been no question of the parents agreeing to the match, the very thought of which had frankly horrified Mozart's father. And although her rejection of Mozart was a bitter blow to the young man at the time, there is no evidence that his subsequent feeling for her was more than professional esteem for an excellent singer for whom he wrote some splendid arias.

Her own views on the younger generation of singers reflect the current opinion, which admired Giuditta Pasta's noble and dignified acting as much as her voice. Like the rest of Vienna, she took a jaundiced view of young Henriette Sontag, Weber's first Euryanthe, who had made her London *début* the previous year.[113] Her opinion of the general run of Italian singers parallels that of the Mozart family in Salzburg (pp. 255-56) and is that of an older generation in whom sheer technique had not yet supplanted musicianship. Her praise of the Paris school must have been more than welcome to little Clara's mother.

M.N. Madame Lange, the sister of Madame Mozart and Mozart's first love, has just been here and conversed with me for two hours. She seems a very pleasant woman but broken by misfortune—she is parted from her husband who allows her so little that she is obliged to give lessons which at her age she finds a great hardship.

She complains bitterly against the Viennese for their neglect of the family of Mozart and says he was frequently in the last extreme of poverty and died miserably poor, that they cannot even find the precise spot on which he was buried, all they say is he was buried in St Mark's burial ground.

She enquired after Sontag but said she did not consider her a great singer and that she did not succeed in Vienna ; Pasta has much pleased, not so much for her voice, as her sensibility and manner of acting. She declares that most of the Italian singers cannot read the music they sing— nature has done much for them in a voice, but that they are quite ignorant of the science. She thinks Paris one of the best schools at present and much more enthusiastic for Mozart than in Germany.

She regrets not having come to London, she was much pressed by the English when at Hamburg to come but had no one to go with, as Mme. Mozart left her to present the Requiem to the King of Prussia who made her a handsome present for the same.

She speaks very highly of young Mozart, and says she loves him better than even her own children.

She told me Mozart always loved her until the day of his death, which to speak candidly she fears has occasioned a slight jealousy on the part of her sister. I asked her why she refused him, she could not tell, the fathers were both agreed but she could not love him at that time, she was not capable of appreciating his talent and his amiable character, but afterwards she much regretted it. She spoke of him with great tenderness and regret, as of her sister whose understanding she thinks very superior.

Madame Lange told me that a conceited coxcomb could never make way with Mozart, but that if a poor musician came to him who understood the art he would play for hours and days. Everything we hear relating to Mozart confirms the account of his amiability and exceeding modesty, he was always gentle, gay and pleasant, and frequently in the midst of company would become abstracted and lost in musical composition.

No further mention of Aloysia Lange is made in either journal, so they evidently never saw her again.

At the Henicksteins' dinner party—which clearly, as was then the custom, took place in the afternoon— they met not only the Abbé Stadler, but also Franz Kandler, who, like Henickstein himself, was a cultivated amateur musician, and something of a scholar as well, as Novello was to discover. Mary Novello describes the occasion :

We were invited to our Banker Henickstein to dinner today to meet the Abbé Stadler, but when we arrived there we found a large party to meet us and a grand parade of servants, etc.—fortunately I had expected some such thing and was not taken altogether by surprise but was dressed accordingly and as they mostly spoke English or French we were soon at home. Vincent was placed between Abbé Stadler and Mr Kandler who is a great amateur and Dilettante. After dinner this latter played several pretty things for us, but only ballads like our own evening societies, nothing sterling of the divinities Mozart or Haydn.

As a tribute to my vanity I must record that no one will believe I have been married longer than two or three years, and it is in vain I assure them that my eldest daughter is married to convince them of my great age. They shake their heads and say we jest—but in order to make some apology for their blindness you must remember that dressed with a little care and you not in sight, I look younger than I am, so I mean to cut the body corporate of you all and set myself down for something about 30.

Dinner parties break up early here, and some return to

business and some to the opera. We went home, for the music we heard the evening before at the Volksgarten did not induce a second visit.

Novello's explorations earlier in the day were probably with the object of finding the house in the Rauhen-steingasse where Mozart died, and of which his son had given him a note (now preserved in the Album) ; for already on the next day, the 24th, he remarks that he makes a point of passing the house as often as he can. A puzzling point is that his actual description of the house as given below was not written up until the 28th, whereas he states that the Abbé Stadler—whom he first met on the afternoon of the 23rd—had pointed it out to him. The most likely explanation is that as Mozart's son had not given a number, but merely described the house by the name of the owners (' das Kussersteinische Haus '), Novello was not sure that he had identified it correctly, and while walking down the Kärntnerstrasse with the Abbé Stadler two days later, on Saturday 25th—asked him to turn aside into the Rauhensteingasse to point it out to him, ' on purpose to remove all doubt '.

Mozart's house was pointed out to me by l'Abbé Stadler himself who was so kind as to go with me there on purpose to remove all doubt : it is now No. 938 in the Rauhensteingasse, with a *porte cochère* in the middle. It was in the first floor to the left that he usually composed. It is a handsome looking house with five windows in front. On entering you turn to the left to go upstairs, which you may be sure I did with veneration—there are three storeys besides the ground floor and the attic—it was not without strange sensations that I ascended the identical stairs which he had so often passed, and down which he was at last brought down as a corpse. But as the family could not be disturbed I was prevented from obtaining access to the apartment where he expired when the pen dropped from his hand. Three handsome windows in the centre and two plain ones on each side.

Over the gate at the entrance is a painting of the Virgin and Child (the colours sadly faded, like his own memory in Vienna). The upper part of the house looks like the top of a church. The ground floor to the right of the entrance is now a bread and biscuit shop, and the other side consists of private apartments. I quite longed for the ability to make a drawing of this, to me the most interesting house in Vienna, as a companion to the one which his widow has had copied of the house where he was born in Salzburg.

Curious that over Mozart's house at Vienna there is a painting of the Virgin and Child and under the painting there is a very tasteful ornament in sculpture of Venus with the world under her feet, and surrounded by very graceful folds of drapery and clouds above of an elegant form.

The next morning they both followed up their acquaintanceship with the Abbé Stadler.

M.N. July 24. Went this morning to Abbé Stadler to see the other parts of the Requiem. . . . The Abbé is a delightful old man, in person resembling Vincent's father, in manner like Abbé du Berlay. I felt great veneration and love for him the moment we met, and he with the kindest manner placed his arm within mine and walked down the stairs as though we had known each other for years.

V.N. Friday, July 24th. At 9 o'clock we visited l'Abbé Stadler according to his kind invitation of the preceding day when we dined with him at Henickstein's.

This interesting and venerable gentleman resides at a small distance from Vienna in the ' Gemeinde' Street No. 60 leading out of the Landstrasse.*

*His apartment, as Novello notes elsewhere, was in the former Rasoumofsky Palace (later the Geological Museum).

He received us in the most kind and friendly manner. Our conversation of course turned upon his friend Mozart and soon he produced some of his treasures. They were several exercises and lessons in Thorough Bass and composition which Mozart had given to a lady, the cousin of the Abbé.[114]

The greater part were in Mozart's own handwriting, in some places he had written only the Melody, and the lady had to try her skill in adapting a bass and marking the Roots of the chords. In other specimens he had written the Melody, the Bass and had added the figures, the lady was to fill up the intermediate parts according to the harmonies he had indicated. Next followed his remarks and corrections of the defects, and what was still more interesting, his own mode of scoring and treating the same subject, so as to make it ' a little better ' than what had been accomplished by the lady.

One in G minor beginning on a Pedal Bass for several bars, with a most numerous and elaborate collection of figures for the Thorough Bass struck me as being particularly beautiful.

In another parcel of MSS., all in Mozart's handwriting, were some very curious and erudite studies and exercises of his own : several were in Canon of the most difficult and complicated construction, but he seemed to have the same intuitive perception of the capabilities of every interval, both as to its position in the scale and its duration as to time, as that which was possessed by Sebastian Bach and other great writers in Canon.

He [Abbé Stadler] at one time was in possession of the first part of the Requiem. . . .

But l'Abbé Stadler has in the very highest taste (preferring the fame and reputation of Mozart to his own private gratification) sent Mozart's original score to be preserved in the Imperial Library for public reference, as the most satisfactory and incontrovertible answer to those who insinuate that Mozart did not write his own Requiem.[115]

L'Abbé Stadler also showed me the portrait of Mozart, engraved by Mansfeld (so frequently mentioned before) and expressed his opinion of its being the best likeness.

He also pointed out to me a most interesting relic in his possession, viz., the identical writing desk on which Mozart had composed all his Operas, Sinfonias, Masses, in a word all his finest work. It is a most unostentatious-looking piece of furniture, made of common wood and painted over a white colour in the most simple manner.

The Abbé added with a smile that since it had been in his possession, he had always used it to write his *own* compositions upon. Of these he showed me his Oratorio of *Die Befreiung von Jerusalem*, which as far as I could judge of it by a mere passing glance appears deserving of being better known, and which I hope to hear brought forward at our English Oratorios on some future occasion and at no very distant period.

He also showed me a very ingenious Fugue in C minor which [he] had written on the name of the composer Schubert, and very kindly requested my acceptance of it, at the same time writing on the title page that it had been presented to me by himself.

The fugue, published by Diabelli and entitled *Fuge für die Orgel oder das Pianoforte über den Nahmen des zu früh verblichenen Tonsetzers F. Schubert* (Fugue for organ or pianoforte on the name of the prematurely deceased composer F. Schubert), is one of those ingenious affairs in which the letters of the name (or such as can be read as degrees of the scale) are turned into a fugue theme : an odd and touching tribute to the composer who, on his deathbed, was planning to submit his fiery genius to the discipline of counterpoint lessons from Simon Sechter (1788-1867), the Court organist, on whom Albrechtsberger's mantle, as performer and as contrapuntist, appeared to have fallen : such is the impression given by Stadler's account of him.

He appeared to think very highly of Mr Eybler as a church writer as well as of Gänsbacher and Seyfried, and spoke of the principal organist of the Royal Chapel, Mr Simon Sechter, as one of the most profound counterpointists of the present day.

He corroborated this opinion by producing several fugues composed by the latter-mentioned Professor, which were so much in the style of Sebastian Bach that they might very easily have been taken for some of the easier class of the compositions of that most masterly and sublime writer for the organ.

One piece in particular was a most ingenious piece of Counterpoint, consisting of variations in score for four instruments upon the melody of *God save the King*.

It has so far proved impossible to trace this ' most ingenious piece of counterpoint ', which Novello goes on to describe as follows :

Much as this subject has been hackneyed by different composers, Mr Sechter has contrived to treat it in a novel and peculiar manner.

There are nine variations altogether, in each of which the melody is going on, in one or other of the Violins or the Viola or the Bass interspersed with other melodies of a totally different character, yet in perfect symmetry with themselves. In the seventh variation is a Russian air, *Schoene Minka* ; in the eighth he has very cleverly introduced the German national air, Haydn's *Hymn to Father*

Emperor, in the first violin while *God save the King* is going on in the viola part. In the ninth variation he has contrived to introduce the French national air *Vive Henri Quatre** in G minor in the second violin, while *God save the King* is still going on in the first violin part in the key of B flat major. Altogether this is one of the most curious and ingenious pieces of counterpoint which I have lately met with.

The discourse next turning on Joseph Haydn (of whom l'Abbé Stadler was also an intimate friend) the latter showed me a portrait of him underneath which hung a small print containing a view of the cottage at Rohrau in which Joseph Haydn was born.

The Abbé then walked across the room and opened a Grand Piano Forte which he informed me was the instrument that belonged to Haydn. It was one of Longman's and Broderip's, the compass from FF in the bass with the added keys up to C in alt. Haydn had brought it with him from England and had retained it till death, when it came into the possession of l'Abbé Stadler.[116] The latter told me he had often heard Haydn play upon it when he used to call to see him. I need not add that I sat down and played upon it with peculiar pleasure.

I of course tried to do my best and after I had finished the Abbé said something so very complimentary that I dare not repeat it.

Mary Novello had no such inhibitions:

He has Haydn's piano forte upon which Vincent rolled forth some chords and resolutions that delighted the old man. He said: ' Je vois que vous êtes grand maître '. He presented him with a fugue of his own writing and promised to write in our album.

*A traditional song which became popular all over Europe at the time of the Congress of Vienna.

From the Abbé's reply to Novello's inquiry about the occasion for which Mozart had turned his unfinished C minor Mass into the oratorio *Davidde Penitente* it emerged that the text, as surmised by Alfred Einstein (*Mozart, His Character, His Work*, p. 349) was by Da Ponte, the librettist of *Figaro, Don Giovanni* and *Così fan tutte*. The adaptation was made for one of the Lenten concerts of the Society of Musicians in 1785 (not, as Novello's account suggests, on his first arrival in Vienna four years earlier, at which time the Mass was not yet written). Constanze's account of the composition of the Mass itself has become still further telescoped and garbled in Novello's memory.

On enquiring on what occasion Mozart had put the 'Davidde Penitente' into its present form, he informed me that when Mozart came to Vienna he was applied to for some piece in the Oratorio style. As the time allowed was not sufficient to write an entirely new piece he took the greater part of a Mass (which I have before said that Madame Nissen told me was written for her first accouchement in Salzburg) to which the poet Da Ponte adapted other words and that Mozart added the fine Terzetto in E minor and two new solos in order to complete the work required.

On my offering to take charge of any message from him to his friends in London he requested to be cordially remembered to M. Clementi, J. B. Cramer and M. Moscheles.

After offering to call upon him the next day to visit the Imperial Library I at last took my leave very reluctantly of this delightful and venerable person, whose manners are those of the perfect gentleman ; he is a most perfect specimen of the mild elegance and polite urbanity of the 'Vieille Cour' without any of its tiresome etiquette and ceremonious formality.

The visit to the Imperial Library, however, did not, for some reason, take place till Tuesday, July 28th, which may have been why the Novellos prolonged their stay in Vienna.

It is Mary Novello who records their next visit—a combined business and courtesy call on Herr Henickstein, into whose mouth, on this occasion, she puts some of the opinions on Mozart recorded by her husband as belonging to their first meeting:

M.N. Called on Mr Henickstein upon money matters and to thank him for his civility. He told us that he was formerly well acquainted with Mozart and sang the Leporello and Figaro in a dilettante company of performers. Mozart taught his sister the Piano Forte. He thought him too gay in his manner, he was always in love with his pupils. They have often gone out together to give a serenade which was then much in fashion.

Later that day they received a call from another of their newly-made acquaintances from the previous day's dinner-party, Franz Kandler. A great lover of Italian music and a master of the language, he had in 1820 written a life of Hasse (as Novello duly noted), and had even earned a tribute of praise in Gottfried Weber's periodical *Cäcilia* for his work in making German music known in Italy by translating opera and oratorio texts into Italian. Despite his Rossini-fever, he did his best to be of service to Novello in his pursuit of Mozart.

M.N. Monsieur Kandler has just been here and very politely offered to assist Vin in his researches for anecdotes concerning Mozart and Haydn. He is much imbued with the Italian music, but has good taste and is, I believe, a clever musical critic.

V.N. Mr Kandler called today. Speaks Italian very well. Favourite Rossini. . . .

It was probably in the course of their discussion that Kandler voiced the opinion attributed to him by Novello in an isolated note embedded among the recorded doings of the following day:

Kandler—Every age has its own idols; that of Haydn and Mozart is past, they have been supplanted by other favourites and now when an opera of Mozart's is performed at Vienna, *nobody goes.*

Vincent Novello's last entry for this day begins:

We this evening visited the public Garden on the Glacis or Esplanade, opposite the Caroline Gate.*

About ten years since a building was established in this spot for the purpose of drinking Mineral Waters; a Coffee House for refreshments has also been established here and the place altogether appears to be one of the most frequented of the kind about Vienna.

By the way it is, I believe, a well-ascertained fact, though not generally known, that the first coffee house in Christian Europe was established in Vienna in the year 1685; a native of Poland, of the name of Koltschitzky, who had rendered some important services during the siege of Vienna, obtained as a recompense the privilege of establishing a public coffee house.[117] At present there are, I am told, upwards of 80 coffee houses in Vienna and its environs, and which are open from morning till midnight.

The Caroline Gardens, as, for want of a better name, I shall term them, are a kind of Vauxhall upon a very small scale. The walks are lighted with small lamps. There is a little orchestra in the centre, filled by about ten or a dozen performers on clarionets and other wind instruments and there are benches placed round for those who choose to sit and take refreshments.

*The garden was on the site of the present Stadtpark, near the former Karolinenthor.

The performers here were of a better class than those I had heard before at the Volksgarten but the pieces they played were not a whit better, nothing but waltzes, eternal commonplace waltzes.

On our return home we passed very near to Mozart's house (as I invariably do as often as I possibly can) and we heard someone playing on the Piano Forte within a few yards of where this divine writer lived, but to my great disgust the person was merely playing nothing but a waltz. Germany really appears to me at present the land of Galops, Waltzes and Quadrilles, and yet with all this eternal thrumming and puffing of waltzes I see no one *dancing* to the music. Immense popularity [*sic* : population] all theatres full, all the Streets full and all the Gardens full.

The cracks of whips, horrible nuisances, utterly regardless of the pain they give.

A remark by Mary Novello, made on the following day, bears out this observation and has a rather odd sequel :

What an immense population does Vienna appear to contain, especially of females. The girl at our inn has just been telling me alluding to Vin and I using one bed, ' In your land the beds are wider and in my land also but in Vienna the husband sleeps in one end of the house and the wife at the other ; the husband cares for every woman better than his own wife and she repays the compliment. *Das ist nicht angenehm, nicht schön* [that is not pleasant, not nice] she added, to which I agreed.

It is a sad little page with which Vincent Novello's diary starts the next day, and his emotions play havoc both with his grammar and his quotations, his valediction to Mozart's unknown burial place emerging as a synthesis of *Macbeth* and Gray's *Elegy*.

25th July, Saturday. Although I had heard that all that was known of the burial place of Mozart was that his remains were deposited in the burying ground of Saint Mark's, a small church belonging to what was formerly a convent of nuns, and that as no stone or mark of any kind had been placed to mark the grave of this illustrious genius, no one could tell which was the precise spot where he rests. I had already heard all this, yet as I always prefer seeing and hearing and judging for myself when it is in my power to do so, I determined to visit the church of St Mark myself and ascertain whatever particulars were still attainable.

I accordingly rose at half past five, and at last succeeded in finding out the church, but not without considerable difficulty, for it is situated at the very extremity of one of the most obscure parts of the suburb.

I arrived about 7 o'clock and was glad to find that they were just going to begin Mass, as it afforded me an opportunity of accosting the Sacristan. In answer to my question whether this was St Mark's church where Mozart was buried, he replied that the church was St Mark's, but of Mozart he knew nothing and could give me no information as to where he was buried.

I accordingly made my way to the burying ground by myself. The church, or rather chapel is a very small one with only one altar and no side aisles, three windows on each side and no galleries.

There is a little choir over the entrance opposite to the altar with a small positif organ and the whole of the decorations, as well as the entire appearance of the place are of the most humble kind.

The only part of the very confined space surrounding the church which appears to be appropriated as a burying ground is on the left-hand of the church where there are a few grave stones stuck up against the surrounding walls ; the whole cannot be above 50 feet square, if so much.

You may be sure I walked over every part of it with the utmost veneration and in every path ; but there was not only no stone to [be] found with his name upon it, but there were scarcely any traces to be found of a single grave.

The inscriptions on the old stones placed against the side walls are merely to some obscure ' Burgermeisters ' and priests formerly belonging to the convent.

Here then after ' life's fitful fever ' he ' in his narrow cell forever laid '.

The reports I had heard were but too true.

Flowers there were none, or I would have gathered some. I therefore plucked a few green leaves to bring away with me as a memorial of my visit to this sad but interesting spot. I returned completely disgusted with the tasteless apathy, the heartless ingratitude and disgraceful neglect with which this great man was treated by the generality of his countrymen and by the Viennese in particular.

His early morning walk to St Mark's took him eastward along the present Landstrasse Hauptstrasse, and a note at the end of his previous day's jottings shows that on his way he looked in at the handsome baroque church of St Roch, now a parish church but formerly belonging to the Augustinians, for whom it was built by Ferdinand III in 1642. The Dominican Church in the Postgasse (1639) he rightly dismisses ; it is baroque at its most fussy and uninspired.

Augustine Church Landstrasse suburb, Saturday morning. Only six o'clock Benediction. Quite full, especially women. Chorale in E flat. Organ nothing particular, all the same monotonous harmonies. Fine church decorated with paintings ; three side chapels. Dominican church near our hotel nothing striking.

As the Rasoumofsky Palace, where the Abbé Stadler lived, lies just off the Landstrasse, it was the most natural thing in the world, visiting hours being what they were, for Novello to look in on him on the way back. Their conversation is recorded in Novello's usual telegraphic style.

Heads of conversation on a visit to Abbé Stadler after having been at Mozart's burying ground.

Most of Mozart's *Masses* written when young.

Mozart had the very highest estimation for Handel.

Handel the first of all writers for oratorio styles and choruses. Has ' Messiah ', ' Judas Maccabeus ' (which he much admires, but ' Messiah ' still more) ; I recommended his ' Israel in Egypt '.

He did not know whether Mozart was acquainted with the ' Israel '.

Mozart used most frequently to play on the organ in the Jesuits' Church at Vienna. He did not much like the organs at Vienna, but esteemed those at Salzburg, especially those round the central Columns at the Cathedral.

Mozart played all the fugues of Sebastian Bach and as an exercise extracted the parts from the Organ copies and put them into separate Lines so as to form a score in order the better to see the contrivance and management of the Counterpoint.

Stadler was speaking here of Mozart's arrangements for strings of some of Bach's fugues. These are mostly from the Well-Tempered Clavier, but, as this, in the absence of pedal-boards on most English organs, was the staple diet of those organists in England who played Bach at all, Novello's reference to ' the Organ copies ' is understandable.[118]

The conversation then turned on one of Mozart's Masonic compositions, and the two gentlemen are soon completely at cross purposes. Novello, presumably because of his previous conversations with Mozart's widow, jumps to the conclusion that the work is the one she spoke of as having been composed when his last illness was already upon him—the ' Little Masonic Cantata,' K 623. But Stadler clearly means a much earlier work, the incomplete cantata *Dir, Seele des Weltalls, O Sonne* (To thee, O sun, soul of the universe), K 429, composed in 1783; for in the list he made for Constanze of Mozart's unfinished compositions (later reprinted in Nissen's biography) he expressly points out, as he does to Novello, the sudden *forte* in the passage ' From thee comes fruitfulness, warmth and light ', and the vigorous bass line in the ensuing tenor aria, in which the instrumentation is merely indicated. (In the opening chorus the same is the case, and the bass is figured.)

There is a further confusion in Novello's note ' Three voices with only Piano Forte Accompaniment', for the only masonic work accompanied by piano alone is the *solo* cantata, K 619 ; the other Masonic cantatas (the two already mentioned and *Die Maurerfreude*, K 471) have orchestral accompaniment. Moreover, it is inconceivable that Stadler should have told him that the earlier cantata, *Dir, Seele des Weltalls*, had only a keyboard accompaniment, for he had not only seen and described Mozart's partly-scored autograph, but (as Constanze implies in a letter to the publisher André) had made a piano arrangement of it—almost certainly the one published in the Collected Edition of Mozart's works. Thus when Novello says that ' Stadler after Mozart's death put it into full score ', he has apparently reversed the process. There is, however, another orchestral arrangement of *Dir, Seele des Weltalls*, originally in the possession of Mozart's eldest son, Carl[119], and an orchestral arrangement of the solo cantata, K 619. Can either of these have been made by Stadler?

Mozart's Masonic ode composed by Mozart just before his death. Three Voices with only Piano Forte Accompaniment. Bass like Handel. Stadler after Mozart's death put it into full score and gave it to Mozart's widow who had it performed with an orchestra. Has a copy of the original as done by Mozart but has no copy of his own full score—it has never been published nor has he even the one Copy in MS. or he would have given it to me (Write to the Widow to ask for Mozart's own adaptation and Stadler's accompaniment).

Points out in the Masonic ode the first germ of the idea of introducing a *piano* and *forte* to the expression of the word Light, to give more effect by the sudden contrast—which idea Handel had before used in his ' Samson ' and Haydn afterwards used, with such extraordinary effect, in the oratorio of ' The Creation '—' Let there be light '.

Showed me MSS. which he had copied for Imperial Library ; had discovered that Hofheimer who lived in the fourteenth century was one of the first who began to write in four parts and in canon.[120] Curious composition in MS. by Werner (who lived at Prince Esterházy's and to whom Haydn was indebted in his works).[121]

Knew Beethoven well but seemed to prefer Haydn and Mozart both as musicians and pleasant friends.

Wrote his name in album (on Mozart's own writing desk) and said he would send me one of his compositions before I left. Promised to come and visit me tomorrow at 5 (Sunday).

But instead, the Abbé turned up again that same day.

About 4 o'clock l'Abbé Stadler called upon me unexpectedly and paid me the high compliment (in my estimation) of looking in upon me like a familiar friend, without invitation, playfully observing he was about 24 years of age ' et quelque chose de plus ' to tell me that he had fixed for me to visit the Imperial Library on Tuesday next at 11 and that he would come and fetch me that we might look over the most curious MSS. together. He would not take coffee and said that he never took wine or anything of that nature; and on my observing that, as he was now upwards of four-and-twenty by his own admission, it was time to begin, his features relaxed into one of the most sweet and delightful smiles that I ever saw upon a human countenance. The whole of the manner, sentiments and charming demeanour of this venerable and interesting person proves him to have been worthy of the enviable distinction of being one of Mozart's most favourite friends. I cannot pay him a higher compliment.

Promised to write out Mozart's Masonic Ode himself in person for me.

On his rising to leave us I found out by accident that he was not going home direct, but had promised to visit some sick acquaintance in the Hospital. I accordingly prevailed upon him to let me give him my arm to assist him in his benevolent little promenade.

As we walked along together he communicated to me the following curious Anecdote : On my enquiring what were the most favourite pieces with Mozart when he was in private amongst his intimate friends, The Abbé said he usually played *extemporaneously*, but that his imagination was so inexhaustible and at the same time his ideas were so symmetrical and regularly treated that Albrechtsberger could not be persuaded but what they were regular pieces that had been studied beforehand—One evening when Mozart, the Abbé Stadler and Albrechtsberger were together, the latter asked Mozart to sit down to the Instrument and play something. Mozart directly complied, but instead of taking a subject of his own he told Albrechts-

14

berger to give him a theme. Albrechtsberger accordingly
invented a subject on the spot, and which he was quite
certain that Mozart could not possibly have heard before ;
he also selected the most trivial features he could think of
in order to put Mozart's ingenuity, invention and creative
powers to the severest test.

This extraordinary Genius immediately took the theme
that had been given him thus unexpectedly, and played
for upwards of an hour upon it, treating it in all possible
variety of form—fugue, Canon, from the most simple to
the most elaborate Counterpoint—until Albrechtsberger
could hold out no longer, but exclaimed in transport, ' I
am now perfectly convinced that your extemporaneous
playing is really the thought of the moment and that you
fully deserve all the fame you have acquired from this
wonderful talent.'

On another occasion Albrechtsberger, who was himself
one of the greatest contrapuntists as well as the greatest
organists of his time, was with L'Abbé and Beethoven when
the latter asked Albrechtsberger to play him a fugue, and
when he had finished, Beethoven exclaimed ' I perceive
that in comparison with you I know *nothing* '.

Evidently the Abbé continued his ' benevolent little
promenade ' beyond the hospital and Novello continued to enjoy his company and his conversation.

Walked with the Abbé (who cordially took my arm as
if I had been his son) to his relative in Kärntnerstrasse
where he was going to pay a visit to another sick friend.[122]
Stadler considers Beethoven an extraordinary Genius—
but irregular, extravagant. He also noticed a difference in
the *mode* of composing, that Beethoven often began before
he knew his own mind and altered backwards and forwards
the passages [*sic*] placing them in different places as mere

fancy or whim directed—but Mozart never began to write anything till he had arranged the whole design in his mind just as he wished it and then let it stand without alteration.

Beethoven never saw Mozart, he came to Vienna *two* years after Mozart's death.

This last statement is inaccurate. It is true that Beethoven did not settle in Vienna until 1793, when he came to study with Haydn ; but he had made a short visit to Vienna in 1787, at the age of sixteen, had visited Mozart and received a few lessons from him. Relatively slow in developing, he may not have impressed Mozart as a budding composer, but his keyboard improvisation had made Mozart exclaim to those present ' Keep your eye on him, some day he will give the world something to talk about '.

Beethoven's mental processes were indeed very different from Mozart's ; but their actual nature eluded the Abbé. Ernest Newman, in *The Unconscious Beethoven*, argues convincingly that Beethoven's vision of the fundamental design of a work was no less clear-cut than Mozart's, but that the details of the melodies themselves were left to be worked out later by the laborious process with which the Sketchbooks have made us familiar. Other composers have had the experience of seeing the pattern of a work and of knowing the *kind* of melody they want at a given place long before the actual melody takes shape, and Beethoven himself once said, ' I change many things, discard and try again. . . . Then, however, there begins in my head the development in every direction, and, insomuch as I know exactly what I want, the fundamental idea never deserts me . . .'

What Stadler goes on to tell Novello about the personal relationship between Haydn and Mozart, and Mozart's humble and generous acknowledgement of his indebtedness to his friend, is true in essentials.

Mozart had, however, encountered Haydn's work long before his coming to Vienna in 1781 ; in particular, the string quartets he wrote in 1773 (K 168-73) of which two have fugal finales, are obviously written under the impact of Haydn's wonderful Op. 20 set, composed in the previous year. But it is not for nothing that the nine years' gap between that set and Haydn's next—the ' Russian ' quartets, Op. 33, of 1781—is paralleled by a nine years' gap between Mozart's earlier set and the G major, K 387, written in December 1782, and that this, his first fully mature string quartet, should be the first of the six which he dedicated to Haydn.

Beethoven although a great admirer of Mozart was not himself sufficiently advanced to excite much of Mozart's attention, but that Haydn and Mozart were like Brothers. Mozart delighted in Haydn's writing and owned repeatedly that he was much indebted to him in forming his style. Stadler said that on his first arrival at Vienna and becoming acquainted with Haydn's work, Mozart naturally changed his manner of composing.

Haydn was not a great Pianoforte player (his best instrument the Violin)—but he delighted in hearing Mozart play the pianoforte. Haydn owned Mozart's superiority and said ' he was a *God* in Music ' (Stadler exclaimed to me ' Mozart est *unique* ; il etoit universel et savoit *tout* '.) Mozart and Haydn frequently played together with Stadler in Mozart's Quintettos ; particularly mentioned the 5th in D major, singing the Bass part,

the one in C major and still more that in G minor.[123]

Although Mozart was indebted to Haydn yet he added

so much of his own genius in the formation of his style—
that the *mélange* became his own. Stadler once asked him
how he contrived to write everything he wished in so
exquisite and perfect a manner—and Mozart simply
answered—'Je ne peux pas écrire *autrement*'—The Abbé
added that at 8 years old Mozart was already well versed
in all the rules of Musical Grammar and that his Genius
was such as to render it easy for him to excel in all styles
just as he pleased.

Mozart did not know some of Haydn's finest works such
as the Creation (Chaos the finest movement)—his best
Sinfonias and the Seven Last Words.

Of these works the *Seven Words of Our Saviour on the
Cross* is the only one Mozart could have known, for
Haydn's 'best sinfonias' (doubtless the twelve London
symphonies) were all written either in the year of
Mozart's death or after it, and *The Creation* did not
appear until 1798. The *Seven Words*, however, was
composed in 1785, and at once achieved such fame that
it is unthinkable that Mozart should not have heard it,
at least in Haydn's own version for string quartet.
Originally an orchestral work, it was commissioned
by the clergy of Cadiz Cathedral as a series of interludes to be played between the sermons of a Good
Friday Three Hour service. Haydn himself, in his
preface to the Breitkopf and Härtel edition of his vocal
version of it, wrote that ' the task of writing seven
Adagios, each of which was to last about ten minutes,
to preserve a connection between them, without
wearying the hearers, was none of the lightest ', and if
the idea of giving the rhythm of each of the ' Seven
Words ' (in its Latin version) to the initial theme of the
corresponding movement really came from the Abbé
(as he told Novello it did), he rendered the composer
a real service in providing his invention with a
springboard.

Haydn himself, as Stadler goes on to relate, made

the oratorio version of the work to a text by Baron van Swieten (the firstfruits of that collaboration which was to produce *The Creation* and *The Seasons*), having heard, and disliked, a version made for performance at Passau by a local musician and cleric.

Stadler was with Haydn when he received the commission to write the seven Adagios—and as he seemed comparatively at a loss to proceed in introducing sufficient variety in writing seven Adagios directly following each other, it was the Abbé Stadler who advised him to take the first words of the text and write a melody to each which should be the leading feature of the movement ; he followed the Abbé's advice and with a success that requires no eulogy from me.

A *chanoine* afterwards adapted words, but not in a satisfactory manner, and Baron [van] Swieten engaged Joseph Haydn to adapt some words to the music himself which he accordingly did. Stadler said he preferred these beautiful compositions without the words just as they originally were conceived by their Author.

Mentioned with great praise the Quartetto of Haydn in F minor with the Fugue (which Pinto arranged for the Piano Forte).[124]

Haydn did not play the Organ much but his brother Michael was a very good performer.

Novello must have had his vocal score of Haydn's *Seven Words* in preparation for publication before he set out, for his edition—after printing a translation of Haydn's introduction—bears the following preface :

During a little excursion to Germany this year, the Editor of the present publication was so fortunate as to meet with the Abbé Stadler, who was the intimate friend of both MOZART and HAYDN. This highly accomplished, amiable and venerable Gentleman . . .

informed the Editor that he happened to be with
HAYDN at the very time he received the commission
from Cadiz to compose the work, and that although
the Composer seemed at first to think that the difficulties attending the proper accomplishment of such a
task would be insuperable, yet that he set to work with
remarkable enthusiasm, and finally succeeded in producing a work which is considered by the best judges
in Germany, the most profound effort of his genius,
and the most lasting monument of his fame.

L'Abbé Stadler also corroborated the truth of the
tradition that Haydn himself considered this ' the
very finest of all his works.'

V. NOVELLO.
London. Sept. 6th, 1829.

It will be noticed that Novello does not credit the Abbé
with the suggestion of using the rhythm of the Latin
words.

In the original version each of the Seven Words is
set as an accompanied recitative and prefixed to the
relevant movement, but as these recitatives have no
thematic connection with the movement that follows,
this probably did not form part of the Abbé's suggestion.

Florian Leopold Gassmann (1729-1774), of whom
the Abbé goes on to speak, was much admired by his
contemporaries, especially by the Emperor Joseph II,
who appointed him Court Composer and, in 1771,
Court Capellmeister. His premature death was the
result of a fall while alighting from his coach.

Gassmann who lived before the time of Mozart unfortunately died young, otherwise in the Abbé's opinion he
would have come next to Mozart as a composer.

He was born in Bohemia and went to study in Italy
where he produced operas, etc., and on his return to
Vienna he wrote several Masses (l'Abbé knows of four or
five) besides Vespers, graduals, offertories, which he

173

thinks are preserved in the Library of Music belonging to the Imperial Chapel, as some of them were composed for that establishment.

Mecchetti, a music seller near Burg Thor, has a good collection of sterling music by Priendl, Reuter and other clever masters.

L'Abbé has promised me to come and fetch me to go with him to the Imperial Library on Tuesday morning next at ½ past 10 o'clock.

Mary Novello gives her own version of parts of the conversation:

The Abbé Stadler who is the most charming man in Vienna, though upward of 80, whom I have threatened to run away with, has told us delightful anecdotes of Mozart. He was with him much. He used to spend many evenings together with him, Haydn and Albrechtsberger. This latter at first doubted Mozart's great powers of working a subject without previous study and conceived he must have learnt them [sic] by heart. One evening he gave him a subject of a most inferior kind, thinking he could [do] nothing with it, when Mozart, perhaps having heard of his doubts, played for a full hour upon the theme, in such a manner that Albrechtsberger got up and embraced him, confessed his former unbelief and his present conviction that he was superior to every other as a composer and as a musician.

Haydn was always his most affectionate friend and greatest admirer. This latter played but little on the Piano Forte, Mozart preferred the organ and played divinely on that instrument.

Mozart always declared his style was greatly indebted to Haydn, though this latter thought so superiorly of him that he begged to go to London first, otherwise he should not dare to succeed Mozart, the English would not tolerate him.

That evening they went to the Opera at the Kärntnerthor Theatre and, for the first time on their tour, heard a work of Mozart performed :

V.N. 25th. Went to the Opera at the Hoftheatre near the Kärntnerstrasse. On Sunday which is the *grand* day for Operas in Germany they give the ' Barbiere di Siviglia ' by Rossini, but on Saturday (a very inferior night here) they gave Mozart's ' Don Giovanni '. However I preferred the inferior night with the superior music.[125]

M.N. Young Mozart said his father's music could not be spoiled, even when indifferently performed ; this is most true and was verified last night when the performance was little better than provincial, both in actors and scenery. The Don Juan had a vulgar Jew face, with the figure and carriage of John Reeves [*sic*][126] and it was impossible to look and act more vulgarly ; the recitative was cut out and several impertinent comic incidents introduced. Yet notwithstanding, such is the charm and character of the music, that it is by far the best entertainment we have witnessed in Germany.

The Choruses, Concerted pieces and Finales went delightfully ; indeed the Band is so loud, that scarcely any other can be heard. All the singers sang the notes set down for them, without trumpery ; and, with the exception of Elvira, well in tune. Though there was no Dragonetti in the band, the four Double Basses had a charming effect ; the Violoncello and Hautboys weak and reedy. The *Damen* were the most vulgar-looking I ever saw in a theatre, only fit for the outside of a booth ; indeed all the actresses were so disfigured with rouge, which was literally laid on in a thick coat under the very eyelids and the lower part equally whitened, that I forbore to look at them ; they spoilt the effect by reminding me of Grimaldi in ' Signor Paulo '.[127] Indeed both men and women have such unmeaning countenances, that it is impossible to conceive, from their expression, either grief or sentiment, it is mere stupid satisfaction.

A fine scene was introduced, which is always omitted in England, for ' Don Juan ', excellently expressive ;* but German words, I dislike excessively, perhaps from being accustomed to the Italian. But, indeed, I cannot reconcile myself to the German sounds as an agreeable language ; it may be expressive and energetic but its sounds are uncouth and painful.

V.N. The House is not large, and is very plainly ornamented, it is about the same size as our English Opera House in the Strand.† The pit is divided into two parts ; that nearest the orchestra ranks highest and contains the seats which lock up. There are also five tiers of which the two lower ones are occupied by the boxes.

I did not admire the tone of the principal Violoncello— it is weak and thin—and in the obligato accompaniment to Zerlina's exquisite song of ' Batti Batti ' seemed to labour too much—as if the task he had to execute was rather too difficult for him.

The obligato Violin Accompaniment to Don Giovanni's serenade song ' Deh vieni alla Finestra ' was not played by the Leader (who was a remarkably corpulent person and very like our friend Terrail)[128] but was assigned to one of the ripienos. I might probably have liked his playing better had I not so frequently heard my friend Spagnoletti's highly finished and refined performance of this tasteful little Air.

*This, as Vincent Novello records (p. 178), was the aria *Metà di voi qua vadano.*
†Later the Lyceum.

The Oboe I did not like—but the Trombones were good —as were also the Bassoons and Clarionets ; the latter charming instruments especially.

I have the same fault to find with this, as with almost every band that I hear, viz, that they play so loud as to overpower the Singers, the consequence is that the Singers are obliged to bawl in self defence in order to be heard, and the result is a coarse, noisy and violent effect. It is but justice however to say that this Orchestra, though not possessing any performer of very prominent ability, is less violent and noisy than that at Mannheim.

Of the singers the one who pleased me best was [*blank*] who played Donna Anna particularly in that divine song ' Non mi dir bel Idol mio ' (which is to my taste one of the most enchanting songs ever written, even by Mozart himself). The Zerlina also performed her part very agreeably, and with the exception of introducing an irrelevant flourish in the Duet ' Là ci darem ', she gave the text of the author with accuracy and precision.

Indeed this praise is due to the performers generally, and for my own part I would much rather hear the *real text* of a great composer given by an unpretending modest performer of genuine feeling than hear his well conceived and appropriate melodies altered and spoilt and frittered away into unmeaning affected nonsensical runs by the affected impertinence and ignorant conceit of many who arrogate to themselves the admired title of firstrate singers.

As I know the whole opera by heart, I of course did not lose anything by its being in German instead of Italian— although the effect was singular to hear such very different sounds and syllables attached to the musical phrases from those to which I had been accustomed. One alteration was for the worse, all Mozart's beautiful and expressive recitatives (with the exception of the *accompanied* ones) were left out and the dialogues were only *spoken*. A long scene of silly buffoonery between Don Giovanni and some officers of justice was introduced in the first Act quite different from the Italian Edition of the opera.[129] But in another instance the performance was better than our Opera in the Haymarket*—for they have the good taste to retain Don Giovanni's fine song in F when he is dismissing the Companions of Masetto, ' Metà di là, metà di qua '†—this is always done as a recitative at the Haymarket but I hope this masterly air will be restored on some future occasion.

I have been altogether much more gratified by the opera I have heard this Evening than by any Musical performance which I have yet heard in Germany. This I am sure is mainly attributable to the sterling merit of the Music itself [rather] than to the performance of it—but as Mozart's son observed to me, his father's music is of that kind it must please you, let it be done how it will. It is very difficult to disguise it or to spoil it so completely as not to leave some delightful feature, there will be always something to admire.

Their Sunday was, as usual, spent in a continual movement from church to church:

V.N. Sunday, Vienna, St Stephen's Cathedral, 8 o'clock, Chorale in G and sermon, at 9 o'clock High Mass . . .

Introit in C quite in Palestrina's solemn and churchified style . . . the service began with a procession round the church by the priests who sprinkled the people with Holy water as they proceeded . . .

The Mass was in a poor commonplace old style like what might have been written by Hasse or Vinci ; all the

*The King's Theatre, later Her Majesty's.
†*Sic.* The aria begins : *Metà di voi qua vadano, E gli altri vadan là.*

178

movements were short and unsatisfactory. The best voices
were the trebles. The orchestral performers were of the
mediocre kind.

The resonance is much less than what might have [been]
expected in so large a building, probably on account of
there being no *transepts* but only a small recess under the
large towers.

Beautiful Altar piece of sculpture at the Cathedral ;
two fine stained glass windows close to the Altar. Pity the
rest were destroyed except the first one on the left of choir
and the beautiful little chapel—with ' dim, religious light '
—under the South-west Tower near the great door, which
seemed to be seldom or never used. Exquisitely fine painting
of a single head at the Altar in the side Chapel to the left
of the High Altar, worthy of Guido—as much force and
energy of expression as I ever saw.[130]

10 o'clock, High Mass at St Anne's Church.

As I was informed by Mr Eybler that there was to be
a mass by Eybler (No. 4 in C) performed here on occasion
of its being the Festival of St Anne, I made a point of
being present as I was anxious to hear something by a
composer whom my friend Mr Latrobe esteems so highly.
But no sooner had they begun the Kyrie than I recognised
it to be Haydn's fine Mass in B flat (No. 16 my edition)[131]
. . . This altogether the most sterling church music I have
yet heard performed in Germany.

There was a very tawdry figure of St Anne with a face
like a Moor's draped up for the occasion and seemed to
attract much attention from the congregation which as
usual consisted almost entirely of females.

The Church is in the Roman style[132] not of the large
class and the gingerbread work seemed rather the worse
for wear. Three chapels on each side—but no aisle.

11 o'clock attended the High Mass at the Chapel Royal
. . . Mozart in D No. 6¹³³ . . . Service conducted by
Eybler . . . most musicianlike performance I have yet
heard. There were not many performers but all *efficient*.

Gothic chapel small and like the Portuguese rather
higher ; quite plain. A bronze crucifix. Not a bit of gold
except at tabernacle, and round a statue with a niche.
Four soldiers with fixed bayonets and their cocked hats on
at the altar . . . Lowest gallery for choir, two above for
the attendants of the Imperial Family, for whom there are
private tribunes overlooking the Altar and Sanctuary and
which connect with the interior of the palace. Vaulted
roof—nine sculptured Gothic figures half way up the
walls in niches, over the [*illegible*] in stone. Chaste and
solemn effect. Pity no painted glass in the windows at the
Altar.

Good taste of the Emperor in not having any crown or
other trappings and insignia of Royalty ostentatiously
displayed in his chapel.

Eybler made no fuss or clatter but beat the time steadily
and calmly like a sterling and accomplished musician
himself who knew that he was surrounded by others who
knew their business without much interference from
him . . .

Eybler has an enviable situation : he appears to have
nothing to do but write Masses and other music of the
sterling class when he feels inclined, and this, with the
certainty of having it well performed by an excellent band
consisting of brother musicians with cultured taste (who
can justly appreciate his best productions). Long may he
continue to enjoy this happy lot, of which he appears to
be so justly deserving by his professional ability and
estimable private character. Would to heaven that his
friend, poor Mozart, had enjoyed the same opportunities

and advantages for the tranquil and independent prose-
cution and exertion of his incomparable musical genius.

If I resided in Vienna this is the place I should come to
every Sunday when I wished to hear classical music correctly and judiciously performed ; and I should go to the
Cathedral when I felt inclined to indulge in a service of a
different and grander class.

Between 2 and 3 went again to St Stephen in hopes of
hearing Vespers but there was only a service preceded by
a short chorale without any accompaniment whatever.

I therefore went on to the parish church of Schotten
which has the reputation of possessing the best organ in
Vienna ; but on my arrival thither about 3 o'clock I found
the same tiresome droning preaching going on and after
enduring this humdrum loss of time for nearly half an
hour my patience was completely exhausted and I returned
home.

I however comforted myself with the hope that I should
find some other opportunity of hearing and judging of this
favourite instrument of the Viennese.

The Schotten Church is a venerable looking one inside
with curious antique carvings in dark wood.[134]

It is only from Mary Novello that we learn how they
spent that Sunday evening :

This being the Feast of St Anne, 25th, there is a grand
fireworks given on the Prater, and we go.

Her description, evidently written next day, follows at
once.

If any one wished to have an idea of the excessive
population of this small town he should be present at
such an exhibition. I should imagine that, throughout the
Prater, there could not be less than ten thousand persons,

yet, in all this crowd not one accident, no pushing, pick-pocketing or blackguardism ; yet two-thirds were servants and their sweethearts. For about 15d. we had a very good seat and the fireworks were very pretty, for nearly an hour. In some parts we surpass them in England, but some sailing balloons that changed colour were most tasteful. (A propos to speak to Charles about the Stranger's Diary in Galig-nani). After the fireworks were finished two brilliant lights were left burning to light the company out and all along the broad path were burning lights that the company might see their way and the greatest order was observed in the line of carriages which was really immense. On each side were innumerable booths for refreshment and others for waltzing and these would probably remain open all night. The whole way into town, and in town, a succession of beer, billiard and wine houses ; but the music is not better than that at our tea gardens and the musicians are, most of them, sunburnt like blacks. . . .

On Monday, 27th, Novello attended the 10 o'clock Mass at the Cathedral (see below, pp. 311-12). Thence he went on to Tobias Haslinger's establishment in the Graben, where a little group assembled which emerges from his notes as a musical ' conversation piece '. Adalbert Gyrowetz (1763-1850), whom he encoun-tered on arrival, was director of the Court Opera and, as Novello remarks, had just achieved success with his opera *Der blinde Harfner*, produced in Prague in 1828. He had lived in London from 1789 to 1792, and gave Haydn a friendly welcome on his first visit to England.

After the Cathedral I called in at Mr Haslinger's where I saw a pleasant elderly-looking gentleman leaning against the counter, who was so like my old friend Salomon that I should have taken him for his brother. On enquiring who he was I found to my great gratification that it was

12. THE MOZART FAMILY

13.   MOZART'S SONS

14.   VIENNA: GASTHOF ZUR STADT LONDON

Mr Gyrowetz, who had been in England at the same time with Haydn and whose symphonies were performed at Salomon's concerts alternately with those of his celebrated friend.

Mr Haslinger was so kind as to introduce me to him, when I had the additional pleasure of finding that he still spoke English fluently. He at once entered into conversation with me in the most cordial and familiar manner. Said it was about forty years since he had been in England, but spoke with great warmth of his old friends Clementi, Salomon, Cramer Jun., and both his sons. On my expressing regret at hearing so little of the music of Mozart and Haydn, either operas, masses, quartets, quintets, he shook his head and said that the age of good music was gone by. He pointed to a large quantity of waltzes, airs with variations, dances, marches and the trifling pieces that were lying spread out in the music shop upon the counter, and said (with a laugh of just contempt) that that was the kind of music that was now the fashion in Germany ; and he added that if he had been aware of my coming to Vienna he would have contrived to have got up some of my favourite quartets of Haydn, Mozart, etc. But as the performers who could do justice to them in summer were difficult to get together he feared there would not be time to accomplish his wish to gratify me as I was to leave Vienna the day after tomorrow.

Promised to write something in album. On my offering to convey any message to Cherubini whom I expected soon to see in Paris he desired his kindest remembrance to this celebrated composer, whom he (in common with most of the best judges I have yet met with in Germany) unites with me in considering the greatest master of the present day.

Mr Gyrowetz although he must now be rather an old

man, has not the least appearance of age about [him] but appears quite strong, robust in health, cheerful in spirits. He has (I believe) not very long since written an opera, which has completely succeeded.

I also met the nephew of Mr Müller the composer to the Leopoldstadt Theatre. He speaks French fluently and was very polite in translating my wishes to the assistant of Mr Haslinger in the shop, who cannot speak any other language than German. He introduced [me] to Mr Assmayr the second organist to the Imperial Chapel who accidentally came in to Mr Haslinger's whose establishment seems to be the favourite lounge and rendez-vous for all the best musical Professors at Vienna.

Ignaz Assmayr (1790-1862), Sechter's assistant as Court Organist, to whom Novello was introduced by Wenzel Müller's nephew, was a minor composer and a friend of Schubert's. Kandler too had evidently joined the gathering in time to share Novello's delight in the arrival from Munich of the copy of Benedict Schack's Mass which he had been so eager to secure. (Cf. p. 61.) The Miss Koehne whose present the absent-minded Novello had ' nearly lost in the Cathedral ' was a cultured young girl whose acquaintance Mary Novello had made in Berlin while travelling with Edward Holmes in 1827, and whose friendly courtesy she records in her unpublished diary.

Polite letter from Eybler which Kandler translated for me. Got Schack's Mass.

Haslinger promised to forward Mary's present for Miss Koehne to Berlin for me which I had nearly lost in the Cathedral.

At half past one the Novellos had an engagement to dine with the Streichers. Now in their sixties, the Streichers were both people of importance in the musical life of Vienna ; and, of the two, the wife, Nanette, was the more remarkable. As a little girl her brilliant, affected style of piano playing had at once impressed and horrified Mozart when he visited her father, J. A. Stein, the celebrated maker of organs and pianofortes at Augsburg, whose instruments he himself preferred to all others. At 22, on her father's death, she had shown herself capable of undertaking the management of the business and even of mastering its technical aspects. In 1793 she married Andreas Streicher, a good pianist and teacher, and together, in partnership with her younger brother, they transferred the business to Vienna. Eventually the brother set up on his own, retaining the family name of Stein, while the Streicher firm continued to thrive, thanks to the high standard and repute of its instruments. Beethoven had met Nanette in her Augsburg days and, although he always regarded the piano of his time as unsatisfactory, he liked the Streichers and their instruments well enough to suggest improvements which, according to Reichardt, succeeded in giving their pianos greater flexibility, depth of tone and sustaining power.

Streicher was always a loyal friend to Beethoven and helped him in every way he could (it was he who introduced Stumpff to him, and who unpacked and overhauled the pianoforte sent to him from London in 1818 by Thomas Broadwood). Meanwhile Nanette patiently and devotedly endeavoured to look after his clothes, his laundry and his domestic affairs, and when, in 1817, Beethoven made his disastrous decision to take his nephew Carl (whose guardian he had become on his brother's death) away from school and look after him at home, it was to her that he turned for advice on the unfamiliar business of running a household. (The original German edition of Thayer's biography contains sixty of his letters to her, all dated 1817 or 1818.)

On his way from Haslinger's shop in the Graben

either to his hotel or to the Streichers' house in the Ungargasse, Novello could have made his ritual journey past Mozart's house without too much of a detour.

Heard next door to Mozart's house in Rauhensteingasse the fugue in Handel's overture to Alexander's Feast played on the Piano Forte ; the only sterling thing I have yet heard on that instrument in Germany. Past the house every day several times.

Mr Streicher to dinner at ½ past 1. Mr Streicher resides in the Ungargasse not far from the Landstrasse and ranks as one of the most eminent Pianoforte makers at Vienna. His son has invented several very clever mechanical improvements in the construction of the keyboard and interior movements. The tone brilliant and powerful without [being?] harsh—the touch [answers?] well to the fingers in executing the delicate shadows and gradations of loud and soft required by a performer of sentiment, taste, feeling and expression, and from what I heard of Mr Streicher's instruments altogether they are (in my opinion) far superior to any others that I have yet met with in Germany.

Mrs Streicher is herself an excellent judge of instruments and occasionally superintended the finishing. She has had the rare pleasure of being on friendly terms with Mozart, Haydn, Clementi and Hummel and has enjoyed the still rarer advantage of having had this first-named great musician as her music-master . . . Her father was a Professor at Augsburg and not only Organist but built an Organ himself for the church where he was engaged (Barfüsserkirche). Madame spoke very highly of this instrument and very politely requested I would make a point of playing upon it in case I visited Augsburg on my return.[135]

Mr Streicher was acquainted with Mozart during the

last part of his career and gave Mozart's younger son his first lessons on the Piano Forte. The latter studied with him for five years, and afterwards had lessons in counterpoint from Mr Gallus.

Mr. Streicher's opinions of the widow are not so favourable as what I could have wished ; but as he said very little upon the subject, which seemed to be a sore one, I of course do not feel authorised to repeat a single word of what passed. Truth I shall always endeavour to ascertain upon every occasion and shall record faithfully for the gratification of those who [*word omitted*] upon subjects which concern the public ; but private affairs and gossip upon matters with which the world at large has nothing to do I have not the least inclination either to learn or to record.

M.N. Dined today with Mr Streicher who is the first Piano Forte maker and knew Mozart. He is a worthy man but too pompous in his manner, which after all is only commonplace ; indeed it is because he has only arrived at the wisdom of commonplace that he is thus pompous. He was very severe upon Mme Mozart and afraid if he told Vin any anecdotes respecting her husband or Beethoven that his name should appear for fear of hurting her feelings.

After dinner, her husband having doubtless returned to business, Frau Streicher escorted them on a drive during which—so Mary Novello relates—they ' visited Mozart's and Beethoven's houses and the grave of the latter '.[136]

V.N. Took a little ride with Mme. Streicher and a gentleman who spoke English.

Beethoven lived three years in the Schwarzspanierhaus No. 200 on the Glacis opposite the Scots Door (Schotten

Thor) on the first floor.[137] The Stair Case is a [*illegible*] one.
Family was absent and the Room locked up so that we
were not able to see the apartment where this great Genius
expired. Very pleasant situation with a fine view of
Vienna and St Stephen in front and a very agreeable
garden behind in which probably Beethoven frequently
strolled while musing on his grand orchestral effects and
designing his magnificent Sinfonias.

M.N. Mrs Streicher was intimate with Beethoven to a
very great degree as she has above 50 notes written by him
to her on familiar subjects. She amused us much by
describing some of his peculiarities with his servants and
sometimes driving them all out of the house in a body.
He must have been a most wilful and disagreeable person
as an acquaintance. In appearance she describes him as a
beggar he was so dirty in his dress, and in manner like
a bear sulky and froward, he laughed like no one else it
was a scream, he would call people names as he passed
them, yet for all this she thinks him an honest man but I
doubt this for he was avaricious and always mistrustful.
He delighted to pinch a person's hand till he hurt it, said
no one could make a good crush that had not a good
conscience ; worried about the minutest things of his own,
some counterpanes Mrs Streicher promised to get washed
for him he teased her husband to death over, and even
wrote to her to Baden a note set to music to the words of
' Where are my counterpanes? '[138] Another time he visited
Baden where she was, but instead of calling upon her
threw his card in at the window, which as he was so odd
looking a man, frightened her servant. He would frequently walk out in the fields for many miles and several
times sat down to write, and having fallen asleep was wet
through with the rain. His servants not liking him he was
frequently much neglected.

What we hear of Beethoven does not increase our love of him, he was like Rousseau says Mr Streicher, always jealous and thinking his friends were deceiving him, even before his deafness attacked him.

As on previous occasions, Vincent Novello's scribbled and disconnected notes would hardly make sense without his wife's more consecutive account. But the construction he puts upon Beethoven's behaviour is consistently more charitable. The comparison between Beethoven and Rousseau seems to have been a commonplace among his contemporaries, but only Novello would have thought of comparing him with his old friend and fellow-organist Samuel Wesley (nephew of John Wesley, the founder of Methodism), with whom he had for years been associated in his devoted championship of J. S. Bach. Wesley suffered from periodic fits of melancholia due to a head injury.

V.N. Madame Streicher told us many anecdotes of him [Beethoven], she was his Pupil (as well as that of Mozart).

Beethoven rough outside and manners not attractive especially at first but excelled despite [*illegible*]. Eccentric and suspicious of the motives of all around him—a mixture of Sam Wesley and Rousseau—read a great deal (sometimes all Dinner) principally poetry—Goethe his favourite.

The only three musicians he liked were Handel, Sebastian Bach and Mozart—hated all etiquette or formality—wore shabby clothes—contempt for aristocrats and their formal parties—never shewed them the least respect—anecdote of Coverlid to his bed teasing Mr Streicher and droll card set to music about it—throwing his visiting Card in *at the window*, frightening the servant—and Madame Streicher returning her card in the same manner. Nephew he loved so much not turning out well—hurt him and hastened his death. Tormented by Servants and no kind

Lady to take care of him ; advised by Madame Streicher to marry, shook his head bitterly (probably thought no Lady could love one who was so deaf)—came full dressed in new Clothes, on New Years Day.

His favourite occupation taking very long walks in the country—but quite alone, frequently lay down and went to sleep in the Rain after writing an Air [*illegible*]. When he came home no one to let him in, remained in rain all night.

All Beethoven's character was of the same energetic forcible cast—his laugh was like no other person's so violent loud and boisterous. When he shook hands Mme Streicher said that he almost crushed her fingers to pieces—he was like a large Bear even in his playful moods.

She attended his funeral stood in the spot in the court yard where his body was deposited before the Procession began—curious crowd. Streicher visited just before he died—but was ill himself when the Funeral took place. Purchased MSS. at his sale—gave them to Madame who gave me two pages of it.[139]

Monument at the detached burying ground at Währing, of pyramid form against the wall on the left side. Butterfly and snake for eternity above, a Golden Lyre lower down and only his name in large gold Letters (good taste). Large slab of granite broken in two without any inscription is placed over his body. When he was first buried a guard was placed every night for some time lest his body should be stolen away.

Währing, now a suburb, was then outside Vienna.[140] Beethoven's grave is now in the musicians' section of the huge Viennese Central Cemetery (a short distance beyond St Mark's cemetery where Mozart was buried). The old design for his monument was retained. The watch kept over his grave immediately after his burial may well have been due to the unfortunate episode of the theft of Haydn's skull.

Frau Streicher evidently brought them back home to pass the evening, which was spent in talk and music-making. Besides the ' sore subject ' of Mozart's monument, Johann Anton André's collection of Mozart manuscripts naturally came up for discussion with the Streichers, as the two families were connected by marriage. It is clear, however, that Streicher had no idea of the full extent of André's acquisitions.

M.N. Mr Streicher spent the evening with us and was very chatty—he says it was Madame's fault that no monument is erected to Mozart but does not quite prove why.

V.N. Mozart's monument a sore subject with Streicher as well as with Gyrowetz and every other person of good taste and feeling I have yet met with.

André the music seller at Offenbach is related (Streicher's son I believe married M. André's daughter) to Mr. Streicher. Wanted the autographs by Mozart in André's possession; regretted they were not published and thought it injudicious to delay their appearance so indefinitely. I could not ascertain exactly what the MSS. were but Streicher thought they were principally some of Mozart's early Piano Forte pieces; in which case I do not think the publication would be a profitable speculation. The case would be very different if they were vocal pieces or complete scenas from operas, sacred pieces in score, or other compositions of the elevated class.

I regret that I shall have no opportunity of calling upon M. André in order that I might have the gratification of seeing the MSS. and then being able to form my own opinion of their nature and value.

Streicher said young Mozart was of an inert disposition but possessed great genius. He taught him the first Concerto he played in public when he was about 13. Young Mozart composed the concerto for the Piano Forte and Streicher's Brother added the accompaniment for the orchestra. In the Andante movement which Crescentini (whom Streicher mentioned as the most perfect singer he had ever heard)[141] was delighted with and would hardly believe to have been written by such a mere boy as Mozart's son then was. Called Mozart himself to answer the question—said ' I wrote [it] and his Brother added the instrumentation '.

At the end of the concert he wished young Mozart to play something Extempore, that the audience might form a more just opinion of his very superior talent. Mozart protested he could not do any such thing and even broke into tears, but Streicher who knew his talents better than himself insisted upon his exerting himself and gave him the subject of his father's fine minuet in ' Don Giovanni '. The boy at last sat down to the Piano Forte, moved the music and blew out the candles to show he was playing entirely without any notes to assist him and performed the most masterly and charming variations upon the theme that had been given to him so unexpectedly, to the astonishment and delight of all who heard him.

(Streicher mentioned that after Mozart had arrived at this high degree of skill it was at one time contemplated to bring him up as a *Farmer* instead of his continuing music as a profession).

Streicher wished him much to write a Sinfonia or some other grand Composition and dedicate it to Haydn, but Mozart who always appeared to underrate his talent and feared that whatever he produced would be compared with what his father had done, and of course to his own disadvantage, had not the courage to follow Streicher's advice. Streicher excused the inactivity and languor of young Mozart at the same time that he accounted for it philosophically and from natural physical causes, for about a twelvemonth before he was born Mme Mozart was confined to her bed by indisposition and it was during this period that she became *enceinte* and was delivered of this weakly child under the same unfavourable circumstances of debility and ill health.

M.N. . . . He is very fond of young Mozart, whom from the age of five he instructed. He thinks him the same genius as his father, but from some physical cause is so exceedingly indolent that he can never be eminent.

V.N. Streicher accompanied in a very musician-like manner three of Mozart's charming little songs contained in No. 5 of the *cahiers* published by Breitkopf and Härtel[1][42] which were sung with good feeling and expression by a young Lady, his pupil in singing. During the whole time I had Beethoven's bust on the table just before me, and some of his own handwriting on the table, from which Mr Streicher was so kind as to say I could choose whatever I thought proper. I selected two half sheets : one a part of a full score and the other containing some little sketches of motives for Finales, a subject for a Fugue, etc., and I shall surely preserve them with the greatest veneration.

Of the two manuscript fragments which he chose, Novello later presented the sketch in full score to the British Museum (Add. 14396, f.30) retaining the 'little sketches' in his album. The bust to which he refers was the one made by Franz Klein in 1812 from the life-mask which, at Streicher's request, Beethoven had allowed Klein to make ; Streicher wished to add Beethoven's bust to the array with which, like Haslinger, he had already adorned his establishment. The '*large* Portrait writing his Mass in D ', subsequently referred to as the best, must be either the Schimon portrait of 1818 or 1819, made while he was at work on the Mass, or that by Stieler which shows him with the score in his hand.

Fine bust of him from a mask—only 1 cast, mould destroyed—pity and not liberal to do so—*large* Portrait writing his Mass in D the *best*.

Very like *Power* the comedian[143] but more energy and sternness in the expression ; pitted with small Pox—and the chin quite scarred with it especially on the right side— where it is absolutely drawn. Difficult to make him sit— she has his Hair framed—when she asked him to let her have some he at first refused—but afterwards said ' cut off a *bushel* if you like '.

M.N. Beethoven is considered very ungrateful by Mr Streicher, he was a pupil of both Haydn and Albrechtsberger, yet never acknowledged it, either in his publications or by speech.

Streicher's statement is true as regards Haydn, of whom Beethoven said ' Although I had some instruction from Haydn I never learned anything from him '. What he absorbed unconsciously from Haydn's music is apparent in his own ; but, like many great creative artists, Haydn was not a good teacher, and in particular was not rigorous enough for Beethoven's taste in the matter of strict counterpoint. When, in 1794 (after Beethoven had had lessons from him for over a year), Haydn went to England for the second time, Beethoven took counterpoint lessons from Albrechtsberger. Years later he said that without Haydn and Albrechtsberger he would have committed many follies. But by then he had learned humility and, as Stadler had already told Novello,* was quick to recognize that Albrechtsberger was a master in his own sphere.

Now Frau Streicher sits down herself at the pianoforte : her playing releases a flood of Haydn anecdotes,

*See above, p. 168.

including the well-known story of his comparison between *The Creation* and *The Seasons* : ' in *The Creation* I had to make angels sing, in *The Seasons*, merely peasants '. The real trouble probably was that, at 68, he had found the work on *The Seasons* a heavier strain than *The Creation*. In addition, he had had friction with the Baron van Swieten, his librettist and patron, who had contrived a text for him on the basis of James Thomson's poem *The Seasons*, adding suggestions regarding the musical setting—especially the programmatic illustration of the sounds of nature—which Haydn did not like at all, and only followed with reluctance.

Van Swieten's taste for the music of Handel led him to organize private performances of his oratorios, for which, as Novello goes on to add, he translated the words. These performances were conducted, first by Joseph Starzer, then, on his death, by Mozart, and it was for them that he wrote his additional accompaniments to *Messiah*, *Acis and Galatea*, *Alexander's Feast* and the *Ode for St. Cecilia's Day*. Those for *Judas Maccabaeus* were not by him, but by Starzer.

V.N.　Haydn much admired the pianoforte playing of Madame Streicher (she is still an excellent performer I heard her play a very tasteful Rondo by Cipriani Potter the one in C dedicated to Mrs Miles).[144]

Baron van Swieten translated the words of the ' Messiah ', ' Alexander's Feast ', ' Judas Maccabaeus ' for Mozart, and ' Acis and Galatea ' for some other German composer to adapt Accompaniment in addition to Handel's score for *stringed* Instruments. He also prepared the Words of ' The Seasons ' for Haydn, who did not think he could do much with them. . . . After the first performance of ' The Seasons ' Streicher called upon Haydn to congratulate him upon having accomplished another great work. [He said] that the words of the Creation had inspired him,

as he had to make *Angels* sing. ' The Seasons ' cost him
more labour than the Creation, one fugue alone (the one
in B flat which I have published in Motets Book [*blank*]
cost him 6 weeks work—and yet nobody seemed to think
anything of it[145]. Haydn was much hurt with the ill-natured
remarks and criticism that were made upon this Oratorio
—and scarcely ever afterward felt inclined to exert himself
for so ungrateful and tasteless a set as the generality of the
Viennese in matters relating to music.

Haydn was delighted when Streicher told him how
highly he esteemed this work and threw himself in his arms.

Streicher also told us that the first Mass which Haydn
produced in Public, the Empress Maria Theresa was
present—Hasse stood by her and she asked his opinion
of the young composer.

Hasse told the Empress that Haydn possessed all the
qualities that are required to form the highest style of
writing viz. beautiful and expressive melody, sound
harmony, original invention, variety of effect, symmetrical
design, knowledge of the powers of the different instruments, correct counterpoint, scientific modulation and
refined taste. Hasse also predicted that Haydn would
become one of the greatest Composers of the Age. This
liberal opinion so encouraged Haydn that from that time
he exerted himself to the utmost to fulfil the flattering pre-
diction, and he at the same time resolved never to give
a harsh or severe opinion himself upon the production of
any young Composer but always to do his utmost to
encourage their first attempts, and to persevere in their
studies with energy and enthusiasm.

Haydn always acted up to this resolution during all his
life—and no one was ever more liberal and just to the
merit of the productions of others than was this great
Master of the Art.

This story is somewhat doubtful. Hasse was permanently resident in Venice from 1771 onwards, by which date Haydn had written only three Masses, if that—the little F major Mass of about 1750, the Great Organ Mass written in 1766 for the Esterházy chapel, and perhaps the Cecilia Mass, probably written for performance on the feast of the saint by the Cecilian Brotherhood in Vienna ; this is the only one of the three of which there is even a suggestion of a performance outside Eisenstadt or Esterház. But even if the story is apocryphal, Haydn's regard for Hasse, and his unfailing generosity towards young composers, are matters of fact.

Johann Nepomuk Hummel, of whom the Streichers go on to speak, was, at seven, already a brilliant pianist. Mozart took him into his house as his pupil for two years (1785-7)—not five years, as Streicher stated. From 1804 to 1811 he held Haydn's old post as musical director to Prince Esterházy. He was on friendly terms with Beethoven.

Anecdote of Hummel showing one of his early Masses to Haydn who was obliged to alter so much of it that at last there was nothing left. Hummel evidently formed his style of sacred music upon that of Haydn—see his No. 1 in B and No. 2 in E flat.

M.N. Haydn, he thinks, did much for Hummel especially at first correcting his attempts at writing Masses. Hummel was five years with Mozart and frequently when this latter returned home and wished to try over something he would waken him from his sleep and make him play. The child would rub his eyes and seem unwilling. Give him a glass of water, ' come there's a good lad ' and they would play together.

Of the poet Schiller I heard that he was amiable but overworked himself particularly at night and this, together with an original defect of the lung, hastened his death.

The casual reference to Schiller with which Mary Novello's account ends must have sprung from a reminiscence of Streicher's, for he had formed a youthful friendship with the poet while the latter was undergoing his medical training at Stuttgart, at the Ducal academy, the *Karlsschule*. Subsequently, when Schiller, forced into the uncongenial occupation of an army doctor, secretly left the duchy to further his ambitions as a dramatist, Streicher aided and accompanied him on his escape. His account of this episode, *Schillers Flucht von Stuttgart und Aufenthalt in Mannheim von 1782 bis 1785*, was published by his widow in 1836, three years after his death.

The next day, Tuesday, July 28th, was the date fixed for their visit to the Imperial Library with the Abbé Stadler. Here Novello was presented to the Curator, Count Maurice Dietrichstein, who was so soon to acquire the autograph of the opening movements of Mozart's Requiem, and who showed him the autograph portions of the *Dies Irae* already presented to the Library by the Abbé. The Count's courtesy may, as Novello modestly assumes, have been in the first place a tribute to the high standing of the Abbé Stadler, but Novello quickly established himself as a scholar and musician in his own right, as is abundantly clear from a covering note in which the Count forwarded a letter from the Abbé in September of the same year :

'. . . I gladly seize the opportunity of bringing myself to your remembrance and of opening a correspondence which, besides the pleasure it will afford me, will doubtless be highly advantageous to the Institution of which I am in charge.

An hour's conversation with you, Sir, was enough for me to recognise your distinction as a scholar and your personal charm, and only made me regret all the more keenly that I was not informed earlier of your arrival in Vienna '.

As the letter goes on to mention, the Count was

15. UNPUBLISHED CANON ASCRIBED TO MOZART, IN F. S. KANDLER'S HAND

contemplating the publication of an edition of the Requiem based on the autographs then known. (The letter is given in full in Appendix IV.)

M.N. I should have mentioned that we yesterday visited the Imperial Library to see the original of the Requiem, where the Abbé had deposited it ; it is shortly to be published in the exact form in which Mozart has left it, in some places only marks, in others sketches. Here were also manuscripts of Haydn, one of his Masses and the Creation. The *salle* is most beautiful, richly ornamented with gilding and statues and the dome painted.

V.N. Visit to the Imperial Library with the Abbé Stadler . . . His Excellency the Count Dietrichstein who has the superintendence of this magnificent Library, was extremely polite and courteous in his behaviour to me (for which I am aware that I am entirely indebted to the kindness of l'Abbé Stadler) and took every possible pains to gratify my curiosity and interest, not only respecting the MSS. of Mozart, but relative to the other music contained in this princely collection which is indeed one of the very finest and most extensive I ever visited. Haydn original MS. of Mass in B flat, No. 16 ; sketches by ditto : Fugue ' et vitam ' No. 1, ditto of Creation (very interesting and curious). Finely illuminated Missals. Hofheimer sacred music.[146]

There is here a copy of Mozart's early opera ' Ascanio in Alba,' the only Copy I ever could meet with. I inquired also for his other Operas ' Il Ré Pastore ', ' La finta Giardiniera ', ' Sulla ' [Lucio Silla], ' Mitridate ', but they had not any Copies and as I have now made researches and inquiries in almost every part of Germany by different channels, without being able to find these, I fear these *germs* of Mozart's incomparable Genius are now irreparably lost.[147]

The ' Ascanio ' is bound in two Volumes, one for each Act. The introduction is in D major, and I should have been delighted to have appropriated the whole day to the examination of this Opera, but before I could turn to the 2nd Movement I was called to look at some other curious MSS., with which invitation I own I complied very reluctantly. There was a good collection of Handel's work in Score (Arnold's Edition, not Walsh's).[148]

It was probably that afternoon that they again met Kandler:

V.N. Mr Kandler gave me an engraving of Beethoven's tomb, published by Haslinger. Showed me MS. of Padre Martini, Crescentini, Paganini, Beethoven, Winter and other great musicians both of the German and Italian Schools. Wished me to go with him to visit Haydn's house, which he had had the goodness to make enquiries about, but I had an engagement to meet Abbé Stadler at his own apartment and I could not of course break my promise.

It was doubtless this refusal which drew from Kandler, in the letter he wrote to Novello on the following day, the playful accusation of ' preferring the guidance of others in initiating you into the musical technicalities of our country '. His letter is reproduced in full in Appendix IV, together with the canon of which he sent Novello a copy as being a youthful work of Mozart's. It is not included in Köchel's Thematic Catalogue.
The Novellos' promised call on the Abbé was their farewell visit.

On taking leave the kind Abbé behaved to me as he would have done to a favourite son, I have seldom felt so strong a veneration and affectionate attachment in so very short a time for any person that I ever met with as for this delightful specimen of what a human being ought to be.

He has all the fascination resulting from the rare combination of intellectual supremacy, highly cultivated talent, exemplary virtues, gentle and refined manners, sentiments the most noble and elevated, and, what is best of all, a heart overflowing with ' the milk of human kindness ' towards all his fellow creatures.

Promised to write to him. Next morning sent him with my address a little souvenir (china coffee cup) as last acknowledgement for the extraordinary kindness with which he had distinguished me.

Mr Kandler—engraving of Beethoven's monument and music composed by Seyfried.

M.N. The Abbé Stadler took a most affectionate leave of us and kissed Vin on the cheek with a truly paternal manner. God bless the dear old man. I longed to bend my knee to him and should, had there not been witnesses who might have considered it affectation. Mr Kandler was also very polite and even affectionate at parting. He is quite an elegant and accomplished man, but I should think in ill health. Bothered to death about our departure but really this Vienna is but a stupid place after all, and one I would least of all choose as a residence.

Evidently she had found the social life of the Imperial capital not to her taste :

The women of Germany have not improved upon me this second visit. It is true they are pretty in the common acceptation of the term : small regular features and fair skins, but they want air and carriage ; the *trottoir* makes them all walk as if they had tight shoes on and though they stare with the vulgarity of the milkmaid, if you address them they are shy and at a loss. As for the peasantry, after 12 or 14 they really become frightful and are more like men than women in dress and appearance. In Vienna

you see some women rolling barrows with stones, conveying up mortar and working on the scaffolding amongst
the men, and some of the loads they bear would astonish
an Irish porter. Scarce a shoe is to be seen on one of them,
but the men cover their feet unless in the fields when their
shoes are strapped to their backs.

How few women I have met like my dear Theresa.[149]
The Miss H[enickstein]s [?] here are very like all other
young women ; monstrously insipid. They extend their
eyebrows at the commonest remark as an expression of
wonder (alias ignorance) sing common ballads and talk
frequently on commonplace subjects—that the Princess
is most charming, that the other is *mignonne*, that the
Emperor walked one way and the Empress another.

Only one more complete day remained to the
Novellos, as they were due to leave Vienna on the
evening of the 30th. Novello made a final attempt to
hear some church and organ music, and his last-
minute shopping at the music publishing establishment of Artaria provides us with the only evidence
we possess that a fragment at least of Haydn's lost Mass
Sunt bona mixta malis, hitherto known only as an entry
in Haydn's own thematic catalogue, was still in
existence in 1829.

Wednesday, July 29th. St Stephen's, 4 o'clock. Went
again in hope to hear a musical Vesper or Litany, but
there were merely the priests singing, with a few short
Chords by way of interlude on the Organ. I went up to
the Organ loft, where I found an elderly looking person
seated at the Instrument. I ventured to address him, as he
appeared to have a good-natured physiognomy (something
like that of Hummel) and said I should esteem it as a great
favour if he would have the goodness to oblige me by
playing one of Sebastian Bach's fugues for the last Volun-

tary. He answered me very politely that unfortunately there would be no opportunity to gratify my wishes, as it was not customary to play any sortie or last Voluntary after the service on weekdays.

Artaria has the original MS. of Haydn's Kyrie [from Mass] No. 5, [of] No. 7 in G complete, and of the Kyrie and part of the Gloria of a mass in D minor entitled ' Sunt bona mixta malis ' which has never been published. These I purchased of him for 6 florins.[150]

Artaria has the Original Copies of the song in G, ' Clemenza [di] Tito ', and the Barrel Organ [Fantasia] Mozart F minor.[151]

A farewell visit from Nanette Streicher gave the Novellos the opportunity to draw her out once more on the subject of Beethoven. Novello was particularly anxious to hear more about his last illness, for he was one of the Directors of the Philharmonic Society who, on February 28th, 1827, had responded to Beethoven's appeals from his sickbed for a benefit concert by sending an outright gift of £100 (which eventually paid his funeral expenses). He had probably been astonished to learn that Beethoven had left over 7,000 florins in bank shares. These, however, Beethoven had always regarded as his nephew Karl's inheritance, and had refrained from touching them however straitened his circumstances ; there was no question of his being—as Frau Streicher surmised—too harassed to realize that he possessed them.

Her reference to his doctors is puzzling, for neither of the two originally summoned (Staudenheimer and Braunhofer) came, and Dr Wawruch, who was then called in, remained in charge of the case to the end, in consultation with Staudenheimer and Malfatti. There is a slight confusion, too, in what Hummel told her about Beethoven's condition. He was an old friend of Beethoven's and had hurried to Vienna with his wife on hearing of his illness. When he first called, on

March 8th, Beethoven was up and partly dressed, having said ' I must not receive him in bed ' ; but ' four days before he died ' he was already far too ill to have made such an effort, though it is possible that he might have done so in the intervening fortnight (Beethoven died on March 26th).

V.N. Madame Streicher called to take leave—told us that Beethoven's life might probably have been prolonged for some time had he continued to employ the King's Physician whom he had consulted at the commencement of his illness—but he was fearful that his means would be inadequate to meet the fees that might be thus incurred and he had too high a spirit to accept any attendance as a favour conferred upon him.

Mme. Streicher's opinion arises from the great skill this eminent medical Gentleman possesses, especially in the complaint (dropsy) under which Beethoven was suffering.

Hummel was much with him during his last illness— about four days before he died Hummel told Madame Streicher that Beethoven made an effort to overcome the languor that was creeping over him—he arose from his Bed and dressed himself—saying to Hummel that it was necessary to make some exertion to stand up against illness and that he would endeavour to overcome his painful and languid sensation—this was said with great energy and he appeared for the moment to be much better—but unfortunately this flash of his former spirit did not last, his feebleness rapidly returned, and he gradually grew weaker until he sank at last into death.

On one occasion, when he began to get infirm and his legs failed him, on arriving near his own house his foot slipped and he fell to the Earth where some mud had been left by a Shower of Rain. A Lady who happened to be standing at a window in the neighbourhood, and who

knew Beethoven, saw the accident and immediately sent
her servant to assist him, but some unfeeling Brutes
who had gathered round him, instead of helping, began
to laugh at the accident that had befallen him which so
enraged Beethoven that although he was scarcely able to
move from the united effects of weakness and pain, he
indignantly refused all aid whatever, turning fiercely away
from the proffered assistance of the servant sent by the
Lady, who could not refrain from tears at the miserable
situation in which this great man was placed—deaf,
covered with mud, scarcely able to walk from intense pain,
and subjected to the jeering insults of a ruffian-like mob.

In excuse for his complaints of poverty to the Philharmonic Society Mme. Streicher accounted for that circumstance by declaring that she believed he was so harassed
by different vexations and the infirmity of his irritable
temper, that he really scarcely knew what was in his
possession or what was not.

That he was more anxious for his nephew than for
himself. That almost all his thoughts and cares were
dedicated towards making some provision for this Person,
who after all did not act in such a manner as to give
satisfaction either to Beethoven himself or to any of his
friends.

This is an understatement ; but Frau Streicher probably refrained from telling them of the young man's
attempted suicide in 1826, the shock of which aged
his uncle and, as she had hinted earlier, may well
have hastened his death.

Beethoven rather fond of ' les plaisirs de la table ', his
favourite dish was a Cold Turkey in Jelly—and the Pâtés
de Périgord—Strasburg Pâté de foie gras.

It is not clear whether it was on this day or on the
30th that the Abbé Stadler looked in once more :

M.N. L'Abbé Stadler has just brought his own copy of a Masonic Ode written by Mozart as a present for Vin and a canon of his own for our little book.[152] What a dear old man he is, the only one I feel inclined to run away with throughout Germany. He is very amiable and as friendly as if we had known each other for years. He is very anxious to hear Vin on the organ but there are no good ones here. I wish he could play for him ; I am sure l'Abbé would be delighted for whatever may be said of the German organists I have never heard any to equal Vin and I am sure their puffing and pumping would not suit anyone who had heard his full smooth tones.

This was not to be, for they left Vienna on the evening of the 30th.

PART V

THE RETURN JOURNEY

Vienna to Salzburg, July 30-August 3

Sunday, August 2. This is the fourth day of our tedious travelling on our return to Munich ; I am almost mad at several times thinking of the time we lose and that it will diminish our stay in Paris. Even the beauty of the scenery is lost on me and but for kind Vin, who bears up admirably, I should run stark in the fields.

> Thus Mary Novello—who now has but one thought, Clara's prospects in Paris—cries out against the slowness of their return journey, which had not even the charm of novelty, for they returned almost as they came, and Sunday, August 2nd saw them once more at Lambach. Fortunately her powers of observation and her sense of humour, though tinged with irritation, have not quite deserted her.

Here the women are all disfigured by wearing black silk handkerchiefs round their heads and a white man's hat stuck on top, bent over their eyes. Most of their garments are also black, which has a very sombre appearance. The prices vary much on the road and the eternal confusion with the good and the bad money and its different value is enough to weary a bank clerk ; at one inn we are charged 15 k. in copper and at another in silver, which latter is nearly four times as much as the former for the same article. The people at the inns are great cheats and seeing you are foreign will always charge Münze instead of Schein if they can.[153] All the talk of the travellers is about *Stunde** and Kreutzers.

Our coachman is most amusing and reminds me constantly of the clown at a fair, he has so many antics and so odd a cry. Our companions are a count and his wife travelling to Carlsruhe. He has been a very handsome man and she seems sweet natured and compliant. He has the habit of always finding fault with whatever is set on table ; the wine is bad, the bread smelly, the inns extortionate, the meat detestable ; yet he eats eternally, drinks all the wine and jokes with the people of the inn. He is a good-natured man who loves to grumble.

Her husband, taking the journey calmly in his stride, shares her amusement at their fellow travellers.

Thursday, July 30. Left Vienna at 7 [in the] morning by one of the coaches carrying four persons (with two Horses). The Proprietor of the coach engaged to take us to Munich in seven days for 32 florins (Wiener). Our companions were a German Baron and his lady. He had been in the army and they both could speak a little French.

I could not help admiring the ingenuity with which he contrived to let us know that he had a Title. He began by complaining that they charged very dear for the passengers at Vienna ; that he had paid 10 florins for his ; he then observed that there were different prices paid by different classes of society, that the common people only paid 2 florins, the middle classes 4, the military 6, gentlemen 8 and the nobility such as Barons paid 10, which he himself paid. It was for us to divine the deduction, of course, that he was a Baron or one of the nobility. His face was a remarkable one, strikingly like that of Lavater as far as the features were concerned but the expression was a strange

*Hours, i.e., length of journey.

mixture of shrewdness, drollery and good sense. Their whole discourse about distance of places and money.

Now at last there is some popular music which strikes him as worth noting ; at the unnamed village ' where we stopped to dine, the same day we left Vienna . . .' he jots down the following :

His next entry, undated, but clearly belonging to Friday 31st, provides a more detailed account of the great Abbey of Melk than he was able to give on the outward journey.

Convent at Melk. Made my way up a mountain path by the side of a very steep precipice going down to the Danube. Granite Rock of rich colour. Found my way into the garden, well laid out ; fine piece of water on the very summit. Two priests walking tranquilly in this quiet and beautiful garden.

Very handsome church, Roman architecture, particularly rich ornamentation. Handsome organ divided on either [?] side of the window with small choir organ in front and orchestra. Tasteful and appropriate quotation from the scripture, ' Laudate Dominum cum chordis et organo, laudate, laudate ' : A kind of triumphal arch at the extreme of the building just opposite the grand entrance to the church so that as you come forth from the large doors you see a most beautiful view of the Danube with an old castle and other picturesque objects on both sides of this fine river through this grand archway which is like a magnificent frame for this fine natural Landscape.

By far the finest convent I have ever seen. Like a princely palace. Conceive Hampton Court placed upon an isolated high granite rock.

Arrived at Amstetten : No beds to be had. Went on to a curious small inn.

Saturday. $\frac{1}{2}$ past 4 left Amstetten. Beautiful road all the way to Enns, where we dined. Fine landscape, fir forest to [blank]. Passports and turned off to Little Munich [Klein-München] leaving Linz (to our great satisfaction) on our right and slept at Neubau. A very large and convenient inn. Mary found out that the daughter of the landlady was very handsome.

At Lambach—where Mary's patience gave out—he too notices the peasant women's dress, and the river scenery reminds him once more of the Wye.

Sunday, August 2. 5 o'clock left Neubau, ½ past 10 arrived at Lambach to dinner. Very picturesque place, both towards the river (like the Wye) and behind in the road towards Vienna. Houses romantically placed partly in the valley and others with tasteful little Temples by the side of the mountain and up to the very summit. Style quite Tyrolese.

Went to the Church in hopes to hear High Mass, but all the services over.

Women with frightful white Hats, black caps and *whity-brown* faces.

A harpist while they dined, and rustic dancing at Frankenmarkt, where once again they spent the night, made up for the lack of church music. Novello notes down the ' Peasants' Dance at Frankenmarkt, Sunday night, Aug. 2nd.'

Afterwards, from memory, he writes the ' Dance played on the Harp at Dinner time, Lambach, Sunday, Aug. 2.'

The next day brought them to Salzburg, with the prospect of speedier travelling.

Monday, August 3rd. As we were jogging along slowly in our [*blank*] the *eilwagen* happened to pass us and as it was coming in the direction from Vienna it struck us that the man had misinformed us relative to the number of Diligences that left Vienna, and that perhaps after all there were *two* every week. This led us to determine on making enquiries at the Bureau on our arrival at Salzburg, and it was fortunate we did so, for we found that there was a Diligence to Munich the next Morning at ½ past 5, which would enable us to arrive there on the same evening and meet another Coach to carry us on immediately.

The Bureau at Salzburg became a place of meeting and parting.

There seemed to be quite a fortunate fatality about our return to Salzburg, for on our going to the Bureau the very first person we saw in the office was Mozart's son, who was just going to set off on a little tour to the Tyrol and had arrived in the same place a few minutes before us. We of course stayed to see him safe off and shook hands with him. We ascertained from him that Mme. Sonnenburg was nearly in the same state of languor in which we had left her and that his mother was in excellent health as usual. After very cordially renewing his promise to write to me as soon as he got back to Poland we shook hands and parted.

M.N. August 3rd. Arrived at Salzburg and by a singular chance happening to ask at the *eilpost* concerning the time of arrival at Munich we encountered the young Mozart who was just setting off for the Tyrol. Spent a pleasant quarter of an hour with him. Took an affectionate leave of the Baron and his lady, our ci-devant travelling companions, who gave us a cordial invitation to visit them in Hungary and seemed very loth to part with us.

Some dried flowers and an address in someone else's handwriting, ' Baron Hornig de Hornberg a Ofen, Christina Stiedl ', pinned into the first pages of Mrs Novello's notebook, would appear to be a remembrance of these friendly acquaintances ; while, hours later, Novello jots down his last disjointed memories of this last chance meeting with Mozart's son.

Young Mozart told me that his father's Mass in F (No. 3 of my edition)*, one of his Litanies and a mass of Hummel's had lately been performed at St Peter's (where Michael Haydn is buried). Madame afterwards informed us that the musical performance at this Church was the best in Salzburg.

Mem. Mozart particularly fond of fish, especially trout. Young Mozart wears spectacles, concave, though his father had very strong and excellent sight. Young Mozart mentioned that rain was so frequent at Salzburg that it was proverbial, on a stranger's arrival to ask as the first question : ' Where is your passport? ' and the second question : ' Where is your *Umbrella*? '

The last trace of ' young Mozart ' among Novello's papers relating to this journey is found in a letter from Haslinger, dated Sept. 9th, in very curious English, conveying greetings from ' Mr Mozart, who returned yesterday from here to Lembergh ' (see Appendix IV).
    A call on Mozart's widow was, inevitably, the Novellos' next move. On their way thither they chanced to look in at the Cathedral just as a performance on the organ was being given. Novello's description of the instrument is given below (p. 307).

We then set off to visit Mozart's widow . . .
On our arrival at Madame Mozart's delightful residence we found that she had very kindly gone on a visit to inquire

*K 192.

213

after the health of Madame Sonnenburg. Her sister
(Sophie) [Haibl] however, received us in such a manner
as to convince us that her surprise in seeing us was an
agreeable one, and, while we were waiting Madame
Mozart's return, she showed us a Mass which was composed by her Husband and that she had that very day
received from Suabia, having procured a Copy of it in
order to present it to young Mozart, who wished to possess
a specimen of her Husband's musical ability and talent
as a composer.[154] From the very first cursory glance which
I had the opportunity of taking of this mass (which has
never yet been published) it seemed a skilful and musician-
like piece of counterpoint. It was in the key of C major
and was upon the model of Mozart's small masses, which
he wrote for Convents and other Establishments where the
Orchestra was on a confined scale.

> Sophie Haibl went on to give them her own account
> of Mozart's death, very much as she had already
> described it in a letter which she wrote to Nissen
> while he was engaged on his biography of Mozart,
> and of which he published an extract.[155] With such a
> sympathetic audience she rather naturally stresses her
> own role more than she did in the letter.

In the course of conversation Madame Haibl told us
that Mozart was about the same size and figure as his son,
but rather shorter. (Madame Mozart told me that both
sons are like their father, but especially the younger one).
She also told me that *Mozart had died in* HER *arms.* On the
very day that he had died he had been writing a part of
the Requiem, and had given directions to a friend (this
must have been Süssmayr) how he wished certain passages
to be filled up. He afterwards said to her, ' My dear
Sophy, I wish you to stay here with your sister tonight
for her sake, as I feel that I am dying '. She said she

17.   *The Fortress and Nonnberg*

18.   *The Nonnberg Convent*

19.   MOZART

endeavoured to the best of her power to console and encourage him, to remove this sad impression from his mind, but he repeated his conviction that he was fast sinking, and said that ' he already perceived the earthy taste of Death on his tongue '.

He also bitterly expressed his regret at leaving his wife and family so ill provided for. Madame Haibl accordingly obtained permission from her mother to remain all night with her Sister and Brother-in-law. Towards evening they sent for the Medical person who attended Mozart, but he was at the Theatre and, on receiving the message, merely said that he would come ' as soon as the opera was over '. On his arrival he ordered Madame Haibl to bathe the temples and forehead of Mozart with vinegar and cold water. She expressed her fears that the sudden cold might be injurious to the sufferer, whose arms and limbs were much inflamed and swollen. But the Doctor persisted in his orders and Madame Haibl accordingly applied a damp towel to his forehead. Mozart immediately gave a slight shudder and in a very short time afterwards he expired in her arms. At this moment the only persons in the Room were Madame Mozart, the Medical Attendant and herself.

The Room in which he died was the front one on the street on the first floor.

On my inquiring of Madame Mozart (who soon after arrived and received us with even more cordiality, if possible, than on our previous visit) how it happened that l'Abbé Stadler had only a part of the Requiem, and that the last part was in the possession of Eybler, she said that, although both the gentlemen declared they obtained the MSS. from her, yet that she was so agitated and confused at the time that she has not the least recollection of the circumstances.[156]

I was again gratified with the sight of the charming

215

portrait of Mozart by M. Lange and, on my expressing
my regret that the Painter had not preserved the form of
his hands, which I understood were particularly delicate
and beautifully shaped, she corroborated the truth of this
report and added that they were so soft and exquisitely
formed that they were more like those of a Lady.

At my request she showed me the score, in l'Abbé
Stadler's handwriting of [the] Masonic Ode by Mozart to
which l'Abbé Stadler had added the orchestral accompaniment ; and, as I related the circumstance of l'Abbé
not having preserved any copy of this score himself, she
promised she would send him one.

The discussion turned to the two great soprano arias
from *La Clemenza di Tito*, Vitellia's *Non, più di fiori* and
Sesto's *Parto, parto, ma tu ben mio*,[157] with their obbligato
parts for basset-horn and clarinet respectively, written
for the clarinettist Anton Stadler, for whom Mozart
had composed the clarinet concerto and quintet. This
conversation had a sequel nine years later, when the
Novellos, escorting Clara to Italy after her triumphs
in Vienna, called once more on Constanze von
Nissen. Mary Novello tells the story in her unpublished diary of the journey :
' Arrived at Salzburg on Thursday midday, April
12th, and being fine and sunny climbed the Nonnberg
to visit the widow of Mozart. She had left this charming abode, and was residing in town. . . . We found
her still looking cheerful and well, although she must
be nearly eighty.* On the following morning we
renewed our visit, and Clara had the pleasure of
singing for her ' Non, più di fiori ' and ' Parto '. She
was affected even to tears, doubtless with many
recollections. She said few voices had the power of
moving her thus, but that there was something in the
tone of Clara's, so sweet and heavenly. (Her husband
was the last she had heard sing it) '.

*She was 75.

V.N. The songs for Corno di Bassetto ' Non più di fiori ', ' Al desio ',[158] and Clarinet ' Parto, [parto] ma tu ben mio ', were written for an admirable Performer on those Instruments, of the name of Stadler (no relation of the Abbé), which accounts for Mozart having taken so much pains with those two obbligato parts. He was very fond of the Clarinet and Corno di Bassetto, for which latter instrument he composed several Trios on purpose for Stadler, but they are unfortunately lost, as Stadler is dead and the MSS. are nowhere to be traced.[159]

Madame Mozart was partial to some Minuets by a person named Mann, and Mozart with his usual obliging sweetness of disposition, said ' Well, as you are so fond of minuets, I will write you one ', which he accordingly did. L'Abbé Stadler was, after, so delighted with it that he added a Trio, which Madame Mozart said was a most charming one.[160] She tried to find the minuet to show me, but could not succeed. In turning over her music for that purpose she met with the score of a bass song with orchestral accompaniment which her son Wolfgang had written to oblige Mr Nissen when he got up his father's little operette ' Il Direttore della Commedia '[161] at one of their own parties and, on my mentioning the admirable Trio between the two ' Prime Donne ' and the Manager, each trying to outshine the other, Madame told me that she used to sing one of the Ladies' parts and kindly requested me to accept this very curious specimen of her son's talents. He wrote it in 1808, when he must have been not quite 18 years of age. It is scored in a very masterly manner and is full of comic humour and dramatic effect.

She also met with a Copy of the charming song ' Al desio ', which she said Mozart wrote expressly for Signora Morichelli (who was once in England) in addition to the other delightful song for Susanna in ' Figaro '.[162] The MS.

copy she showed me was the identical one from which Mozart had often accompanied her (Madame Mozart) when she used to sing it to him, and contained a little cadenza at the end in his own handwriting and which he had written on purpose for his wife and at her request.

On perceiving that I was much gratified in looking at this MS. so full of interest and associations, she was so kind as to write her own name upon it and presented it to me to keep for her sake. I need not add how much I shall prize this MS., evincing at once Mozart's skill in his musical capacity, his obliging kindness of character and his tenderness as a Husband, and, at the same time, affording me a most flattering proof of the friendly and cordial sentiments which his Widow has had the kindness to manifest in my favour. After taking our Coffee and enjoying several hours' chat with this well-bred Lady, whose conversation is peculiarly attractive, we took our leave and she promised to write something on the MSS. she had given to me, and to send them to our Inn. But, instead of sending them by her servant, she was so polite as [to] bring them herself and just as we were sitting down to our supper. Both she and her sister came to us like old friends ; placed themselves by our side at table, and paid us the compliment of partaking of our little Meal, without the least formality, and just as if they wished to convince [us] that they felt as much at home with us as at their own house.

After supper I had the gratification of seeing Mozart's widow and her sister safe home ; they had brought their servant with them, to save my doing so, and would have persuaded me that there was not the least necessity for my accompanying them home, but (as I told her) it was not every evening that I could enjoy the society of so rare a Companion as one who had been the companion of

Mozart, and she politely gave up the little friendly contest and at once took my arm as cordially as if I had been her own brother.

As the road to her house lay through the gate leading to the nunnery which I before mentioned, and the entrance to which is closed early every night, we were obliged to call up the Portress, who let us pass and received Madame Mozart's directions to wait my return and allow me to pass again.

There was a beautiful moon shining on the distant mountains and illuminating both the old Gothic Church of the Convent and the ancient Fortress above. The interesting conversation that took place, and the enchanting beauty of the surrounding scenery, rendered this one of the most romantic and delightful walks I have ever enjoyed.

On our arrival at the house I was at last obliged to take my leave, when Madame Mozart once more shook hands with me most cordially and assured me, after renewing her promise to write to me in the course of a very short time, that our visit to Salzburg had been one of the most gratifying compliments that had been paid for several years, both to herself and to the memory of ' her Mozart '.

I need not say what a crowd of interesting associations, curious thoughts and singular reflections passed through my mind in the course of my solitary walk back to my Inn.

This second visit to Salzburg has been even more gratifying to me than the former one.[163]

Now comes the only bit of real gossip in the whole diary, if gossip it can be called, for it appears rather as the expression of a mother's very natural anxiety, called forth by the confidence Vincent Novello's manner and personality had awakened in her, so that after so short an acquaintance she was moved, that evening, to treat him indeed like a brother.

(*Private*) Young Mozart's mistress in Poland is a countess who is, unfortunately, married to a man she does not esteem. He is so much attached to her that his mother feared he would never leave Poland for any length of time without her and as he cannot take her with him on account of the husband Madame Mozart begins to despair of his ever establishing himself in Vienna or other large capital where his parts might be better known and appreciated.

The more anecdotal Mary Novello says nothing at all about this liaison, but she was not of the party on the evening walk and, as likely as not, her husband did not consider himself authorized to speak, even to his Mary, of what had been confided to him. It is probable that sister Sophie and the servant walked either before or behind them as they discoursed quietly, arm in arm, along their moonlit way.

In fact, Mary Novello gives only a brief summary of their second encounter:

In the evening visited La Mozart. The sister who received us at first told us that the son is a little taller than his father but much like him in face, though the forehead resembles the mother. Mozart died in this sister's arms, and lamented bitterly his approaching death on account of the poverty he would leave his wife in ; he requested Sophie to stay with him all night saying he was sure he should die. ' No, no, she said, you will not die '—' Yes he said I feel the taste of death on my tongue '—yet this day he called for the Requiem and dictated to Süssmayr what should be done.

Madame entered and was more friendly than ever. She has given some music to Vin and Madame Sonnenburg the engraving of her brother, which she had so many years by her bedside, so he is quite happy.

Her husband has given a fuller account of how the engraving came into his possession :

In the course of the day I had contrived to inquire about the health of Madame Sonnenburg and was glad to hear that she was not worse ; but, as I found on entering her Room that she was in a calm sleep, I would not disturb her, but promised to call again in the evening, which we accordingly did. I then met with the gentleman, who spoke French, and who had before behaved with so much politeness.* He mentioned the great pleasure she had repeatedly expressed at the little testimony I had brought her from England of the affection and respect entertained there for her Brother's memory, and was very sure that I should feel much gratified in possessing a signed page of music, or any other little souvenir, to keep for her and her Brother's sakes. She was so kind as to present me with the portrait of Mozart that had been in her own possession for many years, in the original frame, just as it had been hung up so long over her sofa, in her own drawing room. I shall of course preserve this with great care and venera- tion as I feel convinced that as long as she enjoyed the bliss of sight this very portrait must have been one of the objects that she must daily have wished to gaze upon.

The engraving in question is of the Posch portrait which is repeatedly mentioned as being one of the best likenesses, and is reproduced opposite page 215. Mary Cowden Clarke has written on the back ' This, in its simple brown frame, was presented by Mozart's son to Vincent Novello ' and makes the same assertion in *Life and Labours*, but from the above account she is clearly in error.

They had now seen the last of the Mozart family,

* Joseph Metzger. See p. 89 and Appendix IV.

for they were due to start at half past five the next morning, Tuesday, August 4th, on the last phase of their journey.

Salzburg to Paris.   August 4-10

Of the next day's travel all we know is that according to Vincent Novello they

Arrived at Munich at $\frac{1}{2}$ past 10 night, Golden Cock. Left next morning after leaving a note of thanks to Mr Schreifel[164]—at 6 for Augsburg, thence to Ulm and Stuttgart.

By contrast, the next two days were to present to them, within the four walls of their stage coach, a cross-section of European political and social history :

M.N.   Our journey from Munich to Stuttgart was performed in company with the physician, the confessor, the treasurer and another young man, belonging to the suite of the young Empress, daughter of Eugene Beauharnais, and married to Peter of the Brazils. They were very pleasant companions and made themselves extremely merry at the expense of the confessor, who was a raw rustic and knew no other tongue than his own. The first *gaucherie* that he committed was to leave his passport behind him, consequently he was forced to run about a mile in the pouring rain to fetch it, and take Extra Post to follow us. The doctor asked him if he had said his Office, and he produced a French romance, which proved to be a very loose composition ; someone had hoaxed him with it. In short the laugh was eternally against him and we spent two pleasant laughing days and were then forced to part.

Prince Eugene Beauharnais, the Empress Josephine's son by her first husband, ex-Viceroy of Napoleon's

Kingdom of Italy and much-prized commander of his Italian army, had died five years previously in Bavaria, the country of his wife Princess Augusta Amelia, where he had settled as Prince of Leuchten- berg after his stepfather's downfall. In 1829 their daughter Amelia had just become the second wife of Don Pedro I, of the Portuguese House of Braganza, Emperor of Brazil.

The poor ' confessor ' was probably not the spiritual director of the young Royal bride, but merely her domestic chaplain. As such, in the great continental households of that time, he would rank not much higher than an upper retainer—apart from the respect due to his cloth.

Vincent Novello fills in the picture.

Pleasant Companions in Diligence : Dr. Casanova, medical Attendant to the Prince of [Leuchtenberg],[165] a Pomeranian who was Treasurer to the young Empress, the Confessor to ditto (droll anecdotes of his simplicity and *gaucherie*, enquiries respecting the precautions against Cold in Brazil, loss of Passport, extra-Post, etc.), and sharp intelligent youth, under-Secretary—all going to Rio [de] Janeiro in the suite of the Empress.

Casanova attended *Catalani* twice in Munich—also, Mme. Fodor and Pasta. Catalani fond of [*illegible*][166]. Prince Eugene Beauharnais died in his arms. All spoke affectionately of this Prince (our former companion, bright Frenchman, who had taken some Horses, etc. from him, spoke in the same favourable manner).[167] Superior, quite a gentleman ; he had been in the Army and had been taken prisoner and sent to Malta ; well treated by the English, knew General Stuart and Sir S[idney] Smith.[168]

Spoke bitterly of the degraded state of Italy, his native country (he was born at Bologna) which he attributed to the injudicious manner in which the Papal government

223

was conducted, and which he said was only adapted for the fourteenth century.

Contempt for Clergy prevalent throughout the better instructed classes in every place in Germany that we have hitherto visited ; in the Churches only females and no respectable looking people.

They left us at Stuttgart to go on to Frankfurt on the way to Ostend, where they were joining the Empress on board the frigate fitted out to take them to the Brazils.

It is clear that the physician was one of those Italians for whom the Napoleonic era, in which they had taken an active part, although it represented yet another foreign domination, had awakened national dreams, ambitions and hopes, with the creation of a Kingdom of Italy and the adoption of a national flag, the red, white and green tricolour of Napoleon's Italian Army ; men who were now suffering bitter disappointment and a sense of degradation under the reactionary governments and the strengthening of Austrian power and oppression all over the peninsula. From among such men arose many of the early patriots and martyrs of the Risorgimento.[169]

Vincent Novello's remarks also throw light on the anticlericalism of the epoch—a phenomenon at once political and intellectual, but not invariably the equivalent of agnosticism or incompatible with the practice of religion.

V.N. Thursday, August 6th. Arrived at Stuttgart at 4 in afternoon and left again at 6 for Carlsruhe where we arrived at 4 the next morning. Well behaved Frenchman and boy like a little premature man.

Apathy and indifference of the people at the Bureau of Diligence. Frenchman nearly lost his Portmanteau in consequence of their being too indolent to look for it, although it was in the Carriage all the time. Horridly uncomfortable German beds.

Carlsruhe, like Mannheim, is an example of eighteenth-century town planning. The Pyramid mentioned by Novello marks the grave of the Margrave Carl Wilhelm of Baden-Durlach, to whose choice of its the place for his residence, in 1715, the town owes origin and its name.

Carlsruhe well built, regular and handsome Town ; fine Palace, Pyramid, Fountain, Town hall and Gate in succession. Excellent road with fruit Trees and well cultivated grounds on either side between Carlsruhe and Rastadt. On the skirts of a range of mountains to the left, inside which is situated Baden, which seems to be a very favourite place of resort for the purpose of taking mineral waters.

Everybody talking of the marriage of the young Empress with Don Pedro.

Not at all strict about Passports or luggage. Old Frenchman with singular high and droll voice. Good subject for Matthews.[170]

Friday, August 7th. Left Carlsruhe at 6, arrived at Rastadt at 9.

They had now crossed the French frontier, and arrived at Strasburg that afternoon, where we find them in the Cathedral hearing Vespers:

V.N. . . . Strasburg Friday Vespers August 7th ½ past 4 o'clock. . . . No last voluntary on organ, which I was the less sorry for, as I was sure the performer would only have spoilt any movement of the dignified class which he might have attempted.

Fine Painted Glass windows to the great Nave and Aisles, but not to transept or Choir and High Altar. Beautiful circular or Catherine-wheel window at West End.[171] Only *one* Tower like all over Germany.

The exterior of the West Entrance is one of the finest I ever saw. The tower is of the most beautiful proportions and exquisitely light, the design of the entrance façade is somewhat similar to that of Cologne but upon a smaller scale, and the whole is in an extraordinarily good state of preservation.

The sides (like so many other fine Cathedrals on the Continent) are disfigured by shops being thrust against the building, but they are here less offensive as they are constructed in the Gothic style of architecture corresponding with the Cathedral itself. I should much like to hear a funeral service performed in this noble church at midnight and I quite regret not having the opportunity of seeing the beautiful West front by moonlight, when I am certain the effect must be solemn and sublime beyond description.

The only part of the Tower I could wish altered is the pyramidical division of the summit. The ornaments which surround it are not sufficiently varied in their shape, and its height is not in proportion to the other divisions or stages of the tower ; had the pyramid partaken more of the character of a *spire*, and had been carried to double its present height, it appears to me its symmetrical elegance and graceful form would have been absolutely perfect.

M.N. The Cathedral at Strasburg pleases me much more than any other I have seen abroad. It is in fine preservation, even the ornamental part and if the other tower were complete would be perfect. The interior is very grand and many fine stained windows. The appearance of the people is also much changed, more French and more civil.

V.N. Notwithstanding we had travelled the whole way from Vienna with scarcely any intermission, yet as we found (through the information of a very intelligent youth who was one of the commissionaires belonging to the Bureau de Poste) that there was a courier going off that very evening who would travel night and day so as to arrive in Paris in 48 hours after leaving Strasburg, we determined on making the journey with him and secured our places accordingly.

So they set off across that territory which, in the memory of their descendants, was three times to see the advance of German armies:

V.N. Friday, August 7th. Left Strasburg at 11 o'clock at night by the mail for Paris, by way of Metz (which is the shorter road by two posts than the one by Nancy). It is a large kind of Post Chaise calculated to hold three Persons, and the Courier sits outside in a kind of small Cabriolet. The Mail Bags are placed in a recess behind and whole is drawn by four Horses at a very rapid pace. Fortunately the third place was not taken, so that we had the whole inside to ourselves, and travelled quite as comfortably as if we had taken a chariot and four Horses.

In the inside is placed a List of the Places where the Courier is allowed to stop, with other explanations relative to the Rules to be observed on the journey and the address of the official Gentleman to whom the Passengers may apply in case they have any complaint to make against the conduct of the courier or any delay that may take place in providing the relays of Horses. The whole establishment appears to be under the most excellent regulations and I would advise all Travellers who are prepared for this to choose this mode of conveyance in preference to the Diligence or any other kind of carriage. The increased expense is also but trifling in proportion to the additional advantage and convenience derived from its superior speed: by the Diligence, which does not arrive at Paris till the fourth day after its departure from Strasburg, each passenger has to pay for the best places 80 fr. and by the Mail 93 (only 13 fr. more) he can get to Paris in a couple of days, or about 50 hours). In case he should go by the Diligence I have heard several Travellers say that those belonging to the establishment of Lafitte are the best.

At Strasburg our Passports were taken from us and sent off to Paris. A temporary Passport was given us in exchange, but for this a demand of 2 fr. was made. This appeared to be a mere excuse or pretext to extract money from Travellers and is a piece of paltry meanness totally unworthy of any government pretending to be conducted upon liberal practices ; for either the Passports are good or bad. If bad, Mr Novello should not be allowed to proceed because he has merely paid a couple of francs to a police officer ; if good he ought to pass on freely without being molested or forced to pay for another passport which would in that case be quite unnecessary.

In all points of view it is a contemptible and mean imposition.

The Road from Strasburg to Metz is rather flat. On either side the Country is well cultivated and the general features are agreeable, but there is nothing striking or picturesque. The most remarkable change is in the costumes of the Peasantry and in the sudden alteration of the language. After merely passing from one side of the Rhine to the other I have heard scarcely a single word of German spoken.

The manners of the people, those especially of the lower classes, is more civil and well-bred than what I have met with amongst the same classes in Germany. There is the same compliment paid here to the honesty of the people as on the other side of the Rhine, viz., the leaving all the

Fruit Trees and gardens quite close to each side of the road without the least protection.

Arrived at Metz at 2 o'clock (about a third of our journey). Cathedral attended Vespers at 3 o'clock. The building is not of the larger class, but is a good specimen of the Gothic style, with a handsome Tower on the *side* of the Church like St Stephen at Vienna. West entrance bad taste—*Grecian*. Very poor instrument, harsh squally tone, noise and no weight [*illegible*], like a street organ out of tune, and worse player. He was of that abominable class who play *polaccas* on the Organ. He frightened me out of the church completely. I could not stay the service out. (See Shakespeare's Henry IV, Hotspur I think, he misused poor [?] so abominably.[172])

Left Metz (very strongly fortified) at 4 o'clock in the afternoon, and travelled all night. The country was rather flat and uninteresting, but we had most delightful weather and the most beautiful moonlight. Our companion from Metz was a French Countess, who proved to be a very chatty, agreeable and well informed woman. Her husband had been in the army and they had both suffered severely during the struggles that had succeeded the Revolution.

Her father had a narrow escape from being guillotined during the time of Robespierre, whose very name seemed to excite in her mind the most horrible associations and painful recollections. She recounted to us several very interesting anecdotes relative to this extraordinary period of excitement ; and amongst others she said that on one occasion the enemy had obtained possession of the town where she resided with her family ; that they were obliged to escape at a moment's warning, abandoning the whole of their property to the mercy of the enemy, and as the town was given up to pillage by the soldiers they remained for the whole day in uncertainty whether on their return they should not find their house stripped of all it contained and their home utterly destroyed.

> To the survivors of two world wars her experiences seem almost tame, since the worst had fortunately not happened, after all, either to the lady's father or to her home.

Sunday morning, August 9th. Attended High Mass at the Cathedral or principal Church at Châlons. This is a very ancient and venerable Pile, partaking both of the Saxon and Gothic styles of architecture ; it is one of the first instances in which both the Towers are complete, and these are placed at the Eastern end of the church. It is, however, disfigured by the same blemish as that which I noticed at Metz, the entrance at the West End has been restored in the *Grecian* style instead of that which would have corresponded with the rest of the building. It is quite unaccountable to me how any architect can be so utterly devoid of taste as to mix together two such incongruous styles as the Grecian and the Gothic. There are a few stained glass windows remaining in this Cathedral, but of no great beauty either as to design or richness of colour. The best of them is the circular one over the Door of the North transept. Amongst the Paintings which adorn the side aisles I noticed in the Chapel of St Stephen a very good copy of Raphael's ' St Michael overcoming the Dragon ', the original of which I recollect seeing many years since in the Collection of Mr Hope of Duchess Street, Portland Place.[173]

The High Altar here is partly an Imitation of the ' Altare Maggiore ' of bronze in St Peter's at Rome, which, if I recollect well, is from a design by Bernini. . . . The great Bell of this Church is a remarkably fine-toned one, and much better in tune than most of those I have heard

20.   STRASBURG

10 o'clk. High Mass St Anne's Church

As I was informed by Eybler that there were to be a Mass by Eybler (N° 4 in C) performed here on occasion of its being the Festival of St Anne. I made a point of being present — as I was anxious to hear something by a Composer whom my friend Mr Latrobe esteems so highly

But no sooner had they begun the Kyrie than I recognised it to be Haydn's first Mass in Bb (N° 6 my 2d Set)

Fresh Kyrie too harsh

Gradual — Dtt for Tenor & Bass.

Jubi-la-te Deo

'like Cimarosa' style — it is a little too theatrical but charmingly scored

It was excellently sung especially by the Bass — who had the better voice of the two —

Responses for the surge — same as at the Cathedral

The Organ is noisy & harsh — the soft stops were not once used, so that I cd not judge of them

There was a very tawdry figure of St Anne with a face like a moor — dressed up for the occasion, & seemed to attract much attention from the 'Congregation' which was equally composed almost entirely of Females

The Church is in the Roman Style not of the large Class of the gingerbread work seemed rather the worse for wear 3 Chapels on each side — but no aisles.

Credo too fast — hurried unsteady effect
"Et incarnatus agt" in Bb minor the most charming movt in the Mass — it shd have been sung with more delicacy of style — & the Sti 3 voices more subdued. 1st Viol. & D. Bass the best performers

This altogether the most sterling Church Music I have yet heard performed in Germany.

probably by
Naumann

Offertorium

Lauda Si — on Sal-va-torem

on the Continent. The quality of its tone very weighty, solemn and cathedral-like, and it has the same smooth roll *after* the blow has been struck, that I so much admire in the Tenor Bell at Bow Church and at Canterbury Cathedral, and which last fine Bells have all the roundness, softness and breathing depth of a fine double diapason pipe.[174]

We arrived at Châlons sur Marne as early as 5 o'clock, but the courier said we should not depart till 12 o'clock. I could not make out the reason for thus losing about 6 hours to no purpose after having hurried on at such a rapid pace all the preceding night. This instance I must own, forms an exception to the judicious regulations which I have already praised as distinguishing the arrangements connected with the Courier's general mode of travelling.

There are several very pleasant promenades about Châlons, with more trees and of a larger size than what are usually met with in French towns. The walk leading to the Cathedral from the south is particularly agreeable. Nearly the whole way is under the shade of ' melancholy boughs ' and in one part the scenery reminds me of [the] fine avenue in Bushy Park leading from Kingston towards the Palace at Hampton Court, where there is a picturesque fountain placed in the midst of a sheet of water, and appropriately surmounted by a tasteful statue of Diana.

Vincent Novello makes no more notes between now and their arrival in Paris the following morning. His wife has summed up the whole 48-hours journey from Strasburg with :

. . . Booked by the courier to Paris. Our journey to Paris was very rapid and pretty comfortable, assisted by a delicious bottle of champagne.

231

18

facing : PLATE 21
A PAGE OF VINCENT
NOVELLO'S DIARY

Paris, August 10-17

They finally arrived at Paris in the small hours of Monday, August 10, and began their round of visits almost at once.

V.N. We arrived at Paris at 4 in the morning. Specimen of honesty ; coachman found 15 sous, required 60 (or 3 francs) and then wanted to return additional change.

Hotel de France près du Louvre. 3 francs a day for our room.

M. Fétis not at home. Conservatoire. Miss Oury. Mrs Humann. Passed the evening with her.

This last was the English wife of M. Charles Humann and a school-fellow of Mary Novello's. It was M. Humann who came to rescue the terrified little Clara from her boarding establishment during the July Revolution of 1830. Four years afterwards, when Clara was with her mother in Paris, the Humanns had to perform the terrible task of breaking to Mrs Novello the news of her son Edward's death.

Miss Oury was probably a sister or other relative of the violinist Antonio James Oury, who had made his London début the previous year. He had also played at the first Philharmonic concert of the season.

Their visit to the Conservatoire had resulted in an invitation for next day.

V.N. Tuesday [11th] Palais Royal, Garden of Tuileries. Early breakfast *à la fourchette.* Imposition, more than 3 francs each.

Violin playing at Conservatoire began at 9. 11 players. Heard five who all played Viotti Concerto in 4 sharps.

232

[They played] the slow movement in A and a duet in D at first sight, accompanied by four Violins, two Tenors [i.e. Violas], two Violoncellos and a Double Bass. Very fair playing but nothing of very superior genius ; mechanically correct but deficient in feeling. Best players Mr Bonnai and a young lad. List of prizes fixed up at the gate.

Cherubini presided in the Committee Box ; made notes during and after every performance. Fine head with long hair and long, grave and intelligent face, but careworn as if he was not happy. Reminded me of the bust of Homer in Townley marbles. Ella came to our box. Pupil of Fémy, Fétis for counterpoint.

They were evidently in the pretty little theatre which was a feature of the Conservatoire. John Ella, the young violinist and critic who came to their box to pay his respects, had been on his way to Italy, but broke his journey in Paris, heard *William Tell*, and was so captivated that he stayed on for five months. He was well known to Novello, as he had been playing since 1822 in the King's Theatre and Philharmonic orchestras, and perhaps it was he who persuaded Novello to sample *William Tell* the next evening. He had studied the violin with François Fémy, a pupil of Baillot, and had taken lessons from Fétis in counterpoint and composition in 1827. Later, as founder of the Musical Union and organizer of its Tuesday afternoon chamber concerts, he was to introduce analytical programme notes to London audiences.[175]

Their subsequent tour of the city is related by Novello somewhat in the manner of Mr Alfred Jingle.

Omnibus (see List) to Bastille (notice Elephant)—to Jardin des Plantes ; wolves, hyenas, *ours terrible*, eagles, white-headed Vultures, macaw [?], monkeys (horrid disgusting animals), bears (Child killed by one), giraffe, not tall enough to reach the trees. Two elephants very interesting and sagacious ; floundered all over and washed himself at his keeper's bidding ; Put his head repeatedly in his mouth. Opened the gate himself and retired. Returned by the Monnoie in Omnibus (would much envy our fortune in London).

Mary Novello's summing up of her impression of France and of Paris, was written, apparently, on the Tuesday evening :

The more I know of the French people the more I feel their excessive shrewdness and tact. Their country is neither very fruitful or picturesque, the wheat and the bread are much inferior to the German, but they have bragged so much of their own perfection in every respect, that they not only believe the truth of their fanfarronades but two-thirds of Europe give them credit for the most accomplished people and enviable country in the whole world. Their manner and civility is certainly most winning, and the intelligence of the women's eyes and their fluency in general subjects of conversation, is more attractive than beauty.

Paris I find much improved, many of the nuisances round the Palais Royal are abolished. He[176] has dismissed the Filles de Joie that dwelt there and if any one accosts a man the police take her in custody. No woman need be afraid of walking in the streets alone, even at a late hour ; but let no unguarded wight think that the Parisian trades-people ask the lowest price for their goods ; they abate greatly, although they assure you they lose.

Two things I wish we could accomplish in London ; namely the multitude of baths at a franc and 15d. each, and the long coaches, called omnibus, which take you continually from one end of the city to the other for two-pence halfpenny each person.

234

Mary Novello's wish had already been granted in her absence. Already in April 1829 George Shillibeer had informed the Board of Stamps that he was ' engaged in building 2 Vehicles after the manner of the recently established French *Omnibus* ', and on July 4th *Saunders' Newsletter* had announced : ' The new vehicle called the omnibus commenced running this morning from Paddington to the City '.

The Jardin des Plantes amused us much for two hours ; we might spend many weeks but the animals today saved us [*sic*]. There is a fine giraffe elevating his skeleton form to the height of the enclosure and two fine elephants, the one as large as poor Ch . . . [?] was very obedient, took small pieces from the people of bread or fruit and at the word of command bathed himself, floundering about like a huge mammoth, with many other tricks. The zebra, the camel, hyena [?], several horrid monkeys, fierce wolves and great bears ; some of the latter play several tricks for the amusement of the people such as sitting on their haunches and catching crumbs like a dog, climbing a pole, etc.

I wished much for Ned to have seen them.

In 1829 the London Zoo was only six years old, and did not possess a giraffe till 1836.

If the young Edward had been present he would doubtless have left behind him an amusing collection of sketches of wild beasts as a companion piece to the copious illustrations, in pencil or colours, of tales or poems, which he was constantly making while listening to the readings aloud which, then and later, were a regular feature of Novello family life.

We heard a trial of skill upon the violin this morning and many of them played well, but it being all the same piece and 11 candidates we could not remain more than two hours.

I was not more pleased, dear Charles, with the garden of the Tuileries than I was before ; it is pretty and formal, only it wants trees and shade and ' places that deep passion loves ' (you must correct my quotation for I think it is not to the letter).[177]

The façade of the Louvre is extremely beautiful but the Parisians, I believe, prefer the Bourse, perhaps because it is new. We were assured it was the most beautiful thing in the world, but it wants height and relief, it is too monotonous. The additions to the Palais Royal are really beautiful ; when finished the steps and the gallery will surpass the old part by far.

> This is Mrs Novello's last diary entry, though she was in Paris for three days longer. While she was writing, her husband seems to have been immersed in the Paris papers and periodicals :

Good letter relating to the Bibliotheque Royale in the Gazette de Litterature of dimanche 9 aout published rue Champs d'Auteuil No. 20 and a critique on Rossini's ' Guillaume Tell '. Mistaken in saying that violoncellos are expressive of church music. (See Mr Fétis' opinion in *Revue Musicale*).

Another letter relating to Jesuites in ' Figaro ' of the date of mardi 11 August.

Théâtre Français in the evening to see ' L'Ecole des Vieillards ' by Casimir de la Vigne. . . .

Theatre something like Covent Garden. Ornaments rather formal and overgilt. Quiet way of entering the theatre ; no crowding, more like a procession.

Music between the acts ; Haydn's symphonies, about the same degree of talent as our own good theatres. Basses weak and ineffective.

Samson very like Emery. Lafon and Grandville both good actors but Madame Mars (who seems to be the idol of the Parisians) is the best performer I ever saw. She speaks a little mincingly with her teeth shut occasionally, but very natural in several passages. Voice like Mrs Fitzwilliam's but in manner more ladylike. Plot like School for Scandal and Lord and Lady Townly—well-written comedy.[178]

Pleasant after-piece in one act, written by a lady : ' Les suites d'un bal masqué '. Michelot sprightly and lively actor, like our Jones. Mars played in both pieces but first character best. Like to see her in ' Valérie '.

Here Novello, the devoted London playgoer, was exercising his critical faculties on no less a person than the great Mademoiselle Mars (Anne Boutet) who had made her début at 13 and retired from the stage in 1841 in her sixty-third year. Thus at this time she was about 50. Samson, his master Lafon, Michelot and Grandville were all well-known comedians of the ' Français '.

The ' pleasant after-piece ' was a one-act comedy in prose by Mme de Bawr, *née* Sophie Coury de Champgrand (1778-1860). It was acted first in 1813 and remained in vogue for more than 30 years.

Valérie, by Eugene Scribe in collaboration with Mélesville, had been produced at the Theatre Royal, Haymarket, in 1828, under the title of *Valeria*. Mars played the title role in this piece, but only in 1832.

Wednesday, August 12th

Alfred's birthday. A most pleasant collection of 24 hours. Driven to the best part of Paris. New buildings near Place de Louis 16. Column to ditto. Champs Elysées : handome buildings, style of Louvre. Columns and recesses behind, like all French houses. Good amusements for Public, Cafés, etc., Roundabouts, no mistaken pride— public Road.

Père La Chaise, most tasteful specimen of French good sense. No gloom, but flowers, tender remembrance, charming architecture. Tomb of General Foy. Abélard et Héloise. Haydon Drawing of ditto.[179] Fine view of Paris.

An instance in which London might take an excellent hint from Paris.

Coach back to Mr Fétis (they all charge for ' a course ' $1\frac{1}{2}$ fr.), where we had the great gratification of hearing that he had seen the Duke of Rochefoucauld and that he had given his consent to place our Clara at M. Choron's establishment where she would learn music theory, French and other necessary [*illegible*] of education, free of all expense.

> Ambroise Polycarpe, Vicomte de la Rochefoucauld, Duc de Doudeauville, was the head of one of the three branches of the family and Minister of the King's Household since 1824 ; as such he was responsible for the subsidy paid from the King's privy purse to Choron's Institution. His son, Vicomte Sosthène de la Rochefoucauld, was Minister of Fine Arts, and as such had, in 1826, contrived Rossini's appointment as Composer to His Majesty and Inspector General of Singing in all the Royal Musical Establishments. It is not clear which of the two would have had the deciding voice in the admission of candidates to Choron's Institution ; Novello speaks sometimes of ' the Duke ', sometimes of ' the Viscount '.

M. Fétis had also spoken to his friend the Italian singing master Bandinelli, who had promised to give Clara lessons as soon as she was sufficiently educated to receive them.

There were only three vacancies at M. Choron's, for two of which there was to be a contest between the candidates, but as M. Fétis was so kind as to take the responsibility upon himself of her being a girl of promising musical talent, the Duke gave his consent at once. This is a most important circumstance both in our own favour and of our little Girl, who is thus provided for for two or three years in a most desirable and advantageous manner.

M. Fétis promised to introduce Mary and myself to M. Choron on the very next morning, and said he would likewise present me to the Duke of Rochefoucauld before I left Paris.

On our return home from M. Fétis we accidentally met in the Rue Vivienne our pleasant friend Th. Miller, of Bath, who is on a visit to Paris and is studying Italian singing under Signor Bandinelli, the very gentleman who has so kindly promised to assist little Clara, and who ranks as one of the first masters in Paris.

We had a very agreeable half-hour's chat with him, and he agreed to meet us at the Opera in the evening, when Rossini's new opera of ' William Tell ' was to be performed.

We took our station at the end of the queue . . .

The two and a half empty pages which follow this unfinished sentence are the most tantalising things in the Diary.

Thursday, August 13th. At 10 went to Louvre; refused admission without passports ; second time I have been disappointed here. Unnecessary difficulties.

It is hard for us, to whom such difficulties are everyday occurrences, to remember that in the vanished—and now almost legendary—epoch of security and prosperity before the first World War, passports had entirely disappeared except in Tsarist Russia, and movement from one country to another was completely unrestricted.

Voltaire's house corner of Quai Voltaire and rue de Beaune left hand corner turning out of Quai. The house is being newly repaired and is no longer so interesting as if it had been left in the exact state it was when he died.

Alexandre Choron (1771-1834), whom the Novellos were to meet the next day, was, like Fétis and Novello himself, not only a scholar but an active pioneer in the revival and performance of the great music of the past. His projected *Collection générale des oeuvres classiques de musique*, ranging from Josquin des Près to Jommelli, had failed, after a few issues, for lack of subscribers ; but when, in 1817, he founded his ' Conservatoire de Musique Classique et Religieuse ' to train choristers for church and opera-house, he began to give historical concerts, of which Fétis wrote : ' There, for the first time in Paris, were heard the sublime compositions of Bach, Handel and Palestrina . . .[180] In 1825 the school was subsidized and became the ' Institution Royale de Musique Religieuse '. The withdrawal of the subsidy by King Louis Philippe after the Revolution of 1830 killed the Institution, and was a blow from which Choron himself never recovered.

Paris, Friday. For every pleasure I find there must be some counterbalance of pain. Yesterday was a day of most satisfactory agreeable anticipation for our little Girl, but today there seemed to be some kind of obstacles or difficulties arising to her success.

M. Fétis called according to his promise soon after 12 and we proceeded together in a Fiacre to M. Choron, who lives on the Luxembourg side of the river, No. 62 rue de Vaugirard. He is an uncommonly quick and sharp person, remarkably bright and penetrating eyes. His face is very like that of Mr Bannister, the celebrated comedian[181] but rather thinner. He is nearly bald and what little hair he has left is turning grey. He speaks so very rapidly that [it] is scarcely possible to follow him and though the general expression of his countenance is rather careworn, yet his smile is a very pleasant one. I was very much flattered by his showing me, so soon after I had entered into conversation with him, a copy of my first collection of sacred music inscribed to Monsignor Fryer and [he] was so polite as to express a wish to have the whole of the works which I had published of the same description. On M. Fétis explaining that the Viscount de Rochefoucauld had presented our little Clara with one of the nominations vacant, he seemed to be of opinion that it would occasion some little disarrangement of what was intended ; but on M. Fétis assuring him that our little girl possessed great musical talent he said that although the trial for admission between the candidates was to take place that very day, he would defer sending in his report until our child arrived, when in order that everything should be done according to the regulation of the establishment he would have another trial between the candidates, that he might hear Clara go through the same exercises as the other young ladies who were desirous of being admitted.

On M. Fétis expressing a wish to hear the trial, M. Choron consented and invited us also to be present with the rest of the audience.

In the meantime while they were preparing for the exercise we paid a visit to the lady, Madame Bardieu [Tardieu] who has the care of the children amongst whom Clara is to be placed.[182] Her house is very near to that of M. Choron and seems to [be] fitted up very judiciously with a view to the comfort and accommodation [of] the young ladies under her charge. Madame B. received us politely and after M. Fétis had explained the nature of our visit she frankly told us that one of the three places had already been promised to a young girl who had been left by the parents with her under that impression. There seemed to be something like a misunderstanding between

241

this lady and M. Choron, but as these are matters with which I have nothing to do, I of course took no further notice of the subject.

She gave Mary every explanation relating the mode she followed in conducting the establishment, and showed the various schoolrooms, sleeping apartments, etc., mentioned also that those who were admitted not only had instruction from masters in all useful branches of education (in addition to their musical studies) but that after the first [*blank*] was made we should not have anything to pay even for clothes. Altogether Madame B. appears to be an intelligent, shrewd, well-bred lady who has seen a good deal of the world, and I own I shall have perfect confidence in her kind care of our child in case we should be so fortunate as to succeed in placing her in the establishment. But this, it now appears, is not so easy a matter as what we had at first anticipated. From what M. Fétis said, it became necessary to have Clara on the spot as soon as possible and Mary accordingly decided on immediately going off to Boulogne to fetch Clara herself without delay. As no conveyance could be had this evening, she took her place by Lafitte's diligence tomorrow morning at $\frac{1}{2}$ past 11 (40 fr. by the interior and 5 fr. to the conductor).

On leaving Madame B. we went to hear the trial of skill between the candidates for admission, of whom there were eight. M. Choron, not wishing to take the responsibility of the decision upon himself, and in order to prevent the least suspicion that he was in any way swayed by partiality for one candidate more than another, requested that some eminent professor might be appointed to give his opinion instead of himself, and the person chosen to preside on this occasion was Rossini. M. Fétis, also, and some other professional gentlemen of Paris who happened to be present, were requested to favour him with their opinions likewise, and they accordingly took their seats at a table opposite the Piano Forte, where the candidates had to exhibit, and were furnished with a list of the young ladies' names and pen and ink to make such observations on their respective talents as might occur to them during the performance.

Each candidate sang the diatonic scale ascending ; then the first number of Danzi's Solfeggi, and lastly a song from Piccini's ' Didone '. Very few were able to rise beyond A above the staff, and that not without difficulty and rather forcing this.

As Clara's compass already extended to D *in alt*, this last remark is clearly tinged with a certain complacency.

Novello then notes down Cherubini's address (' Cherubini lives No. 19 Rue du Faubourg Poissonnière—same street as Conservatoire ')—doubtless with the intention of calling upon him, though there is no record of his having done so—and the addresses of two music-sellers from whom he hopes to procure copies of Cherubini's masses. He also makes a note of Rossini's address, ' No. 20 Boulevard des Italiens ', whither, a few days later, he and his wife were to take Clara to sing to Rossini in person. But first Clara had to be fetched from Boulogne, and accordingly, Mary Novello set off early the next morning, Saturday 15th. As she journeyed she scribbled some memoranda inside the back cover of her notebook, such as :

Clara to put on chitons[183] when she comes to Paris, and *trowsers*.

Mozart Masses for Clara . . . Ditto a sketch for Vin if I can.

Clara not to be left alone when coming to Paris.

Meanwhile her husband was left to his own devices, and in a mood doubtless tinged with anxiety regarding

Clara's ultimate fate. The day of his wife's departure, being the Feast of the Assumption, at least afforded him the opportunity of hearing some church music.

Saturday [15]. High Mass at Notre Dame. Assumption of Virgin. Mass in B flat with a small orchestra . . . A very disagreeable hard and loud voice amongst the counter Tenors: it predominated over all the rest and *soured* every piece in which it was heard. . . .
Poor service altogether for the Cathedral of Paris which calls itself the capital of Europe.
½ past 1 attended Vespers at S. Étienne near Sainte Geneviève. The most singular original looking church I ever was in. It seems to be patched together at different times and by various architects who had different designs in their heads. The effect is rather picturesque than otherwise.

There is no record of how he passed his lonely time on Sunday, August 16th, for he makes no entry under that date. But the next entries, undated, show him attending Vespers at the Sorbonne and at St Sulpice, both, like St Étienne, on the Left Bank, which he could have done either immediately after leaving St Étienne on the Saturday, or on the following day.

½ past 2 Sorbonne. By far the best music . . .
S. Sulpice ½ past 3 Vespers . . . splendid costumes of priests and service in grand style. Building good for sound; beautiful large shells for holy water.[184]

' Paris, Monday, August 17th.' This last day recorded in his diary, so carefully headed, is lengthy and full of matter ; so full indeed that it may well contain recollections and impressions of what he had done on the preceding day as well. All the places he mentions are, however, within walking distance and could have been visited within a morning's sightseeing.

Monday, August 17th. Church of S. Roch . . . fine handsome cathedral-looking case to the organ. Would rank as the second best in Paris. Present organist M. Vilé [Wély] ; his son occupying office for him.

He also copies the inscription on the memorial tablet erected in 1821 to Corneille, who is buried in the church.

Assumption, small church of circular form. Very fine paintings.

Madeleine, large and handsome church ; very fine columns surrounding the exterior, in shape and general construction like the Parthenon at Athens. It is now undergoing repair and when finished will be one of the noblest churches in Paris.

Chapel to the memory of Louis XVI : one of the most beautiful little buildings in Paris. It is surrounded by rows of Cypress Trees with a small Cloister on each side of the approach ; and within a handsome vestibule and a Court with sculpture. In the centre opposite the entrance is an altar, and in the two recesses on the right and left side is the will and testament of Louis XVI and Marie Antoinette sculptured in gold letters on a ground of black marble.

This elegant little piece of architecture has only been finished about a year, according to the following inscription which is placed on the pediment over the principal entrance.* A monument is also now rising in the Place Louis XVI over the spot where he was beheaded. There is at present little more than the pedestal finished.

The fact that the Chapelle Expiatoire had only been completed in 1826 reminds us that the horrors of the Revolution were still a living memory. That it still conveys its message to the Parisians of today, Georges

*He did not copy the inscription.

245

B. Arthaud's *Paris* (1948) bears witness : '. . . untouched by any of the upheavals of the century, not even by the Commune itself, it still rises, a little island of remembrance in that ocean of hurry and noise, like a prayer or a remorse '.

The ' Place Louis XVI ' reverted, after the revolution of 1830, to the name given it in 1795, and which it still bears—' Place de la Concorde '. The projected monument to Louis XVI at the spot where he was guillotined was not completed.

After so much sightseeing Novello was glad to return to the Gardens of the Tuileries (which, for once differing from his wife, he liked) and sit quietly opposite those windows of the Palace of which, on Saturday, he had already carefully noted : ' Bonaparte's apartments on the left of entrance [to] Tuileries, beyond the Busts ; his bed Room was towards the Garden '.

Gardens of Tuileries very pleasant of their kind. The statues, though not of the first order of sculpture, yet give a very tasteful and refined air to the place.

One of the most interesting seats, to me, is the one at the north west angle beyond the first piece of water. It comprises an agreeable mixture of the gay flowers in the Parterre, and that part of the Palace where Napoleon formerly resided, and the three windows of the apartment on the front *étage* which were once the bedroom of that extraordinary man. How many anxious and restless nights he must have passed in that very room ; how often he must have watched the approach of dawn through those three windows and how many thoughts must have been engraved in his brain while reclining on his pillows or while he was pacing that apartment, and which thoughts were afterwards to have an influence on the affairs and destinies of the whole of the civilized world.

The throne room where Bonaparte received the kings,

etc., who came to have an audience with him is in the centre of the palace ; over this is a high flagstaff and I understand that the Parisians can always perceive whether the King is at the Tuileries or not by a white flag which is hoisted during the time of his stay.

Evidently the white flag of the Bourbons had not been flying that day ; in mid-August Charles might have been at Rambouillet, his summer residence, where he signed his abdication in July 1830.

There is something striking in the attitude of so staunch an Englishman and Liberal. To Novello, the ' Man of Destiny ' was neither the bogey-man he was to remain to English children and their nursemaids for decades to come, nor the tyrant he was in the eyes of Beethoven or Byron ; at that moment at least he is considering him from an angle simply human, with wonder and pity for the extraordinary personality of the man and the poignancy of his history.

The fresh notes on Père Lachaise which follow, and conclude his diary, are almost certainly not a recollection of his first visit there with his wife, but of a solitary return on August 17th to the place which had so much struck his fancy.

Père La Chaise.

Tasteful custom of placing a little Coronet of flowers upon the spot where those repose calmly whom their friends loved dearly.

At the approach they are to be found ready to our hand, of all kinds of Colours and designs.

The upper part of the Rue Roquette is the paradise of stone-masons—Tombstone manufacturers, who seem to have very jucidiously got rid of the disagreeable part of hideous death and to have concealed his horrid features under a mask of flowers and beautiful marble forms.

Vivant Denon author of the famous work on Egypt is

injudiciously placed with his *back* to the wall, so that very few people who pass his monument will be aware of its existence, especially as there is not even his name attached to it, except in front which they don't see. The figure is in bronze and is very well modelled ; the attitude is easy and natural.

Mme. Blanchard, widow of the aeronaut (' victime de son art et de son intrepidité ', 6th January 1819 aged 43).

Jacques Delille the author of ' Les Jardins '. I do not like to call him a poet because I do not think that the French have any poetry or that they can understand what it means. With them poetry seems to consist in the regular arrangement of syllables and the mechanical construction of versification, not with the vigour and beautiful condensation of thought, the exquisite perception of the finest objects in nature, the vivid impression of true and energetic human passion and the power of expressing these perfections in the most nervous and striking manner. Poetry seems to me ' the essence of thought '.

Opposite to Delille is the tomb of Talma the favourite French actor ; but to my surprise (and as it appeared to me a strangely injudicious place) there is no inscription whatever upon it. I agree that his name alone would have been enough, but even that is omitted and unless there be a name how can anyone tell (except he is informed by someone better acquainted with the cemetery than himself) to whom the monument is intended? The Tomb itself is a very tasteful one, it is a square inclosed on three sides with stones, the fourth side of little bronze gratings. In the centre a block of granite on a little grass plot surrounded by myrtles and other plants in boxes. At the time I saw it there were some beautiful coronets of flowers and a laurel wreath placed on the granite block which is placed just above the spot where his remains are deposited. I cannot possibly conceive the reason why his name has been omitted.

David the Painter, a handsome monument, with a likeness of him in bas relief in bronze, very well executed. It is placed near the chapel on the summit of the eminence just where the house belonging to Père La Chaise formerly stood.

I endeavoured to find out where Grétry and Imbert were buried but no one that I met with could tell me and unfortunately at the bureau where the guide books are usually sold there were no more copies to be had.

Whoever wishes to have a just idea of the extent of Paris and of the gaiety, in its wisest and most tasteful aspect, should come and pass a whole morning in the Cimetière of Père La Chaise.

Here the diary ceases at the top of a blank page. And thus we leave Vincent Novello, or rather he leaves us, wandering among the tombstones in serene and pensive mood, surrounded by bright flowers and gazing at Paris beyond, bathed in the clear summer light.

AFTERWORD

IT IS often curious to trace, after all is long since over and done with, the workings of fate—shaped by Providence through the actions and reactions of cause and effect—upon the ultimate destiny of men and of things. There is indeed

> . . . a Divinity which shapes our ends,
> Rough-hew them how we will.

Little Clara Novello, notwithstanding the various difficulties and cross-currents of which we have heard in her father's diary, was accepted at Choron's Institution on her arrival in Paris ; accepted, what is more, ' sans concours '. She was left at Madame Tardieu's establishment, doubtless to the great relief of her parents, who set such store by this, with a view to the gifted child's future.

And doubtless her tuition at Choron's laid the foundations of her brilliant career as a singer, which began, with immediate success, before she had finished her fifteenth year. Still, her time in Paris does not appear to have been so happy as her father's impression of Madame Tardieu's character and of ' the mode she follows in conducting her establishment ' had led him to expect. From Clara's own *Reminiscences* it appears that no-one at Madame Tardieu's was very kind to the homesick, sensitive little foreigner. Possibly the other girls, all French and grown-up, felt a little jealous and found her presence a bore. Madame Tardieu, too, from what Vincent Novello says of the discussions with Fétis and with her, may have resented being obliged, after all, to accept an unexpected boarder.

This, however, is no excuse for her meanness, if not dishonesty, in using the money, left by Mary Novello to furnish Clara with the black silk frock which was *de rigueur* for pupils on state occasions, to buy her only a cotton one, with the result that the other girls jeered at the child for her English parents' stinginess—a grievous mortification, indeed, at that age.

But it is strange to notice, in retrospect, how Clara Novello's whole future life—quite apart from her musical career—was influenced in a most unexpected and unpredictable manner by her coming to Paris that August morning ; stranger still that this should have come to influence the ultimate fate of her parents' records of their Salzburg journey.

On her arrival, as she herself has told, she was at once ' walked in short-sleeved dress, music book under arm ', to be heard by ' dear old Choron . . . Ferdinand Hiller and others ', and next taken on to that other very important adjudicator, Gioacchino Rossini. The latter was ' at breakfast ', and his ' enchanting sweetness ', she adds, ' won my heart at first sight, awed though I was '. Elsewhere she writes of herself: ' My mother used to say I had a dog's instinct about people ', and whether or not this instinct was always right, she certainly came to be known as one who rarely changed her opinions. Rossini—who to her, at the age of eleven, no doubt seemed quite elderly, though he was only thirty-seven—seems to have been equally struck at first sight with this delightful, resolute, good-looking child with the wonderful singing voice ; for they became fast friends on the spot, and remained so to the end of the chapter.

Now if Rossini had met Miss Clara Novello for the first time some nine years later—as the finished, charming young English soprano of concert and oratorio fame in England,

Germany, Austria, and France, newly arrived in Italy, in her twentieth year, to prepare herself for the operatic stage—he would certainly have admired and applauded ; but he would scarcely have conceived the truly paternal interest in her and in all her affairs which he evinced then and as long as he lived. She, on the other hand, could scarcely have felt for the celebrated composer that affectionate, unswerving, friendly trust which led her, over and over again, to turn to him and to his advice during the whole of her ensuing operatic career. It was to Rossini, in Bologna, that she was taken in 1838 by her mother, to be guided in her choice of masters in all the arts of stage singing ; the parents, seeing him through their daughter's eyes and grateful for his kindness to her while at Choron's, had evidently modified their opinion of the man, if not of his music. It was in the title-role of his *Semiramide* that she made a most successful operatic début in Padua three years later, in 1841. It was Rossini who chose her as his soprano for the famous first performance of his *Stabat Mater*, at Bologna in 1842. And when, after Bologna, she was offered a *scrittura* at the Opera House of a small, ancient, provincial hill-town in the Pontifical States (a place she had probably never heard of), it was to Rossini that she addressed herself before accepting ; and it was thus on his advice that she went to Fermo in the midsummer of 1842 for the August-September season at the charming Teatro dell' Aquila.

So, in the end, it was Rossini who was responsible for her encounter with one of Fermo's leading citizens, the handsome Conte Giovanni Battista Gigliucci, then twenty-seven years old, a *Liberale*, independent, serious-minded, patriotic. The consequence (which Rossini must have regretted as keenly as did her own family) was that she threw up her career the very next year, when only twenty-five and at the height of her fame, to marry the man of her heart and choice, quitting (to quote her own words) ' public life for ever, as I believed '.

This, like most of ' the best-laid schemes of mice and men ', was also to turn out quite otherwise, for she resumed her musical career seven years later and gained many more laurels in England and on the Continent as ' Madame Clara Novello ' during her husband's political exile from 1849 to 1861 ; but this has nothing to do with her parents' diaries. What does concern them, however, is the fact that a little girl's sudden friendship with Rossini, in the Paris of 1829, should, among other things, have led to these manuscripts finding their way, many years later, to the Adriatic coast, to be discovered more than a century after they were written, in the house that had become in 1843, and remained up to her death in 1908, the well-loved home of the last survivor among the several long-lived children of Vincent and Mary Sabilla Novello.

THE MUSICAL SCENE IN EUROPE IN 1829

Vincent Novello approached his continental journey with the alert interest and keen critical faculties of a musician of all-round attainments and enlightened if somewhat conservative taste. If the musical scene in Europe, as he depicts it, is largely a gloomy one, the reason lies partly in his own high standards and still higher expectations. But he also provides factual evidence, and his honest and faithful record of his findings, and of his own reactions to them, reflect the situation, and the climate of the age, all the more clearly for being spontaneous and immediate.

The picture he paints, stroke by stroke, is one of a general decline of taste and of standards, opposed by a small minority. Even if we bear in mind that the picture is incomplete, lacking any account of Bohemia, Saxony or Northern Germany, we know that it is in the main a true one. The frivolity and shallowness of outlook which he depicts is that which Berlioz castigated, and against which Schumann was soon to lead his *Davidsbund*. Behind it lay that cleavage between cultured minority and popular feeling which —as we ourselves know—is one of the manifestations of a period of social transition. Then, as now, the whole structure of social life was shifting, and that of musical life with it. Wars and revolutions, political and industrial, had deprived the nobility of their position as the principal patrons of music. A far larger middle-class public, that of the concert-hall and the *Biedermeyer* drawing-room, was springing up alongside the aristocratic salon. In the home and in the public garden Novello found ' sterling music ' everywhere ousted by ' waltzes, eternal commonplace waltzes ' or ' quadrilles from Rossini, Pacini and other poor stuff fit only for the amusement of little school girls '.

The concert-hall, too, was dominated by sheer vocal and instrumental display, as Novello found when he noted down, from a battered poster in the Bourse at Antwerp, the programme of a concert given the previous April : a concert in which artists of the distinction of de Bériot, Joseph Dorus—the pioneer of the Boehm flute—and his sister, an eminent singer, contented themselves with performing ' fragments ' of a Viotti concerto, ornate sets of variations, and such items as ' La cadence du Diable—ballade avec violon obligé par Panseron ' and ' Romance de Philomèle, avec accompagnement de flute, composée par Panseron, chantée par Mlle Dorus et accompagnée par son Frère'.

From one aspect, the conflict between majority and minority can be seen as running parallel with the fifty-year-old rivalry between the established Italian supremacy and the rising German school represented by Haydn and Mozart. In England, indeed, since Handel's sway and Haydn's triumphs, there was no-one to echo Swift's ironic ' Pray let me see a *German* genius before I die ' ; but Lamb's picture of Novello ' pouring in . . . fresh waves . . . from that inexhausted *German* ocean ' still suggests that German music was the novelty, Italian music the accepted norm. This, in spite of the achievements of the great Viennese masters was still the situation in Europe ; moreover, Haydn and Mozart, regarded in their lifetime as representing a new—and to many an unwelcome—challenge to the Italian school, were now looked upon, even by intelligent observers, as a spent force. It was in this vein that Kandler spoke to Novello : ' Every age has its own idols ; that of Haydn and Mozart is passed, they have been supplanted by other favourites, and now when an opera of Mozart's is performed, *nobody goes* '. In the Europe of 1829 Rossini was the unchallenged master ; no-one could have predicted that *William Tell*, of which Novello saw the first production in Paris, was to be his last opera. In his wake followed ' Mercadante and other " illustrious obscures " of the modern school ', and Italian singers still reigned as the despots of the operatic stage : stupid despots, moreover, who had lost the ' severely classical style ' of the eighteenth-century Italian school of singing, which at least made their tyranny the tyranny of trained musicians.[185] Mozart's widow summed up the situation in her warning to the Novellos that in Vienna ' while the Italian singers are there, there is no chance of hearing Mozart's operas, when they leave they are performed ', and the picture drawn by her and her son, though admittedly biased—for Mozart had suffered from the successful rivalry of Italian composers and the caprices of Italian singers—was true in essentials :

M.N. Madame said, that during his life the Italian singers had declared they could not sing his music, but after his death, all his works had been performed by turns without any difficulty . . . Mozart never wrote such instrumental difficulties for the voice as his successors have put down, and the singers get by rote, yet they complained his pieces were impossible for the voice, the fact is, their ignorance is put to fault, and his music requires more study to give it effect than their indolence and ignorance can manage[186] . . .

She does not like Italy, it is certain, the modern Italians bear a bad name from all travellers. She said they have spoiled Rossini and that nothing was to be heard but his operas. . . .

. . . [Mozart's son] was very severe against the Italian singers, declares he has been often obliged to accompany those who could not even name the key he was to play in. He laughed much at Catalani and her 15 songs, and told us that once she requested Spontini to alter the score of one of Mozart's operas—he very properly told her ' Do you think me a fool? '

V.N. Contempt for Signora Catalani, etc., with their few songs by memory—overpaid. Accompanied some who did not even know the key in which they were singing.

Of the all-conquering Rossini himself Stendhal had written, in 1824 : ' The glory of this man knows no limits save those of civilization itself ; and he is not yet thirty-two ! ' An Englishman, William Cooke Stafford, sums up his position in a shrewd paragraph, which also states the issue as one between the German and Italian styles :[187]

'. . . The Germans, justly proud as they are of the fame of their native composers, have been compelled to yield to the force of Rossini's claims . . . very little foreign music is heard with so much pleasure as Rossini's, and we take the reason to be, that, whilst it is not so elaborately constructed as that of Haydn, or Mozart, or Beethoven . . . it is always addressed to the social affections and feelings . . . he is the composer for the populace : he is the *artiste* for those who follow music as a pastime, not as a passion, and who adopt it as an agreeable amusement, not as a profound science.'

This was the outlook against which the intelligent minority were in rebellion—from Novello himself, and the more thoughtful musicians of his own generation, to young firebrands like Berlioz. It would, however, be unjust to claim that Rossini's appeal was only to the populace. Beethoven himself admitted that what he did, he did supremely well, and even Novello's beloved Leigh Hunt in the year after Rossini's visit to England, ventured an opinion which gently challenges that of his friend :

'. . . We fear it is a little out of the scientific pale to think Rossini a man of genius ; but we confess, with all our preference for such writers as Mozart . . . we do hold that opinion of the lively Italian . . . Rossini, in music, is the genius of sheer animal spirits. . . . It is in his liveliest operas that he shines. . . . Not to see his merit in these cases, surely implies only, that there is a want of animal spirits on the part of the observer.'[188]

But it was left to the next generation, that to which Clara Novello belonged, to look up to Rossini as an Old Master and point the finger of scorn at the new popular idol—Verdi, satirized by Browning's Bishop Blougram,

. . . When, at his worst opera's end

. . . .

He looks through all the roaring and the wreaths
Where sits Rossini patient in his stall.

Unfortunately the Rossini opera that Novello heard at Munich was *Ricciardo e Zoraide*, an inferior work with a preposterous libretto, written in 1818 to appease his more conservative critics in Naples and provide splendid singing parts for the stars of the San Carlo Theatre, including his own mistress and future wife Isabella Colbran. Novello's assessment of it is not altogether unjust, despite his thrust—the perennial one—at Rossini's supposed laziness :

Introductory Movement better style than usual for Rossini . . . short Overture, probably omitted Allegro or perhaps Rossini was too lazy to write one[189]. . . . Through the opera I felt the want of more Bass voices. Almost all the male Characters are Tenors or low Counter and high Baritones, which amounts to nearly the same thing, the effect was monotonous and deficient in vigour accordingly—how different from the grand design of Mozart's ' Don Giovanni ' and ' Figaro ' ! The Music was like the generality of Rossini's productions—snatches of good thoughts which are not carried on . . . a few light melodies amounting to the pleasant and exhilarating, but mixed with a most unconscionable quantity of repetition of himself, of commonplace passages, wornout crescendos, everlasting triplets and other trifling puerilities.

It is all the more disappointing that Novello never filled in the pages which he left blank in order to record his opinion of ' William Tell '.

Among other contemporary composers Cherubini, whom Haydn had acclaimed and Beethoven admired, stood highest in the general estimation. Mozart's son told Novello that he considered him the ' best vocal composer now living ', and Mary Novello relates that

Madame spoke of Cherubini with unqualified praise both as a musician and a man, and said he was a great admirer of Mozart and always had his scores and those of Haydn to study from—so had Rossini but the result was not evident, he had some good ideas but he never studied.

The composer Gyrowetz, too, whom Novello met in Tobias Haslinger's shop in Vienna,

desired his kindest remembrance to this celebrated composer, whom he (in common with most of the best judges I have yet met with in Germany) unites with me in considering the greatest master of the present day.

Spohr, Hummel and Spontini—who dominated the operatic world of Berlin—are assessed with fair shrewdness by Mozart's widow and son. Constanze's opinion of Spontini is summed up by Mary Novello:

[She] thinks his Vestale the best performance, but says he is so full of self love that he would never have any other operas than his own performed if he could help it.

Mozart's son considered Spohr

the greatest living artist although he finds him occasionally recherché. Beethoven and Hummel he does not admire with the exception of the former's early works and the two Masses of the latter.

Mary Novello has here over-simplified his opinion of Beethoven into something more unfavourable than, as recorded by her husband, it actually was. His view of Hummel was apparently shared by his mother:

Hummel was Mozart's pupil but she did not think favourably of him or speak of him but as an indifferent person.

Of the great figures of the immediate past, Beethoven, only two years dead, was still, in 1829, an enigma to many. The works of his middle period had, indeed, caught the imagination of Europe. Musicians from all over the world had sought him out with veneration, and his tragedy and his eccentricities alike had made him a focus of legend and anecdote. But in the works of his last years he had passed beyond the comprehension of all but a few (a writer in *Cäcilia* described his last quartets as the product of a mind ' vegetating ' in an unreal world)[190], and the Abbé Stadler, to whom Mozart was the centre of the musical universe, voiced a fairly widespread opinion when he told Novello that he considered Beethoven ' an extraordinary genius— but irregular, extravagant '. Mozart's son also, according to Novello, measured him by the same standards:

Of Beethoven he also thought very highly—especially of his earlier productions—he even said that if he had curbed his tendency to whim and extravagance, he might have perhaps ranked with his father in his instrumental compositions. He admired the overture to Prometheus but not Fidelio ; did not think Beethoven had any genius for vocal music or the Operatic style—and thought all his latter works too extravagant . . . always same passages that were repeated and you wished an end ; that he knew him very well but that Beethoven's manners were not attractive at first—but that he was an amiable character at bottom and he was more agreeable and cordial upon a more intimate acquaintance ; that Beethoven had the highest estimation for his father's productions.

Mozart, in fact, has become an Old Master. Kandler might say with truth that ' now, when an opera of Mozart's is performed in Vienna, *nobody goes* '. But among connoisseurs he is an almost legendary figure, and there is no tendency to regard his art as something delicate and small and endowed with fragile period charm : that aberration belonged to the later nineteenth century. In the 1820's and 1830's, in the eyes of those to whom he means anything at all, he stands for consummate mastery and expressive power : it is the age of E. T. A. Hoffmann and his sombre, romantic conception of *Don Giovanni.* For Novello—as for his pupil Edward Holmes, whose biography of Mozart, written in 1845, is still of value—Mozart was ' the Shakespeare of music ' ; and to realize fully what that well-worn expression implied, on their lips, we have to recall that Shakespeare, undervalued by the ' Age of Reason ', was in the very process of rediscovery by the Romantic era. To Berlioz, to Keats (Holmes' schoolfellow), to Leigh Hunt and his circle, Shakespeare was no accepted classic, but an overwhelming revelation. For the Continent, the Abbé Stadler summed up the views of enlightened opinion on Mozart with his ' Il etoit universel et savoit tout '. Even the violence of the dispute between him and Gottfried Weber over the Requiem springs from the assumption, on both sides, that Mozart was a figure of the highest stature.

Carl Maria von Weber, who had died prematurely of

phthisis after the first production of *Oberon* in London in 1826, was apparently nobody's hero, though *Der Freischütz* had taken the German-speaking world by storm ; as Novello found, its most tuneful numbers had passed into the repertory of strolling musicians and military bands all over the continent. In Vienna he is not once mentioned, and all that Mozart's family in Salzburg can find to say of their ill-fated cousin is that he did much better for himself than Mozart. Mary Novello records her conversation with Mozart's widow and son :

Weber was her first cousin . . . the Germans complain of Weber's treatment in England although he realized £2,000 for one opera, such as it is, whilst Mozart never received as many florins from *them* for all his operas . . . [Mozart's son] very naturally seemed hurt at the greater success of Weber and others who had done so little comparatively to his father, and said it was enough to discourage any professor to see any Italian singer with 15 songs by heart, yet paid more in a night than a professor earns in a month, and yet so ignorant they know not one key from another

The personal note intrudes even more sharply in Vincent Novello's telescoped version of their remarks :

Weber—only *one* opera, *Freischütz*, well paid and provision for his family all over Germany—but Mozart's family *nothing*.

It is, however, worth noting that whenever Novello himself heard a composition of Weber's, his comments are favourable.

Towards the great composers of the more distant past the attitude which Novello encountered, and himself expressed, reflects another aspect of the revolt of the minority against the frivolities of the ' modern school '. This took the form of a nostalgia for a

' Golden Age ' of noble simplicity and classic dignity, frequently finding its outlet in antiquarian scholarship. The spirit that breathed through young Berlioz's adoration of Gluck was the same as that which stimulated Novello's researches among the Fitzwilliam Music at Cambridge, his publication of Purcell's sacred music, and the love of Bach which he shared with Samuel Wesley and a handful of fellow-devotees. It is sad that Novello and Berlioz did not meet each other, for they had much in common, despite their difference in age—their passion for Shakespeare and the theatre, their devotion to Beethoven and loathing of Rossini. But Novello's contacts were inevitably with men of his own generation. A common outlook provided the bond between him and Fétis, who was soon to organize a series of Historical Concerts, anticipating Arnold Dolmetsch by over half a century in his use of the instruments of the period. And it was Fétis who wrote of the fortnightly choral concerts given by the pupils of Choron's *Institution Royale de Musique Religieuse* : ' There, for the first time in Paris, were heard the sublime compositions of Bach, Handel and Palestrina . . . there alone did they dare to depart from the hackneyed repertory on which the concert-going public had been fed for over thirty years '. It was, moreover, at Choron's institution that *Messiah* was first introduced to Paris, in a Latin adaptation.[191] Small wonder that this was the establishment of Novello's choice for the musical education of his daughter.

In Austria, Handel was a considerable figure—thanks largely to the antiquarian tastes of Baron van Swieten, for whose private concerts Mozart had provided the additional accompaniments to *Messiah*. Mozart's son, after telling Novello that his father was a ' great admirer of Handel, well acquainted with his works, especially his Oratorios ', went on to say that he himself ' thought higher of Handel's oratorios than of any other Composition after his father's, and said

20

that he should have purchased the whole of his works in score but that they were difficult to procure and at too high a price for a Professor who, like himself, was not rich.'

Bach, on the other hand, is merely one of a collection of prints on Eybler's wall in Vienna. Novello never once succeeded in hearing a note of his music, and it is left to Mary Novello to record the solitary observation made by Mozart's son :

Mozart's son thinks Bach's *vocal pieces* dry, but he much admires his fugues.

Faint praise indeed from the son of the man on whom the discovery of Bach had made an impact comparable with that of Chapman's Homer on Keats.

★   ★   ★

From the point of view of opera-house and concert hall the Novellos made their tour at the wrong time of year. The season was long since over, and the only purely instrumental music they heard was that performed by military and other bands in public parks and squares. They heard no oratorio, and only routine performances of opera. On these, however, Novello made copious notes—in some cases during the performance itself—which throw some light on contemporary conditions of performance.

The first opera house the Novellos entered was at Mannheim. There they heard Auber's *La Muette de Portici*, which had created a furore in Paris on its first production in 1828 and was to help stir up the democratic ardour that fired the revolutions of 1830 ; a performance in Brussels was actually the signal for the revolt by which the King of the Netherlands (whom the Novellos just missed seeing at Louvain) lost his throne. Novello's account of the music is that of a conservative musician, but is not wholly unappreciative. The complaint of excessive noise is a recurrent one.

The Overture began with a discord and the tappage occasioned by the furious blowing of the wind instruments and the violent drumming was hideously noisy. The style of the Overture is in the unconnected, abrupt, forced, unnatural French style, and it is altogether a commonplace affair 'full of sound and fury—signifying nothing'. . . .

Oboe, thin tone—poor Griesbach, never will there be such a perfect master of this generally disagreeable Instrument as you were.[192]

Clarionet clever and feeling performer . . . instrumental music better than the vocal pieces, especially that appropriate to the dumb girl—tho' much in the Rossinian style.

Principal tenor voice [Alfonso : Werth][193] too much in his throat and too flat. Prima Donna [Elvira : Eichborn] well in tune but now rather old and wanting polish. The Actress who played the Dumb Girl [Fenella : Reinhardt] wanting in energy.

Finale to 1st Act too violent and noisy—the crowing, shouting, bawling, and the furious crashing of the Orchestra was enough to split our ears—it was absolutely frightful.

2nd Act. Lively chorus of the Lazzaroni in F.

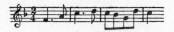

Masaniello's song in G, tasteful in parts but too *dancy*.

Young man who sang Masaniello [Schmuckert] . . . sang well in tune and with very fair taste, wanting power above E on the 5th line A little fellow who sang

Bass and was dressed as a fisherman reminded me of your friend Tiny [?] Smith.

Finale a working up of Masaniello's song but monotonous and too much repeated.

3rd Act. Opens with a gay chorus in D—a street in Naples. Fine dramatic effect but the Act altogether rather tiresome.

In Act IV, as Novello observed, the subject-matter of the Overture is used in the first number, Masaniello's recitative and aria *Spectacle affreux*, but he missed the dramatic point of the returning discords, against which Masaniello (anticipating Hindemith's *Mathis der Maler*) muses on the horrors wrought by the rebellion in which he himself has taken part.

Family tradition records that of Novello's children only two, Alfred and Sabilla, had by nature ' the power of making a shake '—the lack of which he comments on so sharply in the Mannheim singers. Even Clara had to learn the art by practice.

4th Act. Begins with a sudden harsh discord like the subject of the Overture . . . Singers' high notes inefficient. The scene too " long drawn out " and not in the " linked sweetness " that Milton speaks of.

Not a single singer amongst the whole Company appears to have the power of making a shake.

The last movement in G major of this scene [Masaniello's berceuse, *Du pauvre seul ami fidèle*] is one of the best melodies in the piece. It is also very well scored and there are some effective and judiciously contrasted passages for the voice and clarionet and bassoon. Double bass the best performer on the stringed Instruments, the 1st Horn was also a fine player, but the Drum was an absolute nuisance . . . Good Round in B flat [*Je sens qu'en sa présence*]—parts well put together and the counterpoint ingenious.

The finale again consisting of more trumpetting, drumming, bursting of trombones and smashing of cymbals, and upon the whole the melodies want delicacy, sweetness and expression. Orchestra too violent and noisy throughout and, though accurate as to time, but coarse in execution.

5th Act. Opens with another movement in $\frac{6}{8}$, of which there are too many in this opera.

The representation of the eruption of Vesuvius not effective and inferior to the fine scenes at Astley's and other Minor Theatres in England.[194]

The same complaint of noise and want of delicacy on the part of the orchestra is made against the orchestra of the Kärntnerthor Theatre in Vienna as it accompanies *Don Giovanni* :

I have the same fault to find with this, as with almost every one that I hear, viz., that they play so loud as to overpower the singers, the consequence is that the singers are obliged to bawl in self defence in order to be heard, and the result is a coarse, noisy and violent effect. It is but justice, however, to say that this Orchestra, though not possessing any performer of very prominent ability, is less violent and noisy than that at Mannheim.

At the Munich production of *Ricciardo e Zoraide*, the question of vocal ornamentation by the singer makes its appearance. Novello would have been surprised— and probably disgusted—to hear that in this opera all the ornaments (including the ' unnecessary and sickening ' chromatic scale that he accuses the prima donna of interpolating) are written out in the printed score.

Of the two Ladies I preferred Mamsell [Sigl-Vespermann][195] (who sustained the Character of Zoraide), she is occasionally a trifle harsh when she forces her voice, and at other times she lets it drop so as to be rather flat—but

267

she has a very extensive compass from C below the stave to E flat the 3rd Ledger Line above the stave. I could have wished she possessed a little more feeling and that she had good taste enough to have refrained from the introduction of the hideous descent of the Chromatic Scale, one of the most unnecessary and sickening passages that the conceit of a singer ever thought of introducing.

Had he but known it, only a couple of years earlier Rossini had clashed with the ageing Catalani because of her resentment at his writing out all the vocal ornamentation in the arias she was to sing instead of leaving them to her powers of improvisation.[196] Rossini was indeed among the first to resist the pretensions of singers to improvise ornamentation, and his elaborately ornate vocal line is actually a measure of discipline, not of exuberance. It is ironical that when Novello praises the Vienna opera singers in the performance of *Don Giovanni* which he heard at the Kärntnerthor Theatre for performing ' the *real text* of a great composer ', and was delighted to find that his ' well conceived and appropriate melodies ' were not ' altered, spoilt and frittered away into unmeaning, affected, nonsensical runs ', he may well have had the despised Rossini to thank for this happy state of affairs.

The remaining singers in the cast are dismissed in a series of thumbnail sketches :

The second singer (Mad. Pellegrini who performed the part of Zomira) was not deficient in talent though that talent cannot with justice be rated as of the first class. She executed the passages assigned to her with accuracy and precision.

The Tenor [*blank*] I do not admire—his style is laboured and (what is with me a defect for which nothing can compensate) he sings out of tune—he was several times nearly a quarter of a note too flat—which in the concerted pieces especially was ruinous of the effect.

The [*blank*] who is like Pym in personal appearance, and whose voice is a mixture of the quality of Pym and that of Horn of Drury Lane,[197] is to my taste a sweeter and more polished singer, though he does not possess so much power.

The Best Voice I heard was Pellegrini the Bass, who did not appear till near the end of the Opera. I quite regretted that he had not more to do.

As regards the direction of the orchestra, the position during the first thirty or forty years of the century was fluid. Adam Carse, in his masterly and comprehensive survey, *The Orchestra from Beethoven to Berlioz*, points out that:

> In the year 1800 it would have been difficult, or even impossible, to find any orchestra in which the playing was controlled by a musician who did nothing but beat the time and indicate by gestures how the music should be interpreted. By 1850 it would have been equally difficult to find any but small orchestras in which the playing was controlled by any other means than by a time-beating conductor.

At the turn of the century the position everywhere was one of uneasy dual control between the violinist-leader and the musical director ' presiding at the piano forte '. In Germany, as early as 1807, Gottfried Weber was writing in the *Allgemeine Musikalische Zeitung* that the only instrument suitable for the direction of a big musical work was the baton; Spohr, Weber and Spontini adopted this method between 1810 and 1820, and by the 1820's it was clearly in the ascendant. In France it was the violinist-leader who became conductor, using his bow as a baton. But between these continental developments and their adoption in England there was a time-lag. Despite Spohr's famous experiment of conducting the Philharmonic Orchestra with a baton in 1820—which in any case he only tried out at a rehearsal[198]—and Weber's similar procedure in 1826, the old unsatisfactory divided-control method persisted, although there were repeated complaints of the unpleasantness of the piano tone, and the disastrous effect of divergent tempi on the part of violinist-leader and pianist-conductor.

In that very year (1829) Mendelssohn made his first appearance in London, conducting his C minor Symphony with a baton. The press approved of the venture : the critic of the *Morning Post* wrote : ' Mr. Mendelssohn conducted his Sinfonia with a baton, as is customary in Germany, France, etc., where the *discipline* of bands is considered of more importance than in England . . . we hope to see the baton ere long at the Italian opera '. But the leaders of the orchestra were offended, and on his second visit in 1832 he was only with difficulty dissuaded from giving up the baton in deference to their wishes.[199]

It is in the light of this situation that Novello's remarks on the direction and arrangement of the orchestras he heard must be understood. At the Mannheim Opera he writes :

No Piano Forte in the Orchestra but a Person in the centre who beats time all the way through with the score before him. Recitatives accompanied throughout by the Band—not with Violoncello and Double Bass as in England.

Here he is clearly thinking in terms of the traditional Italian operatic recitatives ; but Auber was a 'modern', and *La Muette de Portici* provided an orchestral accompaniment to all the recitatives.

At the Kärntnerthor Theatre in Vienna he makes the same observation, adding his comments on the arrangement of the orchestra.

The orchestra was well filled : there were about 10 first violins, 8 second, 4 Violas and Violoncellos and 4 Double

Basses, with the usual Complement of Wind Instruments. There was no Piano Forte but the conductor sat with the Score before him in the centre of the Orchestra and beat the time throughout. The arrangement which struck me as most peculiar was the mode of placing the Double Basses. The whole four were ranged in a Row just in the middle of the orchestra, opposite the conductor and the Leader, with their backs to the stage. I liked the result of this condensation of force, for each Performer, by having companions and supports, will play with more confidence and decision—also when these four grand Instruments came in altogether in leading or taking up the points of imitation, the effect was strikingly magnificent.[200]

At the Munich Court Theatre the obtrusiveness of the violinist leader comes in for criticism. Evidently he was beating time audibly with his bow, in accordance with the older practice; this suggests that either there was no baton conductor here at all, or that relations between him and the leader were severely strained. In general this famous orchestra, so highly praised by Spohr and (as late as 1827) by Edward Holmes, does not come up to Novello's expectations.

The Leader made himself too prominent and conspicuous by his violent beating and restless fidgeting about. There is no occasion for all this tappage, and if the Orchestra consists of clever performers it is not only unnecessary but an impertinent affront to the other Professors. His own playing partook of the same violent and coarse character. There was power but no delicacy ; plenty of crashing across the strings, but no Legato, dolce or sustained sweet notes like Spagnoletti.

He is a bold decided Leader and an accurate energetic Orchestra Player, but there his talent and ability seem to end. He is, in my opinion, far inferior to Weichsell,

Spagnoletti or Mori as a Leader, and as a *Concerto* or Quartet Player he is, I should guess, not to be placed for a moment in competition with them.[201]

The Violoncello player is a good performer and seems to enjoy what he has to do like a musician, but he has neither the Tone nor the exquisite polish of Robert Lindley. The Double Bass is also a bold and spirited player, but it would be quite absurd to compare him to Dragonetti (indeed who is to be compared to that Miracle of a Performer?)[202]

The principal Clarionet appeared to me to have more feeling than any one in the Orchestra, and I regretted that he had not more to do.[203] The Band of Wind Instruments fell short of what I expected to meet with in a *German* Opera.

The Orchestra is altogether a fine one, but has not fulfilled the expectation I had anticipated from that celebrity it has acquired. It is too noisy, and there is not sufficient *gradation* of tone. There are the *extremes* of PPP and FFF but the minute shades from which some of the most exquisite effects are derived are wanting.

If this latter criticism is just, the orchestra had lost some of the finesse remarked on by Spohr in 1815, when he said of a performance of Beethoven's Fifth Symphony that ' it is scarcely possible that it could have been performed with more spirit, more power, and at the same time with greater delicacy, as also, throughout, with a closer observance of all the shades of *forte* and *piano*.'[204]

At Munich, besides the opera, the Novellos saw Kotzebue's *Das Schmuckkästchen* at the Court Theatre, and Novello gives an account of the orchestra that played the incidental music. His comment on the absence of a keyboard instrument merely implies that he cannot see such an instrument anywhere in the orchestra pit, for on that evening it would obviously not be wanted ' to accompany the recitatives '.

272

The orchestra is large and well arranged, but to my surprise there was no Piano Forte or keyed instrument to accompany the Recitatives. The Leader sat in the Centre (as usual) right behind the Prompter, and at his back were the two violoncellos and Double Basses. On his right were the 2nd Violins, 6 and Violas 2 . . . and on his left were the 1st Violins, 6. Behind the former (to his right) were the two Trumpets and the Drums, and behind the latter (to the left) were the wind Instruments, 2 flutes, 2 Oboes, Clarionets and Bassoons, 2 Horns.

The Overture was a sinfonia of Krommer in F, but they began at once with the Allegro *omitting the Adagio* (a bad sign)—see the subject annexed.

It was played with spirit but received no applause from the audience.

After the 1st Act a slow Minuet in D, rather commonplace, principally for the Wind Instruments, followed by a Trio in G which was rather graceful . . . after 3rd Act a Pastoral Rondo in G beginning

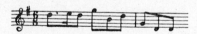

the elements light but prettily scored.

I observed that instead of running out of the Orchestra (as is the custom in England) directly they had put down their Instruments, nearly the whole of the musicians remained in their seats and appeared to take as much interest in the performance going forward on the stage, as the Audience. They seemed a careless set of merry cheerful fellows who took everything very easily and in a *sans souci* manner. Perhaps they may take more pains on *opera* nights but as far as I could judge this Evening the orchestra here is not superior in talent to those of Covent Garden or Drury Lane, and in one respect ours are superior, for they generally play the Sinfonias or Overtures of Mozart, Haydn and Beethoven.

Even the Royal Military Band is compared to its disadvantage with its English counterpart.

July 11. . . . In the Evening at 6 we went to the Garden belonging to the King's Palace (the Hof Garten) to hear the Military Band. It consisted of two Portions, the Brass Band and the Regular Military Band—which consists of about half a dozen 8ve Clarionets, the same number of common Clarionets, 2 Flutes, an octave Flute, 2 Bassoons, 4 Horns, 4 Trumpets, 2 Trombones, 2 Bass Horns, Long Drum, Side Drum and Cymbals.

The Brass Band relieved the principal one by playing alternately with it—but both the Melodies and the harmonies of the airs played were of the poorest common-place description, and the effect was altogether coarse, harsh and disagreeable.

Some of the Pieces selected by the other Band on this occasion were of a better kind that what I had before heard them perform and one movement " the Overture to Preciosa " by Weber, was a Musician-like affair of the light airy class—and was performed in a manner very creditable.

There were two Performers who were very superior to the rest, the Person who played the principal Clarionet and the Leader who played the 1st 8ve Clarionet and whose name I was informed was Witter—the former was principally distinguished by the beauty of his tone and tasteful expression and Mr Witter by his spirited and brilliant execution.

With the exception of the above-mentioned Overture
I found nothing to admire, most of the pieces being
arrangement[s] from Opera Airs by Rossini and his
imitators—mixed with waltzes as usual.

I longed to ask them to play some of Mozart's overtures (especially the Idomeneo which I had heard not
long since by the King of England's Band at Windsor)
or Haydn's Sinfonias—but was fearful of appearing too
presumptuous.

Upon the whole I could perceive nothing in this celebrated Band at all superior to our own military Music
which is to be heard every day on the Parade at the Horse
Guards and at St. James' Palace and very, very far inferior
to the King's Band at Windsor under the direction of my
friend Mr. C. Kramer.[205]

The smaller Austrian towns offer a similar picture.
At Linz, Novello writes:

. . . in walking through the Town I heard only one
person playing on the Piano Forte and that one was
hammering inefficiently at a nonsensical trumpery Waltz.
. . . The Military Band we heard at night at Linz rather
thin, inferior to Munich. Poor March in E flat Auber
Muette de Portici.

Likewise at St Pölten:

. . . heard one Lady singing in a moderately cultivated
style an easy Air with a Guitar accompaniment. I also
heard on the Grand Place to which I accidentally strolled,
the Military Band playing before the Officers' Apartments.
It is numerous but the Clarionets were of a small kind
and of rather a harsh squealing quality—the only piece
worth attending to was the Polacca in the Freischütz.
The others were of the usual trashy waltz kind, with which

I have been hitherto so much disappointed and annoyed in Germany.

One minor disappointment of a curious sort must be mentioned. Novello was familiar with Burney's *Present State of Music in Germany,* in which (pp. 203-4) he describes the Austrians' habit of singing in parts, stating that

At this place [Stein, on the Danube] the soldiers, and almost all the young people that were walking by the water side, were frequently singing, and never in less than two parts.

Edward Taylor, in his *Airs of the Rhine*[206] also says that:

The peculiarity which strikes an Englishman in Germany is the general sensibility to vocal harmony. If he hears a party of country girls singing in a vineyard, or a company of conscripts going to drill, he is sure to hear them singing in parts.

Vincent Novello had thus gone out full of pleasurable anticipation of popular part-singing—and did not get it. Between Liège and Aix-la-Chapelle he remarks for the first time:

I've not yet heard any striking instances of that tendency to sing in *parts* which is said to be so peculiarly characteristic of the common people on the Continent.

At Stuttgart he returns to the charge:

Hitherto I have been much disappointed in not having heard any singing in *parts* in the streets, or any other indication of the great superiority which I was led to expect amongst the Germans in a musical point of view.

Even in Austria, at St Pölten, he is

. . . still surprised at finding no Music—nor any single person ever attempting to sing—not even humming a tune. Our Postillion was a remarkably merry fellow—but he never once tried to get up anything like a song or air of any kind whatever.

★ ★ ★

Among church musicians in England Novello was in an exceptional position, for the whole treasury of Catholic church music, from Gregorian chant to the masses of Haydn and Mozart, lay—in theory at least —at his disposal. As scholar and publisher he had unearthed and published much Italian church music of the polyphonic period and the seventeenth and early eighteenth centuries. Moreover, his work on Purcell's sacred music, and his friendly contact with his Anglican colleagues, had given him a wide knowledge of English church music, despite his own position outside the established fold: a knowledge which enabled him, later, to edit and publish the *Cathedral Choir Book* and to bring out his edition of Boyce's *Cathedral Music*. At the Portuguese Embassy Chapel he had built up a large working repertory of the earlier church music, from the polyphonic period to the lesser eighteenth-century masters. But his real loves were, of course, Haydn and Mozart. His edition of their Masses in vocal score had been the first of his many publishing ventures, and the regular perform-ance of them by his choir had become a feature of Lon-don life: so much so that an anonymous writer in the *Musical World* of 1836 (admittedly a biased source, for his son Alfred was the publisher) ranks ' the intro-duction of the German Masses to the Roman Catholic chapels' with the foundation of the Philharmonic Society and the introduction of *Don Giovanni*, *Der Freischütz* and *Fidelio* to English audiences, as one of the main factors in ' the improvement of our national taste '.

What, therefore, he looked to find in the Catholic churches of the Continent was, in the first place, 'sterling music'—which to him meant Mozart, Haydn, and their lesser contemporaries such as Cherubini and Hummel. He was also prepared to welcome a discreet use of the classics of the polyphonic period and what he calls 'Palestrina's solemn and churchified style'; but in 1829 the influence of Baini's hero-worshipping biography of Palestrina, published the previous year, had not yet put the master on the pinnacle which he was to occupy only a few years later as the church composer *par excellence*, and Beethoven's solitary explorations into his works, and through them into the potentialities of modal harmony, had gone unrecognized for what they were. As for Gregorian chant, he valued it also—up to a point, and in what he considered its right place. But his attitude towards it, like that of his contemporaries, was that of modern man towards something venerable and archaic: in their eyes, Gregorian chant was far from being what it has become to the Catholic Church of this century, the inspired ideal and timeless norm of all church music. Indeed Novello himself, by the publication of his own masses and those of Haydn and Mozart, was largely responsible—according to William Cooke Stafford—for the gradual disappearance of the Gregorian chant from the Catholic chapels of England in the early nineteenth century: 'These modern compositions appear to have generally superseded the ancient ritual: and the only portions of the Gregorian service now generally retained are, in the morning service, those parts sung by the priests at the altar, and the responses; and, in the evening service, the chants for the psalms, and the Gregorian hymns'.[207] Hence Novello expects the responses to be Gregorian and considers it 'wretched bad taste' if they are not; he is pleased, moreover, to encounter the Gregorian psalm tones at Vespers, and to hear such hymns as the *Salve Regina*. But he does not look for plainchant at Mass—except at a Requiem, where its sobriety is appropriate in his eyes—and is disappointed when he meets it too often, or in places where he feels other music would be more appropriate. In Salzburg, for instance, where, on his last morning, he finds, at Mass, ' no choir or Orchestra—merely a few Priests singing in the Plain Chant without even the organ to accompany them ', he promptly concludes that ' Music indeed is in a very sad state of decay in this, the very birthplace of the most enchanting composer that ever existed '. Salzburg and Châlons-sur-Marne were, in fact, the only two towns where he heard Gregorian Masses—apart from Heidelberg where he heard the Requiem—though at Mannheim he says that Mass was sung to a ' kind of chant but not Gregorian '.

Novello's remarks on the accompaniment of Gregorian chant throw light on a peculiar chapter in the history of the corruptions and distortions suffered by the chant since its early days, when the coarse tone and ponderous action of mediaeval organs reduced accompaniment to a minimum. Technical advances in the construction of organs went hand in hand with the development of polyphony to bring about the progressive degeneration of the chant. The Medicean edition of 1615 and the Ratisbon and Mechlin editions of the nineteenth century imposed upon it the harmonic ideas of their respective periods. Not until the researches of the Benedictines of Solesmes had been embodied in the Vatican Edition of 1909 was the chant restored to something approaching its pristine purity, with unaccompanied chant put forward as the ideal, and accompaniment, where present, reduced to a mere background. Novello's outlook was very different from this. His general respectfully antiquarian attitude towards plainchant may have been not unlike that of his pupil Edward Holmes, who, objecting to the erection of contemporary musical structures on Gregorian themes, writes ' The Gregorian tones should be preserved as they were in the time of the elder monks, severe and awful : these Gothic melodies are the only unclothed tunes which are welcome to a musician's ear in that state '.[208] But to Novello, ' these Gothic melodies ' were not particularly welcome in their unclothed state ; and Stafford, whom we have found commenting on the supersession of the chant, in Catholic chapels, save for the re-sponses, psalm-tones, and hymns, adds that these latter ' have been arranged and harmonized by Mr Novello, in a style which entitles him to the thanks of every lover of these ancient and admirable melodies; which, though despised by some for their simplicity, are, nevertheless, affecting in the highest degree, to the truly devotional mind, and capable of inspiring the most sublime emotions '.

Novello's versions, though curious indeed from our standpoint, are superior in one point to some of those which he heard on the Continent, for he does at least realize that Gregorian chant must not be forced into a metrical strait-jacket, and we find him very properly criticizing, at Munich, a ' Salve Regina, old Gregorian in D but too fast and in *measured* time which altered and destroyed its character entirely ': it may have been somewhat on the lines of the version of the *Veni Creator* still sometimes encountered in Italy :

But neither he, nor the church musicians of the Continent, whose plainchant, both as to melody and harmonic notions, was based on the Medicean editions of 1615, had any conception of its real rhythmic nature, which, to them, depended on word accent, not on the points of rhythmic accent in the music itself. Hence, whereas in modern plainsong editions the accompanying chords move only on these ' ictic points ', the intermediate notes being merely passing-notes, Novello's arrangements provide a chord to each note : a chord, moreover, which pushes the harmony into one of the only two modes he recognized—the normal major and minor : witness the D sharp forced upon the melody in the example from the *Dies Irae* given below, the accompaniment of which is that which he provided for that arrangement of the Requiem Mass by Samuel Wesley which he considered superior to the version he heard at Heidelberg :

Similar harmonizations were in vogue on the Continent : witness the curious versions of the Gregorian psalm tones which Novello records at Strasburg and Metz. Even cruder methods prevailed in some places. At Cologne, Holmes found ' the Gregorian service . . . performed in a manner the most remote from good musicianship, every verse being accompanied with the same harmonies, so that there was nothing more than a tiresome repetition of tonic and dominant '.

Novello's plainchant accompaniments are designed for the organ only. On the Continent he sometimes found no accompaniment at all, sometimes the organ alone, sometimes, as at St Michael's, Munich, a string bass moving with it on the lines of the *basso continuo*; in France this function was performed by the serpent. In this respect the position had changed a little during the past sixty years ; in 1773 Burney found the serpent in France, and the double-bass in Italy, used as the only accompanying instruments, and in Antwerp, at the Dominican church, he heard plainchant accompanied by two bassoons and a

serpent, which was 'not only overblown, and detestably out of tune, but exactly resembling in tone, that
of a great hungry, or rather angry, Essex calf'[209]. By
Novello's time, although the instrument persisted
(and earned the same opprobrious description from
Edward Holmes),[210] it was yoked to the organ, and in
Paris Novello even encounters an 'improved serpent'
—possibly the bass horn or ophicleide.

The 'modern' masses—those of Haydn and
Mozart, Cherubini, Hummel and Eybler—were of
course accompanied by a full orchestra. This led
inevitably to the performance of orchestral works as
voluntaries, and we hear of movements of Haydn's
symphonies being played as a sortie, drum-rolls at
the Elevation, fanfares of trumpets, and a display of
virtuosity on the clarinet with which, at Munich,
Novello was fascinated almost in spite of himself.

The organ is a study in itself, and Novello's comments on the organs and organ music he heard, being
those of an expert, are illuminating; but to be fully
understood, they must be viewed against the English
background from which he came. This was not what
might at first be inferred from his constant references
to 'grandeur and power' as the qualities he looks for
in an organ—to him 'that most noble and sublime of
instruments'—and from his use of the expression
'cathedral-like', conjuring up associations with the
rich sonorities so familiar to those who frequent
Anglican cathedral services. In fact, the English
cathedral organs to which we have grown accustomed
are almost all of late Victorian and Edwardian date.
The English organs of Novello's day, those built in
the eighteenth or early nineteenth centuries, though
well made and sweet in tone, were small. Moreover,
as W. L. Sumner observes in his authoritative book on
the instrument, 'even in the second decade of the
nineteenth century only nine of the thirty-three
cathedral and abbey organs in Britain had pedals,
and in all but two of these cases they were pull-downs

acting on the great organ keys '. Novello's friend Samuel Wesley could even ' remember the time when the only organ in London to which pedals were affixed was that of the German Church in the Savoy built by Snetzler '[211]—i.e., that of the German Lutheran Chapel in the Savoy, described by Novello as ' our very favourite Instrument in London '.

From Novello's criticism of the continental organists he heard, the inferior music they played and the poverty of their improvisation, we may infer that, by comparison, the standard of taste and of performance in England was reasonably high, and that English organists had their own style of performance, different from that of the continent. Edward Holmes, Novello's pupil, sums up the difference :[212]

> In the management of the organ the best German players are, with all their readiness in fugue, deficient in two or three important points ; in a close they are too abrupt, and do not allow the tone to die away by degrees into original silence ; they are unacquainted with our cathedral effects, and also with the proper mode of using the organ in choral music, as we are behindhand in the use of the pedals and the building of those vast and voluminous-toned pipes to which they give utterance.

Novello's strictures on the abrupt manner in which the organists he heard ended their performance bear out Holmes' observations, and further indicate that ' cathedral-like ', both to Holmes and to him, was not a general descriptive term, but denoted the deliberate use of a church's resonance in allowing the sound to die away gradually at the close of a performance.

In one respect Novello was less fortunate than Holmes, who had visited Dresden and heard Schneider's use of the pedals in his performances of Bach. Novello's journey, on the other hand, led him through those western and southern regions of Germany where sheer neglect of the pedals—like their absence in England—limited the organists' repertory to that of the piano or harpsichord. Holmes, at Antwerp Cathedral, recognized the 'frivolous and inconsistent' sortie as being 'neither more nor less than one of Nicolai's harpsichord sonatas', and at Cologne quotes a waltz-like tune in D, harmonized by passage-work in tonic harmony throughout, with the comment: 'This kind of waltz movement was, by some curious alchymy of mind, thought to be a becoming handmaiden to the fifth tone'. So too Novello, in Paris, quotes a similar piece of passage-work as constituting one of the voluntaries at Notre Dame, complains, at Châlons, of 'childish roulades, scampering flourishes and old, worn-out passes [sic] in the Harpsichord style', and writes off the organist at Metz, with supreme contempt, as being 'of that abominable class who play *Polaccas* on the Organ'.

This neglect of pedal technique presented a formidable barrier to the performance of Bach's organ works. As late as 1845 a review in the Parisian *Gazette Musicale* of an arrangement of a Bach organ prelude and fugue for keyboard duet observes that 'no publisher has ever found himself encouraged to engrave and print a single line of these organ works, since they all demand the use of the pedals, a technical feat that practically no one in this country seems at the moment to have mastered', and the Bach recitals given by the Belgian organist Lemmens in Paris in 1852, with the pedal parts properly performed, were a revelation to the young César Franck.[213] In England, too, the position with regard to the performance of Bach's works was very different from that which Novello's enthusiastic references to his music might at first sight suggest.

The Bach revival in England, although it had been going on for some thirty years, was in fact a minority movement still, and had not spread very far beyond the little group of organists to whom it owed its inception. The first of these was that solitary pioneer A. F. C. Kollmann, the Hanoverian who became organist at St James' Chapel soon after he came to England in 1784. In 1799 he had announced his project of bringing out a complete edition of the *Well-Tempered Clavier*, which had hitherto circulated in manuscript only. He was forestalled by three continental publishers, Naegeli, Simrock and Peters, who brought out the first printed editions in 1800 and 1801. But then the Forty-Eight came to the knowledge of Samuel Wesley—first the isolated Preludes and Fugues printed by Kollmann in his didactic treatises (even before the complete editions appeared), then the whole work ; by his own account it was the gifted young musician George Frederick Pinto who brought it to his notice.[214] Wesley, who did nothing by halves, found a kindred spirit in C. F. Horn, and with him, between 1810 and 1813, brought out the first English edition of the Forty-Eight : an analytical edition, the first of its kind. He also lit the spark in two younger organists, Benjamin Jacob, of the Surrey Chapel in Blackfriars Road, and Vincent Novello, under whom he had actually worked at the Portuguese Embassy chapel during the period of his brief conversion to Catholicism. Wesley and Novello, in 1810, even won over the aged Burney by playing him the *Goldberg Variations* in a four-handed arrangement, and the organ recitals which Wesley and Jacob gave at the Surrey Chapel became famous.

It was, however, the Forty-Eight, and not the organ works, that formed the basis of their repertory. The reason was partly that the bulk of Bach's organ music, being still in manuscript, was simply not available ; but the absence of pedalboards on the majority of English organs presented a further obstacle. When, in 1809, Wesley and Horn brought out their edition of the *Six Sonatas for Two Keyboards and Pedals*, their Preface states :

> The following Trio was designed for the Organ, and performed by the matchless Author in a very extraordinary Manner : the first and second Treble

Parts he played with both Hands on two Sets of Keys, and the Base (wonderful as it appears) he executed entirely upon Pedals, without Assistance.

The editors were therefore driven to suggest various distributions of the parts between two performers on organ or pianoforte keyboards. Other and more dubious methods of surmounting this hurdle were devised. Dragonetti, Novello's devoted friend and another Bach enthusiast,[215] used to play the pedal part of Bach's organ works with a pianist at public concerts, adapting them in Procrustean manner to bring them within the compass of his three-stringed double-bass, whose lowest note was G. And Novello himself disputes with Wesley the title of the first to make an orchestral transcription of a Bach organ work. His arrangement of the ' St Anne ' Prelude and Fugue was, as he notes on the title-page, ' done to please my Dear Friend, Sam ', and was performed at Samuel Wesley's concert at the Hanover Square Rooms in May 1812 ; Wesley and Novello himself (as Novello also records on the title-page) ' played the obbligato organ part as a Duett on that occasion, each filling the harmonies according to the feeling of the moment, and endeavouring to enrich the effect to the utmost, for the sake of Master Sebastian '.[216]

But, despite the apostolic fervour of Wesley, Jacob and Novello, the Bach cult in England remained local and restricted, and so Novello found it on the Continent also—or rather, failed to find it, for he missed out those centres, such as Leipzig and Dresden, where it was alive, and in Vienna the impetus given by van Swieten's antiquarian enthusiasm a generation earlier had spent itself. Novello's constant complaint, as he travels from church to church along the Rhine and through Southern Germany and Austria, is that none of the organists ' give us a good fugue by Sebastian Bach as I had anticipated '.

It is against this background that Novello's comments, both on the actual instruments he heard, and on the range and style of performance, must be assessed. The only point that causes surprise is that he should have felt such disappointment, for his former pupil Holmes, who had come across the same defects in the course of his tour in 1827, might have been expected to warn his old master of what was in store for him. But Novello was essentially one to see and judge for himself, and his comments, as he moves from church to church across Europe and back, amplify and consolidate the picture outlined above.

ANTWERP

A bare four hours after their arrival in Antwerp at half past six on the morning of Sunday, June 28th, the Novellos were in the Cathedral attending High Mass. Novello's scribbled notes, made while the music was going on, are partly illegible, but his description and musical examples make it clear that the mass performed was Eybler's Third Mass (*de Sancto Leopoldo*) in D. It is fully scored, with the trombones used to reinforce the tenors at the *et resurrexit*, which opens with a melody of plainchant character. There are some effective modulations and felicitously-scored passages, but the whole falls short of the highest inspiration.

Service by Eybler, organist Flipps [*sic*] . . . Kyrie D minor, Gloria D major . . . Clarionets too flat . . . Fugue best movement . . . difference in Power and Voices not good—no *intermediate* altos and tenors . . .

Change to C *minor* bad for ' Gloria tibi Domine ' which ought to have been *major* as being more expressive of joyful and triumphant praise.

Credo in D. Chord struck on the organ first—opening commonplace. . . . Sudden change upon E flat as a unison, and change enharmonic to D sharp the major 3rd in B 5 sharps. Charming movement Crucifixus . . . at the Et Resurrexit, trombone good.

Offertory in F. Clarionet solo . . . Soprano principal voice, thin and not effective. Accompaniment too loud, second Mo[vement?] too theatrical.

Responses to Preface not Gregorian and bad : discordantly out of tune. Sanctus in D major, Benedictus transition to B flat . . . too quick, no prominent feature ; one plagiarism from Mozart's Requiem.

Bad effect breaking in upon the Osanna before he has finished.[217]

Agnus Dei in G pizzicato, with wind instruments legato contrasted with voices—well scored . . . Dona [nobis] pacem returns to the original key of D. Close not dignified or in the church style. . . . One powerful voice amongst the Basses, good B natural above stave.

Discordant [?] effect of different Bells at the altar to interrupt attention.

The sortie was the charming andante in F from Haydn's Sinfonia in B flat, the last we heard at the Philharmonic concert.[218]

Organ all outside show, large case to the size of which additions are making so as to fall upon the whole width of the end of the house.[219] But the tone is of a poor quality and totally deficient in weight, dignity, gradation or power, especially in the Bass; no swell or double diapasons.

Novello appears to have remained in the Cathedral for the Military Mass at midday. His comments are largely indecipherable. All that emerges with any distinctness is the curious statement:

Military Mass at 12. Overture Zauberflöte.

In the afternoon the Novellos, having made their pilgrimage to Rubens' tomb in the church of St Jacques, stayed to hear Vespers. Novello's comments are characteristic of him in their blending of scrupulous honesty with real regret at having to criticize—especially music and his brother musicians. The choir organ was erected in 1720 ; that at the West end was replaced in 1884 by an entirely new instrument.[220]

I regret not to be able to speak favourably of the Musical performance at this fine Church. I heard the whole of Vespers, which was accompanied by a small orchestra, but throughout the entire Collection of Pieces there was not a single one worthy of a musician's attention. The choir organ is poor and meagre in its tone, and the Full Organ is, without exception, the worst I ever heard. The Reed Stops were buzz combs, harsh and detestably out of tune. A pretty voice among the Trebles—pity not to employ women as in England.

The Music was by some obscure Composer whose name I was unwilling to ascertain exactly, for his sake [*deleted but legible* : and the careless inefficient hand and common manner in which it was accompanied did not at all compensate for the poverty of the composition].

On the conclusion of the Vespers at St Jacques (which began at 4 and terminated about 30 minutes before 5) I hurried to the Cathedral once more in order to be present at the afternoon [service] there also, which began at 5. The service was by Cimarosa, with a repetition of the piece in G at the Benediction which had been performed at High Mass in the morning. Good movement in E sung by tenor voice solo and choir ; best voice we heard.

During the Procession the Orchestra played in a very fair manner the first movement of Haydn's spirited Sinfonia in B flat beginning

It does not form one of the twelve celebrated Sinfonias which he wrote in England for Salomon, but it is in a very elevated style of writing and full of energy. Effect spoiled by the Trombone nearly ½ a tone *too flat* throughout.[221]

As the movement did not last quite long enough for the Procession it was eked out by the Organist who played again the very same movement which he had performed before in the morning.[222]

The following morning found the Novellos at St Paul's, still in pursuit of music and Rubens. As he gives no musical examples, the mass they heard is unidentifiable.

Dominicans at 9. Introit in B flat, with Orchestra. Kyrie and Gloria E flat—commonplace. . . . Credo in E, poor affair, no difference for Crucifixus.

Priest's *Preface* accompanied on Organ, partly *unison*. The responses by the Choir *not* Gregorian which is in wretched bad taste. Badly harmonized by Organ in G minor (5ths).

Benedictus in G. Bass solo, poor voice, very fine Flute

obbligato . . . style too operatic and flourishing—old-fashioned divisions.[223]

Priest accompanied on Organ in the Pater Noster. Gregorian—partly unison and no variety in the harmonies.

Dona nobis good ; note good change to D flat . . . impressively profound.

Very fine Organ . . . Choir organ well toned and in tune . . . high notes rather harsh . . . handsome case, Pipes not gilt. . . . Voluntary before Offertory in A and D, mere modulation, no subject or melody, no invention or idea . . . Organist's name Grillott [sic].

Last voluntary Haydn—Finale from Symphony [No. 99].

Novello's notes on Antwerp end with the first appearance of his regular refrain :

I have heard nothing yet by Haydn, Mozart, Beethoven, Cherubini, Hummel or other of the most elevated Class of Composers.

AIX-LA-CHAPELLE

The next lap of the journey, from Antwerp to Cologne without overnight stop, gave Novello no opportunity of hearing any more church music in Belgium, but during the three hours' wait at Aix-la-Chapelle he heard the organ at St Paul's Church—and the process of his disillusionment with the organists of the continent begins :

. . . Organ very fair tone, but the upper part thin and squealy and the whole, as usual, deficient in *weight* and power. The last Voluntary was *flourishing* and in the light sprightly operatic style which is unfortunately so very prevalent on the Continent and which is so totally opposite to the real organ style.

COLOGNE

At Cologne, musically speaking, the Novellos drew a complete blank. By the secularization under Napoleon the Cathedral musical establishment, and those of the other churches in the city, had been dissolved, and their endowments had become State property. A proposal to use these funds to found a conservatory came to nothing, and it was only in 1807, after years of silence and stagnation, that a group of amateurs banded together to celebrate Epiphany, the Feast of the city's patrons, the Three Kings (who, by tradition, lie buried in the cathedral), by performing a Haydn mass. This initiative was followed up, and the group remained in being, was joined by a number of professional musicians, and continued to perform a mass in the Cathedral every Sunday. This, however, was far from being the same thing as having a regularly trained and paid musical establishment, and many other centres besides Cologne, including many of the large monastic establishments throughout Germany and Austria, suffered a sharp decline in their musical repertory and standards of performance as a result of secularization.[224] In any case, these Cologne performances were on Sundays only, and as the Novellos were there in the middle of the week, they heard nothing.

I am sorry to add that music seems to be completely ' at a stand ' here, or rather in a state of retrogradation. I could not find out [that] there was anything of any kind in the musical way that was in the least degree prominent or worthy of notice.

MANNHEIM

The journey up the Rhine as far as Mannheim was again broken only by short overnight stops, and their Sunday at Mannheim provided their next opportunity for hearing church music. But here, Catholic cathedral and Lutheran church alike disappoint Novello, and another recurring *motif* makes its first appearance —the thought that, after all, English musicians can do as well as this, if not better.

Sunday, July 5th. Went to the principal Church (formerly that of the Jesuits whose order is now suppressed) to hear High Mass which began at 9 o'clock. There was no Orchestra and the music merely consisted of a kind of Chant [*deleted*: partaking somewhat of the Chorale style] but not Gregorian: Kyrie in G, Gloria, Credo, Sanctus and Agnus in C, responses all in B flat. It was sung entirely in *unison* by Men's voices, accompanied on the Organ, as were also the Responses which were Gregorian. The soft stops were of a smooth pleasant quality, and the Full Organ, though partaking of the shrill harsh and squally kind of tone, so usual in the Continental Organs, is not deficient in grandeur and power, especially the Pedal Pipes in [the] Choir organ *behind*. The Organists appear to have no idea of *varying* the effect by the introduction of stops differing in the degree and quality of their tones thereby producing a gradation and contrast of effect. They use the same extremes of soft and loud throughout the service, and appear to prefer *noise* to every other effect.

The Organist on this occasion was the most steady player I have yet heard—although in the accompaniment of the Amen even he could not refrain from introducing some unnecessary nonsensical *flourishes* totally inappropriate to the Organ and quite destructive of the dignified and grave solemnity which ought to be the peculiar characteristic of the real Church style. His modulations were not distinguished by any invention—the chord of the diminished seventh too frequently used. The musical part of the service

293

was remarkably short as it was all over in little more than half an hour.

Lutheran Church afternoon service began at 2 . . . was in time to hear a very charming old chorale steadily sung and judiciously accompanied on the organ here, which is a very good-toned one and reminded me almost of our very favourite Instrument in London, viz. the one at the Savoy Chapel.[225] The harmonies introduced by the organist were solid and musicianlike, and it was upon the whole a respectable performance.

I had the curiosity to stop and hear the sermon . . . the organist, who came forward and leant his head upon his hand over the railing of the Organ loft, had an intelligent countenance and bore some resemblance to the celebrated Wölfel, whom I recollect passing a very pleasant evening with at Sam Wesley's with M. Clementi.[226] But I was sorry to find that he was a lazy fellow, for he only played a few chords, which appeared rather *in*voluntary on his part, when the People quitted the Church, instead of giving us a good fugue by Sebastian Bach as I had anticipated.

Afternoon service at the Jesuits began at 3. It is quite a different service from our Vespers. The commencement was a Hymn in the same style as the morning service, after which came a long sermon of which the congregation seemed as weary as I was, who had the advantage of not understanding it. The Preacher was a most unconscionable fellow and went on in the most persevering droning manner for near an hour. To my great relief, however, he left off at last, when the Litany of Loretto began ; it was recited by one of the Priests and answered by the *Congregation* not by the Choir, and without any accompaniment whatever. After some dreary prayers, during which most of the people round me seemed inclined to indulge in a nap, came the Benediction. The Melody sung by the

Choir (in *unison* still) bore some resemblance to my old favourite the ' Pange Lingua ' (which to my taste is the very finest of all the Gregorian Hymns) but much inferior both in melody and modulation and dignified solemnity of expression to that exquisite specimen of sublime simplicity, and the service concluded with the same Hymn in G as that which I had before heard at the commencement and termination of the morning service. The Organist again introduced his favourite chord of the diminished seventh to absolute satiety, without seeming to be at all aware of the great variety of resolutions of which that chord is susceptible under the hands of a profound and really scientific musician.

In personal appearance he is so like my kind Ries that I could easily have taken him for a younger Brother. I noticed, in addition to what I saw in the morning, that the set of Pedals extend a 10th from G up to B. He made but little use of them, and throughout the service, he introduced not a single fugal point or even a passage of imitation or piece of ingenious counterpoint. Indeed the Organists here seem to have nearly sinecure places, as far as their own extemporaneous power of invention or the elaborate performance of Fugues and other compositions of elaborate or difficult performance are concerned—any one of our own English Protestant Parish organists could have very easily got through the duty as I have heard it performed both in the morning and afternoon here.

I quite long to hear something in the style of Sebastian Bach's masterly ' Choral-Vorspiele ', hitherto I have not [found] even an approach to anything at all resembling his solid and grand style of Organ Pieces.

HEIDELBERG

At Heidelberg Novello's impressions of the Requiem

22

Mass he heard in the Heilig-Geist-Kirche are more favourable, though by present standards there may have been little to choose between ' the harmonies with which this fine specimen of the solemn Gregorian style ' were accompanied there and those provided by Samuel Wesley and himself (see above, p. 281). A curious point is that he remarks, with distaste and as something of a novelty, on the tremulant stop on the organ, which was one of the original features of the organ at the German Lutheran Chapel in the Savoy.

At the principal Church heard a Requiem Mass. It was the fine Gregorian Mass for the Dead, which was sung in unison and accompanied by the Organ only. The Instrument, though small, was a very mellow-toned one. The Organist (who was an unpretending performer) used only the two Diapasons and Principal (which mixed very well together) to accompany the voices, and during the Elevation he played a short little voluntary upon the Stop Diapason alone. There was a contrivance to give a tremulous motion to the bellows, which stop is, I believe, called a ' tremulant ', but I did not like the unsteady effect it produced.

The vocal part would have [been better?] had it been sung by men only, for the Boys singing in consecutive 8ves all the way was unpleasant. The Cantor had a powerful voice of good quality and led the Choir very steadily, but the harmonies with which this fine specimen of the solemn Gregorian style were accompanied were far inferior to those contained in [the] English Edition by Samuel Wesley.

MUNICH

The first church music Novello heard here was Vespers at St Michael's on Saturday, July 11; it was then that he encountered the ' measured ' distortion of the Gregorian chant.

The Vespers which I attended began at 3 o'clock but the Service was not interesting. It was without any orchestra and the chanting was all in unison and was merely accompanied by the Organ assisted by a Bass stringed instrument.

Lauda Jerusalem 7th tone. Hymn 'Celestis Urbs Jerusalem' in E minor, only 1 verse.

Organ rather harsh but powerful. Good Bass. Sesquialtera too predominant. Want of more Diapason and [*illegible*]. Good soft Diapason pipes D and A.

Good for sound—resonance and gradual dim[inuendo] into distance like a Cathedral.

Magnificat—8th tone in B flat. Accompaniment by Contra Bass, in tempo, a kind of moving Bass, and Organ holding Chord on the Choir Organ, Full Organ breaking out at the *sicut erat*. The *measured* singing destroyed the *Chant* character.

Salve Regina, old Gregorian in D, but too fast and in measured time which altered and destroyed its character entirely; all its pathos lost. Accompanied by Organ and Double Bass.

There was no Litany or *Tantum Ergo*, and at the end the Organist merely struck a few Chords on the loud organ accompanied by a blast from some trumpeters in the most sudden and hurried manner, as if they wished to escape from the place—and all was over. This formed indeed a most " lame and impotent conclusion ". From the way in which the last voluntaries and other opportunities of showing what a Player is capable of are shirked and slurred over and avoided, I almost begin to think that the Organists really *cannot* play any Fugues of Bach or other Pieces requiring skill and ability.

On the following day, Sunday, July 12th, the Novellos returned to St Michael's to hear the military Mass. Mary Novello, like her husband, was surprised by the drums and the ' grand roulade at the Elevation ', and fascinated by ' the pieces played during the service . . . first ballet music and secondly a bravura, the solo parts so sweetly played by the clarionet, with so much delicacy and expression that I question if any prima donna could have given it equal effect '. Novello himself, despite his faint disapproval, was so much impressed that he noted down on a separate sheet of paper ' *Handreitter* the 1st Clarionet who played so finely in the Jesuits Church at the Military Mass, Munich '.

The service began at ½ past Ten with the Sermon (which was a tedious affair) and at 11 the Band commenced the Salute with a crash of all the Instruments and a furious Roll on the Drums—the effect was very striking and novel to me in the Church.

Next came a light Movement in B flat, quite in the Dance style and would have been very appropriate as Ballet Music. The second piece was an air in E flat followed by a Rondo and a Polonaise—the whole was more like a Bravura air for the Prima Donna in an Opera than anything else.

They had previously been to the Cathedral to hear High Mass, which, as he found out on inquiry, was by Benedict Schack, a friend of Mozart's and the Tamino of the first production of *The Magic Flute*. During the Mass itself Novello noted down several themes, interspersed with such comments as ' Crucifixus—good modulation ', ' Sanctus, good movement, well worked —sterling writing ', ' Beautiful Melody and well scored ', ' Dona nobis pacem—not so good a subject but well enough [worked] as far as the motive was susceptible '. His subsequent attempts to procure a copy of the work, and their successful outcome, have already been described ; his account follows on his description of Vespers, for which he returned to the Cathedral that afternoon.

Cathedral—Musical Vespers 3 o'clock. Too late for first Psalm. No Orchestra. Accompaniment only with soft Organ holding the chords ; moving Bass played on Violoncello. *Beatus Vir qui timet Dominum* . . . 2nd Gregorian Tone. Organ D major. *Laudate Pueri Dominum*, *hurried* effect not half so devotional or solemn effect as the Gregorian Chant. The Antiphons were Gregorian.

" In exitu Israel ' was *read*, but only a part of the Psalm, the object seemed to be to get over the Service as quickly as possible.

Vespers by Abbé Stadler. Hymn in D—good counter-point in the fugal style . . . good trebles, well in tune, deficient in Basses particularly, alto and tenor also weak.

Magnificat in C . . . only [accompanied] on the Organ, like Psalm, with Double Bass moving *in tempo*, [227] not chant-ing—bad effect.

Salve Regina

Sal - ve Sal - ve Sal - ve Re - gi - na

Placid melody. Organ *breaking* out as usual at the end. Response

A - men, A - men.

No Litany, Tantum Ergo or Benediction. Only a few short chords, no fugue or subject for last Voluntary, and the whole, which lasted only about half an hour, concluded in the most abrupt manner.

SALZBURG

The first service which the Novellos attended in Salzburg was morning Mass at the Benedictine convent chapel of Kloster Nonnberg.

Thursday, July 16, at 7 in the Morning, went to hear the high Mass at the Church belonging to a Convent of Nuns close to the present residence of Mozart's widow, which derives its name of the " Nonnberg " from its vicinity to this Nunnery.

The Service was commenced by a little introductory interlude on the organ in the key of A major, to indicate the Tonic of the Mass. Its style was unpretending, and it was played in a modest and appropriate manner.

The Kyrie on the following subject came next.

Ky-ri - e   e - le - i - son

Its principal characteristics were simplicity and sweetness. The Mass was for three voices—two Trebles and a Bass— and was accompanied only by four Violins (two *first* and two *second*) and the Organ. The latter was merely a small Instrument (placed in a little Chapel near the Altar) containing about half a dozen stops, viz., two Diapasons, Principal, 15th and three-rank mixture, without any reeds whatever. The Bass Notes were weak, but the tone was of an agreeable silvery quality, especially the combination of the two Diapasons and the Principal, which were the stops that were most frequently used during the service. There is another Organ of a much larger size at the opposite end of the Church, but this was not once touched during the whole Mass.

The Responses were constructed of the most simple

300

element, merely the Tonic, Subdominant and Tonic, thus :

but the effect was not the less on that account, on the contrary, these few chords sung by the voices alone produced a solemn and *churchified* effect.

The Offertorium was upon the following sweet and charming melody, and was the best Piece that was performed.

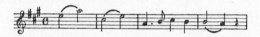

Between the Sanctus and Benedictus a pause was made by the Choir during the time that the Priest was performing the Elevation, after which the music was resumed, to conclude with the "Hosanna in excelsis '.

The Agnus Dei was upon the following melodious subject

and concluded with the Dona Nobis, which was a very charming specimen of simple elegance. I was particularly pleased with the following passage, which formed one of the principal features of the Movement.

At the end of the Mass they performed a Motet, which was evidently by another Master of a much earlier date. It was in F major in the old church style like that of Palestrina, and was less remarkable for its melody than for its fine chords and Ecclesiastical harmonies. It ended with my favourite *plagal* cadence.

After the service was over, I accosted the Person who was carrying home the Music, and he informed me (as well as I could make out his German, which he spoke at a most furious rate, quite *prestissimo*) that the Mass was composed by Deitroffer [*sic*], and on my enquiring whether I could purchase a Copy of the score, he shook his head and said that the Mass had never been published, and that the MS. belonged to the Musical Library of the Convent. I should have liked to have had a copy [of] this Mass, on account of its natural unaffected melody, and its pure, elegant simplicity.

On his second visit to the Convent Chapel there was less to remark on :

Mass in Nonnberg . . . Interlude in D minor, very fine . . . No orchestra. Voluntary in B flat on soft stop, very pretty melody. Mass, De Angelis, Gregorian—too short.

At the Cathedral on the same day, Novello heard High Mass and Vespers. Extracts from his account have already been given, but the whole is retold here for the sake of completeness.

Cathedral, Salzburg, Mass, July 16, 9 o'clock.

The Service began with [a] Procession round the Church, carrying the Sacrament under a Canopy, surrounded with Priests chanting a Gregorian Hymn. A fine effect was produced by the Choristers stopping at intervals, and then breaking out again with their solemn strain, which was sung by men's voices only, and entirely unaccompanied.

The Orchestra was placed in the right-hand Gallery near the Altar against one of the large Pillars which support the Dome. It consisted of two first Violins, a second Violin, Tenor* and Double Bass (no Violoncello), three Trombones (alto, tenor and bass), and the Organ. There are six Organs altogether: one against each of the four Columns under the Dome, another small one (which is usually termed a Positif, and is something like a Chest of Drawers or sideboard) placed on the ground in the Choir not far from the High Altar, and a large Organ over the great West entrance, which Instrument was not used during any part of the service on this occasion, and seems to be reserved for the High Festivals when a more numerous Orchestra is required.

The tone of the Organ which was used to-day was of a sweet quality, especially the two Diapasons. The loud Organ, though deficient in weight and power, particularly in the low Bass Notes, is not so harsh or squally as most of the Organs which I have hitherto met with. The Organist was an unobtrusive respectable performer. He accompanied the voices judiciously, and introduced each movement of the Mass with a few Chords to decide the key. Just before the Gospel he played a little Interlude in the fugue style upon the following agreeable subject:

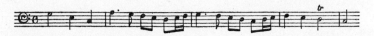

It was so well treated and so regular and symmetrical in design, that if it were an *extemporaneous* production, it was highly creditable to him.

There were about 6 or 8 voices, with a Person to beat

* Viola.

the time for them, but they were not efficient, and were quite overpowered by the Instrumental Orchestra, who played too loud all the way through and especially in the *piano* parts which required delicacy. The best performers were the three trombone players, who produced a fine tone and added much grandeur to the general effect. The next best Player was on the Double Bass. He was a Priest, and it appeared to me quite a novel and singular thing to see this Instrument played by a Person in a Cassock and other sacerdotal habiliments, which however did not seem in the least to impede the freedom of his bowing.

The Responses were given by the voices alone, and were the same as those I had heard before at the Convent, viz. the mere tonic and subdominant forming the plagal cadence.

A - men.

The Boys' Voices were charming and perfectly in tune; the effect of the diminuendo and gradual dying off of the sounds at the termination of each response was quite beautiful and cathedral-like. In the *Accompanied* parts of the service there was rather too much resonance and vibration from the Dome, which occasioned one Chord to run into the other so as to destroy the distinctness of the different harmonies.

The Mass was in C, but contained nothing very striking. The offertory was in E, and was the best movement that was performed. In its style it resembled the first movement of Graun's Te Deum. I endeavoured to ascertain the name of the Composer both of that, and of the rest of the Mass, but without success.

I own I was disappointed at not having heard a single

Piece of Mozart's composition at any of the Churches in his own native town.

During Benediction the Performers left the Organ Gallery and stationed themselves close to the High Altar where they performed a short Motet, accompanied on the 'Positif' or small organ before mentioned.

There was no last Voluntary or 'Sortie', and the whole service was concluded in about 40 minutes.

Salzburg Cathedral, 2 o'clock afternoon.

I expected the Vespers to have begun at the above hour and accordingly attended punctually, but I found the Person at the Cathedral tuning the reed stops of the large Organ at the west end of the Church. That which they were putting into order was not a good one; the tone was *buzzy* and stifled like a poor bassoon or badly voiced Cremona.

I walked round the building and had an opportunity of examining more closely the Positif—small Organ in the Choir near the high altar. Its compass is from E in the bass ♩ up to C above the staff ♩. It has an octave of pedals to pull down the keys but no Diapason Pipes. On the desk was an old Vellum Book in the Gregorian Character.

The Priest who had played the Double Bass in the Morning came out of the Sacristy to tune his Instrument beforehand. He seemed to be a genuine lover of the grand notes that are to be pulled out by a skilful hand from this noble Instrument. He brought out some very fine soft subdued and rich notes before he had tuned it to his mind, and as he leaned over it he appeared to doat upon its full, round and deep tones, nor did he leave it till he had put it into most admirable order.

305

The Choir Boys, of whom there were about a dozen, had cocked hats like the Choir Boys belonging to the King's Chapel Royal in England.

At ½ past 3 the Service began. There was a Catafalque under the Dome with a Mitre, Cardinal's Cap etc., and the Service seemed to be in commemoration of some elevated Ecclesiastic. The painting at the High Altar was covered with black cloth, and the Priests wore dresses similar to those I have seen in England when there has been a Requiem or Service for the dead celebrated.

After the Recitation of several Psalms by the two sides of [the] Choir taking the alternate verses—like the Decani and Cantori at our Cathedrals—there came some versicles with the following fine Responsories.

The rest of the service was solemn Gregorian and excellent of its kind, but it was not what I expected or wished to hear at the birthplace of Mozart. I wished to have heard his Vespers [*illegible*] or one of his masterly Litanies, especially the one in B flat with the glorious fugue *Pignus futurae*.[228]

His last visit to the Cathedral, the following morning, intensified his disappointment.

Salzburg Cathedral, went at 9 expecting to hear High Mass, but there was no choir or Orchestra, merely a few Priests singing in the Plain Chant, without even the organ to accompany them.

Music indeed is in a very sad state of decay in this the very birthplace of the most enchanting composer that ever existed.

During the few hours the Novellos spent in Salzburg on their return journey Novello had his wished-for opportunity of hearing the large organ at the West end of the Cathedral. Unfortunately this provided yet another disappointment.

". . . We then set off to visit Mozart's widow, and on our way thither, by another very fortunate coincidence, we stepped into the Cathedral, where we found that the Archbishop of Salzburg and the Prince of Sweden (which latter happened to be passing through the Town) were both expected to come and hear a performance on the large organ at the west Door, which had just undergone a thorough repair. This Instrument is very seldom used, and if this accidental visit of the Prince had not taken place, I should have had no opportunity whatever of hearing it played.

I should have been much pleased if that would have allowed me to give a favourable opinion of this Organ, which, it seems, has cost a very large sum to be put into playable order ; but the fact is that it is a very harsh and disagreeable Instrument. Nor can I, without sacrificing what is due to veracity, say anything in favour of the Performer, who, instead of *sustaining* the notes and introducing full chords, imitation, suspensions and other features appropriate to the genuine Organ style, played a series of staccato passages, Rossinian triplets, commonplace runs, and abrupt terminations [?], totally at variance with the dignified solemnity required for the proper treatment of the Organ, the most noble and sublime of all Instruments.

LINZ

On the Sunday morning which the Novellos unwillingly spent in Linz, Vincent Novello went to the

Cathedral. His notes, disconnected and partly illegible, reflect his disgruntled view of the town and its music, and of the eighteenth-century organ which from 1856 to 1868 was to be the instrument of Anton Bruckner.[229]

Cathedral at Linz—Service at 9. Bad organ, full diapason coarse and harsh. Sermon a tedious affair.

Introit, fine old style—Palestrina. Orchestra—no *wind* instruments.

A - men.

Good solemn effect—like a sigh.

Kyrie in C.

too short, spoiled at end by squally organ. Gloria . . . commonplace. Gradual, same style in C . . . organ bursting in as usual at end . . . Offertorium.

good treble voices ; violoncello fine player, too abrupt in his ending. Sanctus . . . soft stops good ; after a pause between Sanctus and Benedictus, most tasteful melody altogether :

Agnus Dei in A minor :

Solo Basso best voice, poor style.
Dona nobis :

Fine sequence with voices. Organ took the subject and
worked it pretty fairly . . . but too short and hurried.
The last Voluntary was in D minor, and seemed to promise
something, but it terminated in a few short points of easy
imitation, and like all the rest of the service, was tinged
with that disagreeable sense of impatience, as if the
Performer disliked what he was about and wanted to run
off as fast as he could. In this Organist, although there was
nothing to offend, neither was there anything indicative
of genius nor anything approaching the strict elevated
style of Bach.

Long service altogether, lasted inside [?] of an hour
and a half.

On the page on which these notes are made Novello
has also taken down a chorale, which, from some very
confused notes on the other side of the page, appears
to have been sung by the congregation accompanied
by the organ.

The churches of the Imperial capital provided Novello with the most satisfactory impressions of his trip, though even here he finds plenty to criticize. It is worth remarking that here, as at Linz, chorales, probably for congregational singing, make their appearance: possibly during the celebration of Mass, or as settings of those metrical-paraphrase vernacular masses, the *Deutsche Messen* so frequently used to this day in Austria, southern Germany and German Switzerland. Michael Haydn's mass *Hier liegt vor Deiner Majestät*, of which Novello noted down Haslinger's advertisement in a Viennese newspaper, is one of many such. The organ playing, here as elsewhere, continues to disappoint him.

Augustinerkirche, July 22nd
After quoting what appears to be the beginning of a chorale, Novello merely adds:

No last Voluntary—poor organ.

Augustinian Church in the Landstrasse (now St Roch). July 25th
Augustine Church, Landstrasse suburb, Saturday morning. Only 6 o'clock Benediction. Quite full, especially women. Chorale in E flat, organ nothing particular, all the same monotonous harmonies.

St Stephen's Cathedral, Sunday, July 26th
8 o'clock, Chorale (in G) and sermon.
At 9 o'clock High Mass. The band consisted of about half a dozen Violins, Viola, Violoncello and Double Bass, and Trombones.
Introit in C, quite in Palestrina's solemn and churchified style and probably by him. Four voices and without any accompaniment, charming effect. The service began with

a procession round the Church by the Priests who sprinkled the People with holy water as they proceeded.

During the Procession I heard the large Organ at the west end, which is only used on Sundays and high Festivals. An introduction followed by a Fugue in C minor was played in a very creditable manner by the organist. The tone of this large Instrument is too harsh and coarse to please me ; the effect was also much injured by the continual tremor and unsteadiness of the bellows. The tone of the small Organ in the Choir near the altar is of a much better quality.

The Mass was in a poor commonplace old style like what might have been written by Hasse or Vinci—all the movements were short and unsatisfactory.

The best voices were the Trebles. The Orchestral performers were of the mediocre kind.

Responses like Linz.

Between 2 and 3 went again to St Stephen's in hope to hear Vespers, but there was only [a] Sermon preceded by a short Chorale without any accompaniment whatever.

Monday Morning at Vienna Cathedral, 10 o'clock, July 27. Chorale.

Sweet dulcian. No swell. Good voluntary in A minor, rather too much modulation and deficient in melody and symmetrical construction. After the elevation the Chorale began again. The last Voluntary consisted merely of chords, some of them very crude, without any Fugue or melodious [*illegible*].

Wednesday, July 29th

St Stephen's, 4 o'clock, went again in hope to hear a musical Vespers or Litany, but there were merely the priests singing, with a few short chords by way of introduction on the Organ. I went up to the Organ loft, where I found an elderly-looking person seated at the Instrument. I ventured to address him, as he appeared to have a good-natured physiognomy (something like that of Hummel) and said I should esteem it as a great favour, if he would have the goodness to oblige me by playing one of Sebastian Bach's Fugues for the last Voluntary. He answered me very politely that unfortunately there would be no opportunity to gratify my wishes, as it was not customary to play any sortie or last Voluntary after the service on week days. There is only *one* Row of keys to this Organ, besides the set of Pedals ; the soft Stop answering to our Dulciana is of a very subdued, round and sweet tone, and is by far the best Stop in the Organ. The Pedal Pipes are wanting in dignity and force.

St Anne's Church. Sunday, July 26th

10 o'clock High Mass, St Anne's Church.

As I was informed by Mr Eybler that there was to be a Mass by Eybler (No. 4 in C) performed here on [the] occasion of its being the Festival of St Anne, I made a point of being present, as I was anxious to hear something by a Composer whom my friend Mr Latrobe esteems so highly. But no sooner had they begun the Kyrie than I recognized it to be Haydn's fine Mass in B flat (No. 16 my Edition) [i.e., the Theresa Mass].

Kyrie Fugue too fast.

Gradual, Duet for Tenor and Bass.

Like Cimarosa's style. It is a little too theatrical, but charmingly scored. It was correctly sung, especially by the Bass, who had the better voice of the two.

Responses for Amen, etc., same as at the Cathedral.

The Organ is noisy and harsh ; the soft stops were not once used, so that I could not judge of them.

Credo too fast—hurried unsteady effect. " Et incarnatus est " in B flat minor, the most charming movement in the Mass : it should have been sung with more delicacy of style, and the Instruments and voices more subdued. First Violin and Double Bass the best performers. This [is] altogether the most sterling church music I have yet heard performed in Germany.

Offertorium probably by Naumann.

313

Hofburgkapelle, Sunday, July 26th

11 o'clock, attended the High Mass at the Chapel Royal. Asperges in A minor, accompanied, of which the *Versicles* were Gregorian and sung by voices alone. One of the best-toned Organs I have yet met with of the smaller class. Introt, " Eructavit cor meum ", in B flat ; good old style.
Mozart in D No. 6. [K194].

Good band, though small, several of the Opera orchestra Service conducted by Eybler, who told me he had added the part [for full?] band, as Mozart had written the Mass for only 2 Violins and Bass for some small Church.[230] Most musicianlike performance I have yet heard. There were not many performers, but all *efficient*.
Gradual Michael Haydn.

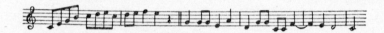

Well worked, good solid style.

Offertory introduced by a short Overture. Began in Tenor, a kind of chant form.

Responses Gregorian 7th tone [*sic*; they appear to be in fact a distortion of the *Tonus Peregrinus*].

Contrasted tenor voice and soprano and they all join at the end. Original and good music.

Charming phrase at the end of Credo, like Gluck's Orfeo.

Soft voluntary before Benedictus. Good organ. Simple smooth melody.

Agnus Dei in B minor began with soprano solo, and Dona nobis which I have produced at [*several words illegible*]. No Tantum Ergo at Benediction.

Last Voluntary in E minor, and ended in D. No Fugue, which disappointed me as he shone [?] as a very fine performer.

> Novello learned the next day at Haslinger's shop that the organist was none other than the celebrated theorist Sechter, from whom Schubert at the time of his death was planning to take lessons in counterpoint:

Mr Müller told me that it was Mr Sechter whom I had heard play the Organ yesterday at the Imperial Chapel, and spoke of him as a very learned contrapuntist—and that he was much greater as a composer than as a performer.

＊　　　＊　　　＊

> The return journey from Vienna to Paris was made much more quickly than the outward trip; the holiday was over and there was business to be done. At Melk the Novellos broke their journey to visit the abbey, and saw the interior of the church with its organ, built by Gottfried Sonnholz in 1731, in its beautiful case; but they did not stay to hear it.[231] Nor did they attempt to stop at Augsburg and hear the organ at the Discalced Carmelite Church (Barfüsserkirche) built by J. A. Stein, Nanette Streicher's father, despite the

315

letter of introduction to the organist which her son had given them. Indeed they heard no church music until they had crossed the French frontier, where, on August 7th, they attended Vespers at Strasburg Cathedral. From here to Paris the journey is marked by lamentable organ-playing, and even the Silbermann organ at Strasburg wins only qualified praise from Novello.

STRASBURG

Chant at Strasburg Friday Vespers, August 7th/29, 4 o'clock.

7th Tone Gregorian. Magnificat Chant and [*illegible*] in E flat. 6th Tone Gregorian. Wretched noisy stuff all on the full Organ—crashing, banging and flourishing throughout without the least variety.

Diapason and Principal by far the most weighty and Cathedral-like I have heard on the Continent. Reed work and Full organ harsh and bad. Organist—flourishes : did not stop for priests but broke in upon them—impatient effect.

Handsome Gothic case on the *side* of the nave, probably not to interfere with the fine effect of the great west window. Probably " L'Orgue de [*illegible*] "—Bass pipes fine, " not loud but deep ", Trebles, high octave too shrill, and scream-ing effect. Good Bass voice like *fat* Monks. No last Voluntary or Fugue, which I was the less sorry for as I am sure this performer would only have spoilt any move-ment of the dignified class which he might have attempted.

METZ

Arrived at Metz at 2 o'clock . . . attended Vespers at 3 o'clock . . . 4th Tone Gregorian thus, viz.:

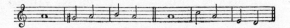

Serpent used with the antiphon, the first time I have heard it since I have been on the Continent—the Psalms were sung without any accompaniment and entirely in unison. Boys give out the first word of [the] Antiphon an Octave higher—too shrill and squally, and too violent a contrast with the Bass voices of the Priests. This was the Boys' chant in unison.

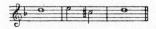

Organ first used to play the Interludes between the verses of the Hymn and Magnificat. Very poor Instrument —harsh and squally tone, noise and no weight, like a street organ out of tune—and worse player; he was of that abominable class who play *polaccas* on the Organ. He frightened me out of the Church completely. I could not stay the service out. . . . The Diapason and Principal were pretty fair stops, but these he seemed to avoid intentionally, and kept constantly bursting and crashing and twiddling about on the coarse and squally loud organ.

CHÂLONS SUR MARNE

Sunday Morning, Aug. 9th. Attended High Mass at the Cathedral or principal Church at Châlons . . . the organ is near the great West door, but it appears to be undergoing a thorough repair and I heard only a few of the stops. When completed it will probably be upon a large scale, judging from the dimensions of the case, which is of a handsome and tasteful form. The tone of what I heard was poor and thin, but it is hardly fair to judge of it from its present very incomplete state.

★   ★   ★

The service consisted merely of the Gregorian Chant, accompanied by the serpent, and the organ was only used for the interludes. I was again disappointed by the Performer not even attempting anything like a Fugue or a solid movement at all approaching the genuine Organ style—but a mere jumble of childish roulades, scampering flourishes and old, worn-out passes [sic] in the Harpsichord style. No last voluntary.

The more I hear of the Organists of the Continent the more I am convinced that the present race have not the least notion of the great capabilities of which the Organ is susceptible, or what is the real genius of this most noble and sublime of all Instruments.

The only performer I regret not having heard is J. Schneider at Dresden, as I understand he is really a great player, and as this opinion is corroborated by the fact of his being in the constant habit of playing the glorious fugues of Sebastian Bach, I can readily believe that he is quite worthy of the great reputation he has acquired.

Edward Holmes, on his travels through Germany, had heard Johann Gottlob Schneider, Court Organist at Dresden, who numbered among his pupils Mendelssohn, Schumann, and Liszt. Holmes must have described to Novello, as he does in his *Ramble*,

Schneider's ' playing of the Kyries of Sebastian Bach, playing the whole of six and seven real parts with such a towering skill in the pedals as to make one think the old author returned from his grave '. The fact that he was so much impressed by Schneider's performance of these relatively easy works (which are in five parts at the most) indicates how rare an accomplishment the use of the pedals was.

PARIS

Notre Dame, August 15*th*

Saturday, High Mass at Notre Dame—Assumption of [the] Virgin. Mass in B flat with a small orchestra, from movable Desks placed before the entrance of the Choir ; not voices sufficient for the Instruments, which (as usual) play too loud in the Piano and delicate passages. Music not of the elevated class, and the execution rather unsteady as to time and unfinished as to manner. The best movement was the " Qui tollis ", a quartet in F minor, with the ripieni voices coming in occasionally to relieve and contrast with the principals. A very disagreeable harsh and loud voice among the Counter Tenors ; it predominated over all the rest and *soured* every piece in which it was heard. There was a tolerably good Bass Voice, but without cultivation or refinement in his style, and the Choir Boys sang their parts in tune and with accuracy. The Choruses were very poor counterpoint and there was not even an attempt at a Fugue, either at the " Cum Sancto Spiritu ", the " et vitam venturi " at the end of the Credo, the " Hosanna in excelsis " or the " Dona nobis pacem ".

The Organ was only used to play a few short interludes between the pieces and whilst the Priests were making their procession round the Church. These voluntaries were played neatly enough as to execution, but were

319

totally unfit for the Organ, as may be judged from the following specimen of one of the subjects chosen.

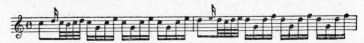

Poor service altogether for the Cathedral of Paris which calls itself the capital of Europe.

St Étienne-du-Mont.   August 15th

Half past one, attended Vespers at St Étienne, near St Geneviève. . . . Improved serpent like Bass Horn—metallic, good tone. Saw Double Bass but not used—but effect of serpent to take the 8ve. *below* the voices at the end of antiphons.

> The ' improved serpent ' may have been the all-metal ophicleide invented in France by Halary in 1817, but there were other forms of the instrument, straightened out and bent back upon themselves like a bassoon and known as the ' Russian Bassoon ' or bass horn, which were sometimes made of metal covered with wood.[232]

The Sorbonne.   August 15th

Half past 2, Sorbonne, Vespers—by far the best music.

Orchestra, good first violins, inferior in the kind of Serpent, [*illegible*] Horns.

Movement in C by Danzi, same as at the Concours—softly and well accompanied.

Best Organ—not so much bursting, cracking and noise, better quality. More judicious Organist.

St Sulpice, August 15 *or* 16

Here Novello's notes are disconnected and partly illegible. Of the organ, built by Cliquot in 1781,[233] he remarks ' Best Diapasons ' ; an observation on the reed stops tails off into illegibility. Apart from this it appears that some, at least, of the music was Gregorian and that the trombones made a fine effect ; whether they were used to accompany the Gregorian chant or not does not emerge, for no other music is mentioned.

*   *   *

So Vincent Novello's musical record ends. It is the record of a practical musician, not of a historian. He possessed no spirit of divination. No suspicion crossed his mind that Rossini was a spent force as a composer, that Italy's musical supremacy was passing and that young Mendelssohn was to be among the leaders under whom German music swept to unchallenged sovereignty : that Bach would be recognised within fifty years as one of the greatest musicians of all time, and that Mendelssohn's efforts—united with his own and those of Wesley and Jacob—had already dislodged the pebbles that were to set the avalanche in motion. He had no inkling that Gregorian chant and the masterpieces of sixteenth-century polyphony would supplant his beloved Viennese masters for liturgical use, and that musical scholarship would awaken sleeping beauties beyond the range of his dreams in that very past to which he looked for salvation.

Yet it was as a practical musician, living in the present, that he did as much as any man of his generation to recapture the past and safeguard the future by arousing the love of the new musical public for the best in music. As his daughter writes, his cheap editions of great works ' created both demand and supply ; for, by his early efforts he introduced little-known works of great masters, thereby originating a taste and desire for them ; and, by his persevering toil, continued to bring them forth in such abundance and usable shape, that they became necessities not only to musicians, but aspirants in musical cultivation. Out of this abundance and usableness grew the requisite cheapness which should place these sterling works within command of the large class of users that had been rendered so extensive '.[234]

This is his greatest achievement : and it still lives.

L. 27.XI.55

APPENDIX I

VINCENT NOVELLO'S FATHER

Giuseppe Novello came from Tonengo (now in the Province of Asti) in what was then the Kingdom of Sardinia. He appears to have been a servant of sorts in various inns before coming to England in 1771. Family tradition says he sold cakes in the London streets before opening his shop.

Giuseppe Novello was, by the standards of his time, no ordinary man of the people. He could read and write (and there was education in the family, for a letter of his shows that one of his father's brothers was employed by the Piedmontese government in the *Gabella del Sale*, the State monopoly of salt and tobacco). He kept a note-book, in Italian, recording the date of his marriage, the births and deaths of his children, etc. Two sons survived, Francis and Vincent (christened Francesco and Vincenzo). He sent them, as boys, to learn French at Boulogne, and although Vincent began to earn his living very early, first as a chorister, then as organist and music teacher, the father must have encouraged him in his pursuit of education, to judge by the high degree of general culture and refinement which he achieved. Vincent lived with his father and took care of him till his death, just before his own engagement and marriage.

Nothing is known of Giuseppe's wife, and little of his son Francis, except that he had a very fine voice and was the principal bass at the Portuguese Embassy chapel during the whole period of his brother's tenure of office as organist. His wife's name was Adelaide Valle, and family records indicate that they had three daughters.

323

APPENDIX II

Despite, or perhaps because of, the aura of mystery surrounding the parentage of Mary Novello's father, Simon Hehl, the tradition of the family's German origin has become obscured. Mr Percy Allen[235] writes of Mary Novello's brother (Captain Simon Hehl) that he was ' a German, in all probability, whose forerunners in England had come over, my father thinks, with the Georges. Be that as it may, the family, I suppose, was, by that time, completely Anglicized, since we hear nothing of German connections '. In a footnote he adds that Mrs Stirling's intimates believed that she had Irish blood in her. We, the grandchildren of Mrs Stirling's first cousin Clara Novello, have always known that Mary Novello, her brother Simon Hehl the younger, and their sister, the lovely Catherine (later Mrs Collins), were born in England, the children of a German father and an Irish (or partly Irish) mother. The latter's name was Elizabeth Field. According to her husband's account, she was the daughter of an Irish lady, widow of a British Army officer, with whom Simon Hehl the elder took lodgings on his first coming to London. Two small portrait drawings, one of Simon Hehl and the other of his wife, are now in our possession in Fermo. Moreover, we have come upon something which was believed to be lost—the memoirs of old Simon Hehl: though unfortunately what we have found is not the original, but merely two copies, one of them transcribed (and considerably mutilated) by our great-aunt Sabilla Novello. With this abridged copy is the draft of a letter written by her in 1899 to her friend Mrs Fields in America, in which she writes :

> Among our family papers is a very interesting MS. by our maternal grandfather (German), giving the recital of his life from boyhood upward. . . . It is wonderfully graphic, and his adventures are so romantic as to appear invented, but we know they are real. I have made a copy of this MS., considerably shortened, with a view to having it published . . ."

Evidently nothing came of this idea ; but from our great-aunt's letter it is clear that the family tradition accepted the main lines of Simon Hehl's story as genuine, despite the aura of improbability that surrounds some of his statements, in certain of which it must have been obvious to them that he was romancing.

According to his own account, Simon Hehl the elder was born in Frankfurt am Main in 1740 and came to England at about thirty years of age as travelling companion and teacher of Italian and German to a not very open-handed Scottish baronet whom he had met in Italy. On his marriage he settled in London as a teacher of languages, of which he knew six, including Turkish. Of his parentage he merely says that he was ignorant of his family pedigree, that his father had died when he was an infant, and that :

> The mention of his name always caused my mother such deep affliction, that by degrees I forbore all allusion to him ; but, from what I gathered at intervals . . . I understood that he was of a noble family, and had imprudently married my mother for her great beauty. . . . The enmity of my father's family had driven the offending couple from Saxony to Frankfort, where he had obtained the high-sounding, but

unlucrative post of Keeper of the Burgher's Armory. I think some change of name may also have taken place, otherwise I might, in the course of my wanderings, have gathered some tidings of my haughty relatives ; but perhaps not, as my own indignation against them kept me from all enquiries . . .

My father, Mario Gigliucci, has often told me that there was more than a little doubt whether Hehl was not an assumed name, for the German verb *hehlen* or *verhehlen* means to hide or conceal. Mr Allen describes the portrait of the younger Simon Hehl, who became a captain of Footguards and ultimately Assistant Quartermaster General of Horse Guards, as that of ' a portly gentleman of aristocratic and somewhat haughty demeanour ', and both his sisters had, from their pictures and from all accounts of them, an equally striking and highly refined appearance. Whether they knew or suspected more about their father's parentage or not, the subject was, I believe, more or less taboo with them.

Although, despite her German blood, Mary Novello had no family ties at all with Germany, and could not even speak the language, we know (by family tradition and through her daughter Clara's *Reminiscences*), that a German lady, Baroness von Helldorf, was her very dear friend. So intimately attached were they to each other that, at about the same time as the Salzburg journey, she and the Baroness exchanged portraits, which their two families interchanged again after their deaths. The portrait of Mary Sabilla Novello which was her part in this exchange is now in our possession ; it is the oil painting reproduced in this book. Some years later her daughter Clara went to Germany to accompany her very young sister Sabilla, who was going to stay with their mother's ' old friend Baroness H. ' to teach English to this lady's six-year-old daughter and be taught German, in return, by the old secretary.

The Helldorfs are an ancient Saxon family, but the friendship between the Baroness and Mary Novello, being an old one, must have started in England ; possibly the Baroness' father was resident in London in a diplomatic or other official capacity. If so, Mary Sabilla Hehl may have been her schoolmate, or even (as the little Helldorf daughter was so much younger than the youngest Novello) her beloved governess ; in either case the Baroness was, almost certainly, the ' dear Theresa ' whom Mary Novello, in Vienna, compares so favourably with all the other ' women of Germany '.

That Mary Novello had visited Germany before, in 1827, appears from remarks made both by herself and her husband in these diaries. (See above, p. 20.) Nothing more, however, was known about this visit until—after this book had gone to press—her diary of the earlier journey came to light in the family home in Fermo. From this diary it is apparent that she had accompanied Edward Holmes on the journey which he records in his book *A Ramble among the Musicians of Germany*. Her account, running parallel with Holmes', is written with the same trenchancy and shrewdness as the present record. It is addressed throughout to her husband, whom, on the eve of their journey down the Danube by raft, she addresses thus : ' God bless you, dear one, I hope to receive a letter from you in Vienna, mine you will receive on Monday next, I wish it were myself instead, but without vanity Edward could not do without me, and you have done him a great service in letting me accompany him. I do not half like the thought of our journey down the Danube, but it may be fancy, if I reach Vienna I shall write from there, both to you and in my journal.'

24

APPENDIX III

THE PRESENTATION TO MOZART'S SISTER

The list of subscribers drawn up by J. A. Stumpff, which accompanied the presentation to Mozart's sister, was receipted by Constanze von Nissen on her behalf and returned to Novello. It therefore remained in his possession, Stumpff subsequently providing a rough translation of Constanze's receipt. It is given below.

The undermentioned Persons, who are enthusiastic admirers of the delightful compositions of Mozart, have formed (quite privately amongst themselves) a little Collection amounting to 60 Guineas, for the purpose of offering a small present to the Sister of Mozart, as a trifling token of their respect for the memory of her illustrious Brother, and of their cordial sentiments towards his estimable Sister, Madame Sonnenburg.

They have confided their little present to the care of Mr V. Novello, in order that he may place it in Madame Sonnenburg's own hands, in any way which he may find will be most agreeable to herself. Whatever mode will afford most pleasure to the Sister of Mozart, will be that which will also afford the greatest gratification to her cordial friends, whose names will be found subjoined.

London, Wedy. June 24th, 1829.

Mr Stumpff	..	..	.. £10
,, V. Novello	..	..	.. 10
,, Stevens	..	..	.. 5
,, Attwood (pupil of Mozart)	..	5	
,, Braham	..	..	.. 5
,, Capel ..	..	..	.. 5

Mr Trueman	..	..	..	£2
„ Potter ..	..	..	..	I
„ Moscheles	..	..	..	2
„ J. B. Cramer	..	..	..	2
Mrs Haddon	..	..	..	2
„ Doxat ..	..	..	..	5
Mr Cazenove	..	..	..	5
„ Horsley	..	..	..	I
„ Dampier	..	..	..	2
„ Holden	..	..	..	I

£63

Mit grössestem Herzen und dem innigsten Dank für meine Schwägerin Sonnenburg Constanza Etatsrathin von Nissen gewesene Wittwe Mozart Salzburg am 15 julli 1829.

Translation:

With the most heartfelt gratitude I acknowledge in the name of Mozart's sister the receipt of the sum mentioned herein—signd:
Constanze v. Nissen Mozart's Widow.
J. A. S.

1. From Count Moritz Dietrichstein, Curator of the Imperial Library.

Monsieur,

Monsieur l'Abbé Stadler m'ayant remis cette lettre, je n'attendais que le départ d'un courrier, pour vous la faire parvenir d'une manière sûre. C'est avec bien de l'empressement que je saisis cette occasion, pour me rappeler a votre souvenir, et pour établir un commerce littéraire qui, outre le plaisir qu'il me prépare, procurera sans doute de grands avantages à l'institut, confié a mes soins.

Une heure d'entretien avec vous, Monsieur, a suffi pour me faire connâitre le savant distingué et l'homme aimable, et elle n'a pu qu'augmenter vivement mes regrets de ne pas avoir été prévenu plus tôt de votre arrivée a Vienne.

Dès ma rentrée en ville je m'occuperai de l'édition du Requiem de Mozart, d'après le manuscript autographe que vous avez vu, et jeme manquerai pas de vous en envoyer un exemplaire, et plus tard autant que vous desirerez.

La langue anglaise ne m'offrant quelques difficultés que sous le rapport du style, je ne prendrai la liberté de vous écrire en francais que lorsque je serai pressé, et vous voudrez bien en agir à cet égard à volonté.

Mon fils, Secrétaire d'Ambassade à Londres, ayant quitté cette ville dans ce moment, j'enverrai mes lettres a Monsieur de Neumann, Conseiller d'Ambassade, ou a Mr le Baron de Koller, qui remplace provisoirement mon fils. Les paquets vous parviendront par Messieurs Bossange,

Barthès & Lovell, libraires, No. 14 Gt. Marlborough St., London, Correspondents de Mr Schalbacher, libraire a Vienne.

Veuillez présenter mes hommages a Madame de Novello et agréer l'assurance de la consideration distinguée avec laquelle j'ai l'honneur d'étre,

    Monsieur,
   votre très-humble et très-obeissant serviteur,
       M. DIETRICHSTEIN.

Vienne le 15 September 1829.
Je joins ici mon adresse. [Separate slip enclosed.]

2. From Tobias Haslinger [in a clerk's handwriting, signed by Haslinger].

Mr V. Novello at London.
     Vienna, the 9th September 1829.

Gentleman,

With the sincerest wish, that you and your venerable Lady might be arrived safe and sound at home, I advertise you that your bespoken music

1. Ahasuerus, composed by J. Seyfried, Esqre. after Mozart, has been adjoined to a sending, just now made to London to Mrs Boosey & C., to whom I have given order to get in from you the amount of it per fls. 6 C.M.

Mr Mozart, who returned yesterday from here to Lembergh, as also Abbé Stadler, Eybler, &c. present their amicable greetings and respects to you ; peculiarly may you accept them for my part ; let me be recommended to your valuable remembrance, please to kiss the hands of your dearest Lady in my name and agree the assurance of the highest reverence, with which I sign,

    Gentleman,
     Your most devoted servant,
      (Signed) TOBIAS HASLINGER.

     331

3.   From Joseph Metzger.*

Salsbourg, ce 16 Juillet 1829.

Monsieur,

La Madame de Sonnenbourg, née Mozart, enchantée de l'honneur de la visite de Vous, et de vôtre Madame, com'aussi de l'inattendu cadeau, dont vous l'avez favorisée par la generosite de vous même, et de plusieurs autres admirateurs de Londres des compositions de son frère Mozart m'a chargé, de vous en remercier en son nom aussi en écrit, et de vous prier de faire son remerciment d'après votre retour aussi aux autres Messieurs, qui prennent part du sudit genereux cadeau, en vous assurant, qu'elle est bien faché, de ne savoir parler avec Vous personellement, pour vous convaincre de la joie, de se voir si distinguée des étrangers, et de la reconnaissance, avec laquelle elle reste et resterait toujours obbligée a vous et a tous les autres amateurs de la musique, qui sont preferablement ravis des compositions de son frère, et qui le conservent par leur bonte si vifement dans leur memoire.

J'ai honneur d'etre avec la plus parfaite estime,

Monsieur,

Votre tres humble Servr.

Joseph Metzger, Privatier.

4.   From Franz Kandler.

This is a translation of the original Italian. The accompanying copy of the canon which Kandler sent to Novello as being an early work of Mozart is reproduced at page 198. It does not appear in Einstein's revised edition of Köchel's Thematic Catalogue. If it is in fact by Mozart, it was probably composed during his tour of Italy with his father in 1770, at the age of fourteen, as this was the only occasion on which he visited Florence.

* The letter is given as it stands, without corrections.

Vienna, July 29th, 1829.

Most honoured Maestro,

I am extremely sorry that you are no longer able to come at the appointed time, and I cannot but regret that you should have preferred others to instruct you in the musical technicalities of our country. Meanwhile I hope I may have the pleasure of being of service, on some other occasion, to one who has so many claims on our interest, affection and most sincere regard.

Be that as it may, I enclose two letters, one for M. Fétis, to whom I owe the honour of your personal acquaintance, the other for Mr Moscheles in London.

I am sending the draft of the canon which Mozart composed at an early age for a noble family in Florence; it is badly written out as I could not find the original, but I am sure I have it in my possession. If it would interest you to have it, I will hunt for it with a little patience. It is as yet unknown to the world.

Finally, here are the three catalogues of the original manuscripts in my possession—the musical autographs as well as the letters and treatises. The names alone indicate little, but they represent a rich harvest, comprising all that, as an ardent collector, I have been able to acquire in the various countries I have visited.

Should there be, in France or in England, a library of high standing and endowed with ample means, or any private individual who would set the right value on such a collection—which is certainly unique of its kind—I might be disposed to sell it, either as a whole or in separate lots, but with the sole object of serving the ends of art: that is, by first making the originals known to the world by means of lithography, through which it is easy to produce any kind of facsimile. If, however, there is anyone over there possessing true genius and knowledge and the necessary means, I

333

would make no difficulties about giving up even the plan
I have just mentioned, provided, of course, that the project
were put into effect over there for the furtherance of
knowledge. On this point I shall await your next esteemed
communication, which will decide my course of action.

The music dealer Schlesinger in Paris, to whom I gave
the commission for the printing of Naumann's celebrated
Paraphrase of the Pater Noster, would certainly reply
more promptly if you, my dear Maestro, would be so good
as to call on him personally and become acquainted with
his business and his publications. If you, or the estimable
M. Fétis, would kindly speak on behalf of the work, which
is being anxiously awaited in Italy, it would certainly have
the result that the Italian edition would also cross the
Channel. I beg you therefore, among your countless other
commitments there, to undertake the correction of the Pater
Noster, which I have as much at heart as any good father
has a happy delivery. With your permission I shall await
your kind reply with regard to the above points, either
from Paris or from London.

Wishing you a very happy journey, and, for myself, the
pleasure of seeing you again (*si superis placebit*), I must once
more assure you of my very highest friendship and esteem,
and always remain, Sir,

Your most devoted friend and servant,

Kandler Fr[anz]. S[ales].

APPENDIX V

Mary Novello's account of the Salzburg journey in 1829 did not fill all the pages of her notebook. On several pages she jotted down summaries of various Rhenish legends; these have been omitted. The later entries—apart from a set of accounts kept on a journey to France in 1830 —deal with musicians, friends of her husband and herself, many of whom have already appeared in the 1829 diaries. They are accordingly given here.

[1] *January 21st/30.*
Attwood told Vin today that Mozart gave the preference to his pianoforte concerto in D minor—that he had heard him play it more frequently than any others. Mozart wrote the Piano Forte Quartetto in G minor whilst Attwood was at Vienna, and that of the three Piano Forte quartets he thought that Mozart upon the whole gave the preference to [the] G minor.
[2]. This Xmas 1829 and 30 Vin has enjoyed two delicious musical treats at the house of his former pupil C. Wilson and his father-in-law Elliston. There were present F. and J. Cramer, Moralt, R. Lindley and Dragonetti, and these all played most exquisitely several quartets of Mozart and quintets of Bach in which Dragonetti failed not to pull out.[236] Never did I see Vin more delighted than upon his return, or more kindly regret that I had not participated this pleasure with him. Dragonetti has promised Vin to give him a high treat one day by inviting him to meet Cervetto at his chambers,

335

when they would play duets all the evening.[237] Vin tells me that Dragonetti's hand is as soft as his but peculiarly formed, very expanded at the finger ends, so capable of a grasp. He began practising this instrument at 18—spent seven years of his life at Vienna, and trusts yet to pass some time at Rome. Knew Beethoven intimately, thinks he was the finest extempore player he ever heard.

F. Cramer says that Hummel's style nearest resembles his brother's, but that there is a peculiarity about J. B. Cramer's playing which he never heard in anyone else.

The two greatest composers, in the opinion of J. B. Cramer and Dragonetti, are Handel and Mozart. Dragonetti mentioned that in the several thousand pieces he had played he had occasionally altered or added to the bass, in his opinion for the better, but in Mozart all was perfect and every alteration must be for the worse. He instanced the opening duet in *Figaro* as the acme of perfection and which none but himself could have thought of. Thinks Handel's " Messiah " the most finished of his oratorios, but altogether prefers " Israel in Egypt "—so does Vin, for its choruses.

Cramer mentioned that when he resided in Vienna, he lodged in the house where Mozart died, but got so possessed with the idea of his superior genius, his sufferings, etc., that he was unable to remain, as he could not write a single line, and he was engaged in composition for . . . (*sentence unfinished*).

[3] *March 4th/30.*

John Cramer spent this evening with us, and was most chatty and pleasant, he delights in his remembrances of Vienna and the friendly society he met with—repeated the anecdote of his not being able to remain where Mozart died, so haunted was he with the idea of the great composer.[238] Tells an anedcote of his being seated between Dussek and Crosdill [239] at a concert where the boy Hummel played a concerto wonderfully for his age. The latter said spitefully, " Well, the piano is a poor instrument and I never heard a good performance yet upon it." " That is just my case," answered the other drily, " I could never meet with any one who approached to perfection on the Violoncello."

[4] *Saturday, January 23rd/31.*

Sir George Smart was here today and talked most pleasantly respecting Beethoven and the occasion of his giving him the autograph Canon [240] which he gave to Vin to be copied. It was after a dinner party when they were all a little mystified with the wine they had taken. Beethoven went to his desk, wrote out the composition and, giving it to Sir George, told him to find out the involved meaning, which, he declares, he never has, although he thinks something more is meant than meets the eye, or else it was a trick upon him.

[5] *January, 29th/32.*

Dragonetti passed the evening with us, and delighted us infinitely with his fund of anecdote and Italian gesture ; indeed without seeing him half the relation loses its value, for his expressive and significant *oeillades* and his mixed dialect of French, Italian and English convey infinitely more than the simple facts. He came to seek his beloved wife, alias his double bass, which he had left in our care for these last two months. He has refused a sum, which few men would for their wives, and perhaps which few wives would value, namely [£]800. It has been in his possession for 40 years and upwards, and belonged to the nuns of La Pietà at Vicenza, mentioned by Dr. Burney as celebrated for their concerts;[241] indeed Dragonetti told us they generally muster 24 Violins, 6 double basses, altogether about 86 performers, all nuns. An English nobleman had offered 100 guineas for this celebrated double bass, but Dragonetti, who coveted it also, won the father confessor to his side, who finally succeeded in persuading the nuns that it would be sacrilege to sell this invaluable instrument to a heretic who could not give voice to it, and refused to hear their confessions until they acceded to his wishes, and the instrument became Dragonetti's, who alone is worthy to possess it.[242]

At a convent in Padua Dragonetti boasted that his bass was more powerful than the organ, a dispute arose, and a wager was settled between him, the superior and organist. Dragonetti purchased an extra large string, indeed one that had served as a sign of the man's trade, and having fastened it to his bass, in the dead of night alarmed the fraternity by imitating a sudden storm of wind and thunder on his instrument in the corridors.

Dragonetti passed six years at Vienna, and refused [£]200 a year for life from the prince Esterházy, because he would not bind himself to any one man and render himself a slave. He played a duet in public with Beethoven during his stay in the city, but declares no one ever heard him who had not been fortunate enough to persuade him to play in private, for although he had three pianos he kept them in such a dreadful state that it served as an excuse to visitors not to comply with their request. At a private party Beethoven played for Dragonetti. Beethoven's manner of composing he described, that he walked up and down a large apartment, in which were two amanuenses, and as the thought struck him he set down the figures of the chord which they copied out.

Haydn's playing he said was good, Hummel, Cramer and the rest he thinks nothing compared with Beethoven's.

Banti he thinks the most wonderful of singers, and related his astonishment at her wonderful memory, as she could not read a note of music, or a word of print, yet hearing an air once played over, and that but indifferently, she sang it most divinely.

His thoughts of the Philharmonic members are not very exalted, with the exception of a few professors, whom he significantly described as with their heads kept under by the quacks, he thinks them charlatans, especially Ayrton, Dance, Latour, F. Cramer, Sir George Smart, who certainly are a disgrace to the society.

Dragonetti is not only a clever man in his art, surpassing indeed all others on his instrument, but he is a *wise* man, from the strength of his mind, his integrity and observation. These supply to him the ordinary education of schools and books to other men, and his playful manner with children is charming. His advice to Lindley and Edward was most judicious, his contempt for F. Cramer's want of sincerity noble and manly, his remarks on Mori's failure in excellence worthy the attention of parents and young people. How delicious is such an evening, unassisted by parade, ostentation, dress, company and the usual accompaniments of society. I only regret dear Vincenzo was absent, for Dragonetti is with him a deity.

NOTES

INTRODUCTION

[1] See Genealogical Table, inside back cover.
[2] See Appendix I.
[3] See Appendix III.
[4] In the account of their journey which Mary Novello wrote up from her diary and published in the *Musical World* in 1837, she refers to him as ' the enthusiast S—'. That this was Stumpff is proved by the publication, in the *Harmonicon* of 1830, of a letter to Stumpff from Mozart's widow, telling him of her sister-in-law's death and that she had repeatedly expressed her gratitude to all who had subscribed to the present sent to her.
[5] In the preface to his edition of Benedict Schack's Mass in G minor, which Novello acquired on his journey (see above,

pp. 61-2) and published in 1831, he refers to ' The Life of Mozart by Mr Nissen (an English translation of which is now preparing by the present Editor).'
[6] As can be seen in the writings of Stendhal and his contemporaries, this ' expression ' extended in men's minds through Istria to the Gulf of the Quarnaro, as it did in Dante's time :
' E come a Pola, presso del Quarnaro
Che Italia chiude, e i suoi termini bagna '
(And as at Pola, near the Quarnaro, which closes Italy and bathes her boundaries. *Inferno*, Canto IX).
[7] See Appendix II.
[8] *The Cowden Clarkes*. By Richard D. Altick. 1948.

THE JOURNEY TO SALZBURG

[9] See Genealogical Table, inside back cover.
[10] It has proved impossible to trace this Italian quotation ; possibly it occurs in one of the many opera arias or part-songs with which Novello was familiar. The Cowper extract is from The Task, Book I (lines 183-6).
[11] General Count Dominique René Vandamme (1770-1830), one of the heroes of Austerlitz and a devoted follower of Napoleon, had been first imprisoned, then banished to his native Cassel, by the restored Bourbon Monarch.
[12] There is a series of scenes from the life of St Roch, by E. Quellin, in the south aisle at St Jacques', but no Van Dyck. The portrait panel on the monument to the painter Lantschot was, however, at one time attributed to him.
[13] Continental reed stops of this period, when of inferior quality, are often described by specialists as ' comb-and-paper reeds '.
[14] The panels painted by Rubens for the ceiling of the Banqueting Hall of old Whitehall Palace (which now houses the

Royal United Service Museum) were removed for restoration when the hall itself was closed for repairs in 1829. There may have been some proposal to exhibit them at the National Gallery, but there is no record that this actually occurred.
[15] W. E. Schultz, *Gay's Beggar's Opera* (1923), p. 319.
[16] I have found no record of a painting by Guido Reni in this church.—Ed.
[17] Possibly the *Interior of a Riding House*, at Dulwich.
[18] For Mary Novello's previous trip to Germany see Appendix II.
[19] William Clarkson Stanfield (1794-1867) exhibited at the Society of British Artists from 1823, and in 1826 and 1827 foreign scenes begin to appear among his works.
[20] The Le Keux brothers, John (1783-1846) and Henry (1787-1868) were both engravers specializing in architectural work. John collaborated with John Britton in his *Architectural Antiquities* and the two of them worked with Augustus Pugin in his *Architectural Antiquities of*

Normandy, while Henry worked with Britton in his *Cathedral Antiquities of England*.

[21] As already mentioned, Novello means Buckingham Palace, which—formerly Buckingham House—had just been extensively rebuilt by Nash for George IV, with the Marble Arch (modelled on the Arch of Constantine) as its main approach.

[22] Edward Holmes, who toured Germany and Austria in 1827, writes of the great bell of Cologne Cathedral that the 'tone, which was continuous, resembled a gigantic bass diapason pipe' (*A Ramble among the Musicians of Germany*, p. 30). Novello, who must have heard Holmes' account at first hand, now runs on into a comparison of various English bells: 'York Minster (C like Bow), Tom of Oxford, Dr. Aldrich [1642-1710, Dean of Christ Church, architect of Tom Tower and composer of the round " Hark, the merry Christ Church bells"] the lowest bell, tho' a low note (A) is not in tune [?] and has a [?] and coarse [?] quality. The Tenor at Canterbury is remarkably sweet and cathedral-like—that at Westminster Abbey is likewise very fine for its peculiar solemnity of effect ; but for pure tone (like a fine diapason pipe), for softness and power combined, perfect intonation (that of C principally combined with its subdominant F), weighty metallic quality (it weighs no less than 52 Hundred weight) the Tenor bell of Bow Church in Cheapside is by far the finest instrument of its kind I have yet heard.'

Bow bells, recast after the destruction of the first set in the Great Fire of 1666, were destroyed when the church was bombed in 1941.

Novello refers again at Châlons sur Marne to the tenor bells at Canterbury and Bow (see above, p. 231).

[23] The Rembrandt painting to which he refers is at the Louvre. There is no painting by either Adrian or Isaak van Ostade that answers precisely to Novello's description.

[24] Thomas Campbell (1777-1844) had visited the Drachenfels in 1800 ; his poem *The Brave Roland* was written in 1820.

[25] Turner made a number of paintings and sketches of the Fortress of Ehrenbreitstein, of which one, *Ehrenbreitstein during the demolition of the fortress*, made in 1817, was engraved by J. Pye in 1824 on a single plate, and appeared (dated October 1828) in *The Literary Souvenir* for 1829—perhaps the Annual to which Novello refers.

[26] Letter to George and Georgiana Keats, October 1818.

[27] Robert Barker's Panorama, just off Leicester Square, and its subsequent rivals and successors, were among the cinema's earliest ancestors. The principle of the invention was the portrayal of an unbroken sequence of scenes or events on the inside of a cylindrical surface (or on canvas rolled out before the spectators). In certain of these, the audience viewed the scene through peepholes. (Willson Disher, *The Pleasures of London*, 1950, pp. 226-8).

[28] George Frederick Pinto was the nom-de-guerre of a brilliant young violinist, a pupil of Salomon, who died in 1806 at the age of twenty. His real name was Saunders. It was he who introduced Novello's friend Samuel Wesley to the music of J. S. Bach. An engraved portrait of him appears on the title-page of 'Four Canzonets and a Sonata ', brought out after his death by Samuel Wesley for his widowed mother's benefit.

[29] Sir Ulick O'Shane, ' a fine gallant *off-hand* looking Irishman,' thrice married and with a third, unloved wife much older than himself, is one of the principal characters of Maria Edgeworth's *Ormond* (1817).

[30] The ' curious fountain ' is the Castor-Brunnen, erected in 1812 by the last French prefect to commemorate the French campaign against Russia ; in 1814 the general of the advancing Russian army added to the inscription the words *Vu et approuvé par nous Commandant Russe de la ville de Coblence, le 1 janvier 1814*.

The mediaeval castle of Stolzenfels, blown up by the French in 1689, was restored by Frederick William IV of Prussia, when Crown Prince.

[31] Foreheads villainous low: Shakespeare, *The Tempest*, IV, 1.

[32] Giovanni Antonio Galignani (1752-1821), born at Brescia, lived some time in London, then went to Paris, where he started an English Library in 1800 and, in 1808, a monthly publication, *The repertory of English literature*, which became the Tauchnitz Edition of the period. In 1814 he also started a daily English

paper, *Galignani's Messenger*, which continued until 1884, when it became the *Daily Messenger*. It was finally discontinued in 1904.

[33] Holmes, *Ramble*, pp. 261-4.

[34] John Boydell (1719-1804), a publisher as well as an engraver, dedicated this plate to the Earl of Bessborough.

[35] A coach with glass windows, as distinct from a mere 'curtain coach.' The term designated a coach hired by the day instead of from a public stand.

[36] Probably the Pfälzer Hof (literally, Palatine Court), mentioned in several nineteenth-century travel-books and guide-books.

[37] The ruins Novello saw, here and at Heidelberg itself, were those of the Romanesque abbey church of St. Michael, on the Heiligenberg, built on the site of a former Roman fortress.

[38] The Society of Jesus, suppressed in 1773, had been restored throughout the world in 1814. Persisting in the interval under other titles, they had continued their educational work, and the 'Gentlemen of Stonyhurst' had established their famous school there in 1794. But the doings of Catholics in distant Lancashire clearly did not impinge on Vincent Novello's London.

[39] Lucas, *Letters of Charles Lamb*, II, pp. 456-7.

[40] Probably a troupe belonging to Abraham Saunders (1748-1839), a circus proprietor, who afterwards ran a penny-gaff.

[41] The river glideth at his own sweet will. Wordsworth, *Upon Westminster Bridge*.

[42] Leigh Hunt, *The Story of Rimini*, Canto II:
And in the midst, fresh whistling through the scene
A lightsome fountain starts from out the green
Clear and compact till, at its height o'er-run
It shakes its loosening silver in the sun.

[43] This is the chorale *Gott des Himmels und der Erde*, as given in the Darmstadt Cantional of 1687 (Johannes Zahn, *Die Melodien der Deutschen Evangelischen Kirchenlieder*, Vol. II, no. 3614b).

[44] Niccolò Jommelli (1714-1774) a Neapolitan, and one of the most famous opera and oratorio composers of his day, was Capellmeister to the Duke of Württemberg for 15 years (1753-1768).

[45] Crosby Hall, built in 1466, was occu-

pied in 1483 by the Duke of Gloucester, later Richard III. It is mentioned twice in Act I of Shakespeare's *Richard III*. A water-colour by John Sell Cotman in the Victoria and Albert Museum, dated 1831, depicts Crosby Hall in the state described by Novello; a wooden floor inserted at the level of the capitals of the columns to provide more storage space gives it a curiously low-ceilinged appearance. It was moved to Chelsea Embankment in 1910 and is now the dining-hall of a residential club belonging to the Federation of University Women.

[46] Prince Eugene Beauharnais, Napoleon's stepson, had married Princess Augusta of Bavaria, and had died in Munich in 1824. See above, p. 223.

[47] Clarkson Stanfield, besides his easel pictures, did a certain amount of stage scenery, including the sets for the first production of Weber's *Oberon* at Covent Garden in 1826.

[48] Novello leaves blanks intending to fill in the names from the playbill which is preserved among his papers. Of the two actresses he refers to, Adelheid Fries, *née* Spitzeder, was at first a 'guest actress' playing young female leads; she was then engaged at the Hoftheater in Munich in 1820 and remained for over 25 years. Charlotte von Hagn (1809-1891) acted at the Hoftheater from 1828 to 1833. Mrs. Sparkes must have been a memory of Novello's youth; she was a Drury Lane actress who died in 1837, aged 83.

[49] Benjamin Thompson (1753-1814) was born in Massachusetts, entered the service of the Kings of Bavaria as Councillor in 1784 and was ennobled as Count von Rumford (Rumford being the home of his wife's family). A scientist and reformer, he anticipated President F. D. Roosevelt and the New Deal by drafting unemployed beggars into public works projects. His principles he outlined by saying 'To make vicious and abandoned people happy, it has generally been supposed necessary to first make them virtuous. But why not reverse the order? Why not make them happy, and then virtuous?'

[50] Max's aria, *Durch die Wälder*, from Act I of Weber's *Der Freischütz*.

[51] A copy of Novello's edition of the work, with its lengthy preface in which he relates the circumstances under which he first heard it at Munich, is in the

Library of the Royal College of Music. [52] Righini's *Missa solenne a quattro voci composta per la coronazione di Leopoldo II* (1790) was later published in Berlin. Méhul's *Messe solennelle à quatre voix composée pour le couronnement de Napoléon I* was not actually performed at Napoleon's coronation and was not published until 1879, so must have been in manuscript. As for Haydn's Nelson Mass, it is anomalous to the point of irony that this Mass should have so long been known in England (for no historical reason) as the Imperial or Coronation Mass, when its connection with Nelson, enshrined in its German title of *Nelsonmesse*, is historical and intimate. It was composed in the summer of 1798, and the news of Nelson's victory of the Nile on August 1st left its impress in the trumpet fanfares which light up the grave *Benedictus*. The mass was performed in Nelson's presence when he visited Eisenstadt with Lady Hamilton in 1800. [53] The *Missa S. Hieronymi* in C major, composed in 1777, is listed as No. 11 of the Thematic Catalogue of Michael Haydn's sacred works by M. Klafsky in *Denkmäler der Tonkunst in Oesterreich* Jahrgang 32, Teil I, Band 62. [54] The Regent's Park Diorama, first

cousin to the rival Panoramas, allowed the spectators in their darkened rotunda to view, through an aperture, a large picture on which various effects of light could be played, bringing about a startling illusion of reality. (Willson Disher, *The Pleasures of London*, pp. 195-6). [55] Sir Joshua Reynolds' *Ugolino and his children in prison* was painted in 1773 ; a mezzotint engraving was made by John Dixon. Leigh Hunt, in the account of Genoa in his Autobiography, also refers to the prototype of the gaunt and tragic head : ' Now and then there was a head like the beggar who sat for Sir Joshua's Ugolino—a fine head, but still a beggar ' (Autobiography, ed. Morpurgo, p. 439). [56] The Rainer family were Tyrolese minstrels who had appeared in London in 1828. The tall black headdress of the traditional Upper Bavarian peasant women's costume probably reminded Novello of the typical Welshwoman's hat. [57] Henriette Sontag, Weber's first Euryanthe, had made her London début in 1828. (See above, pp. 149-50 and, for Mary Novello's further remarks on the ' women of Germany ', as she encountered them in Vienna, p. 201.

THE FIRST VISIT TO SALZBURG

[58] Novello kept the scrap of paper on which his informant had noted : "Frau von Niessen est logé dans l'aut ville [sic] Nonthal No. 23. Dans la maison de Mons. de Robinig loge Mad. de Sonenburg la vieille, No. 214 Kirchgasse [corrected in pencil to 215]. La jeune de Sonenburg loge vis a vis de Loretto". The "jeune de Sonenburg" was probably the wife of one of the two stepsons of Mme. von Sonnenburg, who both lived in Salzburg. [59] Probably K323 (1779) and K221 (1771). [60] Carl Thomas Mozart, the elder of Mozart's two surviving sons, became a civil servant in the Austrian Kingdom of Lombardo-Venetia. Edward Speyer (*My Life and Friends*, 1937), records that his father Wilhelm Speyer, while in Milan in 1818, used to play Mozart's violin and piano sonatas with his son Carl, who ' on such occasions used his father's clavier, under which a pair of

Mozart's neat little slippers had found a permanent home.' [61] This nickname for Mozart's last symphony originated, apparently, with J. P. Salomon (see p. 99). Regarding Mozart's personal preferences among his own works, Mary Novello, on a later page of her diary, made a note of a conversation between her husband and Thomas Attwood (Appendix V, p. 335). [62] Those reproduced as engravings in Nissen's biography : the family portrait by de la Croce, that of the child Mozart by an unknown Viennese artist, that of Nissen by Jagemann and of Mozart's two sons by Hansen. They are all preserved in the Mozart Museum at Salzburg. The original of the de la Croce portrait was in the possession of Mozart's sister (cf. p. 89) ; Constanze possessed an engraving from it. [63] The album is preserved in the Mozart Museum. [64] This is a much prettified engraving

25

from the portrait by her brother-in-law Joseph Lange, now in the Zavertal Collection at the University of Glasgow (H. G. Farmer and Herbert Smith, *New Mozartiana*, 1935, pp. 29-55. Both are reproduced opposite page 86.

[65] This was the cover of a letter addressed by Mozart to his father in Salzburg, It was placed by Novello in his album.

[66] Works of Charles and Mary Lamb, ed. Lucas, Vol. VII, pp. 852-3.

[67] A cantata by Mozart's son, dedicated to the Empress Carolina Augusta and entitled *Der erste Frühlingstag*, is mentioned in Nissen's biography as being about to appear in Vienna.

[68] *Mozarts Geist, seine kurze Biographie und aesthetische Darstelling seiner Werke*. The work, published anonymously in 1803, is by I. T. F. C. Arnold.

[69] Novello here omits Hagenauer's surname. The house was owned by the Hagenauer family from 1713 to 1858. The portrait of an earlier Hagenauer, Johann Lorenz, the Mozart family's landlord and friend, is to be seen in the Mozart Museum.

[70] His account is quoted, almost verbatim, by Mary Cowden Clarke (*Life and Labours*, pp. 26-28).

[71] Novello leaves gaps for the names of artist and engraver. The print, which was the one which Madame von Sonnenburg gave him through Herr Metzger on his return journey, was the one engraved from Posch's medallion by Mansfield (see above, p. 80). The painting of the Mozart family is the one by della Croce.

[72] This instrument, now in the Mozart Museum in Salzburg, is probably the one at which Mozart and his sister are seated in della Croce's portrait of the Mozart family, as this also has black keys for the naturals and white ones for the sharps. It was made by Anton Walter of Vienna.

[73] Henry Nyren was the son of the great John Nyren, the cricketer, who in his elderly years, was a member of the Novello circle, and whose classic *The Young Cricketer's Tutor* (1833) owes its literary form to Charles Cowden Clarke. Francis Joseph Gall (1758-1828) was the founder of phrenology, a word first coined and used in 1815 to denote the subject of the researches of Gall and Spurzheim.

[74] Mozart's son showed discrimination in

calling Novello's attention to Haydn's late part-songs with piano accompaniment, which are still rarely heard outside Germany. They were obviously unfamiliar to Novello, who noted them down as being published by Simrock and added "recommended by Mozart's son."

[75] The album was offered for sale at Sotheby's on 13 Dec. 1950, by Dr. Claudio Torresella, of Milan. The inscriptions in it show that Sabilla Novello gave it, years ago, to her niece Porzia Gigliucci, who subsequently presented it to a fine collection of autographs belonging to a dear Italian friend, now long since dead. Its history in the intervening period is unknown to the family.

[76] Ilia's aria in Act II.

[77] *Di scrivermi ogni giorno*, the quintet of farewell in Act I.

[78] Of the two Fantasias in C minor, K396 and K475, it is probably the first that is meant here, for it was originally the introduction to an unfinished sonata for violin and piano, one of a set he planned to dedicate to his wife in the early days of their marriage, but did not complete. The Abbé Stadler completed the Introduction, which was then published as a Fantasia for piano alone.

[79] The almost indecipherable words here might be "6 4tets", in which case the reference would be to the set dedicated to Haydn, of which, as already mentioned, Stumpff had acquired the autographs from André (above, p. 76).

[80] Probably the offertory *Misericordias Domini*, K222, for four vocal parts with instrumental accompaniment. It was first published in 1811 by Kühnel of Leipzig, but it was subsequently published by Breitkopf and Härtel.

[81] In his notes of their first meeting on the previous day Novello wrote 'No complete Edition of his Father's works—which I advised him to undertake as a most delightful task.' It is not absolutely clear whether on this second occasion Novello, a pioneer of Collected Editions, is continuing to press the same point, or whether, as the phrase 'a genuine collection of authentic documents' suggests, he is not rather urging Mozart's son to endeavour to collect all Mozart's available *autographs* and deposit them in a suitable national library.

[82] Johann Mederitsch (1755-1835), a

Bohemian musician who settled in Lemberg, and whose name, in his native language, means *cock*; hence the Latin form *Gallus*.

[83] No. 7 of Novello's edition is K.App.233 and probably not by Mozart; No. 10 is K275.

[84] The Nonnberg is actually the Eastern spur of the Mönchsberg, on which the Fortress of Hohensalzburg is built.

[85] This was either an inaccuracy on Constanze's part or a misapprehension of Novello's; Mozart's only visit to Salzburg with his wife, in the late summer of 1783, lasted a bare three months.

[86] Mary Novello probably means nationalism, and she may have been right, though not for the reason she

thought, for it would hardly have been nationalism that made an Italian audience applaud a Spaniard. But possibly some political allusion had slipped past the vigilance of the Austrian censorship. There are, for instance, many stories current of Italian audiences before and during the Risorgimento cheering to the echo at the word *libertà*, though used in a sense quite other than political.

[87] Probably the opera of that name by Giuseppe Blangini (1781-1841) produced at Cassel in 1811.

[88] A song for two tenors and bass, entitled 'Die Nacht.'

[89] *Konstanze Nissens Tagebuch ans der Jahren 1824-1837*, ed. Hermann Abert (*Mozarteums-Mitteilungen*, 2. Jhrg., Heft 2, 1920).

THE AUTHENTICITY OF THE REQUIEM

[90] Eybler's work on the scoring is considerably more extensive than is generally realized, as C. B. Oldman points out (*Letters of Mozart and His Family*, trans. Emily Anderson: Vol. III, Extracts from the letters of Constanze Mozart to Johann Anton André, translated and edited by C. B. Oldman); all the additions shown ringed in pencil (by the Abbé Stadler) in the facsimile of the Requiem, published by Alfred Schnerich (1914) are his.

[91] Constanze referred later to some scraps of manuscript among her husband's papers which she had handed over to Süssmayr, but there is no evidence that these related to the Requiem. It is, however, of interest to note that the book of counterpoint exercises prepared by Mozart for the Abbé Stadler's niece, which the Abbé showed Novello, contains a melody of which the opening phrase is identical with that of the *Benedictus*.

[92] In this connection it has been pointed out (William Pole, *The Story of Mozart's Requiem*, p. 75) that in the phrase translated above as ' newly composed by me ' (*ganz neu von mir verfertigt*) the word *verfertigt* can bear the meaning of manufactured or prepared, i.e., on the basis of already existing material.

[93] According to a note on the MS. Eybler intended to bequeath it to the Imperial Library at his death, but he must have decided to give it during his

lifetime, for in 1839 it was already in the Library, whereas he did not die till 1846.

[94] *Acqua toffana*, though unknown to modern medical dictionaries, was familiar in the eighteenth and early nineteenth centuries. The *Enciclopedia moderna e Dizionario Italiano della conversazione* (Venice 1837), and our own Penny Cyclopedia of the Society for the Diffusion of Useful Knowledge (London 1833) describe it as a slow poison invented by Tofana, a Neapolitan woman, and brought to light in 1659 by a Roman police inquiry into the doings of a group of conveniently widowed women. Its main ingredients are said to have been arsenic and lead oxide. Administered in small doses, it escaped detection, and the victims were reputed to die only after a considerable interval.

[95] Mozart had only been promised the reversion of the post at St. Stephen's. He had, however, received the offer of an annuity of 1,000 florins from a group of Hungarian nobles, which would have given him economic freedom.

[96] This, the confirmation of Nissen's account (pp. 565-7) refers not only to the appointment at St Stephen's, of which he had only been promised the reversion, but also to the offer from Hungary already mentioned.

[97] A slip of memory ; the final chord in Mozart's autograph is that of D as dominant to G minor (bar 54).

[98] This is misleading in that the only portion of the autograph ever owned by Stadler was his portion of the *Dies Irae*; the *Requiem aeternam* and *Kyrie* he had merely copied, subsequently presenting his copy, along with his autograph portion of the *Dies Irae*, to the Imperial Library (cf. pp. 124-5).

THROUGH AUSTRIA TO VIENNA

[99] Clara Novello (*Reminiscences*, p. 78) states that her parents did in fact make the journey by water, in one of the log rafts, with cabins constructed in the middle, which, before the advent of steam, were a normal mode of transport on the Danube. She is however confusing this journey with that made by her mother, who—as recorded in a still unpublished diary—accompanied Edward Holmes on his travels in 1827. See Appendix II.

[100] The bill has been preserved and shows that the performance was not an opera but a play, *Das Gastrecht*, by F. W. Ziegler.

[101] See Appendix II.

[102] Novello leaves a blank for the name of this village, lying between Linz and Enns, where in 1809 the Austrians fiercely contested Masséna's crossing of the river Traun.

[103] Clara Novello's *Reminiscences*, ed. Valeria Gigliucci (London, 1910), pp. 78-9.

[104] Two other recommendations, probably also from Mozart's son, Novello apparently had no time to follow up ; among his memoranda he noted ' Mr. Hardwig, Ami de Mozart, to be found at the " Café de la Couronne " am Graben, every day at 3 o'clock,' and ' Mr Haensel, friend of Haydn, Hohe Brücke No. 351.' Peter Haensel was a composition pupil of Haydn's in 1793.

[105] Nor was he ; he was born in 1765, and was thus only 64. But in Italian sixty (*sessanta*) and seventy (*settanta*) sound very much alike, so Novello probably misheard him.

[106] This bust, by Thaller, had belonged to Haydn, who had provided the clothes and the hair for the wig, and kept it under glass in his reception room. It is now in the Museum der Stadt Wien. (Joseph Müller, *Haydn Portraits*, Musical Quarterly, April, 1932).

[107] Eybler's story, and in large measure his surmise, are correct. When in 1820 Haydn's body was brought to Eisenstadt for re-burial, the head was found to be missing. It had in fact been stolen by Prince Esterházy's former secretary, Carl Rosenbaum, who, with his partner in the theft, a certain Johann N. Peter, the administrator of a penitentiary, had been studying the phrenological work of Gall and Sturtzheim. The skull had not, however, been sent to Paris, but was kept by Rosenbaum, who on his deathbed left it to Peter on condition that he in turn bequeathed it to the Museum of the *Gesellschaft der Musikfreunde* in Vienna. (The full story is told by Karl Geiringer, formerly Curator of the Museum, in his *Haydn—A Creative Life in Music*, pp. 174-5.) It was eventually handed over by the Gesellschaft der Musikfreunde and solemnly laid in the composer's tomb at Eisenstadt on June 5th, 1954.

[108] The duet *Placidissime Catene* is, according to the MS. copies extant in the British Museum, by Steffani, not Caldara. Eybler's contribution to Novello's album was a three-part *Hymne zu Gott*.

[109] See above, pp. 180, 314-15. The Mass was K194.

[110] See above, pp. 119ff, 129.

[111] This is the Posch-Mansfeld engraving already referred to (pp. 80, 89).

[112] Haslinger was Eybler's publisher, and besides the Requiem had published the five Masses, of which No. 3, the *Missa de Sancto Leopoldo*, was the work the Novellos' heard at Antwerp (see pp. 287ff.). A Mass in F (possibly the one Eybler was at work on when they called) was also published by Haslinger as No. 6.

[113] Mary Novello notes later : ' Mlle. Sontag is much decried here, they say she is very well for a young person but has no style or expression. They cannot imagine how she is tolerated as first singer in London.'

[114] These contrapuntal exercises written by Mozart in 1782 for Maximilienne Stadler, the Abbé's niece (not his cousin), are described and discussed by Robert Lach, *Wolfgang Amadeus Mozart als Theoretiker* (Denkschrift der Akademie der Wissenschaften in Wien, Vienna, 1918).

[115] See above, pp. 119ff, for a full discussion of this problem.

[116] Haydn possessed two English pianos; one, by Schudi & Broadwood (which he called *mein schönes Forte Piano*) was sold by him in the year of his death, 1809. The Longman & Broderip instrument was sold after his death for 700 florins.

[117] F. G. Kolschitzky was a Pole whose knowledge of Turkish enabled him to penetrate the Turkish lines during the siege of 1683 and bring back information vital to the city's defenders. After the raising of the siege a vast quantity of coffee was found in the abandoned Turkish camp, and Kolschitsky opened his coffee house that same year (not in 1685) on the strength of this captured hoard.

[118] See above, pp. 282ff, Mozart's arrangements of Bach's fugues are as follows : K404a (three-part fugues) consists of three from the Well-Tempered Clavier (I, 8 and II, 13 and 14), one from the second Organ Sonata, one from the Art of Fugue (Contrapunctus 8) and one by Friedemann Bach, with introductory Adagios either composed by Mozart or adapted by him from other works of Bach ; K405, consisting of five four-part fugues from the Well-Tempered Clavier (II, 2, 5, 7-9) arranged for string quartet.

[119] This MS. exists in two portions, having been divided by Carl Mozart. He believed it to be an autograph of his father's, and presented the first half of it to the Mozart Museum in Salzburg, the second half to V. H. Zavertal. This second half is in the Zavertal Collection at the University of Glasgow (H. G. Farmer and Herbert Smith, *New Mozartiana : The Mozart Relics in the Zavertal Collection at the University of Glasgow*, 1935). The first half, completed by a later hand, was the version used by the editors of the Collected Edition of Mozart's works, as the autograph was not then available.

[120] Paul Hofheimer (1459-1539) was one of a group of composers, including Heinrich Isaac and Hermann Finck, who, though not 'the first to write in four parts', made a speciality of German songs in very simple and appealing four-part harmony.

[121] Gregor Werner (1695-1766) was Haydn's predecessor as Capellmeister to the Esterházy family ; Haydn worked under him as his Vice-Capellmeister for four years, and, many years later, arranged six of his fugues for string quartet and had them published by Artaria (in 1804) 'out of sincere esteem for this celebrated master'.

[122] For his own benefit Novello has already made a note to the effect that :

'L'Abbé Stadler has some relation (a brother, I believe) who lives in the Kärntnerstrasse No. 1076 ; probably he will be able to correspond with me in case accident should befall this estimable and delightful old gentleman.'

[123] This is amplified by a remark among the notes of this conversation made the following day : ' Quintets of Mozart—1st Violin Schmidt, 2nd Stock, 1st Viola either Haydn or Mozart in turn, 2nd Viola Abbé Stadler—Bass he could not recollect.'

The account of Novello's meeting with the Streichers on Monday 27th also contains the following note : ' Schmidt, now dead, was one of Mozart's most faithful and intimate friends. He was an admirable performer on the violin and used frequently to play quintets through with Mozart and Haydn (as l'Abbé Stadler had already mentioned to me).'

[124] Op. 20, No. 5, of which the last movement is a fugue. G. F. Pinto's arrangement of *Haydn's celebrated Fuga, in F flat minor [sic], adapted for the Organ or Piano Forte*, was published by Lavenu and Mitchell.

[125] Professor E. J. Dent (*Mozart's Operas*, 2nd edition, 1947, p. 176) points out that *Don Giovanni* was regarded by a Berlin critic of the 1790's as ' a very suitable opera for Saturday nights '—doubtless because the supernatural element would, in his opinion, provide sensational thrills for the groundlings.

[126] This is clearly a slip of the pen for John Reeve (1799-1838) a comedian celebrated in his day, but described by his biographer Bannister as ' a first-rate droll, but very far from a first-rate actor ' ; contemporary engravings show him coarse-featured, with a strongly-marked nose—the traditional conception of a ' vulgar Jew face '. Unfortunately the playbill has not been preserved.

[127] Joseph Grimaldi (1779-1827) the unrivalled pantomimic Clown, who delighted London for forty years with what might be called a species of ' intellectual buffoonery' peculiarly his own.

[128] The *Harmonicon* of 1830 mentions a singer of that name as performing in a part-song by Sir George Smart. He also took part in the farewell concert given by Clara Novello before her European tour in 1837. The original accompaniment to the Serenade is for mandoline and *pizzicato* strings.

[129] At that period when opera was regarded as everyday entertainment (and *Don Giovanni* was Saturday-night entertainment at that) fidelity to the composer's conception counted for little, and interpolations were freely made to raise laughs or give the singers opportunity for display. Mozart himself cheerfully provided such interpolations : Donna Elvira's aria *Mi tradì*, written for the singer who took the part in the Vienna production of *Don Giovanni* in 1788, is one of them.

[130] The baroque High Altar was the work of the brothers Jacob and Tobias Pock. The stained glass dated from the fourteenth century, and originally filled seventeen windows. The ' beautiful little chapel . . . seldom or never used ' was probably St. Eligius' Chapel in the southwest corner of the nave, near the great west door, from which the baptismal font had been moved before to St. Catherine's chapel, under the South Tower, in 1782. It has proved impossible to identify the ' exquisitely fine painting of a single head ' which Novello so much admired.

[131] No. 16 in Novello's edition of Haydn's Masses is the ' Theresa ' Mass.

[132] The church, built in the fifteenth century, was remodelled in the baroque style by the Jesuits in 1747.

[133] K194, No. 6 in Novello's edition of Mozart's Masses in vocal score published in 1819.

[134] The Schottenkirche, formerly a Benedictine abbey founded by Irish and Scottish monks in the twelfth century. It was reconstructed by Andrea Allio in 1638-43.

[135] Madame Streicher eventually provided them with a letter of introduction from her son Johann Baptist to Lehmann, organist at the Barfüsserkirche (Church of the Discalced Carmelites) in Augsburg, of which a translation is given below ; it is dated July 28th:

' Mr Novello, who has been introduced to us as a highly distinguished organist and composer from London, is passing through Augsburg and wishes to make your acquaintance and also, through you, to have the opportunity of seeing the late J. A. Stein's great work, the organ at the Discalced Carmelite Church. I am all the more confident that you will be ready to grant his wish in that, as you will find, both Mr Novello and his wife are delightful and extremely nice people. If, in return, I can do you any service here, you know that I will do so with the greatest pleasure. My parents send their best wishes—in which I join —to you and your wife, meanwhile I remain, with the kindest regards, Yours most sincerely, J. Bapt. Streicher.'

As the Novellos did not break their journey at Augsburg on their way to Paris, the letter remained in their possession.

[136] No account of Mozart's house appears in either diary on this day, but possibly Novello's detailed description of it, dated the following day, is the result of this visit.

[137] Beethoven did not take the apartment in the Schwarzspanierhaus until the autumn of 1825—only eighteen months before his death.

[138] The postscript of a letter written in July 1817 reads ' Wo sind meine Bettdecken?

(Thayer, Vol. IV, pp. 488-9).

[139] See above, p. 193.

[140] Novello's manuscript collection of part-songs, known in the family as ' The Green Books ' and much used for home music, contains Seyfried's arrangement of the second of Beethoven's three Equali for trombones (of which he had arranged the first and third for performance at Beethoven's funeral). Novello gives it the title *A German Lament for the death of Beethoven*, as sung at his grave in the quiet village churchyard at Währing, near Vienna . . . It was in fact performed at a commemoration at the graveside in March 1828. (Ignaz von Seyfried, *Ludwig van Beethoven's Studien im Generalbasse*, 1832).

[141] Girolamo Crescentini (1762-1846) one of the last and finest of the male sopranos. He also composed and taught singing. He lived in Vienna from 1803 to 1805.

[142] The *Oeuvres Complettes de W. A. Mozart*, published by Breitkopf & Härtel ; Cabier V, containing thirty of his songs, was published in 1799.

[143] Tyrone Power, who in 1826 had succeeded Charlie Connor as leading Irish comedian at Drury Lane.

[144] Cipriani Potter (1792-1871) was professor of pianoforte at the Royal Academy of Music (of which he became Principal in 1832). He had studied in Vienna in 1817-18 and was the first to try the piano given to Beethoven by Thomas Broadwood after it had been unpacked by Streicher.

[145] Novello clearly means the big chorus ' Endless praise to Thee we'll sing ' at the close of the ' Spring ' section of *The Seasons*. It does not, however, appear among his published volumes of motets.

[146] The two Haydn Masses are the ' Heilig ' and ' Theresa ' Masses, Nos. 1 and 16 of Novello's edition. The ' very interesting and curious ' sketches for *The Creation* have been described by Karl Geiringer (*Haydn's Sketches for The Creation*, Musical Quarterly, 1932). The Hofheimer manuscripts in the Imperial Library, as described by Eitner (*Quellenlexikon*) consist mainly of German songs, some with sacred words.

[147] The autographs of *Lucio Silla*, *La Finta Giardiniera*, *Il Ré pastore* and parts of *Mitridate* were among those acquired by André. *La Finta Giardiniera* had, however, been fairly widely performed, as a German *Singspiel*, by Böhm's travelling company, and before Novello left Vienna he found that published versions were available, for he notes an advertisement by Anton Paternos, of the Neue Markt, in the Wiener Zeitung of July 30th: ' Edition Mozarts Opern. No. 6, Die Gärtnerin aus Liebe, 3 Akten, Ital. Deutsch, 3 fl. 30 kr.' *Ascanio in Alba* was written in 1771 for the wedding of the Archduke Ferdinand.

[148] Dr. Samuel Arnold (1740-1802) planned and edited a Collected Edition of Handel's works—one of the first Collected Editions ever brought out. It ran to 54 volumes and, even so, remained incomplete. (This was the edition presented to Beethoven by Stumpff.) The Walshes, father and son, were the publishers who brought out Handel's works in his lifetime.

[149] This is doubtless Mary Novello's German friend the Baroness von Helldorf. See Appendix II.

[150] The numbers refer to Novello's own edition of Haydn's Masses ; No. 5 is the St Cecilia Mass and No. 7 the St Nicholas Mass. No trace has been found of any of these MSS. It is not quite clear whether Novello uses the term ' original MS. ' as meaning ' autograph ', but he refers also to the autograph of the aria from *La Clemenza di Tito* as the ' original copy ', so he probably thought he was acquiring autographs. The autograph of the St Nicholas Mass, however, is now in the Westdeutsche Bibliothek, Marburg ; of the St Cecilia Mass only the *Agnus Dei* and portions of the *Benedictus* are known to exist in autograph. They were formerly in the Esterházy collection.

[151] The ' song in G ' from *La Clemenza di Tito* is Vitellia's aria, *Deh, si piacer me vuoi*, of which Artaria formerly owned the autograph ; it was later acquired by the Preussische Staatsbibliothek, which already owned the rest of the autograph. The work in F minor for ' Barrel Organ ' is probably the Fantasia for a mechanical organ in a clock, K608, of which Artaria acquired from Beethoven a copy believed to be an autograph, and had published a piano arrangement by Clementi. Novello also notes particulars of an orchestral arrangement of this work by Seyfried, published by Breitkopf and Härtel.

[152] This was duly preserved in the Album; underneath it Novello has written : ' The handwriting of the Abbé Stadler, the intimate friend of Haydn, Mozart and Beethoven '.

THE RETURN JOURNEY

[153] At this period there were two different currencies in the Austrian territories, a heavy coinage called *Conventions-Münze* and a paper currency known as *Schein-Geld*. Murray's Handbook for Travellers in Southern Germany (1840 edition) warns travellers that ' a dishonest innkeeper or tradesman might allow a stranger to pay in good Gulden an account made out in Schein Gulden. It is therefore prudent to inquire on receiving a bill, whether it is in *Münz* or *Schein* Gulden. '

[154] Jakob Haibl (1761-1826), was a tenor

in Schikaneder's company and wrote a
few *Singspiele* which the company performed. At the time of his death he
was chorus-master at the theatre at
Diakovar (Slavonia).

[155] Nissen, *Biographie W. A. Mozarts*,
pp. 573-5 ; the original is in the possession of the Gesellschaft der Musikfreunde,
Vienna. The relevant passage is published in *The Letters of Mozart and his
Family*, translated and edited by Emily
Anderson, Vol. III, pp. 1447-50.

[156] As already mentioned, the Abbé
Stadler, by his own account, had received
his portion of the Requiem as a gift from
an unnamed friend (see above, p. 124).
Eybler obviously received the MS. when
he undertook to complete it, though it is
curious that he did not turn the whole
thing over to Süssmayr on giving up the
task.

[157] Sesto is a soprano (*travesti*) role ; it
was sung at the first performance by
Carolina Perini.

[158] *Al desio di chi t'adora*, K577, is an
additional aria for Susanna in *Le Nozze
di Figaro*.

[159] These ' lost ' Trios are probably the
five for two basset-horns and bassoon,
K.App.229 and 229a. Constanze,
writing to André in May 1800, told him
that Anton Stadler ' has copies of some
trios for basset-horns that are still
unknown. Stadler declares that while he
was in Germany his portmanteau, with
these pieces in it, was stolen. Others,
however, assure me that the said portmanteau was pawned for 75 ducats '
(*Letters of Mozart and his Family*, Vol. III,
p. 1479). In any case, editions were
published only a few years later by
Artaria, Simrock, and Breitkopf and
Härtel, of which Constanze clearly knew
nothing.

[160] This is the Minuet for piano in D,
K355, dated by Köchel *c.* 1780, but
renumbered K594a by Einstein, who
accepts the date of *c.* 1790 suggested by
Wyzewa and St Foix, on the strength of
its mature style. In any case, if it was
written for Constanze, it must be later
than 1780. The Abbé Stadler wrote a
trio in B minor for the first edition,
published by Mollo. The ' person named
Mann ' is probably the Viennese composer Johann Christian Mann (1726-
1782).

[161] *Der Schauspieldirektor* (*The Impresario*).
Novello presented the MS. of this aria to
the British Museum (Add. 14396). It
is entitled *Ich bin der erste Buffo*.

[162] This is an error. *Al desio* was entered
by Mozart himself in his Thematic
Catalogue as having been written as an
extra aria for Adriana Ferraresi del
Bene, who sang Susanna when *The
Marriage of Figaro* was performed in
Vienna in 1789. The ' other delightful
song ' is *Un moto di gioia* (K579), written
for the same occasion ; Einstein believes
it was inserted at the opening of Act III.
The MS. of *Al desio* which Constanze von
Nissen gave to Vincent Novello was also
presented by him to the British Museum
(Add. 14316).

[163] Novello's account of his moonlight
walk with Mme. Nissen is quoted by
Mary Cowden Clarke (*Life and Labours*,
pp. 30-31).

[164] Undoubtedly for his promptitude in
forwarding to Vienna a copy of the Mass
by Benedict Schack which Novello was
so anxious to procure, and which had
arrived at Haslinger's shop on Monday
27th (see pp. 61, 184).

[165] Prince Adalbert of Bavaria, in his
Eugene Beauharnais, der Stiefsohn Napoleons
(Munich, 2nd edition, 1950) mentions
a Munich surgeon of the name of
Casanova who treated Prince Eugene
during his first stroke in 1823, and again
during his second and fatal stroke in
1824.

[166] The word here is almost indecipherable, but by the look of it—incredible as
it may seem—the capricious prima donna
may have been fond of knitting. She
had been fêted in Munich in 1818, and
Prince Eugene had arranged for her to
sing before his father-in-law, the King
of Bavaria, during his birthday celebra-
tions, coinciding with those of the
promulgation of the Constitution.

[167] See above, p. 49.

[168] General Sir John Stuart, the ' Victor
of Maida ', was in Malta in 1805, won
his victory in Sicily in 1806, and held the
chief command of the land forces in the
Mediterranean from 1808 to 1810.
Rear-Admiral Sir Sidney Smith, famous
for his defence of Acre, served in the
Mediterranean from 1806.

[169] It was one such patriot exile from the
Papal States, Colonel Francesco Pasotti
(also a former officer of Napoleon's
Italian Army), who in Nice took care of
the Gigliucci children, little refugees from
Fermo, during their parents' long

absences. He was a valued friend of the Novellos and, eventually, lived and died in a house belonging to Alfred at the gates of the Villa Novello in Genoa.
[170] Charles Matthews (1776-1835) was one of the most famous comedians of his generation.
[171] The rose window at the west end is 44 feet in diameter.
[172] It is not Hotspur, but Falstaff, who says (Henry IV, part I, Act IV, Sc. 2) : 'I have misused the King's press damnably'.
[173] Both of Raphael's paintings of this subject are in the Louvre. Waagen's Treasures of Art in Great Britain (1854) mentions no Raphael and no painting of St Michael in Mr H. T. Hope's collection (Vol. II, p. 112).
[174] Cf. Novello's earlier remarks on English bells, quoted in footnote 22.
[175] John Ella, 1802-1888, by John Russell (Music & Letters, April, 1953).
[176] Presumably either King Charles X, or the Duke of Orleans, the future King Louis Philippe, to whom the Palace belonged.
[177] Fountain heads and pathless groves, Places which pale passion loves.
John Fletcher, The Nice Valour or the Passionate Madman, Act III, Scene 3.
[178] Lord and Lady Townly are the two chief characters in The Provoked Husband, by Sir John Vanbrugh (completed after his death by Colley Cibber). It had been performed at Covent Garden on October 4th, 1826, in the same season as The School for Scandal, and again at Drury Lane in March, 1829.
[179] Benjamin Robert Haydon was in Paris in 1814, but it has proved impossible to trace a drawing by him of the Cemetery of Père Lachaise or of the tomb of Abélard and Héloïse. The monument to General Foy is by David d'Angers. He had distinguished himself in the Peninsula and at Waterloo.
[180] Quoted by Robert Wangermee, Le premiers concerts historiques à Paris (Mélanges Ernest Closson, 1948).
[181] John Bannister, son of the singer and actor Charles Bannister, was a pupil of Garrick. He started life as a tragedian, but it was ultimately as a comedian that he made his reputation.
[182] Clara Novello, in her Reminiscences gives the lady's name as Tardieu, but Novello, who had misheard it as Bardieu, refers to her throughout as ' Madame B.'
[183] Probably some form of wrap; cf. Georgiana Hill, A History of English Dress (London, 1895) : 'Another fashionable foreign adaptation was the Arabian tunic, a kind of upper robe arranged after the style of the Greek chiton. It was worn out-of-doors in place of the pelisse.'
[184] These are two enormous natural seashells presented to King Francis I by the Republic of Venice.

THE MUSICAL SCENE IN EUROPE IN 1829

[185] Deutsche und Französische Sänger und Sängerinnen in Italien. (Cäcilia Vol. X. 1829).
[186] Stendhal (Vie de Rossini, Paris, 1824) (p. 37) relates that when a certain Italian nobleman wished to arrange a performance of the finale of Act I of Don Giovanni it took the singers two months, and the instrumentalists six, to learn it.
[187] William Cooke Stafford, A History of Music (Constable's Miscellany, Vol. LII. Edinburgh, 1830).
[188] ' Going to the Play Again ' (Examiner, 1828. Reprinted in ' The Wishing Cap Papers,' 1874.)
[189] The imposing and serious opening Largo is only eleven bars long, and leads into a march in C major played by a band off-stage. This in turn is followed by an Andante grazioso, with solo passages for oboe and clarinet, after which the march returns. If the curtain rose at the first appearance of the march, Novello may not have reckoned it as part of the overture.
[190] E. Woldemar, Aufforderung an der Redaktion der Cäcilia (Cäcilia Vol. VIII, 1828).
[191] Robert Wangermee, Les premiers concerts historiques à Paris. (Mélanges Ernest Closson, 1948).
[192] Friedrich Griesbach (d. 1824) was for years leading oboist at the King's Theatre, and also played in the concerts of the Philharmonic Society. The first London performance of Beethoven's Pastoral Symphony was at a concert given for his benefit.

[193] The cast is as given by Novello at the end of his notes.

[194] At this time the two ' patent theatres ', Covent Garden and Drury Lane, still held a monopoly of legitimate drama. Other theatres, classed as ' minors ', evaded the restrictions or throve mainly on musical or spectacular shows, such as the famous equestrian performances at Astley's Amphitheatre.

[195] The names of the cast, left blank by Novello in his notes, are filled in from the playbill preserved with his MS. Catherine Sigl-Vespermann (b. 1802) had been singing at the Munich Opera since 1820. Giulio Pellegrini, first bass at the Munich Opera, had sung there since 1820 ; his wife was Clementine Moralt. He appeared in London in 1831. In this performance he sang the part of Ircano, Zoraide's father.

[196] *Cäcilia*, 1829, Vol. X. *Mancherlei über die Pariser Operntheater*, by G. L. P. Sievers.

[197] There are two principal tenor roles in the opera—Ricciardo, the Christian paladin, sung on this occasion by Wilhelm Bayer, a young singer who made his first appearance at Munich that year, and Agorante, King of Nubia, sung by F. X. Loehle, a singer of some experience who had sung at Munich since 1819 and later became an eminent teacher.
' Horn of Drury Lane ' was Charles Edward Horn, the Caspar in the Drury Lane production of *Der Freischütz* in 1824, who was able to sing tenor and baritone at will. He was also the composer of *Cherry Ripe*.

[198] Arthur L. Jacobs, *Spohr and the Baton* (Music and Letters, Dec. 1950).

[199] Adam Carse, *The Orchestra from Beethoven to Berlioz*, p. 323. F. G. Edwards, *The Baton in England* (Musical Times, June, 1896).

[200] This appears to be the same arrangement as that recorded by Franz Stöber's sketch of the lay-out of this orchestra, made in 1821 (Carse, p. 473).

[201] Weichsell led the King's Theatre Orchestra from 1802 till 1818 or after ; Spagnoletti succeeded him and led the orchestra throughout the 1820's. Mori, for a period, led this orchestra for the ballet and succeeded to the leadership on Spagnoletti's death. All three had served as leaders of the Philharmonic Orchestra. (Carse, *The Orchestra from Beethoven to Berlioz*, pp. 171, 209).

[202] Lindley and Dragonetti were leading cellist and double-bass at the King's Theatre ; both joined the orchestra in 1794, and remained together as an unrivalled team for over fifty years. The cellist at Munich may have been Philipp Moralt, whose brother George was leading viola at the King's Theatre (see Appendix V).

[203] This may have been the famous Heinrich Joseph Bärmann, for whom Weber wrote his Concertino and whom Holmes considered the equal of the English player Willmann.

[204] *Selbstbiographie*, Vol. I, pp. 228-9 ; quoted by Adam Carse, *The Orchestra from Beethoven to Berlioz*, p. 129.

[205] The King's Household Band, known as the Prince Regent's Band before the accession of George IV, was a wind band under the direction of Christian Kramer (d. 1834) and constituted as follows : 8 clarinets, 2 oboes, 3 flutes, 4 bassoons, 1 serpent *obbligato*, 3 serpents *ripieno*, 4 trombones, 4 horns, 4 trumpets, kettledrums (Carse, *The Orchestra from Beethoven to Berlioz*, p. 181). Rossini heard them perform under Kramer, who was a clarinettist, at Brighton Pavilion in 1823.

[206] Quoted by William Cooke Stafford, *A History of Music*, p. 248.

[207] William Cooke Stafford, *A History of Music*. It is faintly ironical that Alfred Novello, as Choirmaster to the Sardinian Embassy Chapel in Lincolns Inn, was one of the pioneers in the re-introduction of Gregorian chant. His *A Concise Explanation of the Gregorian Note* (1842) is dedicated to Augustus Welby Pugin.

[208] Holmes, *Ramble*, p. 68.

[209] *Present State of Music in Germany, the Netherlands and the United Provinces*, pp. 12, 34-36.

[210] Holmes, *Ramble*, p. 32. '. . . that intolerable nuisance in [the churches] of France, the serpent, the sound of which so much resembles the immature efforts and bleating of a bull-calf'. Doubtless Holmes, like Novello himself, had read his Burney.

[211] W. L. Sumner, *The Organ*, pp. 175, 178.

[212] Holmes, *Ramble*, p. 59.

[213] Léon Vallas, *César Franck*, pp. 100f.

[214] H. F. Redlich, *The Bach Revival in England* (Hinrichsen's Musical Year Book, Vol. VII, 1952).
Stanley Godman, *The Early Reception*

of Bach's Music in England (M.M.R., December, 1952, p. 459).

Samuel Wesley's MS. Autobiography (B.M. Add. 27593), quoted by J. T. Lightwood, *Samuel Wesley, Musician* (London, 1937).

[215] It may have been Dragonetti who introduced Novello to Bach's chorale preludes. · A copy of Breitkopf and Härtel's edition of the chorale preludes (*c.* 1805), now in the Library of the Royal College of Music, bears on the title-page of the first volume, in Novello's handwriting, the inscription ' Vincent Novello—the gift of his beloved friend Dragonetti '.

[216] F. G. Edwards, *Bach's Music in England.* (*Musical Times*, Sept.-Nov., 1896). *Cf.* also letter from A. H. Stevens (M.T., 1923) pointing out that Novello's original MS. of this arrangement appears in the catalogue issued by Mr. Harold Reeves.

[217] The phrase in Mozart's Requiem from which Novello thinks Eybler is plagiarizing occurs in the opening bars of the Benedictus. The return of the words *Osanna in excelsis* as part of the Benedictus, to which Novello takes exception, is a device (used by Haydn in the Theresa Mass) to reduce the number of sections and give greater unity.

[218] This, as appears subsequently (p. 290), was the Adagio of Symphony No. 102 in B flat.

[219] According to A. Freeman (*Some Organs of Antwerp*, The Organ, April, 1932), this organ was probably the one described by James Essex in his *Journal of a Tour through Part of Flanders* (1773) as being in the South Transept. It was repaired in the early 1830's and work had apparently already begun in 1829.

[220] A. Freeman, *Some Organs of Antwerp* (The Organ, April, 1932).

[221] This *incipit* belongs to no known Haydn Symphony. It is, however, sufficiently like that of the *Armida* overture to suggest that it may be the work in question. The slow middle section would explain the reference to ' movements '. The trombones were evidently a local interpolation: Haydn never uses them save in his great late oratorios.

[222] This is the Adagio of Haydn's Symphony No. 102 in B flat (see above, p. 288).

[223] A term for variations in which the melody is broken up into decorative passage-work in notes of smaller value.

[224] *Uebersicht der musikalischen Anstalten zu Cöln am Rhein*, Allgemeine Musikalische Zeitung, 1815 (Jahrgang 17), quoted by A. Schnerich, *Messe und Requiem seit Haydn und Mozart* (1909). In Austria the process had already been begun by the reforming measures of Joseph II, by which a number of old and wealthy foundations were secularized.

[225] This was undoubtedly the organ of the German Lutheran Chapel in the Savoy, built by John Snetzler in 1757 and for years the only organ in London with pedals ; these, and a tremulant, were original features of this instrument. It was praised particularly for its steadiness of wind in the Gentleman's Magazine of 1772. The Chapel was moved to Cleveland Street, W.1, towards the end of the nineteenth century, and was destroyed by bombs in the second World War. (Andrew Freeman, *John Snetzler and his Organs*, The Organ, Vol. XIV, No. 54, October, 1934).

[226] Joseph Wölfl (1772-1812) was an outstanding pianist and a serious rival of Beethoven's as a virtuoso ; the two were more than once pitted against each other in set contests at private gatherings, before Beethoven's growing deafness gradually drove him from the concert platform.

[227] Novello apparently means ' in measured time ' ; cf. account of Vespers at St Michael's, p. 297.

[228] Mozart wrote two settings of Vespers, K321 and K339 (but in neither case does the text throw light on the illegible word). The Litany is that in B flat, K125, the first of the two Litanies of the Blessed Sacrament (1772).

[229] The organ was constructed by F. Z. Krismann (d. 1794) using parts of the existing organ and parts of the organ of the former Cistercian Monastery at Engelszell. Bruckner had always been fascinated by it, but on his appointment found it in bad condition, and urged on the repairs and enlargements which were already contemplated (Max Auer, *Anton Bruckner*, Vol. I, p. 142, Vol. III, p. 31).

[230] The work was composed in Salzburg in 1774 and was in fact originally scored for two violins, string bass and organ only.

[231] Andrew Freeman, *Some Austrian Organs* (The Organ, July 1933, Vol. XIII, No. 49).

[232] Adam Carse, *The Orchestra from Beethoven to Berlioz*, pp. 42-3.
[233] This, with the other organs heard by Novello in the French capital, is described by Félix Raugel, *Les Grandes Orgues des Eglises de Paris et du Département de la Seine*, 1927.
[234] M. Cowden Clarke, *Life and Labours*, p. 60.

APPENDICES

[235] *The Stage Life of Mrs. Stirling*. By Percy Allen (London 1922). Mrs Stirling (later Lady Gregory) was Captain Hehl's daughter and Mr Allen's grandmother.
[236] Elliston was probably Robert William Elliston the comedian (1774-1831), and Moralt was probably George Moralt (1785-1847), one of five famous musician brothers, all members of the Munich Opera Orchestra. George Moralt later became leading viola player at the King's Theatre, as well as being a member of the family string quartet. For J. B. Crame, see pp. 35, 115; for Lindley and Dragonetti, see footnote 202.
[237] James Cervetto (1747-1837), one of the leading cellists in London in his day.
[238] Below the slip of paper pasted into his Album on which Mozart's son noted down for Novello the name of the house where his father died (see above, p. 152), Novello has noted that John Cramer ' occupied the same apartments for a short time after his arrival ; but he found the reflections excited by the circumstance of his inhabiting the identical spot where Mozart had suffered so much, and the associations connected with the place, were altogether of so exciting and painful a nature, that he was quite unable to practise or to compose a single piece ; and, as he himself told me, he was at last absolutely obliged to quit the house '.
[239] Jan Ladislas Dussek (1760-1812), pianist and composer, lived in London between 1790 and 1800. John Crosdill (1751-1825) was reputed the best English cellist of his time.
[240] The canon *Ars longa, vita brevis* was given by Beethoven to Smart when the latter visited him in 1825 (Thayer, Vol. V, pp. 246-7).
[241] Mary Novello is here confusing Vicenza with Venice, where Burney describes the performances by the girls of the Orphanage La Pietà—not by nuns, as stated by Mary Novello.
[242] The instrument was bequeathed by Dragonetti to the Basilica of San Marco in Venice, his birthplace, where it now is.

BIBLIOGRAPHY

ALTICK, RICHARD D. *The Cowden Clarkes* (London, Oxford University Press, 1948)

CARSE, ADAM. *The Orchestra from Beethoven to Berlioz* (Cambridge, Heffer, 1948)

COWDEN CLARKE, CHARLES AND MARY. *Recollections of Writers* (London, Low, 1878)

COWDEN CLARKE, MARY. *Life and Labours of Vincent Novello* (London, Novello, 1864)
My Long Life (London, Fisher Unwin, 1896)

LORD DERWENT (GEORGE HARCOURT JOHNSTONE). *Rossini and Some Forgotten Nightingales* (London, Duckworth, 1934)

EDWARDS, F. G. 'Bach's Music in England' (in *Musical Times*, September-December 1896)

FARMER, H. G., and SMITH, HERBERT. *New Mozartiana: the Mozart Relics in the Zavertal Collection at the University of Glasgow* (Glasgow, Jackson, 1935)

FREEMAN, ANDREW. 'Some Organs at Antwerp': 'Some Austrian Organs': 'John Snetzler and his Organs' (in *The Organ*, April 1932, July 1933, October 1934.)

HOLMES, EDWARD. *A Ramble among the Musicians of Germany . . . by a Musical Professor* (London, Hunt and Clarke, 1828)
Life of Mozart (London, Chapman and Hall, 1845)

MOZART AND HIS FAMILY, *The Letters of.* Edited by Emily Anderson. With extracts from the letters of Constanze Mozart to Johann Anton André, translated and edited by C. B. Oldman (London, Macmillan, 1938)

NISSEN, GEORG NIKOLAUS VON. *Biographie W. A. Mozart's* (Leipzig, Breitkopf, 1828)

NOVELLO, CLARA. *Reminiscences*, compiled by her daughter Contessa Valeria Gigliucci (London, Arnold, 1910)

N[OVELLO], M[ARY] S[ABILLA]. 'A Visit to Mozart's Widow and Sister' (in *Musical World*, nos. LXXV-LXXX, 18 August to 22 September 1837)

POLE, WILLIAM. *The Story of Mozart's Requiem* (London, Novello, 1879)

RAUGEL, FÉLIX. *Les grandes Orgues des Églises de Paris et du Département de la Seine* (Paris, 1927)

REDLICH, H. F. 'The Bach Revival in England' (in *Hinrichsen's Musical Year Book*, VII, 1952)

SCHNERICH, ALFRED. *Messe und Requiem seit Haydn und Mozart* (Vienna, 1909)

SCHOLES, PERCY. *The Mirror of Music* (London, Novello and Oxford University Press, 1947)

STADLER, ABBÉ MAXIMILIAN. *Eine Vertheidigung der Echtheit des Mozartischen Requiems* (Vienna, Tendler and von Manstein, 1826)
Nachtrag zur Vertheidigung . . . (The same, 1827)
Zweiter und letzter Nachtrag . . . (Vienna, Mausberger, 1827)

STAFFORD, WILLIAM COOKE. *A History of Music* (Constable's Miscellany of Original and Selected Publications . . . vol. LII ; Edinburgh, 1830)

SUMNER, W. L. *The Organ* (London, Macdonald, 1952)

THAYER, ALEXANDER WHEELOCK. *Ludwig van Beethovens Leben.* Completed by H. Deiters, edited and revised by C. W. J. H. Riemann (Berlin, 1866-1908).

TOYE, FRANCIS. *Rossini: A study in Tragi-comedy* (London, Heinemann, 1934)

WANGERMEE, ROBERT. 'Les premiers concerts historiques à Paris' (in *Mélanges Ernest Closson*, Société Belge de Musicologie, 1948)

WEBER, GOTTFRIED. 'Über die Echtheit des Mozartischen Requiems' (in *Cäcilia*, no. 11, 1825 ; see also subsequent numbers)

INDEX

Upright figures refer to the diaries ; italic figures to the running commentary and notes. Artists (including architects and engravers) and authors referred to by the diarists are indexed under the collective headings *Artists* and *Authors*.

A

356

357

INDEX

INDEX

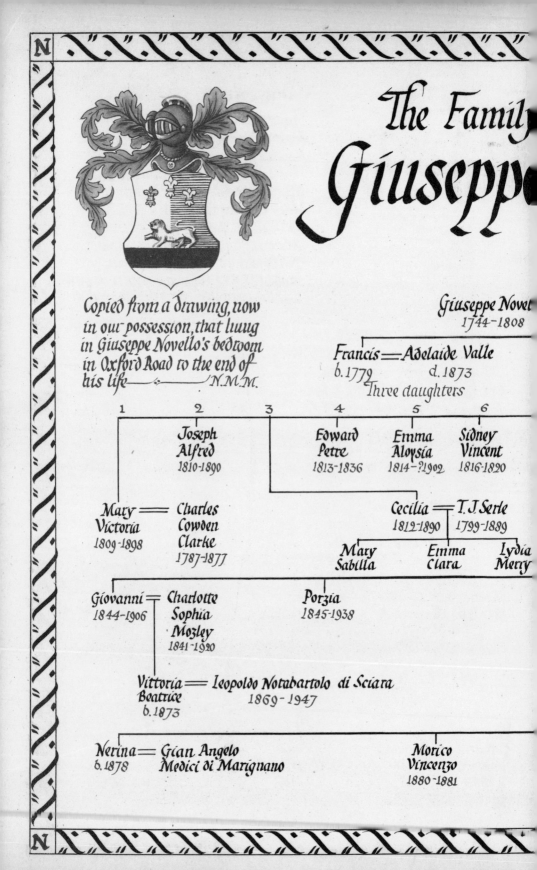

The Family
Giuseppe

Copied from a drawing, now
in our possession, that hung
in Giuseppe Novello's bedroom
in Oxford Road to the end of
his life ——⋆—— N.M.M.

Giuseppe Novel
1744-1808

Francis ══ Adelaide Valle
b.1779   d.1873
Three daughters

|1|2|3|4|5|6|

Joseph
Alfred
1810-1890

Edward
Petre
1813-1836

Emma
Aloysia
1814-?1902

Sidney
Vincent
1816-1820

Mary ══ Charles
Victoria   Cowden
1809-1898   Clarke
            1787-1877

Cecilia ══ T.J Serle
1812-1890   1799-1889

Mary   Emma   Lydia
Sabilla   Clara   Merry

Giovanni ══ Charlotte
1844-1906   Sophia
             Mozley
             1841-1920

Porzia
1845-1938

Vittoria ══ Leopoldo Notarbartolo di Sciara
Beatrice   1869-1947
b.1873

Nerina ══ Gian Angelo
b.1878   Medici di Marignano

Morico
Vincenzo
1880-1881